Freedom and Prosperity in Tennessee

Edited by:

J.R. Clark
THE UNIVERSITY OF TENNESSEE AT CHATTANOOGA

Associate Editors:

Russell S. Sobel
THE CITADEL

Joshua C. Hall
BELOIT COLLEGE

Freedom and Prosperity in Tennessee / J.R. Clark, Editor

Includes bibliographic references.

ISBN-10: 0-615-70357-7

ISBN-13: 978-0-615-70357-2

The Scott L. Probasco Jr. Chair of Free Enterprise was established by an initial bequest from the estate of Mr. Burkett Miller in 1977 to help citizens understand the principles that form the foundation of the American economic system. The chair's mission is to develop, through the educational field, the type of political, social, and economic environment that will permit private enterprise to achieve its proper perspective in American economic life.

Cover design by Cari E. O'Neal

Printed and bound in the United States.

TABLE OF CONTENTS

PREFACE

Tennessee is blessed with vast natural resources, a valuable strategic location, and a strong economic infrastructure. Yet it lags behind its neighboring states in many critical areas of economic growth and prosperity. The average citizen in Tennessee's 42 border counties receives $1,175.87 less income per year than the average citizen in the 52 counties on the other side of the Tennessee state line. Surprisingly, the income difference is largest for Alabama with their border county citizens earning $5,747.96 more each year, but even citizens in North Carolina's border counties earn $723.47 more per year than their Tennessee neighbors. Most of these counties have highly similar demographics and geography as their counterparts in Tennessee, but significantly better functioning state policy.

From the Great Depression in 1929 until 1981, Tennessee was among the poorest states in the union ranking between 42nd to 47th to 44th in per capita income. Beginning in 1981, a progressive 15 year trend of modest taxation, deregulation, decentralization, and privatization propelled the state economy from 44th to 31st among the 50 states in personal income.

Tennessee's Per Capita Income Ranking

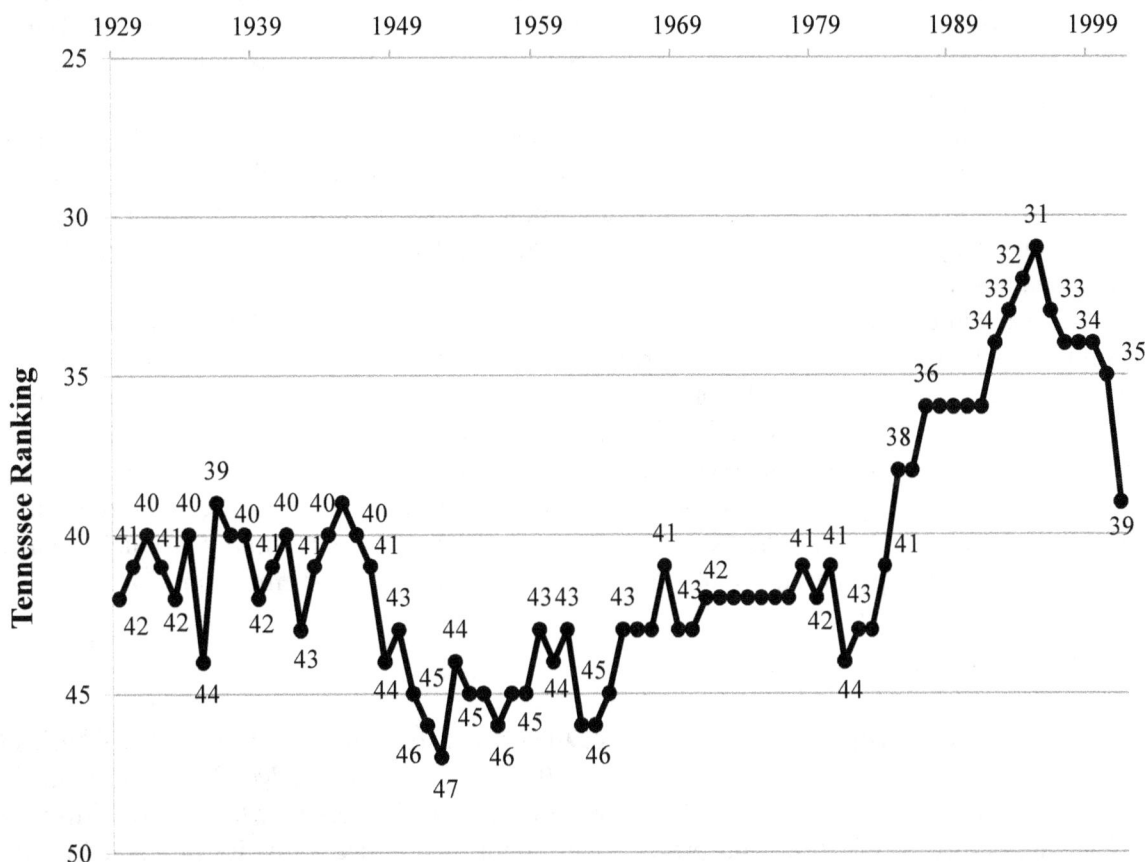

Source: Bureau of Economic Analysis (2012), see reference list at end of Chapter 1 for full citation.

Unfortunately, since 1995, a 15 year trend of expanding government, higher taxes, and greater regulation has pushed Tennessee to rank 39th in income and returned the state to the relative position it held after the Great Depression. The figure, Tennessee's Per Capita Income Ranking, shows Tennessee's ranking throughout the entire history for which average income data are available. As the figure illustrates, the current situation is the result of *long-term*, sustained problems in Tennessee policies, primarily over the last 15 years.

The most frequently asked question of almost any economist is what can be done to improve the economy? This study addresses that question directly and specifically *as it applies to the state of Tennessee*. It identifies the State's most critical economic issues and the public policy behind them. It examines those issues with objective economic research and provides comprehensive policy prescriptions to accelerate prosperity in Tennessee. Fifteen distinguished scholars, mostly economists, from across the nation lent their expertise to this volume, but all chapters relate specifically to Tennessee. Although the analysis and policy prescriptions, by their very nature, must be complex, the research is presented in a style and level easily readable by the average citizen. Three introductory chapters provide the background in basic economic principles necessary to understand why the reforms proposed in the final eleven chapters are critical to prosperity in Tennessee.

The chapters in this book were all written independently and deal with different areas of state policy while addressing a broad spectrum of economics issues and regulatory reform. However, each issue tests a common hypothesis: "Is making Tennessee state policy more consistent with economic freedom the best way to improve the well-being of Tennesseans?" Widely published academic research clearly indicates that greater economic freedom increases capital formation, labor productivity, and wages, and reduces resources wasted on political and legal plunder.

The authors based their research on science, not politics. The issues addressed in the project were chosen without regard to any particular political party, legislation, or the political feasibility of proposed reform. The authors developed suggested policy reforms in Tennessee from their analysis of documented, publicly available facts and extensive references to the published academic literature.

We believe that readers of this research will gain a better understanding of capitalism's potential to generate long-run economic prosperity in Tennessee, and the policy reforms that could achieve it. The primary goal is to provide scholarly, academic research that can inform citizens about state policy decisions and open a much needed dialogue on growth-oriented policy reform in Tennessee. Beyond that basic dialogue, and as scholars, we do not seek to influence any party, legislator, particular piece of legislation, or the electorate, in any particular fashion. The opinions expressed, if any, by the individual authors are their own and do not necessarily represent those of the group, their universities, or employers.

ACKNOWLEDGEMENT

We wish to acknowledge the generous financial support for this research from the Charles G. Koch Charitable Foundation, General B.B. Bell, Mr. Harry Fields, Mr. Brice Holland, Mr. Tony Vest, Mr. Rudy Waldorf, and The Beacon Center of Tennessee. Many other individuals contributed considerable time and professional talent to produce a quality published product including Joshua C. Hall as production editor; Evgeny Vorotnikov for discussions of Chapter 8; Sarah Estelle, Scott Cunningham, and J. Sebastian Leguizamon for discussions of Chapters

10; James Bailey, Huiru Chen, Julia Clapper, George Ryan Connor, Suzanne East, Cuyler Hines, and Rachel Smith for providing research assistance for Chapters 8, 10, and 12; Susan S. Douglass and Ashley S. Harrison for econometric modeling and analysis, proofreading, and editing; Cari E. O'Neal for cover design, chapter art design, and proofreading; and Sherian B. Carmichael, Christine Estoye, and Sara Gard for proofreading. Without their efforts and talents, the completion of the project would not have been possible.

J.R. CLARK
Probasco Chair
The University of Tennessee at Chattanooga

CHAPTER 1

THE CASE FOR GROWTH

by Russell S. Sobel, J.R. Clark, and Susane J. Leguizamon

Freedom and Prosperity in Tennessee

1

THE CASE FOR GROWTH

Russell S. Sobel, J.R. Clark, and Susane J. Leguizamon

Tennessee needs policy founded in a vision of a better future for its children and grandchildren. If done correctly, policy reform has the potential to drastically increase the well-being of Tennesseans within a generation. Within two generations the state could be at the top of the national income rankings, rather than the bottom. This progress requires policy reform undertaken with the explicit objective of increasing the rate of economic growth and sustaining it over the long term. This reform must be based on science, not politics. That is, Tennessee needs to adopt policies that have been proven to increase growth in other states, and to abandon policies that have decreased economic growth in Tennessee and in other states.

To begin our quest to understand which policies promote, and which hinder, economic growth this introductory chapter outlines the main arguments for why economic growth should be considered as one of the most important policy priorities in the Volunteer State.[1]

If Tennessee can get its policies in shape prior to the recovery from the current national economic downturn, it will be in a strong competitive position to attract the new businesses coming to life as the economy recovers.

THE HAVES AND THE HAVE NOTS

How wide are the differences in standards of living across states? How does average income in Tennessee compare with that of other states? Figure 1.1 shows the most recent data available on per capita personal income for all fifty U.S. states.

With a 2010 per capita personal income of only $34,955, Tennessee ranked 37th, making it the fourteenth poorest U.S. state. Three of Tennessee's neighboring states (Virginia, Missouri, and North Carolina) have higher per capita personal incomes. Prosperity does indeed cease at the border. At the county level, average income is $2,361 higher in Virginia's bordering counties and $731 higher in North Carolina's bordering counties.

---

[1] This chapter is based on Sobel and Daniels (2007) and Sobel and Leguizamon (2009).

Figure 1.1: Average Income by State, 2010

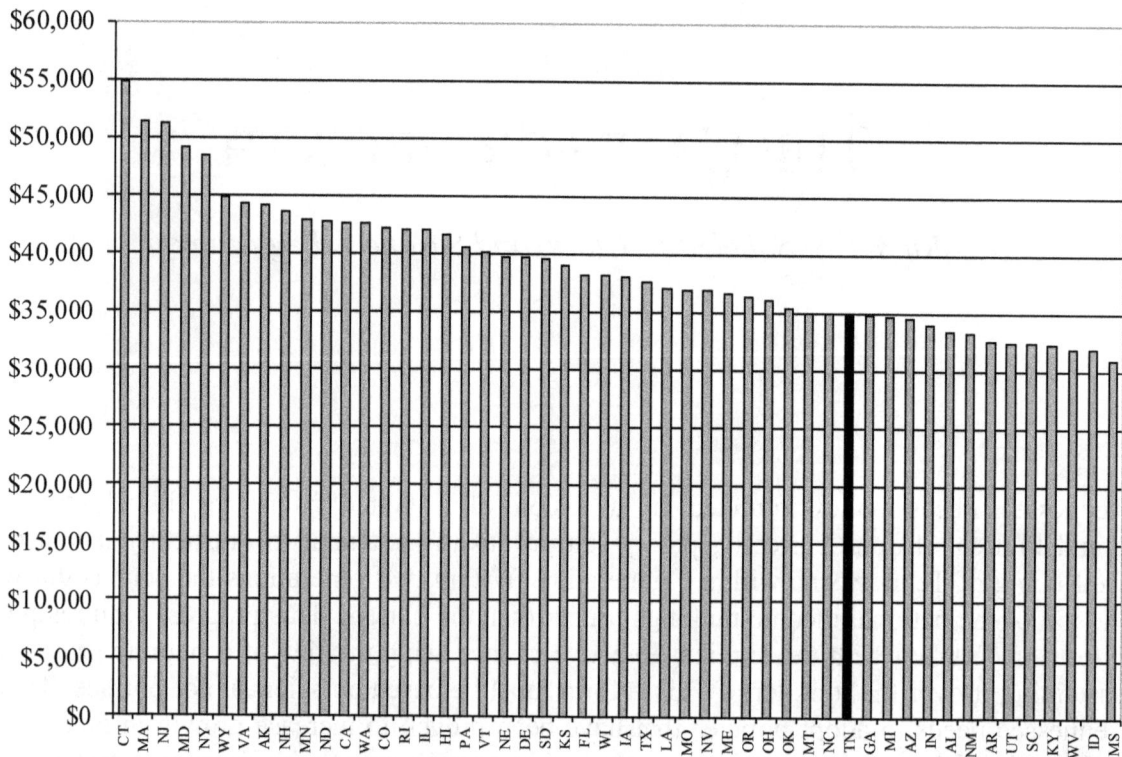

Sources: Bureau of Economic Analysis (2012); Bureau of Labor Statistics (2012). Note: All per capita personal income data in Chapters 1 and 2 are adjusted for inflation to constant 2010 dollars using the Consumer Price Index.

Average income in Tennessee is about 87.5 percent of the U.S. average of $39,945. Tennessee has a hard-working labor force, a bounty of natural resources, major metropolitan areas, wonderful recreation opportunities, major transportation rivers, and other significant advantages. From a purely economic perspective, there is no reason Tennessee should be so low in the national income rankings.

Why does the average Tennessean earn less than the average citizen in other states? One fundamental problem is that despite its many advantages, Tennessee has been unable to get its economic policies right. Getting these policies right is the key to increasing prosperity.

HAS TENNESSEE ALWAYS RANKED NEAR THE BOTTOM?

While Tennessee ranked 37th in per capita personal income in 2010, the path by which it got there is interesting. Figure 1.2 shows the entire history of Tennessee's ranking. In 1929, the first year the data began being collected, Tennessee ranked as the 42nd poorest state among the then 48 states. For the majority of the early history shown in this graph, Tennessee hovered in the mid to lower 40s in the rankings. By 1981, Tennessee ranked 44th, two spots poorer than it did in 1929.

Figure 1.2: Tennessee's Historical Income Ranking

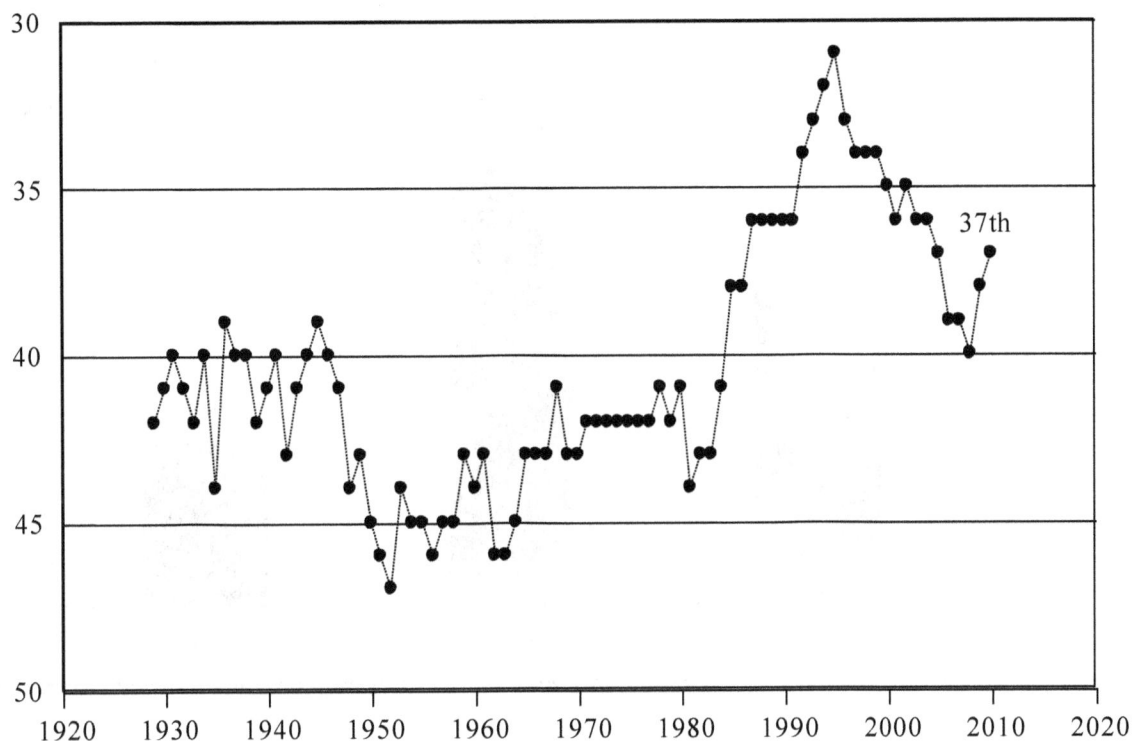

Source: Bureau of Economic Analysis (2012). Note: This is Tennessee's ranking among U.S. states in real per capita personal income. Note that the ranking is out of 48 states prior to 1950. In 1950, the government began including Alaska and Hawaii in the data, even though they did not achieve statehood until 1959.

In the 1980s, however, things changed dramatically. Between 1982 and 1995 Tennessee rose from 44th to 31st in the rankings, an impressive movement of 13 spots upward in 13 years. Unfortunately, these gains slipped away beginning in the mid-1990s, and from 1996 to 2008 Tennessee fell from 31st to 40th. Tennessee rose only slightly to 37th by 2010.

Had Tennessee been able to maintain its upward trend that began in the 1980s, jumping 13 places every 13 years, in 2010 instead of ranking 37th in the nation, Tennessee would have ranked as the 16th richest state. While we will discuss the policies that may (or may not) have contributed to this pattern in the next chapter, the underlying *direct* explanation is easy to uncover—the differing rates of economic growth during these periods.

Figure 1.3 shows Tennessee's average growth rate of per capita personal income for three periods of time: 1972 to 1981, 1982 to 1995, and 1996 to 2010. This is the "real" growth rate or the growth rate after adjusting for inflation.

During the 1982 to 1995 period, Tennessee's 2.4 percent average real rate of economic growth—the 4th highest rate of growth among U.S. states at that time—is what propelled the state upward so rapidly in the income rankings during that decade. During that period, Tennessee experienced nine years of rapid growth, each of 2.3 percent or higher, with some years above 4 percent. This was a significantly higher growth rate than the 1.7 percent Tennessee had achieved earlier in the 1972 to 1981 period.

Figure 1.3: Tennessee's Declining Rate of Growth

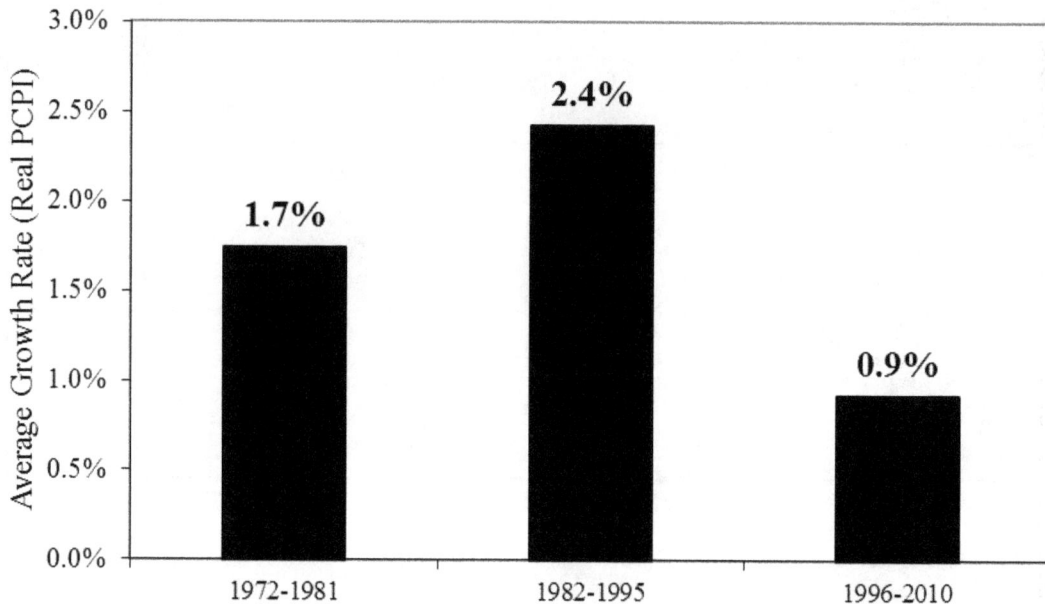

Source: Bureau of Economic Analysis (2012).

Unfortunately, economic growth in Tennessee slowed after the mid-1990s, falling to 0.9 percent between 1996 and 2010. Rather than being one of the fastest growing states, Tennessee's recent growth of 0.9 percent makes it the 10th *slowest* growing state during the 1996 to 2010 period. Even excluding the recent recession years, average growth from 1996 to 2008 was only 1.2 percent, the 6th worst (slowest) rate of growth among the 50 U.S. states.

While some might think the difference between 1.7 and 2.4 percent seems small, nothing could be further from the truth. Even small differences in growth, over long periods of time, add up to significant differences. This is the topic to which we now turn our attention.

JUST ONE PERCENTAGE POINT: WILL OUR CHILDREN BE BETTER OFF?

Large changes in wealth and prosperity cannot be generated overnight. Places that are prosperous today went through stages of development. What prosperous areas have in common is that they were able to sustain higher rates of economic growth over longer periods of time. Let us consider a few examples.

Figure 1.4 shows the history of income growth in Tennessee, adjusted for inflation, along with several alternative future projections. One projection simply takes Tennessee's recent rate of real per capita economic growth over the 1996 to 2008 period (prior to the recession), 1.2 percent, and forecasts it into the future. The other two projections show what the future would hold if Tennessee's growth were increased back to the 1972-81 rate of 1.7 percent or the 1982-95 rate of 2.4 percent. These real growth rates are not unrealistic. Both are actual growth rates experienced in other U.S. states over the last decade.

Figure 1.4: Which Future for Tennessee?

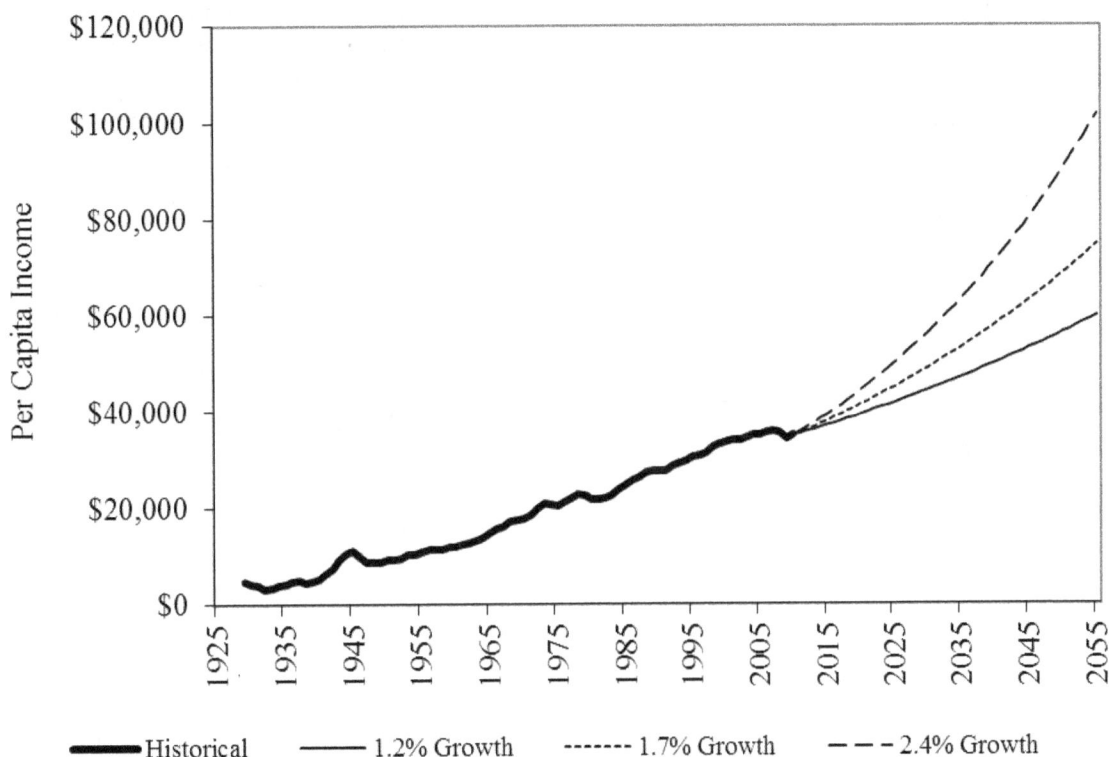

Source: Bureau of Economic Analysis (2012). Note: Per capita income is adjusted for inflation to constant 2010 dollars.

The last year of historical data shown in the figure is 2010, a year in which the average income in Tennessee was $34,955. Consider the simple question of what the average income will be in one generation, or twenty years into the future, in 2030. At the historical growth rate of 1.2 percent, average income in Tennessee would be $44,373 in 2030.[2] What if, instead, growth could be increased to 1.7 or even 2.4 percent? Under these alternative scenarios, average income in 2030 would be $48,970 and $56,171 respectively. Thus, going from a 1.2 percent to a 2.4 percent rate of economic growth results in a difference of almost $11,800 in average income one generation out into the future. Also remember that we are considering average income *per person*. The average family size in Tennessee is 2.99 persons (from 2010 Census data), so the impact of this difference on the average family is roughly three times this amount—or a substantial $35,275 difference in family income under the two alternative scenarios 20 years into the future.

What if we look even farther into the future? What about two generations? By 2050 the differences grow even larger. Instead of average income being $56,329 in 2050 at a growth rate of 1.2 percent, it would be $68,604 at 1.7 percent, or a whopping $90,263 at 2.4 percent. Make no mistake about it, over two generations a 1.2 percentage point increase in Tennessee's rate of growth means a difference of almost $34,000 in per capita income.

---

[2] All dollar values for future years are given in today's dollars—or "real dollars"—that have already been adjusted to take out the impact of inflation on the purchasing power of money in the future because we are using a real, inflation adjusted, growth rate.

Perhaps a better way of looking at the data is to ask: At what date in the future will average income in Tennessee hit $50,000? To put this figure in perspective, it is approximately the current average income level in Massachusetts, New Jersey, and Maryland. At Tennessee's historical 1.2 percent rate of growth it will hit $50,000 in the year 2041. At a 1.7 percent rate of economic growth, this date would instead be 2032—or nine years earlier. At a 2.4 percent rate of growth it becomes 2026—or fifteen years earlier. Increasing economic growth by just 1.2 percentage points moves the date at which the average Tennessean will have an income level of $50,000 forward by almost an entire generation.

Rather than relying entirely on future projections, it is also useful to consider a few specific historical income comparisons. Consider the cases of Tennessee and two states that fifteen years ago, in 1995, were virtually identical to it in terms of income, Vermont and Wyoming. Figure 1.5 presents this data. In 1995 the average income in Tennessee was $30,532, while Vermont and Wyoming had average incomes of $30,129 and $30,559 respectively. Tennessee ranked 31st in per capita income that year, with Wyoming one spot ahead of Tennessee (30th) and Vermont two spots behind (33rd).

Figure 1.5: State Growth Comparisons

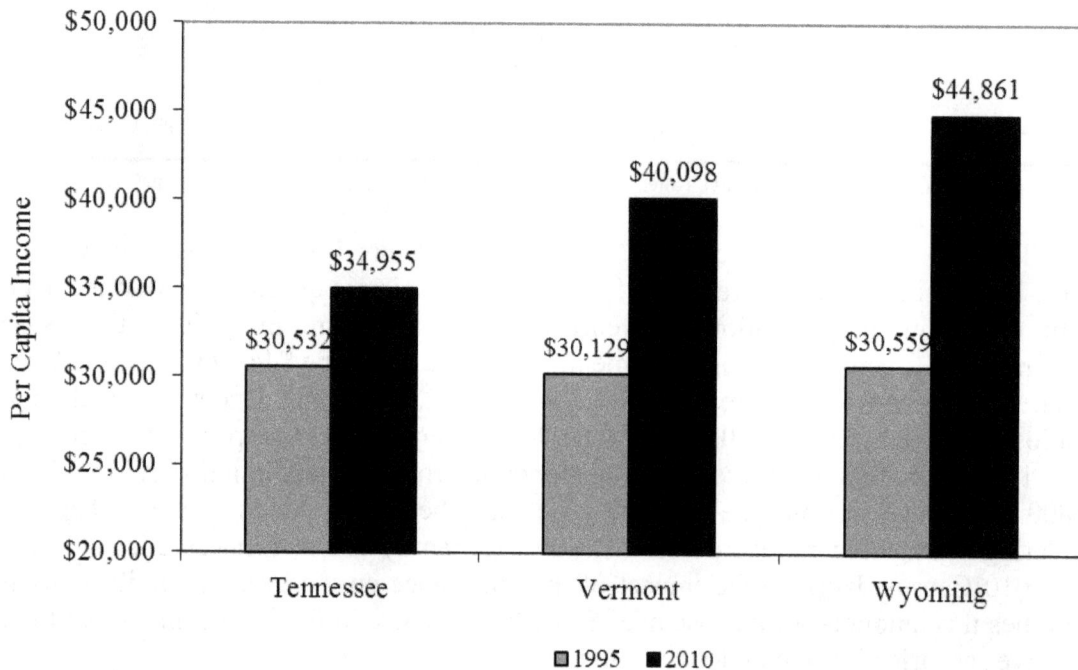

Source: Bureau of Economic Analysis (2012). Note: Per capita income is adjusted for inflation to 2010 constant dollars.

Over the next twenty year period, Tennessee was able to sustain a 0.9 percent rate of growth, Vermont 1.9 percent and Wyoming 2.7 percent. After fifteen years, less than one generation, Tennessee's 2010 average income of $34,955 is about $5,150 less than the average income in Vermont and $9,900 less than average income in Wyoming. The result is that while Tennessee has fallen to 37th in the national income rankings, Vermont has risen to 19th and Wyoming has risen to 6th.

It almost seems unbelievable that such small differences in growth can produce such large differences through time, but they can. A well-known financial formula called "The Rule of 70" helps us to understand the importance of time and economic growth rates in generating prosperity.[3] According to this rule, an area's standard of living will double every X years, where X equals 70 divided by the rate of economic growth:

$$\textbf{\textit{\underline{The Rule of 70}}}\text{: \textit{Years it takes for income to double}} = \frac{70}{\textit{Annual rate of economic growth}}$$

So, a state that sustains a 1.2 percent growth rate, such as Tennessee (prior to the recession), doubles its living standards roughly every 58 years (70 ÷ 1.2). A state that sustains a growth rate of 1.7 percent sees its living standards double approximately every 41 years, and a state that sustains a growth rate of 2.4 percent doubles its income in only 29 years.

As these numbers clearly illustrate, small differences in the rate of economic growth produce big differences in standards of living when they are sustained over long periods of time. The principle at work here is the same one responsible for the "miracle" of compound interest. Tennessee currently ranks 37th in average income. If all states continue their current growth rates, 20 years into the future, Tennessee will have fallen to 42nd. If instead Tennessee could increase growth to just 1.7 percent, its ranking in twenty years would be 29th. If Tennessee could manage to grow again at 2.4 percent, it would rank 16th in the nation within one generation. If that 2.4 percent could be sustained for forty years, Tennessee would rank as the 8th richest state in the nation in 2050.

As the experiences of other states illustrate, these large leaps in the income rankings are possible. Between 1995 and 2010, North Dakota moved up 31 places from 42nd to 11th, Wyoming jumped 24 places from 30th to 6th, South Dakota rose 16 places from 38th to 22nd, Vermont improved 14 places from 33rd to 19th, and Montana moved up 12 places from 47th to 35th. All of them did this the same way—by sustaining high rates of economic growth.

FROM RAGS TO RICHES: IT CAN BE DONE

Because economic growth rates vary considerably more across countries than across U.S. states, some international comparisons of long-run growth are even more impressive. An often cited example is the comparison between Hong Kong and Argentina. Approximately fifty years ago, Argentina was almost as rich as many European nations, while Hong Kong was relatively poor. Due to their differing policy climates, today Hong Kong is one of the richest countries in the world while Argentina has fallen behind. This example is often pointed to as proof of how little a country's natural resources matter for growth. Hong Kong, after all, is essentially a rock island in the ocean. Argentina, in contrast, has a wealth of natural resources. Like Argentina, Tennessee's abundance of natural resources by itself cannot guarantee a fast rate of economic growth.

Figure 1.6 shows the levels of per capita income in 1960 and 2002 for five countries: the United States, Venezuela, Argentina, Japan, and Hong Kong. In 1960, while the United

---

[3] Alternatively this is sometimes referred to as the "Rule of 72" which produces similar results, but is divisible by more whole numbers making it easier to use in simple calculations.

States was the richest of the group with a per capita income of almost $15,000, Venezuela was not far behind at nearly $10,600. Japan and Hong Kong, on the other hand, were relatively poor. Their average citizens had only 25 percent as much income as the average citizen in the United States (per capita incomes of roughly $5,000 and $3,750 respectively).

Figure 1.6: International Growth Comparisons

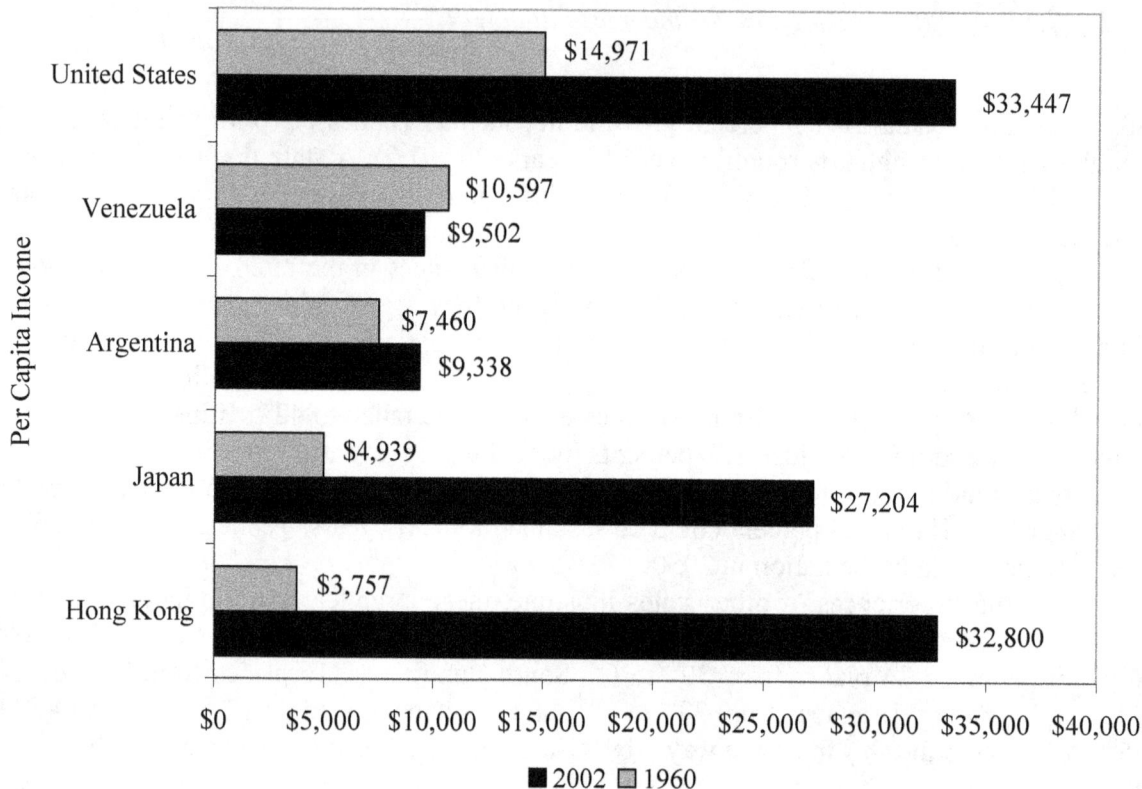

Sources: Summers and Heston (1994); World Bank (2004). Note: Per capita income is adjusted for inflation to 2005 constant U.S. dollars.

These countries followed very different paths over the next forty-two years. Growth rates were most rapid in Hong Kong (5.3 percent) and Japan (4.1 percent), while growth was virtually non-existent in Argentina (0.5 percent), and was actually negative in Venezuela (-0.3 percent). Over the same period U.S. per capita income growth averaged somewhere in the middle of these other countries (1.9 percent).

Fast forward two generations. By 2002, Hong Kong was nearly as rich as the United States (and wealthier than most European countries), and Japan was not far behind. Both are true "rags to riches" stories. In contrast, the average citizen in Argentina is only $2,000 richer than his or her grandparents and the average citizen in Venezuela is almost $1,000 *poorer*.

CHATTANOOGA VERSUS CHARLOTTE: A TALE OF TWO CITIES

Returning closer to home, let's take a more detailed look at the comparison between Tennessee and North Carolina. Because of their similar histories, the cities of Chattanooga, Tennessee and Charlotte, North Carolina are interesting to consider. In 1890, Chattanooga's population was roughly three times *bigger* than Charlotte's (29,100 versus 11,557). By 1950 both cities had approximately the same average incomes, educational levels, and populations. In 1950, Chattanooga's population of 131,041 was almost identical to Charlotte's population of 134,042. Both cities were in states with significant rural populations, and both relied heavily on industries which have dwindled (for Charlotte this was textiles and tobacco). Over the subsequent six decades, however, Charlotte has grown into a crowning jewel of the South, with a population more than four times the size of Chattanooga (731,424 versus 167,674 in 2010). Similarly, in 1950, Memphis was three times bigger than Charlotte, while today Charlotte is now 13 percent bigger.

Virtually all of Charlotte's new jobs and businesses were in industries that could have located anywhere. Charlotte's numerous new bank headquarters are an example. Nine Fortune 500 companies now have their corporate headquarters located in the Charlotte metro area. There was no special geographic reason, such as a specific natural resource or even a sea port, giving Charlotte an advantage over Chattanooga in its ability to attract and nurture these businesses. The question of interest is why these two seemingly similar cities diverged so drastically. As we have seen, over such a long period of time, even small differences in growth rates can produce large differences in income. What made it possible for Charlotte to sustain a higher rate of growth over such a long period of time? The answer is simply that North Carolina had a set of policies in place that were more conducive to economic growth.

ECONOMIC GROWTH AND HUMAN WELL-BEING

At this point, some readers might be questioning whether income is really a good measure of personal well-being. While increasing income certainly helps everyone afford more of the things they want, there is more to life than material possessions. We also care about our families, our health, and our overall safety. While growth may increase our income and standard of living, how does it affect these other measures of personal well-being? By focusing on growth can we also achieve other goals as well? Let us look at the evidence.

People want to lead long, healthy lives and this requires access to quality healthcare. Figure 1.7 shows how two important measures of health and longevity differ between groups of the highest income and lowest income states. Without exception, citizens in high income states live longer, healthier lives. The average high income state ranks 6th out of 50 in terms of the life expectancy of its citizens. The average low income state ranks only 35th. In terms of health care quality, the picture is the same. Richer states do better, while poorer states like Tennessee do worse. The average high-income state ranks 6th in terms of health care quality. The average low-income state ranks 41st. Because Tennessee is a lower income state, it is also one of the less healthy, placing 38th in the U.S. health rankings and 46th in life expectancy.

Figure 1.7: Health Indicators by Income Level

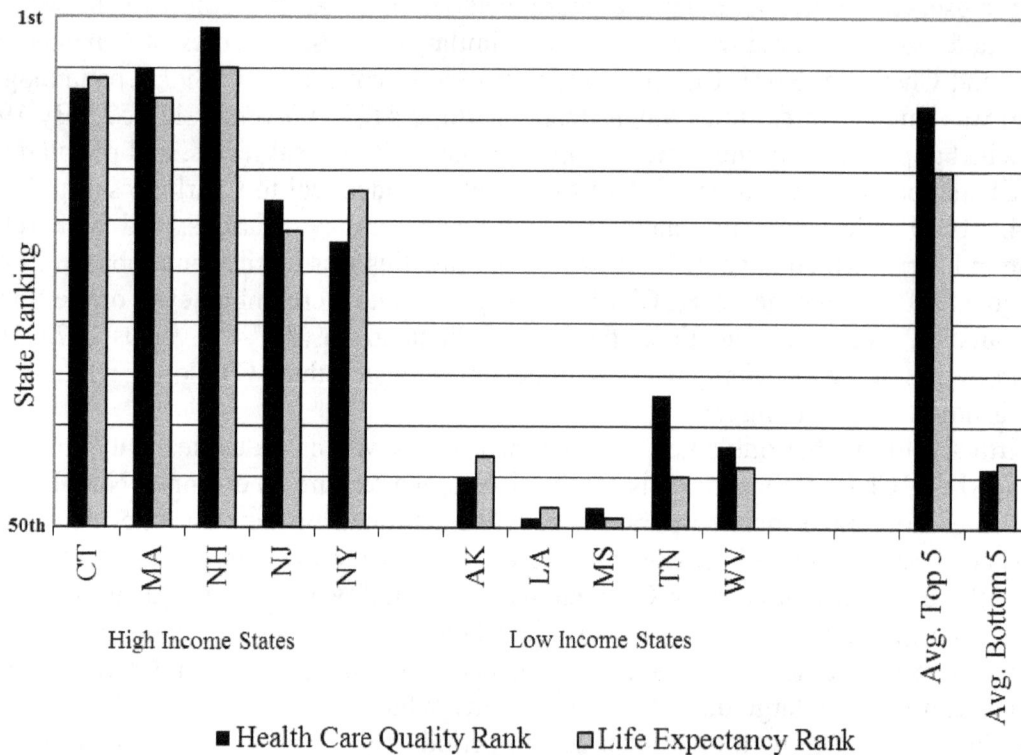

Sources: Quitno (2006); U.S. Census Bureau (2005).

This difference is not limited only to physical health; it also appears in measures of mental health. People in lower income states suffer from the highest rates of mental illness (almost 13 percent in the lower income states compared with only 9 percent in the richer states). This difference is likely due to the lower levels of stress at home and in the workplace that higher income brings.

In addition to our own health, we also care about the well-being of our families and children. All parents want their kids to have stable families, live in safe neighborhoods, and receive a good education. Does having higher income levels lead to these as well? Figure 1.8 presents the evidence. Families living in the five states with the highest incomes experience lower divorce rates than families in the five lowest income states (2.8 versus 4.8 on average). Richer families have fewer money problems destroying their marriages and more money to spend on family vacations and leisure activities. Furthermore, higher income leads to safer neighborhoods. For instance, states with higher incomes have lower rates of violent crime (3.4 versus 4.8 on average).

Our children benefit from economic growth not only in terms of safety and stability but also in the area of education. Children growing up in high income states are far more likely to graduate from high school. The five highest income states have higher percentages of the population graduating from high school than all five of the lowest income states. Higher income states have more children graduating from college as well (33.6 percent versus 19.6 percent college educated population, not shown in figure). Not only does more education increase a child's future earning potential, enhancing the state's prospects for growth in the future, but people with higher levels of education report higher levels of job satisfaction and overall happiness in their lives.

Figure 1.8: Divorce, Crime, and Education

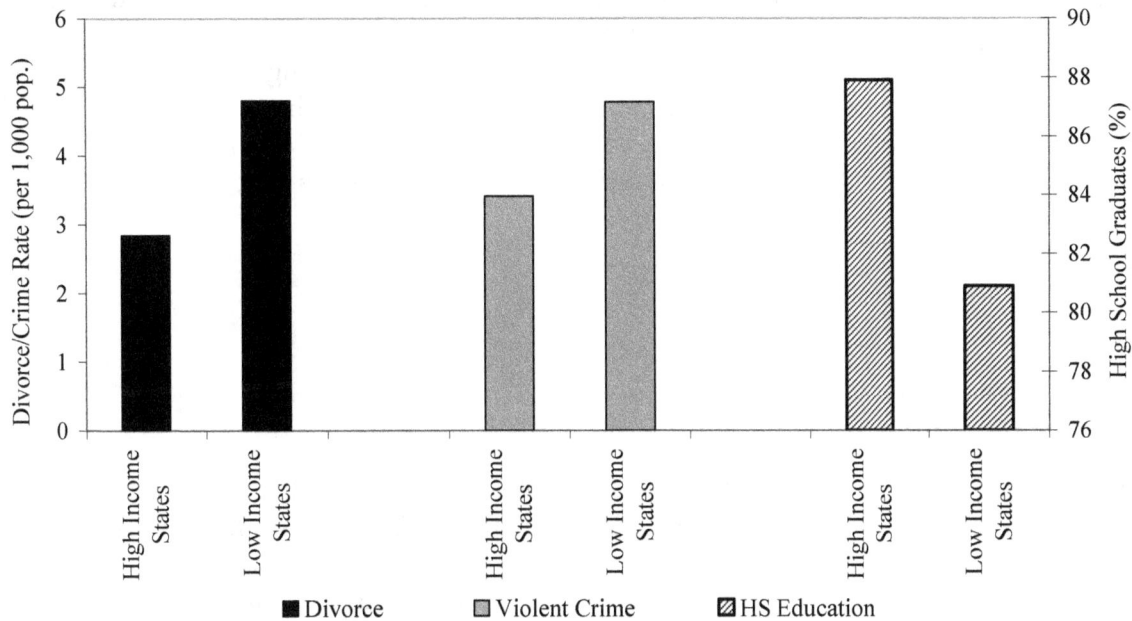

Sources: Federal Bureau of Investigation (2005); U.S. Census Bureau (2004, 2006).

The evidence is overwhelming. Economic growth not only makes us materially richer; it helps to accomplish our other goals as well. The objective of growth is really about creating a future for Tennessee where families are not only wealthier, but also happier, healthier, safer, and better educated.

CONCLUSION

This introductory chapter has explained how even small differences in economic growth rates can produce substantial differences in the quality of life within a generation or two. If Tennessee refuses to undertake policy reform, and continues its current trend, in twenty years the state will have fallen to 42nd in per capita personal income, and Tennesseans will remain at the bottom of the economic ladder.

In contrast, a better and richer Tennessee is possible to achieve within our lifetimes. An increase in Tennessee's rate of real per capita economic growth, back to the 1.7 percent level sustained from 1972 to 1981, would result in a ranking of 29th twenty years into the future. An increase back to the 2.4 percent level sustained from 1982 to 1995 would result in Tennessee becoming the 16th richest state in the nation within one generation, and the 8th richest state in the nation within two generations.

More importantly, this growth does not have to come at the expense of other things people value—to the contrary, these other areas are also enhanced by economic growth.

Reducing crime and increasing human capital through education are policy agenda items of the Tennessee Chamber of Commerce & Industry (2010, 2011) in their recent 10 for TN proposals. But improvements in these areas are a symptom of growth, not a cause. Policy reform that increases economic growth and prosperity in Tennessee will *automatically* result in reductions in crime and increases in educational attainment. These social ills are a result of poverty, not a cause of it, and focusing on policies targeted in those areas to produce economic growth is simply putting the cart in front of the horse.

But, can policy reform actually increase growth by a meaningful amount? Evidence from both the experience of U.S. states and countries around the globe suggests the answer is yes. In the next chapter we turn to the next important question: Which policies are most conducive to creating and sustaining long-term economic growth in a state?

REFERENCES

Bureau of Economic Analysis, U.S. Department of Commerce. 2012. *Annual State Personal Income*. Washington, DC: U.S. Department of Commerce. http://www.bea.gov/ regional /index.htm.

Bureau of Labor Statistics, U.S. Department of Labor. 2012. *Consumer Price Index*. Washington, DC: U.S. Department of Labor. http://bls.gov/cpi/.

Federal Bureau of Investigation, U.S. Department of Justice. 2005. *Crime in the United States 2004*. Washington, DC: Government Printing Office.

Quitno, Morgan. 2006. *Health Care State Rankings 2006*. Lawrence, KS: Morgan Quitno Press.

Sobel, Russell S., and Susane J. Daniels. 2007. "The Case for Growth." In *Unleashing Capitalism: Why Prosperity Stops at the West Virginia Border and How to Fix It*, edited by Russell S. Sobel, 1-12. Morgantown, WV: Center for Economic Growth, The Public Policy Foundation of West Virginia.

Sobel, Russell S., and Susane J. Leguizamon. 2009. "The Case for Growth." In *Unleashing Capitalism: A Prescription for Economic Prosperity in South Carolina*, edited by Peter T. Calcagno, 7-10. Columbia, SC: South Carolina Policy Council.

Summers, Robert, and Alan Heston. 1994. *The Penn World Tables (Mark 5.6)*. Cambridge, MA: National Bureau of Economic Research.

Tennessee Chamber of Commerce & Industry. 2010. *Business Insider*, Winter. Nashville, TN: Tennessee Chamber of Commerce & Industry. http://www.tnchamber.org /_member/_images/_page_images/files/78789_BusInsider_Winter10.pdf.

———. 2011. *Business Insider*, Summer. Nashville, TN: Tennessee Chamber of Commerce & Industry. http://www.tnchamber.org/_member/_images/_page_images/files/84200 _BusInsider_Summer11.pdf.

U.S. Census Bureau. 2004. *Education Attainment in the United States 2004*. Washington, DC: U.S. Census Bureau. www.census.gov/population/www/socdemo/education /cps2004 .html.

————. 2005. *Interim State Population Projections*. Washington, DC: U.S. Census Bureau. www.census.gov/population/projections/MethTab2.xls.

————. 2006. *Statistical Abstract of the United States, 2006.* Washington, DC: U.S. Census Bureau. www.census.gov/compendia/statab/2006/2006edition.html.

World Bank. 2004. *World Development Indicators*. CD-ROM.

CHAPTER 2

THE SOURCES OF ECONOMIC GROWTH

by Russell S. Sobel, J.R. Clark, and Joshua C. Hall

Freedom and Prosperity in Tennessee

2

THE SOURCES OF ECONOMIC GROWTH

Russell S. Sobel, J.R. Clark, and Joshua C. Hall

The previous chapter made the case for why increasing the rate of economic growth in Tennessee should be considered one of the top policy priorities. However, policy reform to promote growth should be based on evidence of what has worked, and what has not worked in Tennessee and other areas. Evidence was presented in the previous chapter that economic growth is faster in states like Vermont, Wyoming, North Dakota, South Dakota, and Montana; and in countries like Hong Kong and Japan. How can this be replicated in Tennessee? Can we uncover which policies tend to promote prosperity? These are the questions we address in this chapter.[1]

As we will soon see, there is one feature that high-income and fast-growth places generally have in common: They have unleashed capitalism and backed it up with sound political and legal systems that firmly protect property rights and prohibit fraud, theft, and coercion. By doing so, they have created a level playing field for prosperity to take root. As economist Dwight Lee writes:

> No matter how fertile the seeds of entrepreneurship, they wither without the proper economic soil. In order for entrepreneurship to germinate, take root, and yield the fruit of economic progress it has to be nourished by the right mixture of freedom and accountability, a mixture that can only be provided by a free market economy. (1991, 20)

THE PROCESS OF ECONOMIC GROWTH

To understand economic growth and the best way for government policy to promote it, we must first delve deeper into the relationship between economic inputs, institutions, and outcomes.

---

[1] This chapter is based on Sobel and Hall (2007b, 2009).

An economy is a *process* by which economic inputs and resources, such as skilled labor, capital, and funding for new businesses, are converted into economic outcomes (e.g., wage growth, job creation, or new businesses). This concept is illustrated in Figure 2.1. As the large arrow in the middle of the figure shows, the economic outcomes generated from any specific set of economic inputs depend on the "institutions"—the political and economic "rules of the game"—under which an economy operates. The important point is that some rules of the game are better than others at producing prosperity.

Figure 2.1: Inputs, Institutions, and Outcomes

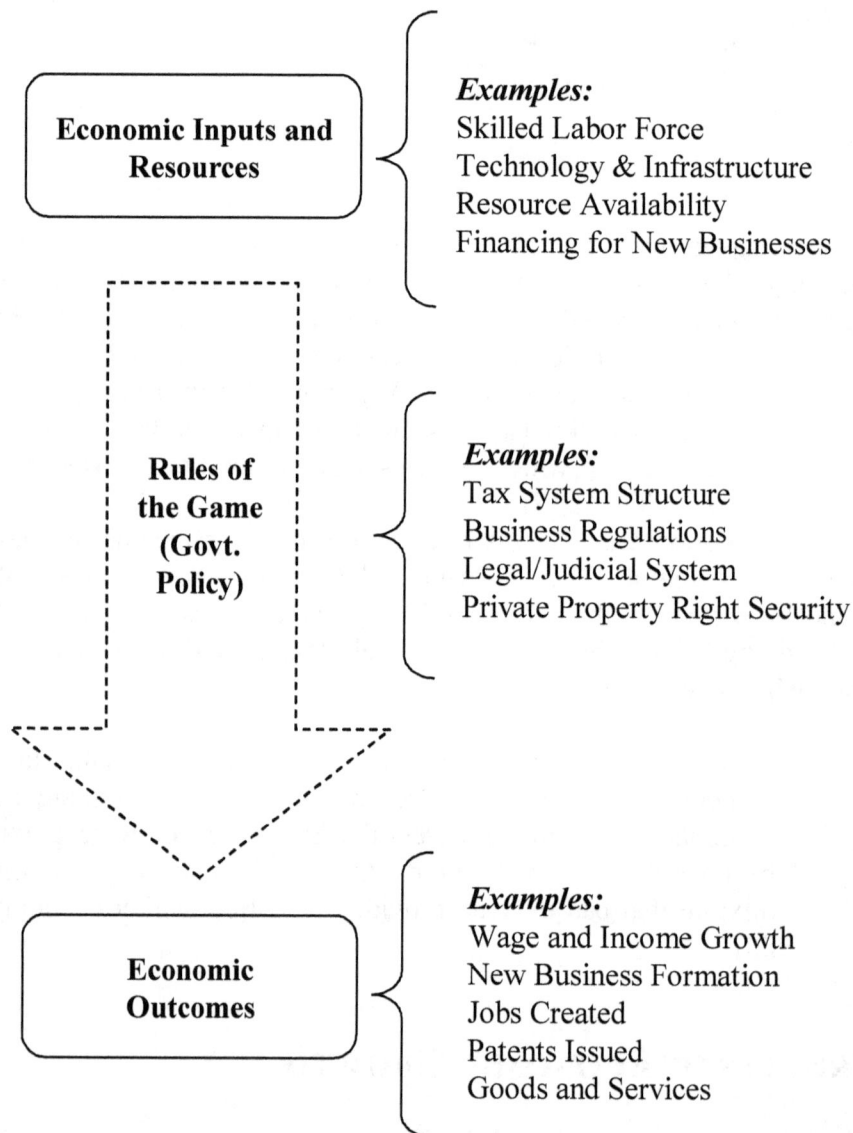

Economic Inputs and Resources

Examples:
Skilled Labor Force
Technology & Infrastructure
Resource Availability
Financing for New Businesses

Rules of the Game (Govt. Policy)

Examples:
Tax System Structure
Business Regulations
Legal/Judicial System
Private Property Right Security

Economic Outcomes

Examples:
Wage and Income Growth
New Business Formation
Jobs Created
Patents Issued
Goods and Services

Source: Hall and Sobel (2006).

Several analogies will help to clarify. First, let us consider a basketball game. The players, the court, and the basketballs are all inputs into the process. The "institutions" in this context are the rules under which the game is played. Some examples of these rules are the time length of the game, the length given on the shot clock, the rules on fouling, and the three-point line rule. Examples of the measurable outcomes are the score, the winning team, the number of fouls, etc. The important point is that the outcomes will be influenced by which rules of the game are chosen. The reason for this is that the rules of the game affect the choices and behavior of the people playing the game. If, for example, the rule that shots made from behind the three-point line were changed so that these were now worth only one and a half points, we would expect players to respond to this rule change in a predictable manner. As the point value of those longer shots decreased, fewer players would attempt them.[2]

While a basketball example might sound hypothetical, Clemson University economists Robert McCormick and Robert Tollison (1984) found that while adding an additional referee to a basketball game was expected to result in more fouls being called, a slower-paced game, and less scoring, when these rule changes were actually introduced in ACC basketball they had precisely the opposite effect. The result was fewer fouls, a faster pace, and more scoring. The explanation? Knowing that fouls were more likely to be called by referees, players changed their behavior and committed fewer of them.

To take another example, consider for a moment the board game Monopoly. The "institutions" in this analogy are again the rules under which the game is played. Imagine if a new rule was created making it legitimate to steal the property cards of other players if they were not looking. The play and outcomes from a game of Monopoly would be significantly different under these different institutional rules, as players would alter their behavior in response to them. Not only would this rule change increase the rate of theft among players, it would also result in fewer properties being purchased, less investment (houses or hotels) on the properties, and more resources being devoted to trying to protect their property cards from being stolen (and more effort into trying to steal the property of other players).

As a final analogy, consider the process of baking cakes. In this context, the ingredients are the inputs, the "institutions" are the oven, and the outcomes are the delicious cakes that result at the end. The main point is obvious—if the oven is not working, simply putting more ingredients (inputs) into the oven does not result in more cakes coming out the other end. Too many government policies at every level of government fail to realize this, and keep pouring money into programs that attempt to increase the inputs into the economy when the real problem is that the oven is broken due to failed economic policies. An economy cannot spend its way out of problems that are caused by weak institutions. Rather, institutions must be improved, and this, and only this, will result in investments in inputs paying dividends at the other end of the process.

This model makes it clear that by improving institutions, or the rules of the game under which the Tennessee economy operates, economic outcomes can be changed for the better. When institutions are weak, even places with abundant natural resources or other inputs have difficulty becoming prosperous. Tennessee, and the countries of Argentina and Venezuela, fit into this category of resource-rich areas that have not been able to sustain economic growth (as was noted in the previous chapter).

The important point is that our daily economic lives are played out under a set of rules that are to a large extent determined by government-enacted laws and policies. These political

---

[2] This change in the rules would also alter the incentives in the selection of players, or investments in resources for an economy. Coaches would now have a much weaker preference for players who could make longer shots.

and legal "institutions" as economists call them, are what create the incentive structures within the state economy. Prosperity requires that Tennessee gets the rules right.

ADAM SMITH'S QUESTION:
WHY ARE SOME PLACES RICH AND OTHERS POOR?

Adam Smith, the "father of economics," published the first book addressing the set of topics we now consider "economics" in 1776. In his book, titled *An Inquiry into the Nature and Causes of the Wealth of Nations*, Adam Smith ([1776] 1998) attempted to answer a single question: Why are some nations rich and others poor? Economic science has come a long way in 230 years, and volumes of published research now clearly provide the answer to the question Adam Smith posed long ago. The answer is fundamentally the same one arrived at by Adam Smith.

In a nutshell, he found that countries become prosperous when they have good institutions that create favorable rules of the game—rules that encourage the creation of wealth. Smith further concluded that the institutional structure that best promotes prosperity is an economic system of capitalism backed up by sound political and legal institutions. According to Smith, an economy becomes prosperous when they use unregulated private markets to the greatest extent possible, with the government playing the important, but limited role of protecting liberty, property, and enforcing contracts. Over 230 years of published scientific evidence now supports Smith's conclusion.

Capitalism is not a political position or platform, it is an economic system—a set of institutions or rules that define the "economic game." Capitalism's institutions produce prosperity better than the alternative of government control, not only in terms of financial wealth, but in terms of other measures of quality of life. Adopting institutions ("rules of the game") consistent with the economic system of capitalism has the potential to generate outcomes that better accomplish the common goals of all political parties: prosperity, wealth, health, family, security, etc.

THE RISE AND DECLINE OF ECONOMIC FREEDOM
IN TENNESSEE

While most people tend to think of capitalism and socialism as alternative and discrete forms of economic organization, in reality government policies tend to lie somewhere on a continuum between these two extremes. What differs on this continuum is the degree to which the government uses its power to enact command and control policies that intervene into the private sector. Some countries, like North Korea, have governments that use a command and control approach to organizing nearly the entire economy. These countries lie at the extreme socialist end of the capitalist-socialist spectrum. Other countries, such as China, are nominally socialist, but rely considerably more on the private sector in organizing their economies. Some countries have moved from one end of the continuum to the other, like the former Soviet Republics of Estonia and Latvia, and Slovenia (formerly part of socialist Yugoslavia), who all adopted radical reforms that moved them toward capitalism.

On the other hand, most market-based economies have a much larger degree of government intervention and control than is envisioned under pure capitalism. Within the last two decades, a significant advance in our understanding of this continuum was the publication of the *Economic Freedom of the World* index created by economists James Gwartney (a former Chief Economist of the Joint Economic Committee of Congress) and Robert Lawson.[3] They derive an index measure for each country placing it on a scale of zero to ten, where ten represents the greatest degree of "economic freedom," i.e., reliance on capitalism, and zero represents the greatest degree of "economic repression," i.e., reliance on government control of the economy. In the most recent index, the United States scores 7.6 out of 10, ranking it the tenth most capitalist, or free-market, economy in the world. The United States has fallen five spots in the past two years however, and now ranks below Canada. The countries ranking as the most capitalist in the world are Hong Kong, Singapore, New Zealand, and Switzerland.

Figure 2.2: Tennessee's Economic Freedom Rank

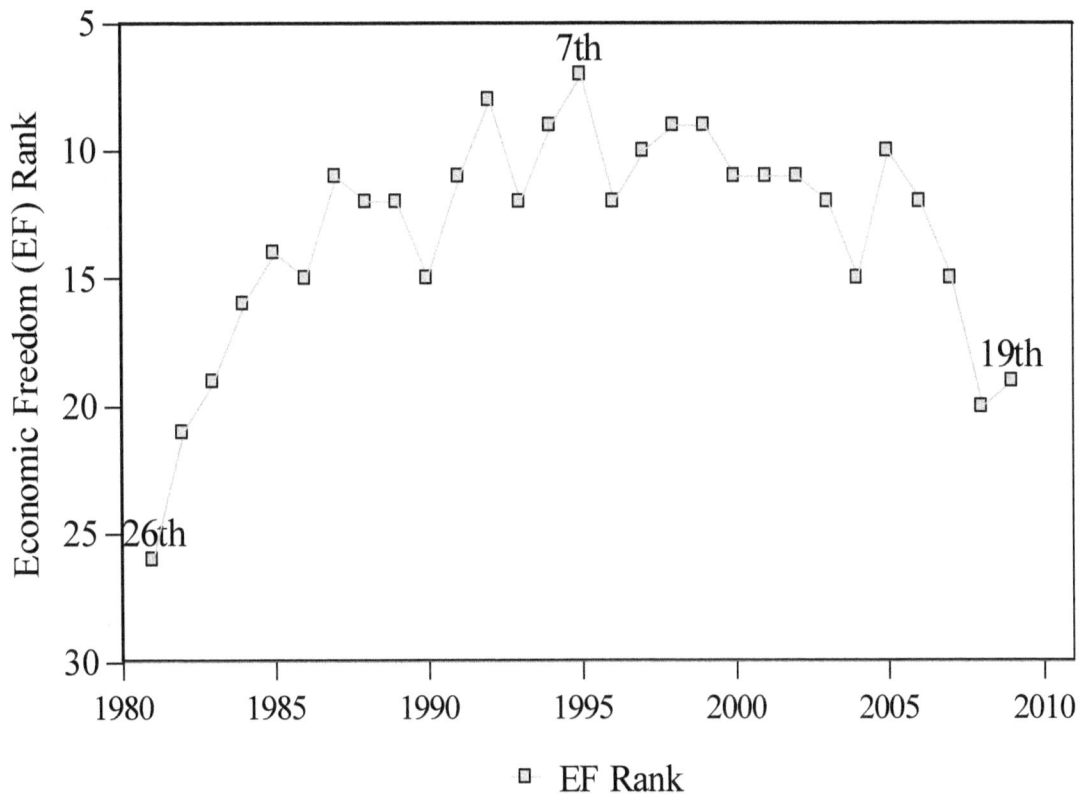

Source: Ashby, Bueno, and McMahon (2011).

Because state and local policies vary within the United States, Amela Karabegovic and Fred McMahon (2008) created an index of the *Economic Freedom of North America*, that ranks U.S. states and Canadian provinces by the degree of free-market orientation within each

---

[3] Online at: http://www.freetheworld.com. The most recent edition is the 2011 report (Gwartney, Lawson, and Hall 2011).

state or province.[4] Among U.S. states, Tennessee ranked 19th in the most recent index, for year 2009 data. In 1995, however, Tennessee was ranked 7th in this index. Figure 2.2 shows how Tennessee's economic freedom rank has changed.

From 1981 to 1995, Tennessee rose from 26th to 7th in the economic freedom ranking among U.S. states. Since that time, and particularly since 2005, economic freedom has been on the decline in Tennessee, falling back to near where it began in the early 1980s.

Does the "market-friendliness" of Tennessee's policies help to explain its recent economic performance? Recall that Figure 1.2 from Chapter 1 showed Tennessee's per capita income ranking from 1929 forward, and that there was a large improvement in Tennessee's ranking in the 1980s followed by a subsequent decline. Figure 2.3 shows the remarkable correlation between Tennessee's economic freedom and per capita income rankings. Here, Tennessee's per capita income ranking is measured on the left y-axis, while its economic freedom ranking is on the right y-axis. Also shown in the figure in boxes at the top are the average growth rates during these two periods.

Figure 2.3: Economic Freedom vs. Prosperity in Tennessee

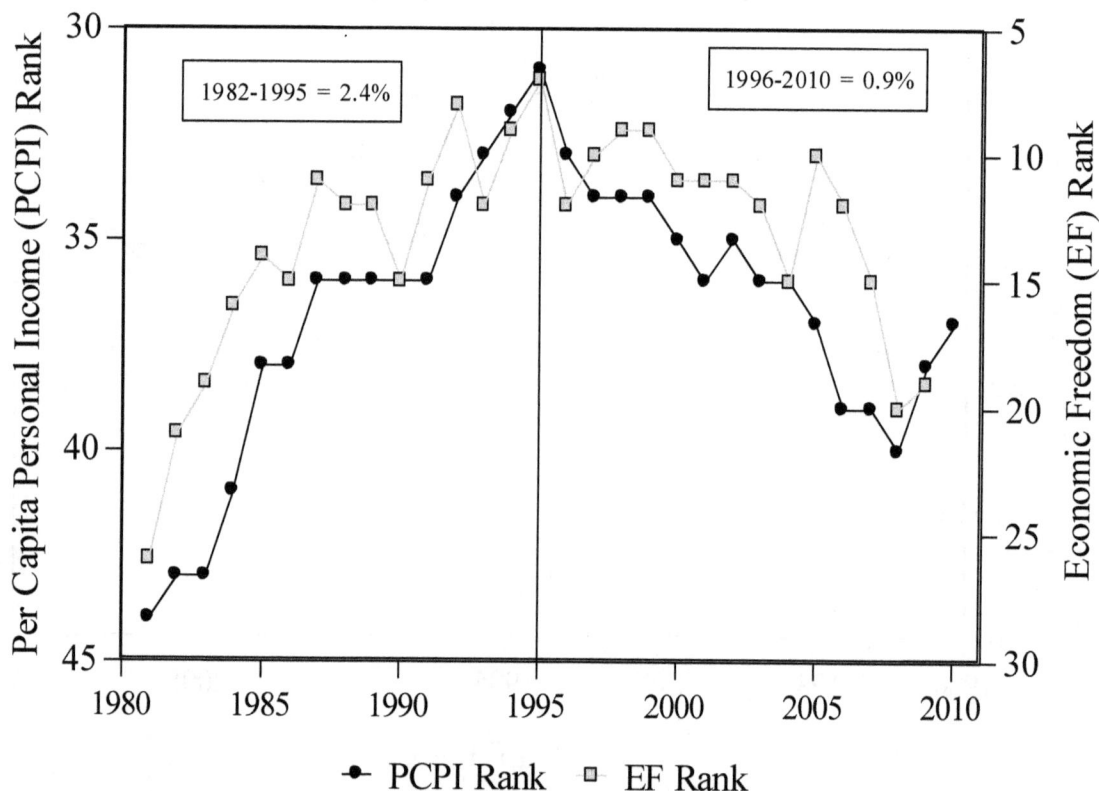

Source: Ashby, Bueno, and McMahon (2011) and Bureau of Economic Analysis (2012).

Between 1982 and 1995 when Tennessee's economic freedom was improving, growth was rapid (2.4 percent), and the state rose 13 spots in the per capita income rankings.

[4] Online at http://www.freetheworld.com. The most recent edition is the 2011 report (Ashby, Bueno, and McMahon 2011) which includes annual rankings through 2009. Rankings reported in this chapter have been recalculated among only the U.S. states (i.e., excluding the Canadian provinces).

Beginning in 1995, economic freedom began falling, and Tennessee's growth slowed substantially (0.9 percent). From 2005 to 2008, Tennessee's economic freedom dropped significantly, and it fell four places in the per capita income rankings in only four years. A recent, but slight, improvement in economic freedom from 2008 to 2009 resulted in the per capita income ranking rising three spots in three years.

The point should be obvious, for Tennessee to improve economic growth it must again move toward policies that embrace capitalism and free markets. If Tennessee continues its downward trend that began in the mid-1990s, the state's economic ranking is likely to suffer, and within two decades Tennessee will be at the very bottom of the national economic rankings with states such as West Virginia and Mississippi. With all of Tennessee's advantages over these states, it is almost unbelievable that the Volunteer State could be in such company. Yet, as the earlier oven analogy demonstrated, when policies are bad, economic outcomes suffer despite having good inputs included in the process.

To help illustrate how Tennessee relies on capitalism less than some of the other U.S. states, it is worthwhile to examine one of the major components of the economic freedom index: government spending as a share of the state economy (shown in Figure 2.4).

Figure 2.4: Government Control of the Economy

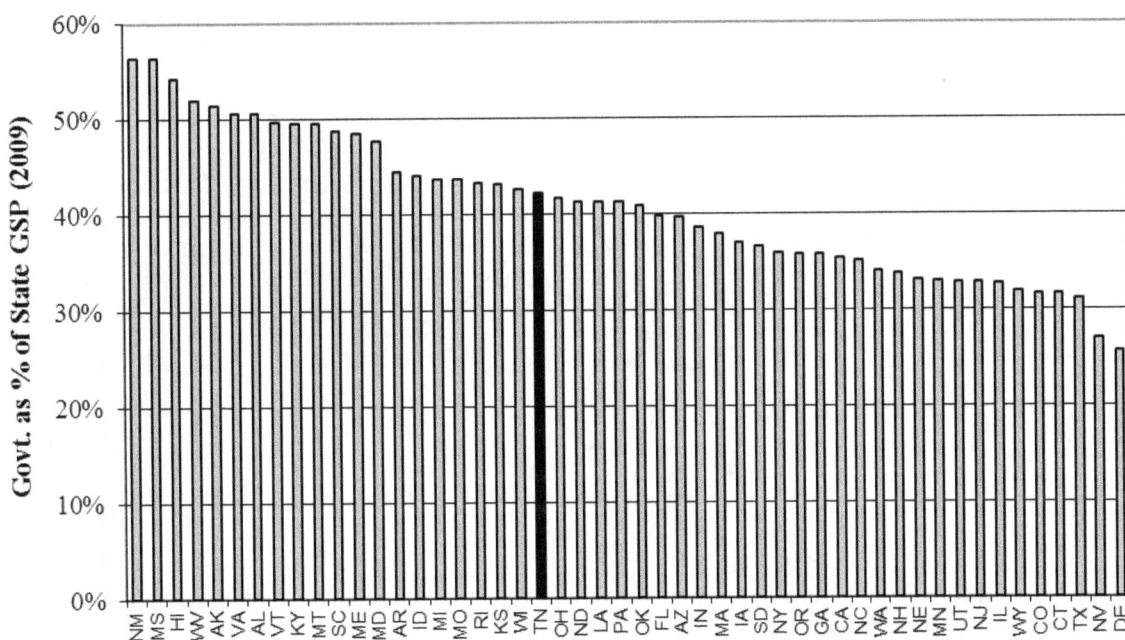

Source: Ashby, Bueno, and McMahon (2011).

How much government spends relative to the total size of a state's economy is a good measure of the extent to which government controls the allocation of economic resources in a state. Government spending is, of course, only one component of the overall economic freedom index, which also includes measures of government regulations, relative tax rates, and threats to private property.

Looking at spending alone, relative to the other U.S. states, Tennessee has the 21st largest government share of state economic activity. Combined, all federal, state, and local government spending in Tennessee amounts to 42.2 percent of the state economy. For comparison, in the most free market state, Delaware, government controls only 25.6 percent of the economy, leaving roughly 75 percent to the private sector. At the other extreme, in the state ranking 50th in economic freedom (the least capitalist state), West Virginia, government spending is among the highest in the nation, taking up 51.9 percent of the state economy, and leaving less than half of the state's economic resources available to the private sector. In both New Mexico and Mississippi, government spending exceeds 56 percent of the economy.

Change in Tennessee's government size as a share of its economy is one of the key factors that led to the trends in economic freedom shown earlier. Figure 2.5 shows Tennessee's ranking in the size of government component of the economic freedom index. Here lower rankings (implying smaller government control) are better, and higher rankings (implying more government control) are worse, as the size of government enters negatively into the computation of the overall economic freedom index.

Figure 2.5: Tennessee's Government Size Rankings

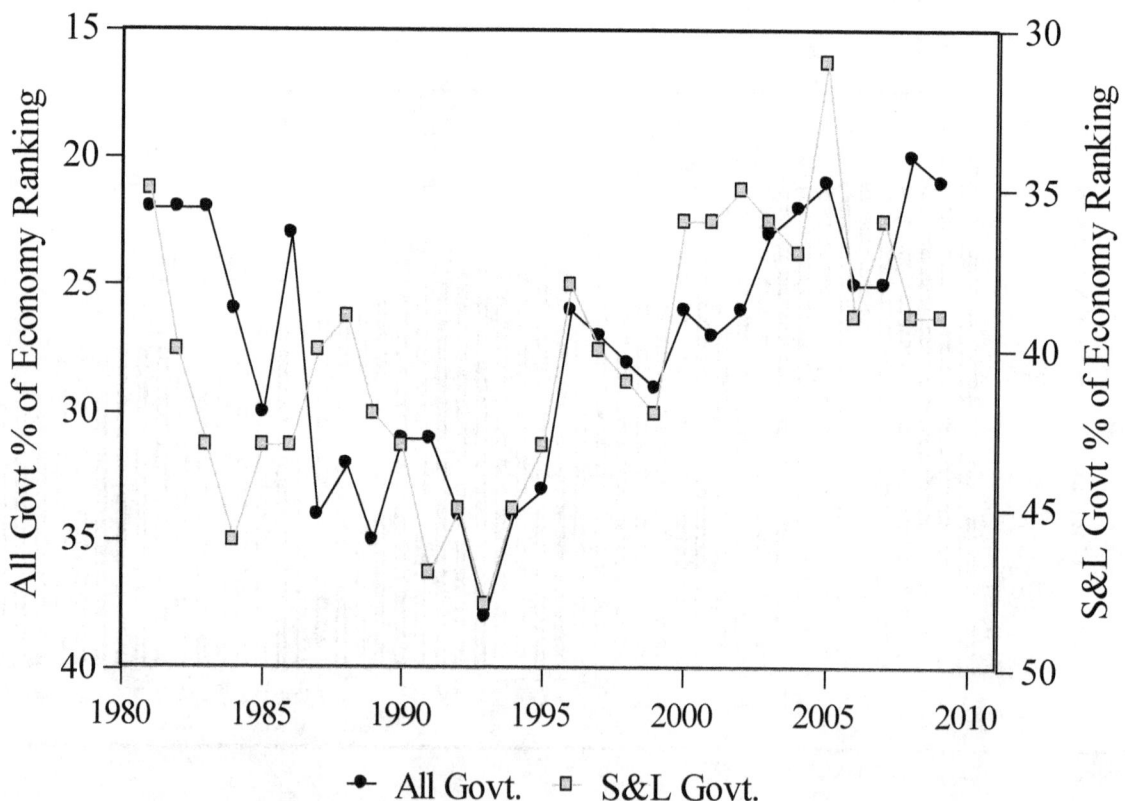

Source: Ashby, Bueno, and McMahon (2011).

During the 1980s and early-1990s, total (all) government spending fell by roughly 4 percent of the state's economy, while it has risen by 12 percent of the state's economy since. This expansion in the size of government has led to Tennessee's ranking in government-sector control of the economy worsening by 17 places. While Tennessee currently has the 21st *largest* government sector among U.S. states, back in 1993 Tennessee had the 13th *smallest* government sector (ranked 38th). Excluding federal spending doesn't change the pattern. While Tennessee used to have the 3rd *smallest* state and local (S&L) government control (ranked 48th), it has worsened 9 spots in the rankings since that time considering state and local spending alone. Tennessee's government spending as a share of the economy was higher in 2009, either including or excluding federal spending, than it had been in the entire history of the state. Recent reductions from 2010 to 2011 in the state's budget are a move in the right direction, and Tennessee needs to maintain this trend to stimulate economic growth.

The pattern shown by the data is obvious. During the period prior to 1995, Tennessee's government was shrinking as a share of the economy, and economic growth was rapid. Since that time Tennessee's government sector has grown substantially and as a result Tennessee's rate of economic growth has fallen dramatically. International studies across OECD countries suggest that a nation's economic growth rate falls by 1 percentage point for every 10 percentage point increase in government as a share of the economy (Gwartney et al. 2009). This, interestingly, is roughly the amount by which Tennessee's economic growth rate has fallen as its government sector expanded by 12 percent of the state economy since the mid-1990s. The slowdown in economic growth is not entirely explained by the increase in government spending, as other indicators in the economic freedom index show downward trends as well. While Tennessee's scores for 8 of the 10 index components rose from 1981 to 1995, since that time Tennessee's scores for 7 of the 10 index components have fallen.[5]

TENNESSEE'S OTHER ECONOMIC POLICY RANKINGS

Not only does Tennessee's economic freedom ranking show the need for policy reforms that embrace capitalism, nearly every other national index of business climate agrees. Tennessee's most recent rankings in all of the major national indices of state business climates are presented below.

Tennessee's Business Climate Rankings: [6]

25th Small Business & Entrepreneurship Council's *Small Business Survival Index* (2011)
17th Small Business & Entrepreneurship Council's *Small Business Tax Index* (2011)
27th Tax Foundation's *State Business Tax Climate Index* (2011)
19th Fraser Institute's *Economic Freedom of North America* (2011)
18th CNBC's *America's Top States for Business* (2011)
44th Corporation for Enterprise Development's (CFED) *Development Capacity Index* (2007)
41st Progressive Policy Institute's (PPI) *New Economy Index* (2010)
44th Beacon Hill Institute's *State Competitiveness Report* (2010)
41st Milken Institute's *National State Technology & Science Index* (2010)
19th Institute for Legal Reform (ILR) / Harris *State Liability Systems Ranking Study* (2010)

---

[5] These 10 index components measure a variety of factors including government spending, taxes, regulations, and the security of property rights.

[6] These rankings can be found online at the following websites: http://www.milkeninstitute.org (two), http://www.taxfoundation.org, http://www.itif.org/, http://www.beaconhill.org, http://www.sbecouncil.org (two), http://www.cfed.org, http://www.instituteforlegalreform.com, http://www.pacificresearch.org, http://www.cnbc.com, http://www.freetheworld.com, and http://www.forbes.com.

22nd   Pacific Research Institute's *U.S. Tort Liability Index* (2010)
9th   Milken Institute's *Cost of Doing Business Index* (2007, inverted to make 1=best)
21st   Forbes *Best States for Business* (2011)

With the exception of the *Cost of Doing Business Index*, Tennessee generally ranks in the 20s to mid-40s in the national business climate rankings. These indices are to one extent or another measuring the same thing: Tennessee's lack of reliance on capitalism.

The one area of Tennessee's business climate that has shown significant improvement in recent years is the legal system rankings. Due to Tennessee's tort and medical malpractice reforms, in the ILR/Harris ranking for example, Tennessee has improved 10 spots in the ranking. This is in jeopardy however if the proposal to move to elected judges in Tennessee becomes law. Studies clearly show that states with elected judges, especially if they are elected in partisan elections, have worse legal systems than those states with an appointment mechanism for selecting judges (Sobel and Hall 2007a; Hall and Sobel 2008; Hall and Sobel 2009). Tennessee's recent expansion in charter schools, and restrictions on collective bargaining for teachers, are also movements in the right direction.

Tennessee's lack of a state income tax on wage income is one of the state's main advantages over most other states. Numerous studies have shown that states without income taxes on wage income grow significantly faster, and are more prosperous, than states with income taxes on wage income, and the most convincing of these studies use border county comparisons across state lines. Tennessee's limited income tax only taxes interest and dividend income, at a rate of 6 percent, and allows for a $1,250 exemption per filer, as well as generous (and recently increased) exemptions for those aged 65 and over with taxable income less than $26,200 (single) or $37,000 (married). It accounts for only a very small fraction of state tax revenue, but it does provide some revenue for local governments in Tennessee who get 2.25 of the 6 percent tax. The 6 percent rate is in line with Tennessee's eight neighboring states (whose rates range from 5 to 7.75 percent). As a foundation for future prosperity, Tennessee should reject proposals that call for imposing a state income tax on wage income.

Tennessee's corporate income tax of 6.5 percent is also in line with the eight neighboring states whose top rates range from 5 to 6.9 percent. Tennessee's state sales tax rate is 7 percent. Neighboring state Mississippi also levies a 7 percent state sales tax rate, and two of Tennessee's other neighbors, Kentucky and Arkansas, levy state sales tax rates of 6 percent, only 1 percentage point lower than Tennessee. Georgia and Alabama have the lowest state sales tax rates of Tennessee's neighbors at 4 percent. Tennessee allows local option sales taxes, and the average local sales tax rate in Tennessee is 2.44 percent. This compares favorably to Alabama's local sales tax average of 4.03 percent, Missouri's average of 3.24 percent, and Georgia's average of 2.95 percent. There are no local sales taxes in neighboring states Kentucky and Mississippi. At neither the state or local level alone do Tennessee's sales tax rates seem out of line with surrounding states, however, when one combines the two rates, Tennessee does rank the highest in the nation at a combined rate of 9.44 percent.[7]

While this high ranking on the sales tax has been a statistic cited in the press during debates about lowering the sales tax on food in Tennessee, it is important to remember both that states without income taxes on wage income (like Tennessee) generally have higher sales tax rates to generate additional revenue, and that if it were not for the high local sales taxes, the state's 7 percent rate alone would only rank Tennessee as tied for the 19th highest

---

[7] Tax rates cited are as of January 1, 2011; source: http://www.taxfoundation.org.

combined sales tax rate in the nation (tied with Indiana, Mississippi, New Jersey, and Rhode Island). Like many other states, Tennessee does levy a lower sales tax rate on food. Despite the popular argument that reducing the sales tax rate on food helps the poorest citizens, it is important to remember that all purchases with federal food stamps are exempt by federal law from state sales taxes in all states. Recent proposals to lower the current 5.5 percent rate on food down to 5 percent over three years really do little to help those most in need whose food stamp purchases are not subject to the tax anyway. The bigger danger is that proposals to lower Tennessee's sales taxes would be tied to increases in other taxes that are more damaging to economic growth than is the sales tax. The more important point, however, is from the standpoint of promoting economic growth; if some taxes are to be reduced, there are much more important taxes to cut than the sales tax.

The taxes most in need of reform in Tennessee to increase economic growth are the taxes that fall on capital investment (such as property taxes on machinery, equipment, intangibles, and inventories), and the taxes on inheritance and gifts that reduce the incentives to accumulate wealth and pass that wealth on to future generations, especially through the transfer of family businesses. As we will discuss in the next chapter, capital investment—expenditures on things like machinery and equipment that increase the productivity of labor—is a key driver of economic growth. Unfortunately, Tennessee levies some of the highest taxes in the nation on capital investment, a big factor limiting the economic growth prospects of the Volunteer State.

As an example, Tennessee's effective property tax rate on industrial property is among the highest in the nation. A study by the Minnesota Center for Public Finance Research that appears in the *2009 Competitiveness Redbook* published by the National Association of Manufacturers (2009) provides a ranking of the tax burden on a representative manufacturing business with $25 million of property consisting of $12.5 million in machinery and equipment, $10 million in inventories, and $2.5 million in fixtures. Tennessee ranks tenth, with an annual property tax bill of $1,033,544 which amounts to a 2.067 percent effective tax rate. For comparison, in the most free-market state, Delaware, this same business's property tax bill would be $238,840 (an effective rate of 0.478 percent, the lowest in the nation). Thus, the annual property tax bill for an identical manufacturing business in Delaware is about one-fourth of the tax bill they face in Tennessee.

Perhaps more importantly, the property taxes levied on this business in six of Tennessee's eight neighboring states are significantly lower; $241,498 in Virginia, $327,100 in Kentucky, $491,071 in North Carolina, $553,776 in Alabama, $686,550 in Arkansas, and $760,381 in Georgia. By choosing to locate right across the state border, this representative manufacturing firm's tax bill would be between 25 and 77 percent lower. Only Mississippi and Missouri have higher effective property taxes at $1,291,050 and $1,111,255 respectively. The high property tax rates Tennessee imposes on equipment and machinery result in less capital investment and reduced prosperity for all Tennesseans.

Like a three legged stool, a state's tax system, legal system, and regulatory code must all be well designed to support economic growth. While we have discussed Tennessee's legal and tax codes, reforms to the state's regulatory structure also warrant discussion. Regulatory reform is also a policy priority of the Tennessee Chamber of Commerce & Industry (2010, 2011) in its recent 10 for TN proposals. In national rankings of regulatory climate, Tennessee doesn't do too poorly, raking 6th best in the country in the *Forbes* index subcomponent on regulatory climate, and 12th when ranking states by their expenditures on regulatory enforcement. However, what matters most is Tennessee's rank relative to its neighboring states, and three of Tennessee's neighbors rank in first, second, and third place in the *Forbes* regulatory ranking, while two others rank seventh and ninth. In addition, these indices also give states higher rankings for having Right-to-Work laws, so part of Tennessee's high ranking is simply due to this one policy. The true regulatory climate that impacts small and large businesses would rank much lower on the list if this one labor-related policy was excluded.

One significant problem with regulations—in all states—is that there is no natural "profit and loss" mechanism that serves to indicate which regulations, once in place, are performing well and which are not. Identifying which current regulations are ineffective or fail to create benefits that exceed economic costs is difficult, and getting these regulations repealed through the political process is often even more of a challenge. One obvious area for improvement in Tennessee has to do with its sunset provision. While sunset provisions—those that force regulations to be reconsidered and fight to stay in place—have been shown to result in significantly improved state regulatory climates, Tennessee's sunset provision, adopted in 1982, that all newly enacted rules sunset after one year, is often circumvented by the state legislature. According to Hahn (2000, 882-3), in Tennessee "the legislature routinely votes to eliminate the expiration date of the sunset provision, defeating its original purpose." Hahn notes that in one year the legislature only allowed seven rules adopted in the previous year to expire, and all seven were minor issues or rules.

A more recent study in 2010 by Jason Schwartz from the New York University School of Law's Institute for Policy Integrity, gives Tennessee a grade of "D" in its regulatory review system. Schwartz notes that "Tennessee has not aggressively used its power to sunset rules. In the 1990s, the legislature voted to extend nearly all rules beyond the expiration date of the sunset provision" (371). He continues, that from "2005 through 2010, only one rule has not been extended by the annual legislation on sunsetting rules." Schwartz notes that until recently the House and Senate Government Operations Committees have been "plagued by squabbling or indifference...and have had trouble scheduling joint meetings to review rules."

While Tennessee has granted its legislative review committees substantial power, and has recently amended their authority in 2009, Schwartz remains skeptical of Tennessee's process of regulatory review. Schwartz (2010, 371) concludes:

> Tennessee's structure is not reasonable...Reviewing rules by forcing them to expire after one year is not the most straightforward or efficient approach to regulatory review. The system also only gives the legislature the binary choice of letting a rule expire or not, instead of helping to calibrate regulations...historically review has been inconsistent and not transparent. There is no effective periodic review, inter-agency coordination, or protection against agency inaction. Analytical requirements are extremely weak, though at least the regulatory flexibility analysis looks at the consequences of creating small business exemptions.

Clearly there is room for improvement in Tennessee's system of regulatory review. Perhaps a longer sunset window, but with a more meaningful requirement for an independent, non-governmental, body to undertake serious and transparent cost-benefit and efficiency analysis, with public input, and considering amendments and changes to regulations, would help to improve Tennessee's regulatory code.

TENNESSEE HAS LOW ECONOMIC FREEDOM RELATIVE TO ITS NEIGHBORING STATES

As we have alluded to in the discussions of Tennessee's regulatory ranking and taxes on capital investment, what matters most is not Tennessee's absolute rankings in national policy indices, but rather Tennessee's rank relative to its neighboring states. Because business firms and citizens alike can easily locate across a state border to avoid policies and take advantage of other regional, geographic, transportation, or weather advantages, having "good" policies sometimes simply is not enough when you have neighbors with "great" policies. Unfortunately, Tennessee is in this situation. At least three of Tennessee's neighbors are among the very top in the nation when it comes to business and economic policy. Sometimes having good neighbors is a disadvantage.

Of the thirteen business climate rankings presented earlier, Tennessee ranks in the top ten in only one of them. Virginia, on the other hand, is in the top ten nationally in seven of the thirteen rankings, and in the top fifteen in ten of the rankings. Similarly, North Carolina ranks in the top ten in four of the rankings, and Georgia in two. When comparing Tennessee to its neighboring states only, Virginia beats Tennessee in eleven of the thirteen rankings, North Carolina and Missouri beat Tennessee in nine of the thirteen rankings, and Georgia beats Tennessee in eight of the thirteen rankings. The only neighbors that Tennessee outranks on a majority of the business climate rankings are Arkansas, Kentucky, and Mississippi. In the critical economic freedom ranking, both North Carolina and Georgia are among the top ten most economically free states in the nation, while Tennessee ranks 19th.

Ranking Tennessee only versus its neighbors on an index by index basis, Tennessee ranks sixth or worse out of these nine states in five of the business climate rankings. Thus, while Tennessee's mid-level absolute national rankings in many of the indices may seem adequate, with such competitive neighbors, adequate simply isn't good enough when you are competing with those states for new businesses and residents.

Because business location decisions are most flexible across neighboring state lines, this is problematic for Tennessee. It also increases the importance of making policy reforms in the Volunteer State an immediate priority.

Because of their better business climates, Georgia and North Carolina have created a more vibrant entrepreneurial environment. Measures of entrepreneurial activity, including venture capital investments per capita, patents per capita, establishment birth rates for large firms, and the growth rate of sole proprietorships, show Tennessee lagging behind its neighboring states.[8]

---

[8] See Figure 2.7 for the actual numbers.

WHAT IS CAPITALISM? THE CONCEPT OF ECONOMIC FREEDOM

While everyone has a general idea of what economists mean by the term "capitalism" it is important that we now define it more precisely. Fundamentally, capitalism is an economic system founded on the private ownership of the productive assets within an economy. These include land, labor (including your person), and all other tangible property (e.g., cars, houses, factories, etc.) and intangible property (e.g., radio waves, intellectual property, etc.). Individuals are free to make decisions regarding the use of their property, with the sole constraint that they do not infringe upon the property rights of others.

The freedom of action given to private owners under a system of capitalism is why the index that ranks states and countries is called the "economic freedom" index. Economic freedom is synonymous with capitalism. More specifically, the key ingredients of economic freedom and capitalism are:

- personal choice and accountability for damages to others,
- voluntary exchange, with unregulated prices negotiated by buyers and sellers,
- freedom to become an entrepreneur and compete with existing businesses, and
- protection of persons and property from physical aggression, theft, lawsuits, or confiscation by others, including the government.

The concept of capitalism is deeply rooted in the notions of individual liberty and freedom that underlie our country's founding and are reflected in the Declaration of Independence and the U.S. Constitution. Economic freedoms are based in the same philosophies that support political and civil liberties (like the freedom of speech and the freedom to elect representatives). Individuals have a right to decide how they will use their assets and talents. On the other hand, they do not have a right to the time, talents, and resources of others.

Because private property rights, and their protection, are critical to economic progress, it is worthwhile to be more specific about private property rights.[9] Private property rights entail three economic aspects: (1) control rights—the right to do with your property as you wish, even to exclude others from using it, so long as you do not use your property to infringe on the property rights of someone else; (2) cash flow rights—the right to the income earned from the property or its use (i.e. being the "residual claimant," which is also critical for enabling the property to be used as collateral for loans); and, (3) transferability rights—the right to sell or divest of your property under the terms and conditions you see fit.

---

[9] Note that the appropriate definition of property rights are those of protective rights—that is, rights that provide individuals with a shield against others who would invade or take what does not belong to them. Because these are nonaggression or "negative" rights, all citizens can simultaneously possess them. In the popular media, some people argue that individuals have invasive rights or what some call "positive rights" to things like food, housing, medical services, or a minimal income level. The existence of positive rights require the forceful redistribution of wealth, which implies that some individuals have the right to use force to invade and seize the labor and possessions of others, and such invasive rights are in conflict with economic freedom. If you can ask "at whose expense" at the end of a statement about a claim of someone's right, it is not—and cannot be—a real right. Real rights, such as the right to your life or free speech, do not impose further obligations on others (other than to avoid from violating your right). The right to property does not mean you have a right to take the property of others, nor is it a guarantee you will own property—rather it is a right that protects legitimately acquired property against the aggression from others who would take it.

A government policy that weakens any one of these components of property rights weakens property rights in general. Taxes, for example, restrict the cash flow rights associated with property and so weaken private property rights on that dimension.[10] Regulations, on the other hand, restrict how owners may use their property, infringing on control rights, and weakening private property rights on that dimension. Outright takings, or other forms of outright expropriation, by removing the property from an owner's possession (such as eminent domain, especially when allowing the state to remove the property from an owner's possession and transfer it to another private owner) actually weaken property rights on all of the dimensions considered above, making property a "contingent right" (contingent on the state's arbitrary will) rather than an "absolute right" guaranteed and protected by law.

In order to nurture capitalism, government must do some things but refrain from doing others. Governments promote capitalism by establishing a legal structure that provides for the even-handed enforcement of contracts and the protection of individuals and their property from aggressors seeking to use violence, coercion, and fraud to seize things that do not belong to them. However, governments must refrain from actions that weaken private property rights or interfere with personal choice, voluntary exchange, and the freedom of individuals and businesses to compete. When these government actions are substituted for personal choice, economic freedom is reduced. When government protects people and their property, enforces contracts in an unbiased manner, and provides a limited set of "public goods" like roads, flood control, and other major public works projects, but leaves the rest to the private market, they support the institutions of capitalism.

CAPITALISM, DEMOCRACY, AND CONSTITUTIONAL CONSTRAINTS

It is also important to distinguish between economic freedom and democracy. Unless both parties to a private exchange agree, the transaction will not occur. On the other hand, majority-rule voting is the basis for democracy. When private mutual agreement forms the basis for economic activity, there will be a strong tendency for resources to be used in ways that increase their value, creating income and wealth. The agreement of buyer and seller to an exchange provides strong evidence that the transaction increases the well-being of both. In contrast, there is no such tendency under majority rule. The political process generates both winners and losers and there is no assurance that the gains of the winners will exceed the cost imposed on the losers. In fact, there are good reasons to believe that in many cases policies will be adopted for the purpose of generating benefits for smaller and more politically powerful interest groups—even when those policies impose much greater costs on the general public. Elected officials must cater to the special interest groups who provide votes and support for their political candidacy—they have to if they want to keep getting reelected.

The reason why the political allocation of resources is problematic is that when the government is heavily involved in activities that provide favors to some at the expense of others, people will be encouraged to divert resources away from productive private-sector activities and toward lobbying, campaign contributions, and other forms of political favor-seeking. We end up with more lobbyists and lawyers, and fewer engineers and architects.

---

[10] In addition, because the value of a property asset is determined by the present discounted value of the net income from the property's ownership, taxes often directly impact the current market value of property to the owners. Insecure cash flows due to taxes also inhibit long-term contracting and lending.

Predictably, the shift of resources away from production and toward plunder will generate economic inefficiency. We will return to this idea in more detail in Chapter 3.

Unconstrained majority-rule democracy is not the political system that is most complementary with capitalism—limited and constitutionally constrained government is. Constitutional restraints, structural procedures designed to promote agreement and reduce the ability of interest groups to exploit consumers and taxpayers, and competition among governmental units (federalism and decentralization) can help restrain the impulses of the majority and promote economic freedom.

As Supreme Court Justice Robert Jackson emphasized in *West Virginia State of Education v. Barnette* (1943, 638), "one's right to life, liberty, and property, to free speech, a free press, freedom of worship and assembly, and other fundamental rights may not be submitted to vote; they depend on the outcome of no elections." The fundamental principle is that there needs to be safeguards preventing democratic governments from enacting policies that infringe on the property rights of citizens, just like the rules preventing it from infringing on the rights to free speech and worship. When property rights are secure so that owners can use their property in the ways they see fit without the fear of the property being seized, overly regulated, or taxed, the foundation for *freedom and prosperity* is created.

WHAT CAPITALISM IS NOT: BEING BUSINESS FRIENDLY DOES NOT MEAN GIVING AWAY FAVORS

Before moving on, one additional point needs clarifying. There is a difference between what economists call capitalism and what some might consider "business-friendly policies." When government gives subsidies or tax breaks to specific firms or industries that lobby but not to others, this is at odds with the institutions, or rules of the game, consistent with capitalism.

When it becomes more profitable for companies and industries to invest time and resources into lobbying the political process for favors, or into initiating lawsuits against others, we end up with more of these types of destructive activities, and less productive activity. Firms begin competing over obtaining government tax breaks rather than with each other in the marketplace. They spend time lobbying rather than producing.

In addition, by arbitrarily making some industries more (or less) profitable than others, private sector economic activity is distorted in those sectors relative to other sectors. For growth, market-determined returns (profit rates) and market prices should guide these investments, not government taxes and subsidies. Capitalism is about a fair and level playing field for everyone. This means lower overall levels of taxes and regulations—ones that are applied equally to everyone.

Business subsidies may visibly create jobs, but the unseen cost is that the tax revenue or other resources necessary to fund these subsidies generally destroy more jobs than are created. They result in a *net* reduction in economic activity. The problem, politically, is that these losses are not as visible. When every taxpayer in Tennessee has to pay, say, $1 more in taxes to fund some multi-million dollar subsidy, this reduced spending spread out all over the state ends up causing job losses at businesses all over the state. Government subsidy programs can, thus, transfer jobs around the state, but, on net, the overall impact is negative.

When business interests capture government's power, things can go just as bad for capitalism as when government power is held in the hands of less business-friendly groups.

For example, when companies can get government to use the power of eminent domain to take property from others, or use lobbying or connections to get special tax favors, subsidies, or exemptions for their business, this policy climate is not conducive to capitalism either.

Economic progress, growth, and development are not about having business take over government policy making. Unconstrained democracy is a threat to capitalism regardless of who is in power. Progress is not about turning policy over to a specific industry; instead it is about being competitive across the board to attract many new types of businesses in different locations. It is about an environment in which small rural entrepreneurs can compete and thrive in the global marketplace that is now becoming more connected to them through the Internet. It is about creating more high-paying jobs across the board.

Tennessee has a bad record when it comes to granting these special favors, including millions of dollars in incentives given to Union City's Goodyear Tire & Rubber plant, Madison's Peterbilt Motors Company, Nashville's Dell Computer plant, Spring Hill's General Motors plant, Amazon.com's facilities in Chattanooga and Cleveland, Chattanooga's Volkswagen auto assembly plant, and numerous film and television incentives. These incentives are not only extremely costly, often costing up to $200,000 per job created, and sometimes ineffective as these firms close or relocate prior to fulfilling their job creation promises, but more importantly they simply create the wrong policy climate—one that encourages all firms to try to invest in seeking favors from Tennessee's state government.

Government officials often cite the necessity to offer these credits to entice firms to locate in the state. However, the only reason the incentives are necessary is due to the high taxes on these types of firms in Tennessee to begin with, such as the property taxes discussed earlier. The problem is the underlying tax structure, and the solution is to lower the high taxes that prevent Tennessee from being competitive in the first place. These incentives would not be necessary if Tennessee had a more competitive tax structure.

When governments give favors to some businesses but not others, it is unfair to the competitive market process as unsubsidized Tennessee firms must now compete with the politically-favored, subsidized firms for employees, resources, land, and consumers. All firms in Tennessee should have a good business climate, without having to devote time, effort, and resources toward political lobbying and favor seeking to get it. Many of Tennessee's businesses—including small entrepreneurs—simply do not have the political power to even begin to negotiate a better business climate like these large companies. The resources devoted toward offering these special favors to big businesses would be better spent providing across the board, broad-based tax reductions that apply to all of Tennessee's entrepreneurs and businesses.

INSTITUTIONS AND GROWTH: A CLOSER LOOK AT THE EVIDENCE

Nobel Prize winning economists F.A. Hayek, Douglass North, and Milton Friedman won their Nobel awards for contributions to our understanding of why (and how) capitalism creates such remarkable prosperity. The reason why so many economists are in agreement on this issue is because the evidence is so clear. Let us take a closer look at the evidence on the relationship between capitalism and prosperity.

First, let us compare states' reliance on capitalism, the *Economic Freedom of North America* index, and state per capita income. This is shown in Figure 2.6. The trend line shown in the figure clearly has a positive slope. Thus, the states whose citizens have the highest average incomes are the states that rely most heavily on capitalism. The poorest states are those that rely most on government.

Figure 2.6: Reliance on Capitalism and Prosperity

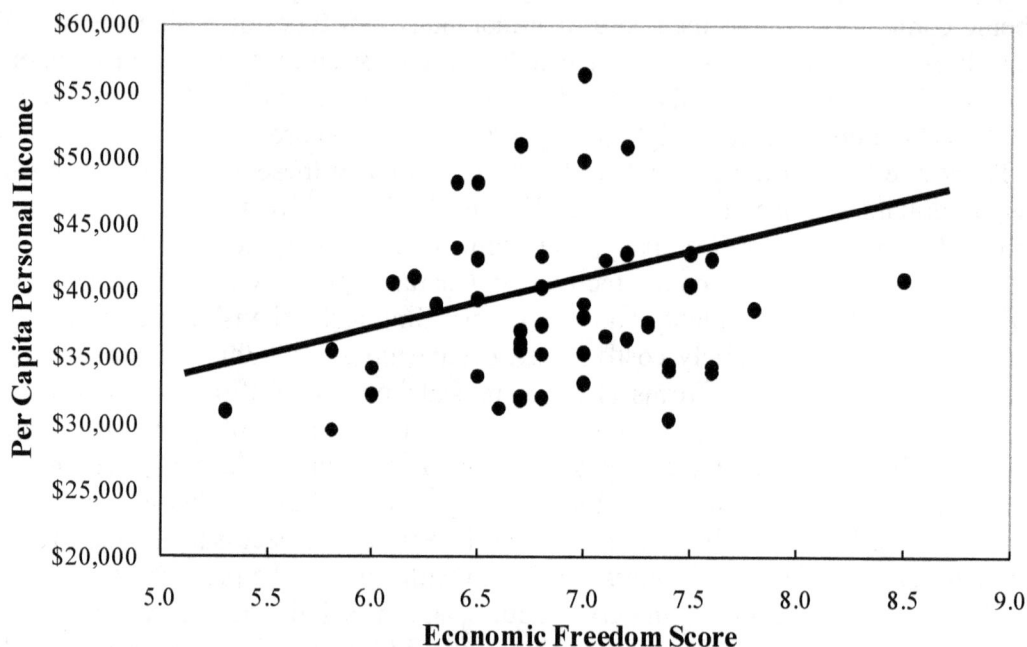

Sources: Karabegovic and McMahon (2008); Bureau of Economic Analysis (2009).

How does the economic freedom index correlate with other measures of economic activity? Figure 2.7 shows, for the top five and bottom five ranking states in the economic freedom index, seven measures of economic prosperity and entrepreneurial activity. To provide a picture uncomplicated by the recent national recession, this data is from prior to the recession. The table shows the averages for these two groups of states on these important indicators of prosperity, as well as the difference between the averages for these two groupings of states. For comparison, Tennessee's data on these measures is shown at the bottom of the table.

The states listed in the top of the table, those with the best institutions, are uniformly more prosperous than the states with the worst economic institutions. The differences in economic outcomes are striking. Looking at the averages given near the bottom of the table, average per capita personal income is $5,618 higher, and the poverty rate is 3.1 percentage points lower, on average, in those states with the best economic institutions. Examining the measures of entrepreneurial activity, a similar pattern emerges—states with the most economic freedom have higher rates of entrepreneurial activity. Relative to the states with the least economic freedom, those with the most have venture capital investment $123.17 higher per capita, a rate of patents 21.1 higher per 100,000 residents, a growth rate of sole proprietorships 1.4 percentage points higher, an establishment birth rate almost 2 percent higher, and a birth rate of large establishments 2.3 percentage points higher.

Figure 2.7: Capitalism's Economic Record

State	Economic Freedom Index (2005)		Economic Performance Measures		Measures of Entrepreneurial Activity (annual averages)				
	Score	Rank (among U.S. states)	Per Capita Personal Income (2008)	Poverty Rate (2007)	Venture Capital Investment Per Capita	Patents Per Capita (per 100,000 pop.)	Sole Proprietorship Growth Rate	Establishment Birth Rate (all firms)	Establishment Birth Rate (large firms only)
Top 5 States									
Delaware	8.5	1	$40,852	10.3%	$60.97	52.6	5.5%	13.1%	14.2%
Texas	7.8	2	$38,575	16.3%	$113.29	25.9	3.3%	12.8%	12.0%
Colorado	7.6	3 (tie)	$42,377	11.5%	$333.22	37.1	4.6%	14.2%	13.0%
Georgia	7.6	3 (tie)	$33,975	14.3%	$103.63	14.6	4.0%	13.5%	11.7%
North Carolina	7.6	3 (tie)	$34,439	14.3%	$82.57	19.5	3.5%	11.7%	10.3%
Bottom 5 States									
Montana	6.0	46 (tie)	$34,256	14.1%	$14.30	12.6	1.9%	12.0%	10.7%
New Mexico	6.0	46 (tie)	$32,091	17.9%	$10.08	16.3	2.7%	12.1%	10.8%
Maine	5.8	48 (tie)	$35,381	12.2%	$34.96	9.3	3.0%	11.2%	9.5%
Mississippi	5.8	48 (tie)	$29,569	20.7%	$18.53	5.6	3.4%	11.1%	9.7%
West Virginia	5.3	50	$30,831	17.1%	$0.00	0.0	2.8%	9.5%	8.6%
Average - Top 5 States			$38,044	13.3%	$138.74	29.9	4.2%	13.1%	12.2%
Average - Bottom 5 States			$32,426	16.4%	$15.57	8.8	2.8%	11.2%	9.9%
Difference (Top minus Bottom)			$5,618	-3.1%	$123.17	21.1	1.4%	1.9%	2.3%
For Comparison									
Tennessee	7.4	10	$34,330	15.8%	$44.37	12.9	4.0%	11.1%	10.1%

Sources: Bureau of Economic Analysis (2009); Karabegovic and McMahon (2008); U.S. Census Bureau (2009); Sobel (2008).

Because Tennessee ranks in the middle of the pack on economic freedom and business climate measures, the measures of entrepreneurship and prosperity for Tennessee generally fall in between the values for the top and bottom states. Of most interest, however, is probably how Tennessee compares to its neighboring states of Georgia and North Carolina (both listed among the top five states in Figure 2.7). As was mentioned earlier in this chapter, Tennessee lags behind its neighboring states on measures of entrepreneurial activity and prosperity.

EVIDENCE FROM ACROSS THE WORLD

While state comparisons are probably the most valuable for Tennessee policy reform, it is worthwhile to spend a moment looking at some additional evidence on the relationship between reliance on capitalism, or economic freedom, and prosperity from around the world. This is meaningful because as mentioned earlier, there are much larger differences between countries than between U.S. states. The majority of countries in the world indeed rely less heavily on capitalism than does Tennessee, but their fate can help us understand what is in store for the state if policy keeps moving in the wrong direction.

Figure 2.8: Capitalism and Income (International Data)

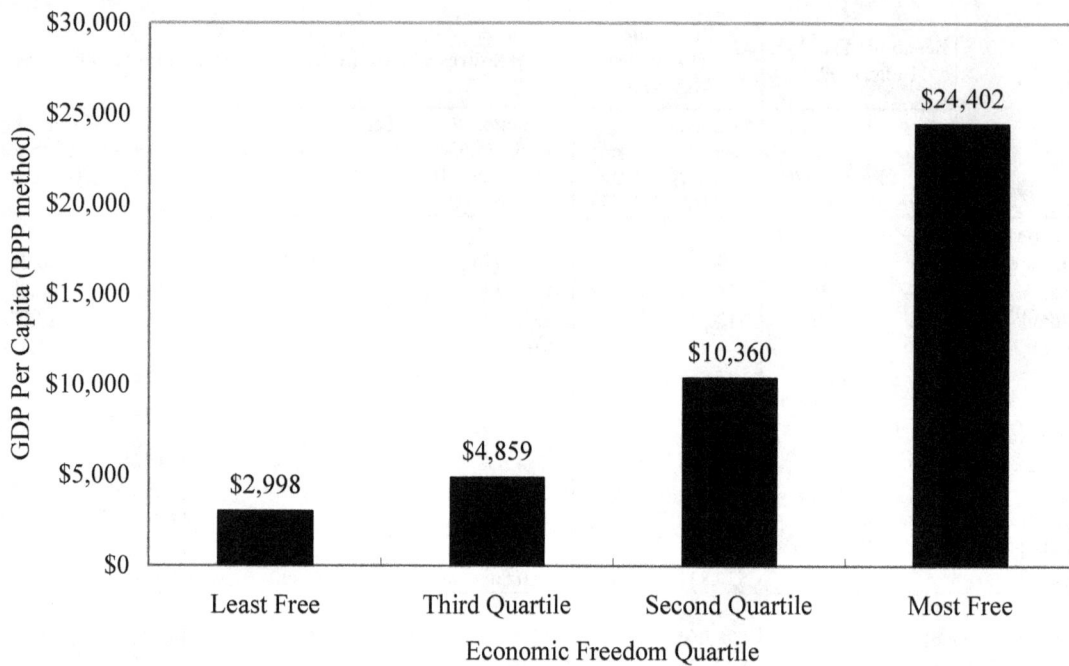

Source: Gwartney and Lawson (2006).

Figure 2.9: Capitalism and Growth (International Data)

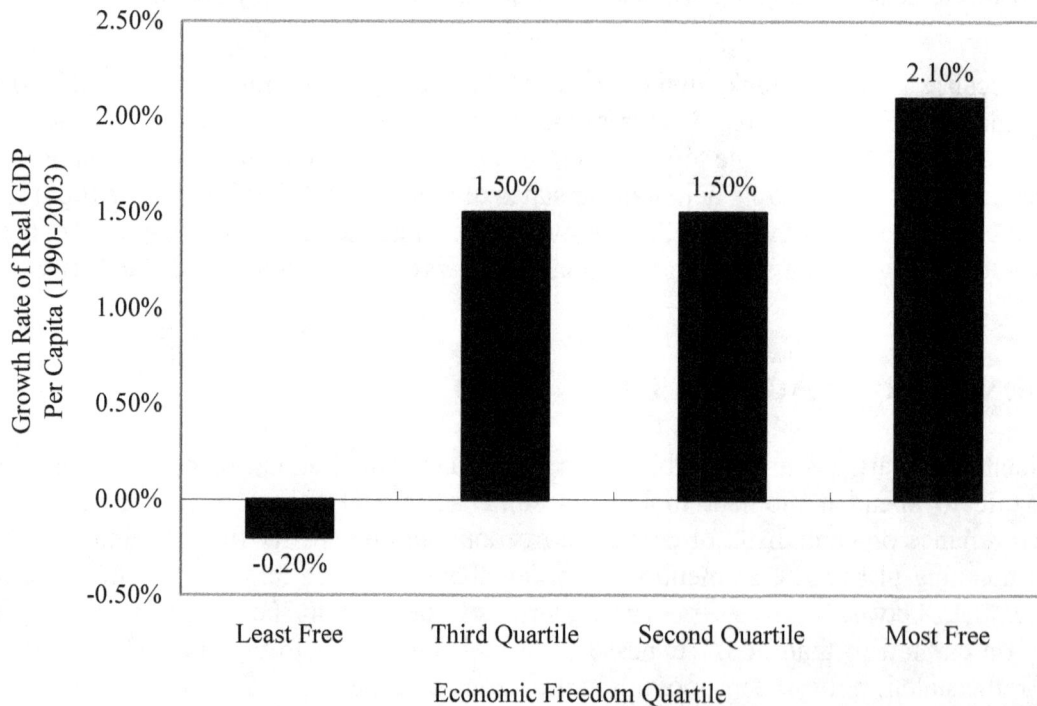

Source: Gwartney and Lawson (2006).

Figure 2.8 shows the average income level within four different groupings of countries in the *Economic Freedom of the World* index. Countries are divided into these groups based on their scores, and again, higher numbers mean a heavier reliance on capitalism, rather than political planning, to organize their economies. The pattern in Figure 2.8 is clear and is the same pattern we saw across the U.S. states previously. A heavier reliance on capitalism makes countries more prosperous.

Figure 2.9 shows a similar graph for the relationship between reliance on capitalism and income growth rates over the 1990-2003 period for countries of the world. Those relying least on capitalism are not only poorer to begin with (looking at average income levels), but they are also becoming worse off through time. As their negative growth rates show, average income is actually falling through time in these countries. At the opposite end of the spectrum are countries that rely heavily on capitalism and have both high incomes and high growth rates as a result.

In summary, the international evidence bears out the same conclusions as the evidence from U.S. states. Those areas embracing capitalism are richer and grow faster, and those areas that do not are poorer and grow slower.

THE GAP BETWEEN RICH AND POOR

This chapter has presented evidence that areas relying on capitalism—the protection of private property through limited political and sound legal institutions—are more prosperous. The data we have presented here on average per capita income supports this conclusion. Some readers, however, might worry that while reliance on capitalism causes average income to rise, it may cause the distribution of income among people to change in an undesirable direction. After all, opponents of capitalism in the popular media quote statistics about how the rich are getting richer and the poor are getting poorer. Would a heavier reliance on capitalism make this happen in Tennessee?

First, it is important to differentiate between income disparities *within* a state changing and income disparities *across* states changing. For example, states (and countries) relying more heavily on capitalism have both higher levels of income and faster income growth, while states (and countries) relying less heavily on capitalism have both lower levels of income and slower economic growth. So it is true that through time, the relatively richer citizens of places like Delaware keep getting richer faster than the relatively poorer citizens of places like Tennessee. As Chapter 1 demonstrated, through time, even small differences in growth rates can cause large differences in prosperity. However, this is the result of some areas getting policy to work properly. States that adopt good policies not only make their citizens richer, but those citizens keep getting even wealthier through time. States adopting bad policies make their citizens poorer and also cause them to experience slower growth, leaving them behind the progress of others. In other words, it is differences in the reliance on capitalism that explain the growing disparities *across* states.

While the growing disparities across states are caused by policy differences in whether states embrace capitalism, the impact of a greater reliance on capitalism *within* a given state is a different story altogether. While certainly under capitalism some earn more than others, the alternative to this, the political allocation of wealth, is actually much more uneven. The benefits of government spending and transfers are much more highly concentrated among the politically powerful than are the benefits of private economic activity. The larger the government control of the economy, the more concentrated and uneven is income growth.

Let us look at the evidence.[11] Consider the comparison of West Virginia—the state ranking 50th in the index of economic freedom—versus Delaware—the state ranking 1st. It is worth noting that these two states also rank 50th and 1st respectively in one of the alternative measures of state reliance on capitalism presented earlier in this chapter—the Institute for Legal Reform's *State Liability Systems Ranking* of state legal systems. While the economic freedom index is certainly the closest measure to what economists mean by capitalism, because the most fundamental underpinning for capitalism is secure property rights (which are to a great degree determined by precedent through the state's court decisions), the Institute for Legal Reform's ranking of state legal systems provides another measure.

There is no question that both studies are in agreement as to these two states comprising the two extremes: Delaware is the best example of capitalism in the United States and West Virginia is the best example of the lack of free markets. From the government spending data presented earlier, in West Virginia government spending exceeds 50 percent of the economy, while in Delaware it is roughly 25 percent. Let us compare how income growth varies across the income distribution in Delaware and West Virginia.

Figure 2.10 shows data on how the growth of income has differed among income classes in West Virginia over the last two decades. Income growth has been very uneven in West Virginia. The poorest 20 percent of West Virginians experienced income growth of approximately 11 percent, in total, over the past two decades. Moving to the right, higher income groups saw income rise even faster. The richest 20 percent of West Virginians experienced a 63 percent increase in income over this period, a growth rate almost six times as large as for the lowest 20 percent.

Now, let us consider income growth in Delaware. As we have seen, Delaware's government size, relative to its economy, is about half as large as West Virginia, and it has one of the most favorable business climates in the United States, with very low labor and business regulations and a highly-rated legal system. As Figure 2.11 shows, income growth in Delaware has been much more even.

The income growth for the poorest 20 percent of Delaware's population was almost 30 percent, a rate similar to all other income groups, including the richest 20 percent. Over the past two decades, those with the lowest incomes in Delaware have seen their incomes grow by almost three times as much as those with the lowest incomes in West Virginia. Capitalism, as Delaware illustrates, is a rising tide that lifts all boats.

In the economies with the most reliance on capitalism and the smallest government sectors, income growth is much more rapid—not just overall—but also for those with the lowest incomes. Places where legislatures and political parties control the distribution of wealth and economic activity end up with the most favoritism and smallest gains for those with low incomes. This is because those with lower incomes do not have the political power to compete with special interest groups for government spending, contracts, regulations, and handouts.

---

[11] Income growth data are from Bernstein, McNichol, and Lyons (2006). Online at: http://www.epinet.org. For a more scientific treatment of this issue, using data from all 50 states, see Ashby and Sobel (2008).

Figure 2.10: West Virginia Income Growth

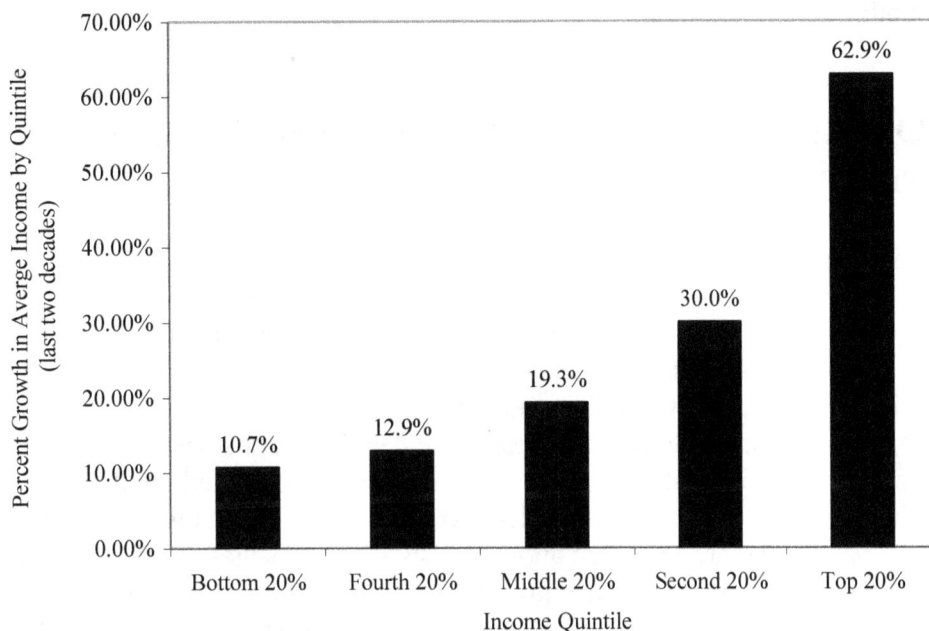

Figure 2.11: Delaware Income Growth

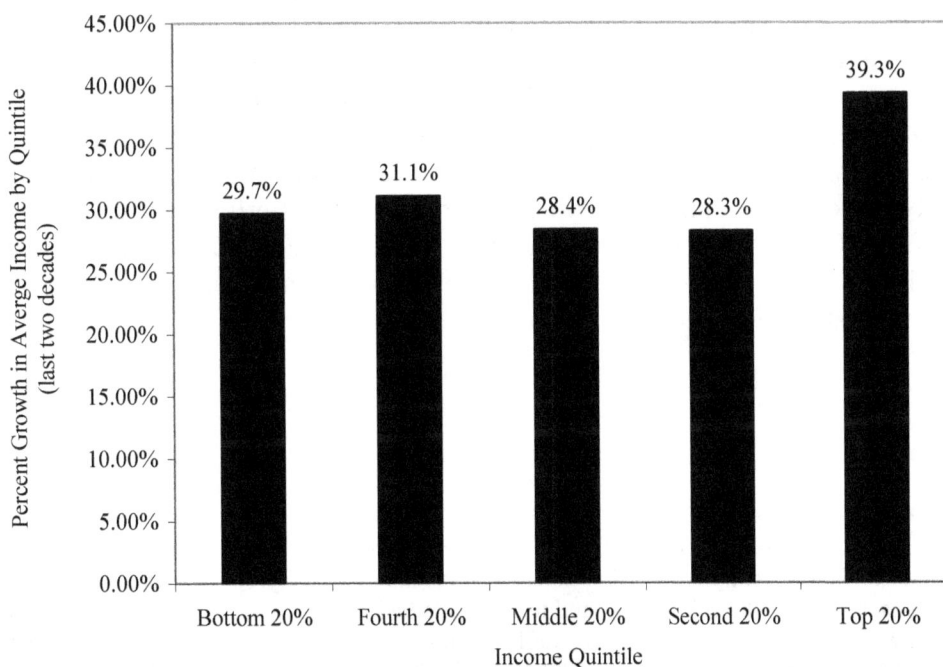

Sources: Figures taken from Sobel and Hall (2007b, 2009) using data from Bernstein, McNichol, and Lyons (2006) and Bureau of Economic Analysis (2006).

Contrary to what many commentators would have you believe, the evidence clearly supports the view that income distributions in economies with more government control tend to be less equal. Nobel Laureate Milton Friedman perhaps put it best in episode five of his

1980 documentary *Free to Choose* when he said: "A society that puts equality before freedom will end up with neither. A society that puts freedom before equality will end up with a great measure of both."

COULD OTHER THINGS ACCOUNT FOR THESE DIFFERENCES IN PROSPERITY?

Up to this point we have relied on presentations of simple correlations to establish the linkage between good institutions and prosperity. Some readers might wonder if these relationships hold up to closer inquiry after controlling for other factors that might account for observed differences. This is the realm of academic journal publications, and for our intended audience, the details behind this analysis would be uninteresting.

Rather than attempting to present these more detailed results here, we instead point the reader to the following published articles on this subject contained in the accompanying footnote to this sentence.[12] All of these articles are published in academic journals, in which authors submit papers that are reviewed anonymously by other scholars from across the globe in a scientific manner. Papers generally go through revisions and must pass a high level of scrutiny. These studies confirm the conclusions we have shown in this chapter, namely that economic freedom promotes prosperity.

It is worth noting that this literature does provide evidence rejecting some popularly held notions of what other factors might explain these differences in prosperity. Areas rich in natural resources, for example, do not necessarily grow faster than those areas with none. The previously mentioned case of Hong Kong (a rock island in the ocean) and how it has grown rapidly versus resource-rich countries with slow or negative growth, such as Venezuela and Argentina, are good examples. Geographic climate variation, or just plain luck, does not explain the differences observed across countries or regions or states either. When we see the borders between countries—like the two sides of the former Berlin Wall separating wealthy, capitalist West Germany from relatively poor, socialist East Germany—it is clear that institutional differences, differences in the rules of the economic game, are the true source of differences in prosperity.

---

[12] The positive relationship between economic freedom and growth has been shown to be robust in a large number of studies. Gerald Scully (1988), for example, finds that politically open countries that respect private property rights, subscribe to the rule of law, and use markets instead of government to allocate resources, grow three times faster than countries that do not. Harvard economist Robert Barro (1996) finds a positive relationship between economic freedom and growth. Gwartney, Lawson, and Holcombe (1999) take into account demographics, changes in education and physical capital and find that economic freedom is still a significant determinant of economic growth. John Dawson (1998) finds that economic freedom positively affects growth and it does so by directly affecting the productivity of capital and labor and indirectly through its influence on the environment for investment. This is consistent with Hall and Jones's (1999) finding that policies consistent with economic freedom improve labor productivity. A very nice overview of the findings of this literature can be found in Berggren (2003) and a list of the dozens of studies on economic freedom can be found at www.freetheworld.com.

CONCLUSION

This chapter has presented evidence that areas relying on capitalism—the protection of private property through constitutionally limited political institutions and sound legal institutions—are more prosperous. We began with a review of the economic evidence on the sources of prosperity and growth. Beginning with Adam Smith, over 230 years of evidence suggests that reliance on capitalism is the best route to achieve increases in living standards. States and countries relying more heavily on capitalism not only have higher income levels and faster average income growth, but also faster and more even growth across the income distribution.

One key component in reforming policy in a manner conducive to growth is to ensure the security of private ownership rights. This implies protection of persons and property from unreasonable aggression, theft, lawsuits, or confiscation by others, including the government. This is why having a weak legal system is devastating to the underpinnings of a free-market economy. Too often these violations of private property sneak in under the guise of regulations that require costly actions on the part of property owners, or restrict their ability to use their property as they see fit.

In addition to the legal foundations necessary for capitalism, governments must also refrain from attempting to control the state's economy by spending citizens' incomes for them through high taxes and government expenditures. Large rates of government employment, ownership of land and of productive assets, and high government spending, beyond some basic functions, reflect the government attempting to drive the economy rather than leaving this to the private sector. There is no getting around the fact that the private and government sector shares in the state economy add up to 100 percent. The goal should be to increase the share controlled through the private sector and diminish the share controlled through the public sector. The evidence clearly shows that prosperity follows as a result.

REFERENCES

Ashby, Nathan J., Avilia Bueno, and Fred McMahon. 2011. *Economic Freedom of North America: 2011 Annual Report*. Vancouver, BC: Frasier Institute.

Ashby, Nathan J., and Russell S. Sobel. 2008. "Income Inequality and Economic Freedom in the U.S. States." *Public Choice* 134 (3/4): 329-346.

Barro, Robert J. 1996. "Democracy and Growth." *Journal of Economic Growth* 1 (1): 1-27.

Berggren, Niclas. 2003. "The Benefits of Economic Freedom: A Survey." *Independent Review* 8 (2): 193-211.

Bernstein, Jared, Elizabeth McNichol, and Karen Lyons. 2006. *Pulling Apart: A State-by-State Analysis of Income Trends*. Washington: Economic Policy Institute.

Bureau of Economic Analysis, U.S. Department of Commerce. 2006. *Annual State Personal Income 2005*. Washington, DC: U.S. Department of Commerce. http://bea.gov/bea /newsrelarchive/2006/spi0306.htm.

———. 2009. *Annual State Personal Income*. Washington, DC: U.S. Department of Commerce. http://www.bea.gov/regional/spi/default.cfm?selTable=SA30.

———. 2012. *Annual State Personal Income*. Washington, DC: U.S. Department of Commerce. http://www.bea.gov/regional/index.htm.

Dawson, John. 1998. "Institutions, Investment, and Growth: New Cross-Country and Panel Data Evidence." *Economic Inquiry* 36 (4): 603-619.

Friedman, Milton. 1980. "Created Equal." Volume 5. *Free to Choose*. Directed by Peter Robinson. Erie: Free to Choose Media. Transcript online: http://www.freetochoose.net/1980_vol5_transcript.html.

Gwartney, James D., and Robert A. Lawson. 2006. *Economic Freedom of the World: 2006 Annual Report*. Vancouver, BC: Fraser Institute.

Gwartney, James D., Robert A. Lawson, and Joshua C. Hall. 2011. *Economic Freedom of the World: 2011 Annual Report*. Vancouver, BC: Fraser Institute.

Gwartney, James D., Robert A. Lawson, and Randall G. Holcombe. 1999. "Economic Freedom and the Environment for Economic Growth." *Journal of Institutional and Theoretical Economics* 155 (4): 1-21.

Gwartney, James D., Richard L. Stroup, Russell S. Sobel, and David A. Macpherson. 2009. *Economics: Private and Public Choice*. 12th ed. Mason, OH: South-Western Cengage Learning.

Hahn, Robert W. 2000. "State and Federal Regulatory Reform: A Comparative Analysis." *Journal of Legal Studies* 29 (2): 873-912.

Hall, Joshua C., and Russell S. Sobel. 2006. "Public Policy and Entrepreneurship." Technical Report 06-0717. Kansas City: Center for Applied Economics.

———. 2008. "Is the 'Missouri Plan' Good for Missouri? The Economics of Judicial Selection." *Show-Me Institute Policy Study* 15: 1-24.

———. 2009. "Judicial Selection Methods and Legal System Quality." In *The Rule of Law: Perspectives on Legal and Judicial Reform in West Virginia*, edited by Russell S. Sobel, 25-49. Morgantown, WV: Center for Economic Growth, The Public Policy Foundation of West Virginia.

Hall, Robert E., and Charles I. Jones. 1999. "Why Do Some Countries Produce So Much More Output Per Worker than Others?" *Quarterly Journal of Economics* 114 (1): 83-116.

Karabegovic, Amela, and Fred McMahon. 2008. *Economic Freedom of North America: 2008 Annual Report*. Vancouver, BC: Frasier Institute.

Lee, Dwight R. 1991. "The Seeds of Entrepreneurship." *Journal of Private Enterprise* 7 (1): 20-35.

McCormick, Robert E., and Robert D. Tollison. 1984. "Crime on the Court." *Journal of Political Economy* 92 (2): 223-235.

National Association of Manufacturers. 2009. *2009 Competitiveness Redbook*. Washington DC: National Association of Manufacturers, Association of Washington Business, and Washington Research Council.

Schwartz, Jason A. 2010. *52 Experiments with Regulatory Review: The Political and Economic Inputs into State Rulemakings*. New York, NY: New York University School of Law, Institute for Policy Integrity.

Scully, Gerald. 1988. "The Institutional Framework and Economic Development." *Journal of Political Economy* 96 (3): 652-662.

Smith, Adam. (1776) 1998. *An Inquiry into the Nature and Causes of the Wealth of Nations.* Washington: Regnery Publishing.

Sobel, Russell S. 2008. "Testing Baumol: Institutional Quality and the Productivity of Entrepreneurship." *Journal of Business Venturing* 23 (6): 641-655.

Sobel, Russell S., and Joshua C. Hall. 2007a. "The Effect of Judicial Selection Processes on Judicial Quality: The Role of Partisan Politics." *Cato Journal* 27 (1): 69-82.

———. 2007b. "The Sources of Economic Growth." In *Unleashing Capitalism: Why Prosperity Stops at the West Virginia Border and How to Fix It*, edited by Russell S. Sobel, 13-36. Morgantown, WV: Center for Economic Growth, The Public Policy Foundation of West Virginia.

———. 2009. "The Sources of Economic Growth." In *Unleashing Capitalism: A Prescription for Economic Prosperity in South Carolina*, edited by Peter T. Calcagno, 21-48. Columbia, SC: South Carolina Policy Council.

Tennessee Chamber of Commerce & Industry. 2010. *Business Insider*, Winter. Nashville, TN: Tennessee Chamber of Commerce & Industry. http://www.tnchamber.org. /_member /_images/page_images/files/78789_BusInsider_Winter10.pdf.

———. 2011. *Business Insider*, Summer. Nashville, TN: Tennessee Chamber of Commerce & Industry. http://www.tnchamber.org./_member/_images/_page_images/files /84200 _BusInsider_Summer11.pdf.

U.S. Census Bureau. 2009. *Small Area Income and Poverty Estimates.* Washington, DC: U.S. Census Bureau. http://www.census.gov/did/www/saipe/data/statecounty/data/2007 .html.

CASE CITED

West Virginia State of Education v. Barnette, 319 U.S. 624 (1943).

CHAPTER 3

WHY CAPITALISM WORKS

by Russell S. Sobel, J.R. Clark, and Peter T. Leeson

Freedom and Prosperity in Tennessee

3

WHY CAPITALISM WORKS

Russell S. Sobel, J.R. Clark, and Peter T. Leeson

The previous chapter showed that increased reliance on capitalism has allowed other states and countries to become more prosperous. To promote capitalism in Tennessee, its political and legal institutions must do two things: (1) strongly protect private property rights and enforce contracts; and (2) refrain from adopting policies or undertaking actions that infringe on voluntary actions and contracting in the private sector.

Unfortunately, governments often enact policies that interfere with capitalism without fully understanding the economic consequences. While policy makers in Tennessee and other states are indeed smart and reasonable people, most do not have formal training in advanced economics. To ensure that the true economic consequences of policies are better understood, elected officials and citizens must become more knowledgeable about a few basic principles of economics. We hope this chapter will help to accomplish that goal. For readers wanting to learn more, we suggest the easy-to-read book, *Common Sense Economics: What Everyone Should Know about Wealth and Prosperity*, by James D. Gwartney, Richard L. Stroup, and Dwight R. Lee (2005).[1] With better knowledge of fundamental economics and the basic structures that operate within an economy—the reasons why and how capitalism works—policy makers can make better state policy decisions.

In this chapter we discuss these basic economic principles, including the concepts of wealth creation and entrepreneurship.[2] In addition, we examine the concept of "unintended consequences"—or secondary effects—the reason why, for policy making, good intentions simply are not enough to guarantee good outcomes.

---

[1] We also suggest the equally easy-to-read classic, *Free to Choose* by Nobel Laureate Milton Friedman and his wife, Rose Friedman (1980).
[2] This chapter is based on Sobel and Leeson (2007, 2009).

VOLUNTARY EXCHANGE, WEALTH CREATION, AND VALUE ADDED

While we tend to think of our wealth in dollars, true wealth has nothing to do with paper money itself. Total wealth in a society is not a fixed pie waiting to be divided among us. Wealth, instead, is constantly being created by each of us; the "economic pie" grows each day. Wealth is created through both production and exchange. An example will help to illustrate.

Suppose that two neighbors trade a bushel of hay for a load of wood. Both are now better off; after all, they were only willing to trade with each other because each wanted what the other person had more than what they traded away. Both have become wealthier in every sense of the word even though no new money has been printed, nor existing money passed around.

On an everyday basis, money only represents wealth to people because it measures the quantity of these trades—or purchases—we can undertake when we exchange money that we earn from producing at our jobs for the goods and services produced by others. A man on a deserted island with $1 million is very poor indeed without anything to purchase with the money. On the other hand, a man deserted on an island with no money, but a group of other people, will be much wealthier because of his ability to produce and exchange with others— even in the absence of paper money on the island.

Taking the example further, suppose a group of island castaways decided that half of them should dig holes and the other half should fill them in. After a full-day's work, they would have nothing to show for this effort; nothing was produced. Holes were dug and filled again. No wealth was created, even though people worked very hard.

Wealth would be created if instead half the tribe collected coconuts and the other half fished. Now they would have dinner. Suppose one castaway invents a new tool that increases the number of fish she can catch. This invention would further increase wealth; there is more food at the dinner table. In fact, the new tool might increase productivity so much that only half as many castaways are needed fishing, and the extra castaways are free to labor at a new task such as building a shelter, further increasing wealth. As these examples illustrate, there is a close link between prosperity, or "wealth," and the quantity, quality, and value (or usefulness) of the output produced. Prosperous places—those with high levels of income and wealth—become that way by producing large quantities of valuable goods and services.

One difference between this castaway analogy and our daily economic lives, however, is that we might anticipate the castaways sharing the fruits of their labor, for example, splitting the fish caught that day. In a large and advanced economy it no longer works this way. Instead, each of us gets paid in dollars, or money income, for what we produce at our jobs. We then go to stores and exchange that money for the goods and services produced by others at their jobs.

The amount of income we earn is determined by both the prices people are willing to pay us for what we are producing and how many units of it we can produce. For individuals, states, and nations, income is determined by the value of output. A worker with a backhoe will be more productive than a worker with a shovel and will earn more as a result. An entrepreneur producing apple pies will be more prosperous than one producing mud pies because people place a higher value on apple pies (and thus are willing to pay more for them).

This logic leads to one obvious, and simple, litmus test that can be used to decide if a suggested new policy or law is good, or bad, for the Tennessee economy—does it increase, or decrease, the net amount or value of output (of goods and services) produced in the state? Regulations, such as those adopted in some European nations for example, which restrict the workweek to 35 hours clearly result in reduced output, and reduced standards of living as a result. For a tax-funded government program, this principle must be applied by looking at the *net* change in output—that is, one must properly account for the reduced output caused by the taxes or other resources necessary to fund the policy.

One of Adam Smith's insights in his previously mentioned 1776 book, *An Inquiry into the Nature and Causes of the Wealth of Nations*, is that labor productivity, the main determinant of wage rates, is increased through specialization and the division of labor. When labor is divided into specific tasks, like workers in an assembly-line, they can produce more as a group than could have been produced individually. The same holds true when individuals specialize across different occupations and industries.

However, according to Smith, our ability to specialize, thereby increasing our productivity and enhancing our wages, depends on the size or "extent" of the market to which we sell. When consumer markets are larger in size, smaller specialized stores can survive that could not have survived in a smaller marketplace. Cookeville's population, for example, is able to support two general purpose pet stores, each carrying a broad line of products. In a place like Memphis, however, a dozen or more stores can flourish, with a greater extent of specialization, one store, for example, might specialize in snakes and other reptiles, while another specializes in birds. Increasing the size of the markets to which Tennessee's goods and services sell could increase wealth by allowing Tennesseans to specialize more specifically in areas where they do best.

Population growth in metropolitan areas would be one way of increasing market size. But another way to increase market size is to enact policy reform that better enables the businesses in Tennessee to sell and compete in larger national and global marketplaces and expand their customer base. To compete in these markets Tennessee businesses need to be on a level playing field with their competitors. Tennessee's taxes and regulations are a competitive disadvantage to firms located in the state. The higher prices Tennessee businesses must charge for their products greatly limits the markets in which they can compete. If these tax and regulatory costs could be reduced through policy reform, firms could offer more competitive pricing, increasing their market shares and the extent of their markets. This would allow both the businesses themselves, and their workers, to become more specialized and earn higher incomes as a result.

In addition to specialization and the division of labor, capital investment also increases labor productivity. Higher levels of education (more "human capital") and better machinery, buildings, and tools to work with (more "physical capital") can help our citizens produce more output and generate more income.

An example of the value of capital enhancing wages is readily available within the forest products industry of Tennessee. For those familiar with the logging industry, a worker operating a "feller buncher," a huge machine with claws and a round built-in saw that the worker drives (pictured), can harvest roughly two and a half times as much

timber in the same amount of time as a worker with a chainsaw. As a result, the wage rate he earns is roughly two to three times higher as well. This capital equipment allows the worker to be more productive and thus to earn more income.

Another example of capital enhancing the earnings to labor is evident in the large and thriving auto industry of Tennessee. Modern robotics and automation allow workers to position, spin, and move the parts they are assembling much more easily and quickly. With this new capital equipment workers are more productive and earn higher wages as a result.

But new factories, better machinery, and equipment are expensive. They require large investments in assets and property. In Tennessee, taxes (such as property taxes on capital equipment), regulations, and lawsuits decrease the return from capital investment and thereby lower the inflow of capital into the state. As we discussed in Chapter 2, Tennessee has among the highest property taxes in the nation on a representative manufacturing facility's equipment and machinery. This results in Tennessee's workers being less productive—and earning less as a result.

The income a state produces from its output depends not only on *how much* is produced (which can be expanded through specialization, division of labor, and capital investment), but also on the price per unit, or *value*, of the goods and services produced. A timber stand containing mostly poplar trees will produce less income than one with a higher proportion of more valuable black cherry trees. Income can be increased not only by increasing labor productivity, but also by raising the value per unit—or "value added"—of Tennessee labor.

However, the answer to the question of which specific uses of Tennessee's resources create the most value, and thus income, is not obvious. In fact, the answer is so complex that it is not something any one person or group of people knows, not even a group of expert economic planners. It is an answer that must be *discovered* by individuals in the private sector through the decentralized process of entrepreneurship, a process of private trial and error. This is the topic of our next section.

Before moving on, however, let us complete our discussion of the process of wealth creation started above. As we pointed out, in a real-world economy things work a bit differently than in the castaway example because we must first earn income by producing goods and services. Only then do we use that income to acquire the goods and services produced by others. The ability to turn our income into prosperity and wealth through exchange is the second important part of this process.

As consumers, we turn income into wealth through the acquisition of goods and services like food, clothing, shelter, and recreation. In our shopping, we search out and negotiate with potential sellers from around the globe. We spend time and effort on this search because maximizing the value we get from our limited budgets makes us wealthier.

Finding a product we want to buy at a lower price increases our wealth because we now have more money to spend on other things.

This is the reason why restrictions on the ability of citizens to freely engage in trade with people from other geographic areas through tariffs, quotas, taxes, and other restrictions, destroy wealth. Individuals cannot generate as much value and happiness from their limited incomes. Not only are there fewer options to choose among, but also the taxes and regulations make things more costly for us to purchase, reducing our ability to stretch our budgets and turn our income into wealth.[3] This is one reason to avoid adopting policies that interfere with, tax, or restrict Internet purchases.

As this section has discussed, our well-being is the result of both production and exchange. Becoming more prosperous can be accomplished by increasing the amount of wealth created in the state through: (1) increasing in the quantity, quality, and value of goods and services the state's citizens produce, and (2) increasing the number and value of the voluntary exchanges the state's citizens make, both with other Tennesseans and with people from around the world.

Policy reform that lowers taxes and regulations can help achieve these goals because it results in: (1) increased specialization of labor and increased capital investment—increasing labor productivity and wages; (2) increased ability of residents and businesses to buy and sell with individuals from across the state, nation, and globe; and (3) more private sector entrepreneurship that allows the decentralized decisions of workers and business owners— rather than government planning—to help search out and identify the ever-changing bundle of goods and services that creates the most value and income for Tennessee.

ENTREPRENEURSHIP AND DISCOVERY

Of the many potential things Tennessee could produce with its resources, it should set its sights on those having the highest value in the marketplace. However, this target is an ever shifting one, with new opportunities arising and others dwindling every day. One important reason the economic system of capitalism is especially good at generating prosperity is because it does a good job at chasing this ever-moving target through the continuous process of entrepreneurship and discovery.

Sifting through these many combinations is a difficult task because the number of possible combinations of society's resources is almost limitless. Two quick illustrations will help to clarify the vastness of these opportunities. First, think for a moment about the typical automobile license plate. Many have three letters, a space, and three numbers. There is a formula for calculating the total number of "combinations"—the total number of possible different license plates—that could be created using these three letters and three numbers. The answer is more than you might think: 17,576,000. Second, let us consider the number of possible ways to arrange a deck of cards. Even with only 52 cards, there is a mind-blowing number of possible ways to arrange them—the answer is a 68 digit number:

---

[3] If the benefits from the spending undertaken with the tax revenue, or from the regulation, are things we value highly enough, the tradeoff might be worth it. Of course, if this were the case, we would expect citizens to voluntarily contribute to the cause, or privately regulate the activity, being considered. But when the value created by government policy is lower than our losses from the resulting higher prices and more limited availability of goods and services, society's well-being is reduced.

80,658,175,170,943,878,571,660,636,856,403,766,975,289,505,440,883,277,824,000,000,000,000.

With this many ways to rearrange a deck of 52 cards, the astonishing implication is that each and every time you shuffle a deck of cards you are most likely making a new ordering of cards that has never been seen before, and is likely never to be seen again. In fact, even if every human that has ever lived on the Earth did nothing but shuffle cards 24 hours a day their entire life, and even unrealistically assuming they could shuffle the deck 1,000 times per second, we would have not even come close to making it through a fraction of the number of total possible arrangements of the deck throughout all of human history.[4]

Now, returning to the economy, we clearly have more than just three letters and numbers, or 52 cards, with which to work. Instead, we have thousands of different resources that could be combined into final products. With this many inputs to work with, the number of possible different final product combinations that could be produced is almost infinite.

Entrepreneurship is important because it is the competitive behavior of entrepreneurs that drives this search for new possible combinations of resources that create more value. A vibrant entrepreneurial climate is one that maximizes the number of new combinations attempted. Some of these new combinations will be more valuable than existing combinations and some will not. In a market economy, it is the profit and loss system that is used to sort through these new resource combinations discovered by entrepreneurs, discarding bad ideas through losses and rewarding good ones through profits. A growing, vibrant economy depends not only on entrepreneurs discovering, evaluating, and exploiting opportunities to create new goods and services, but also on the speed at which ideas are labeled as successes or failures by the profit and loss system.

From an economic standpoint then, business failure has a positive side; it gets rid of bad ideas, freeing up resources to be used in other endeavors. In our example, where half of the castaways were digging holes and the other half filling them in, business failure would be equivalent to the half that were filling in the holes going out of business and losing their jobs. A capitalist economic system causes this failure and then replaces it with a profitable business that installs underground piping in the holes to provide running water.

A vibrant economy will have both a large number of new business start-ups *and* a large number of business failures. Minimizing business failures should not be a goal of public policy. Instead the goal should be to maximize the number of new combinations attempted, which also implies having a lot of failures. In an economy where all entrepreneurs—even those with crazy and marginal ideas—can try them out in the marketplace, there will be a lot of business failures. The benefit is that it increases the odds that we will stumble on that one-in-a-million new major innovation, or the next Fortune 500 company. Business failures are a natural result of the uncertainty involved in knowing whether a new idea will meet the "market test." From an economic perspective, it is better to try 100 new ideas and have 60 fail, than to only try 50 and have 30 fail. By doing so, we end up with 20 additional new businesses.

Noted economist Joseph Schumpeter ([1911] 1934) stressed the role of the entrepreneur as an innovator who carries out new combinations of resources to create products that did not previously exist. The result of these new combinations is entirely new

---

[4] For an insightful and more thorough demonstration of the process of computing combinations for a deck of cards see http://www.worsleyschool.net/science/files/deck/ofcards.html.

industries that open considerable opportunities for economic advancement. In Schumpeter's view, the entrepreneur is a disruptive force in an economy because the introduction of these new combinations leads to the obsolescence of others, a process he termed "creative destruction."

The introduction of the compact disc, and the corresponding disappearance of the vinyl record, is just one of many examples of this process. Cars, electricity, aircraft, and personal computers are others. Each significantly advanced our way of life; but, in the process of doing so, other industries died or shrunk considerably. Economists today accept Schumpeter's ([1911] 1934) insight that this process of creative destruction is an essential part of economic progress and prosperity and that capitalism is uniquely suited to foster it.

A point worth clarifying is that it is much better to have a decentralized profit and loss system sorting through these new combinations, than a government approval board or decision-making process. The reason is that the incentives facing public officials can be very different than the incentives facing venture capitalists and entrepreneurs. While each venture capitalist and entrepreneur brings different motivations to the table, ultimately their success or failure is determined by whether their idea generates wealth.[5] This is the "market test" we alluded to earlier. The same is not true for public officials in charge of handing out tax incentives or low-interest loans. They may have other concerns beyond creating wealth. For example, officials may be concerned about *where* a new business is located in order to maximize political support among voters. But there is no reason to think that this decision corresponds with the most economically advantageous one.

In addition, there is no individual, or group of individuals, that could be in charge of this discovery process. There is nobody, not even those seemingly in the best position to know, who can predict which business opportunities are the most viable in advance. For example, Ken Olson, president, chairman, and founder of Digital Equipment Corporation, who was at the forefront of computer technology in 1977, stated: "There is no reason anyone would want a computer in their home." Today his remark sounds funny because we all have computers in our homes, but at the time even those in the infant computer industry did not see this coming. An even better example might be the story of Fred Smith, the founder of Federal Express Corporation. He actually wrote the business plan for FedEx as his senior project for his strategic management class at Yale. While we all know in retrospect that FedEx was a successful business idea, Smith's professor at Yale, one of the leading experts on business strategy, wrote on his paper in red ink: "The concept is interesting and well-formed, but in order to earn better than a C the idea must be feasible."

The point? Even smart professors, business leaders, and government officials cannot possibly pre-evaluate business ideas and identify those that will be most successful and those

---

[5] It is important to recognize that from society's perspective the profits earned by entrepreneurs represent gains to society as a whole. Because entrepreneurs must bid resources away from alternative uses, production costs reflect the value of those resources to society in their alternative uses. Thus, profit is only earned when an entrepreneur takes a set of resources and produces something worth more to consumers than the other goods that could have been produced with those resources. A loss happens when an entrepreneur produces something that consumers do not value as highly as the other goods that could have been produced with those same resources. For example, an entrepreneur who takes the resources necessary to produce a fleece blanket sold for $50 and instead turns them into a pullover that sells for $60 has earned a $10 profit. Since the price of the resources used by entrepreneurs reflect the opportunity cost of their employment in other uses, the $10 profit generated by the entrepreneur reflects the amount by which they have increased the value of those resources. By increasing the value created by our limited resources, entrepreneurs increase overall wealth in a society.

that will fail. A thriving economy is created when individual entrepreneurs have the freedom to try new ideas, risking their own assets, or the assets of their private investors, and the profit and loss system is used to decide their fate. While some policy makers may think solar power is the future of the state economy, the truth is that Tennessee's future is yet to be discovered, and when it is, it will likely be in something that is not yet invented or known at the present time. In the end, it is Tennessee's *citizens* that must discover the future for the state, not the state political process.

In addition, many good ideas die because entrepreneurs simply cannot put together the initial level of resources necessary to comply with the many rules, regulations, and permissions necessary to open a business in Tennessee. We will never know if one of these could have been another FedEx. If we want a thriving economy, Tennessee must find ways to make it easier and less costly for entrepreneurs to try to test their ideas in the marketplace.

To promote entrepreneurship, government often attempts to enact new programs, such as state-run venture capital funds, government-funded or subsidized business incubators, economic development authorities, or even to create new positions within the education system aimed at expanding entrepreneurship education within schools and colleges. Unfortunately, these policies grow the government sector, and *shrink* the private sector. The simple fact is that the public and private sectors sum to 100 percent of the economy, and expansion of government spending means reductions in private spending, and of the resources available within the private sector. One wonders, for example, whether the hundreds of millions of tax dollars spent on incentives for Goodyear Tire & Rubber, Peterbilt Motors Company, Dell Computer, General Motors, Amazon.com, and Volkswagen would have created more jobs and opportunities had this money simply been left in the private sector's hands.

Entrepreneurship is the means by which we discover ways to increase the value created by the state's labor, physical, and natural resources (or economic inputs, in the framework of Figure 2.1 in Chapter 2). Successful entrepreneurship expands the overall economic pie and allows us to generate more wealth and prosperity. To encourage growth, policy reform must reduce the burdens on entrepreneurial start-ups and learn to tolerate business failures.

ADAM SMITH (AGAIN): THE INVISIBLE HAND PRINCIPLE

Under capitalism there is no captain of the ship, no central economic planning authority making the decisions for the economy as a whole. How, in the absence of this central economic planning, can an economy thrive? Adam Smith's ([1776] 1998) most important insight was the concept of "the invisible hand" of the marketplace which provides the answer to this fundamental question.

Smith's ([1776] 1998) insight was that the incentives under capitalism are arranged in such a way that even though we all pursue different goals and objectives to advance our *own* economic interests, we are in turn faced with strong incentives to pursue those actions that also create the most wealth for society as a whole. An example will help to illustrate Adam Smith's invisible hand principle in action.

Suppose the price of maple lumber increases because of higher consumer demand for maple furniture. This single price change will change the incentives faced by decision makers throughout the economy, likely resulting in changes in which properties are harvested, the percent of maple sent to sawmills versus other uses, the incentive of non-furniture makers to substitute away from maple, etc. The "signals" sent by these market prices are what enable our workers and businesses to identify changes in which goods and services create the most value. Price signals not only tell us when new opportunities are arising; they also help us to find out when what we are doing is no longer as highly valued, or when the resources we are using have found an alternative use in which they create even more value.

Nobel Laureate F.A. Hayek (1945) stressed that unregulated prices are a necessary ingredient for a functioning capitalism-based economy. The information contained in prices about buyer preferences, relative scarcity, and the cost of production is essential to good business decision making. However, these all-important prices are often missing in the government sector.

For policy, taxes should be viewed as prices people pay for the goods and services they receive from government. If a private firm provided roads, water, and sewers, it would extend service to any new development willing to pay a price high enough to cover the firm's costs of reaching and servicing the area. When government runs these services, however, the prices it charges are often out of line with true costs. This can result in development not being undertaken when and where it should be; or being undertaken when and where it should not. Policies should be designed to avoid interfering with market prices; and when possible, we should also attempt to set taxes and user fees for government provided goods and services at levels more analogous to market prices. Additionally, consumer choice mechanisms can often be introduced into government provided goods and services, such as with school voucher (i.e., parental choice) programs—as long as the money follows their choice—to help infuse more of a profit and loss system into government provision.

SPONTANEOUS ORDER: A THRIVING ECONOMY IS A RESULT OF HUMAN ACTION, NOT HUMAN DESIGN

Nobel Laureate F.A. Hayek (1967) contributed to our understanding of economic progress by realizing that much of the economy is the "result of human action but not human design." What Hayek had in mind with this distinction was that many institutions are not consciously designed. Rather, they are the result of the efforts of many individuals, each pursuing their own ends, whose activities create order through time. The English language is one example, as is the common law and a successful economic system. No one person or group of people can sit down and create these things by human design.

Hayek called these outcomes "spontaneous orders." Another example of spontaneous order is the marketplace itself—the nexus of interpersonal relationships based on producing, buying, and selling goods and services. When there are large gains to be had, Hayek pointed out, these relationships spontaneously arise without any central economic planning.

Hayek's concept can be illustrated with an example. Suppose a college in Tennessee added a new dormitory on campus that was separated from the classroom buildings by several acres of undeveloped land. The college could hire someone to plan and pave the sidewalks in advance so that students could walk to campus. Alternatively, students could be allowed to have one semester in which they tracked through the woods on their own, creating their own pathways. The college could then retrospectively pave these pathways. The deeper and wider a pathway is, the wider the sidewalk is made. Many of the road systems in the United States are the result of this process in which trailblazer's paths were then used by wagons, and eventually the larger ones paved to become major highways.[6]

The important difference is that when a system is allowed to arise naturally it will be much more likely to satisfy the true desires of those involved and create the most value. One university in Ohio that pre-planned its sidewalks has subsequently had to install benches and holly shrubs to discourage people walking "in the wrong places" and making trails in the grass. Students simply were not using the "planned" sidewalks. Spontaneous orders work better with human nature and help to accomplish our specific goals in the most efficient manner. The "unplanned" sidewalks simply go where people need them the most.

While we have explored Smith ([1776] 1998) and Hayek's (1945) reasons why an economy organized as a "ship without a captain" is best, let us now turn to the reasons why having a strong captain in control can prevent prosperity.

GOOD INTENTIONS ARE NOT ENOUGH: THE PREVALENCE OF UNINTENDED CONSEQUENCES

As we mentioned in the introduction to this chapter, what often happens is that new policies restricting capitalism are enacted because they "sound like good ideas." Unfortunately, these policies frequently have unintended consequences that work against the very goals they were intended to achieve.

The minimum wage is a good case in point. While many people are in favor of the minimum wage law, they support it because they think it helps low income families. The published scientific evidence, however, rejects this view and instead concludes that the minimum wage actually makes the intended beneficiaries worse off.[7] So, for the same reason—the goal of helping those in need—economists are generally opposed to minimum wage legislation. This position can only be reached by examining all of the other indirect changes that happen as a result of a minimum wage, such as less worker training, fewer employee benefits, and most importantly fewer jobs and higher unemployment for low-skilled workers.

Again, it is important to remember that economics is a science, not a political position. We care little about the publicly *stated* intent or goal of the policy, and rather evaluate policy based on published research that examines real-world evidence. Good intentions are not enough to guarantee good outcomes. A few more examples will help to illustrate this important point.

The employment provisions of the Americans with Disabilities Act (ADA) were passed with the intention of lowering barriers to employment for disabled persons. The legislation prohibits discrimination based on disability status and further requires employers to make reasonable accommodations for employees with disabilities. Has the ADA lived up to its stated intent? Has it expanded employment among the disabled?

---

[6] A more in-depth illustration of this idea for interested readers is given in the famous "I, Pencil" essay by Leonard Read (1958), available at the Foundation for Economic Education's website http://www.fee.org/pdf/books/I,%20Pencil%202006.pdf.
[7] For evidence, see some of the studies complied by the Joint Economic Committee of Congress, available at http://www.house.gov/jec/cost-gov/regs/minimum/case.htm.

Thomas DeLeire (1997), a public policy professor at The University of Chicago, wrote his Ph.D. dissertation on the employment effects of the ADA legislation when he was in graduate school at Stanford University. His research shows that the ADA has actually *harmed* the employment opportunities for disabled Americans.[8] By increasing the cost of hiring disabled workers and making it harder to fire them, this legislation has resulted in a reduction in employment among disabled individuals. Prior to the ADA, 60 out of every 100 disabled men were able to find jobs. After the ADA went into effect, however, employment fell to less than 50 per 100 disabled men. After adjusting for other factors, DeLeire concludes that 80 percent of this decline was caused by the bad incentives created by the ADA. While the entire purpose of this legislation was to increase the employment opportunities for the disabled, the data simply do not support this view. Instead, the ADA seems to have made it more difficult and costly for employers to hire disabled workers, resulting in reduced job opportunities for disabled people. If the goal is to expand employment opportunities for disabled Americans, the research suggests that the ADA is not the answer.

Environmental policy often has the most devastating examples of unintended consequences. Under the Endangered Species Act, for example, large areas around the nesting grounds of the red-cockaded woodpecker can be declared "protected habitats," which then imposes stringent restrictions on the surrounding property owners (a loss of "control rights" in the terminology introduced in Chapter 2). When the Federal Fish and Wildlife Service put Boiling Springs Lakes, North Carolina on notice that active nests were beginning to form near the town, it unleashed a frenzy of action on the part of the residents, but not of the type you might expect (Associated Press 2006). Foreseeing the potential future restrictions on their property use, landowners swarmed the city hall to apply for lot-clearing permits. After removing the trees, the land would no longer be in danger of being declared an environmentally protected habitat because no future nests could form on the property.

Similar incidents have occurred throughout the range of this bird, and the total habitable nesting area for this species in the United States has fallen dramatically as a result of the poor incentive structure created by the law. The red-cockaded woodpecker has lost a significant portion of its habitat, moving it closer to extinction because of the unintended consequences of the Endangered Species Act.

As these examples illustrate, policy designed with even the best intentions can create unintended consequences that work against the original goal of the policy. The concept of unintended consequences vividly illustrates why having an economic "captain" can often produce more harm for an economy than not having one.

One additional problem with government regulations mentioned in Chapter 2 is that there is no profit and loss-type system to eliminate bad policies through time. In the end, some policies just do not live up to their stated goals, or do so but at too high of a cost. West Virginia, for example, imposed a maximum eight hour operating restriction on taxi drivers.[9] The law was intended to reduce driver fatigue and accidents involving taxis. Policy makers, however, overlooked the unintended consequences resulting from changing the incentives faced by cab drivers. With fewer hours to drive in a day, cab drivers started driving at faster speeds and took fewer breaks. Not only did the law result in a significant reduction in the number of cabs operating in the state, which led to more driving while intoxicated incidents, but it exacerbated the very problem it was designed to reduce. Even though there are *fewer*

---

[8] See DeLeire (1997, 2000).
[9] See Corey and Curott (2007) for a longer description of this law and its consequences in West Virginia.

cabs on the road due to the law, the total number of accidents committed by cab drivers has *increased* in West Virginia since the regulation has been passed. Despite this information being widely-known, state policy makers in West Virginia do not "have the time to get the law off the books" due to having to deal with too many other, more pressing, current issues. Simply put, government lawmakers just do not have the time to go back and look into the effectiveness of all laws from the past, nor the time to introduce the legislation to repeal them.

This highlights the need for Tennessee to reform its regulatory review process along the lines of the discussion in Chapter 2. Quite simply, if a regulation adopted in Tennessee cannot prove, with data, that it is accomplishing its stated goal in a cost effective manner within some period of time, say five years, it should be repealed. Regulations, and other policies, should have to fight to stay in place based on scientific evidence regarding the costs and benefits they create.

Vote Early, Vote Often: Bad People or Bad Incentives?

Economists are of the opinion that government agencies tend to be less efficient than private firms. But the reason has nothing to do with "bad politicians" or the particular people involved in the government sector. Getting more out of government is not a matter of getting "better people" in government. Government workers are smart, caring, and devoted to their causes. The problem is that the reward structure—the rules of the game—within their jobs does not provide the right incentives to encourage the best outcomes. Nobel Laureate James Buchanan, with coauthor Gordon Tullock (1962), published a seminal book on this subject called *The Calculus of Consent*. As they pointed out, in government there is no invisible hand. An example will help to illustrate.

Most people know that government budgets are often given as fixed amounts for each fiscal year. At the end of the year, any remaining money in the budget is usually taken back and if money remains, the next year's funding is likely to be reduced because the agency did not need all of the money it was allocated. To avoid this outcome, government agencies are notorious for spending their remaining budgets rapidly at the end of each fiscal year. The point is that even a person who was very careful and frugal with their money at home, or would be at a job in a private corporation, would begin to behave differently under this different set of rules that are present in the government sector. In government, the problem is not the people; it is the incentives they face.

The Nirvana Fallacy

The "nirvana fallacy" is the logical error of comparing actual things with unrealistic, idealized alternatives.[10] For instance, some might see a problem in the current health care system and propose that because of this failure, we should have a government-run health care system, based on the logic that this ideal government-run system would overcome all of the problems.

---

[10] For a more detailed discussion, and source for this definition, see http://en.wikipedia.org/wiki/Nirvana_fallacy.

This tendency to idealize the outcomes of future government policies and programs is a persistent bias in policy making.

In reality, both market and government sector provision have their limitations—neither is perfect, and there will be particular problems under either alternative. To help overcoming this fallacy, there is one simple reminder, or test, that should be remembered when considering new government policies or programs. This is simply asking the question of which *current* government agency do you want running or administering the program. For example, the idealized attractiveness of a government-run health care system is more realistically viewed by imagining the nation's health care system being run by FEMA, the Department of Defense, the Internal Revenue Service, or a state agency such as the Department of Motor Vehicles, Department of Education, or the Department of Social Services.

Only through careful thought about real-world alternatives, by comparing the likely true limitations of both the private and public sectors, can good judgments about policy be made. To be a productive force in an economy, government must do some things (like protect people and their property, enforce contracts in an unbiased manner, and provide a limited set of "public goods") but refrain from doing others.

WEALTH CREATION VERSUS WEALTH DESTRUCTION: TRADE AND TRANSFERS

As was noted earlier, when Jeff buys corn from Mary for $20, wealth is created. But when the government taxes Jeff $20 and gives it to Mary, this does not create wealth—no corn is produced. When governments do too much of this type of redistribution among individuals, there arises a fierce competition to become a recipient of government funding—another Mary. When business firms in the state think about trying to become more profitable, they too often think about how to secure more government subsidies, favors, or tax breaks. Instead, their efforts should be devoted to doing a better job at whatever it is they produce.

In stressing the role of entrepreneurship in an economy, New York University economist William Baumol (1990) notes that entrepreneurial individuals have a choice to devote their labor efforts toward either private-sector wealth creation, or toward securing wealth redistribution through the political and legal processes (e.g., lobbying and lawsuits).[11] This decision is influenced by the corresponding rates of return—or profit rates—of these alternative activities. Capitalist institutions, or institutions providing for secure property rights, a fair and balanced judicial system, contract enforcement, and effective limits on government's ability to transfer wealth through taxation and regulation, reduce the profitability of unproductive political and legal entrepreneurship. Under this incentive structure, creative individuals are more likely to engage in the creation of new wealth through productive market entrepreneurship.

In areas with weaker capitalist institutions, like Tennessee, these same individuals are instead more likely to engage in attempts to manipulate the political or legal process to capture transfers of existing wealth through unproductive political and legal

---

[11] Spending effort and resources to secure wealth through political redistribution is what economists call "rent-seeking." See, for instance, Tullock (1967) and Tollison (1982).

entrepreneurship—activities that destroy overall wealth. This reallocation of effort occurs because the institutional structure largely determines the relative personal and financial rewards to investing entrepreneurial energies into productive market activities versus investing those same energies instead into unproductive political and legal activities. For example, a steel entrepreneur might react to competition by trying either to find a better way of producing steel (productive entrepreneurship), or by lobbying for subsidies, tariff protection, or filing legal anti-trust actions (unproductive entrepreneurship).

To understand this distinction better, it is useful to consider the difference between positive-sum, zero-sum, and negative-sum economic activities. Activities are positive sum when net gains are created to society. Private market activities are positive sum because both parties gain in voluntary transactions. When you purchase a pizza, you value the pizza more than the money you pay for it, while the pizzeria values the money it receives from you more than it did the pizza. Government actions that transfer wealth, regulate, subsidize, or protect industries from competition are instead zero sum activities. One party's gain (e.g., the subsidy) is offset exactly by another party's loss (e.g., the taxes). However, because the zero-sum transfer requires an investment of resources in lobbying to secure, their overall impact on the economy is negative. Magnifying this is the fact that others will devote resources to political lobbying on the "defensive side" of transfers to protect their wealth from being seized. The resources devoted toward securing (and fighting against) zero-sum political transfers have a cost; we have more lobbyists and thus fewer scientists and engineers.

Unproductive entrepreneurship is unproductive because it uses up resources in the process of capturing zero-sum transfers and these resources have alternative, productive uses. Baumol's theory is founded in the idea that entrepreneurs exploit profit opportunities not only within private markets but also within the political and legal arenas. Thus, differences in measured rates of *private sector* entrepreneurship are partially due to the different directions entrepreneurial energies are channeled by prevailing economic and political institutions, through the rewards and incentive structures they create for entrepreneurial individuals.

In places like Tennessee, where the state government's large influence over spending encourages individuals to fight over obtaining state government funds, it encourages a high level of unproductive entrepreneurship. As a result, Tennessee has less productive private-sector entrepreneurship.

How much unproductive entrepreneurship is there in Tennessee? While it is hard to derive an exact number, some data can help to illustrate. In 2011, for example, 1,572 registered lobbyists represented 733 companies and organizations in Tennessee (Tennessee Ethics Commission 2011). In addition, Tennessee was home to 16,630 resident and active lawyers (American Bar Association 2011). Campaign contributions to candidates running for office in the 2010 Tennessee elections amounted to over $75.3 million, or $47.04 per vote cast in the election.[12] Policy reform that reduces the profitability of initiating lawsuits and lobbying government can create more wealth and prosperity as entrepreneurial efforts are re-channeled into productive uses.

Studies that examine the relationship between measures of productive private sector entrepreneurial activity and a state's economic freedom index (measuring institutional

---

[12] Data for federal offices ($22.8 million) is from OpenSecrets.org (2011) and data for state offices ($52.5 million) is from FollowTheMoney.org (2010). Voter turnout data (1,601,549 votes were cast in the 2010 general election) is from the United States Elections Project (2011).

quality) have found highly significant results.[13] Higher economic freedom produces higher venture capital investments per capita, a higher rate of patents per capita, a faster rate of sole proprietorship growth, and a higher establishment birth rate (both overall and among large firms) as was seen in Figure 2.7. Capitalism promotes productive entrepreneurial efforts.

But this same research also suggests that states with the worst economic freedom scores have the worst records on lobbying activity and lawsuit abuse—the unproductive types of entrepreneurship. In the ranking of "net entrepreneurial productivity" where productive entrepreneurship is measured relative to unproductive political and legal entrepreneurship, Tennessee ranks 32nd. It has both lower levels of private, productive entrepreneurial activity and higher levels of unproductive activity than fast-growth states with better scores on economic freedom such as Georgia, North Carolina, Delaware, Nevada, and Texas.[14] Tennessee has the 25th highest rate of unproductive entrepreneurial activity among states, while only the 30th highest rate of productive entrepreneurship. The relationship between having strongly capitalist institutions (as measured by economic freedom) and the index of net entrepreneurial productivity across states is shown in Figure 3.1.

Figure 3.1: Institutional Quality and Entrepreneurial Productivity

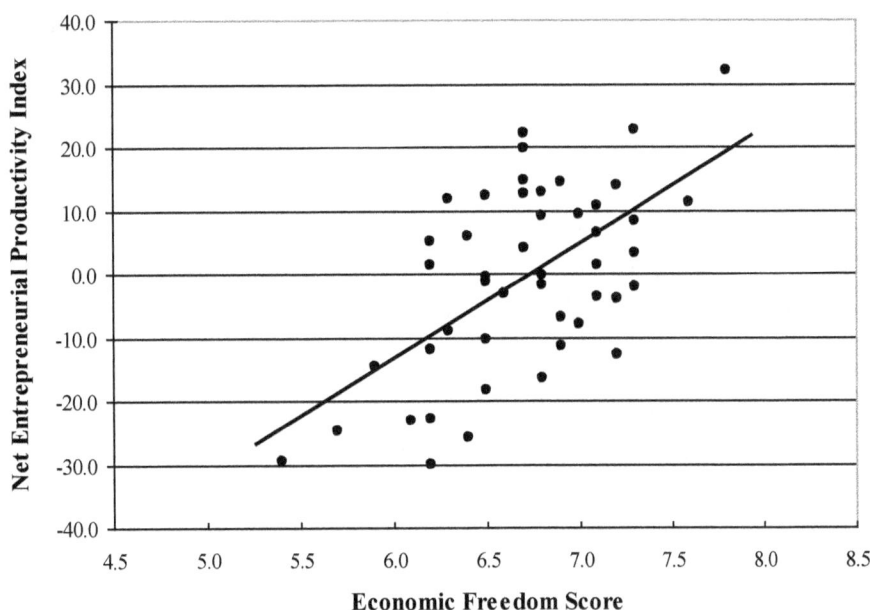

Source: Sobel (2008).

The data in Figure 3.1 suggest that capitalism and limited government promote prosperity not only because they promote productive activities, but also because they discourage unproductive, wealth-destroying activities. While the later chapters of this book are devoted to specific policy reforms for Tennessee, Figure 3.2 gives a general list of state policy reforms that increase net entrepreneurial productivity, thereby generating wealth.

---

[13] See, for example, Sobel (2008).
[14] As a more detailed comparison with its neighbors, while Tennessee ranks 32nd in the index of net entrepreneurial productivity, North Carolina ranks 15th and Georgia ranks 18th. For reference, Tennessee ranks 19th in economic freedom while Georgia ranks 5th and North Carolina ranks 9th.

Figure 3.2: Reforms That Increase the Reward to Productive Entrepreneurship Relative to Unproductive Entrepreneurship

- Reduce or eliminate state personal and corporate income taxes
- Eliminate legal minimum and maximum price and wage laws
- Reduce occupational licensing restrictions
- Place constitutional limits on eminent domain and environmental property takings
- Reduce government ownership of productive resources (e.g., land holdings)
- Make broad reductions in government employment, spending, and levels of taxation
- Strive for broadly applied, simplified tax codes that reduce the ability of groups to lobby for specific exemptions, credits, and rate reductions
- Reduce the returns to lobbying by eliminating forms of pork-barrel legislation that use state money to fund local pet projects, and by eliminating business subsidies
- Increase the use of market-based reforms such as medical savings accounts, school vouchers or school choice programs, privatized retirement funds, privatized government services (ambulance, water, garbage)

Source: Sobel (2008).

CONCLUSION

Chapter 1 made the case for why increasing economic growth should be an important policy goal in Tennessee. Chapter 2 presented evidence that areas relying more heavily on capitalism are wealthier. This chapter examined the underlying reasons why capitalism promotes prosperity.

Capitalism makes people wealthier because it results in higher labor productivity, increased specialization, expansion of markets, increased capital investment, expanded opportunities to trade with others, more entrepreneurial discovery, and a channeling of entrepreneurial efforts toward productive activities. It helps put resources to their most productive uses, generating higher incomes in the process.

Despite the overwhelming evidence in favor of increased reliance on capitalism, Tennessee has been reluctant to embrace this ideal in policy. This might be surprising when viewed from the outside as Tennessee is a state who has a Republican governor, and a Republican controlled legislature. However, when we examine all U.S. states, there is very little correlation between political party control of the legislature (or other measures of party affiliation) and economic freedom scores. Figure 3.3 shows a scatter plot of each state's economic freedom score, and the percentage of the state legislature that was Republican in the same year as the data used to construct the economic freedom score (2005).

Figure 3.3: Economic Freedom and Political Affiliation

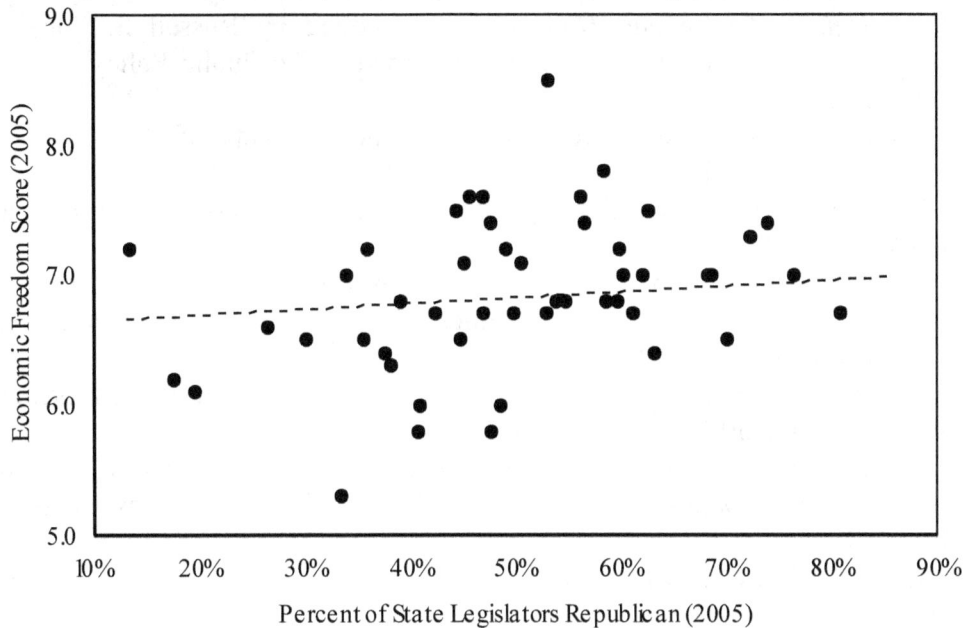

Sources: U.S. Census Bureau (2009); Karabegovic and McMahon (2008).

The trend line in the figure is virtually flat. It does have a slightly upward slope, but it is statistically insignificant. Quite simply, there is no statistically significant link between Republican control and reliance on capitalism in state policy. In fact, the states with the highest percentages on both ends of the spectrum have virtually indistinguishable scores on economic freedom. Across states, both Democrats and Republicans are equally likely to enact policy that embraces capitalism. The reason is because capitalism helps both parties to accomplish goals of common importance. This nonpartisan relationship also holds up for other measures of state political affiliation, including the percentage of the state population voting for the Republican presidential candidate.

REFERENCES

American Bar Association. 2011. *National Lawyer Population by State*. Chicago, IL: American Bar Association. www.americanbar.org/content/dam/aba/migrated /marketresearch/PublicDocuments/2011_national_lawyer_by_state.authcheckdam.pdf.

Associated Press. 2006. "Rare Woodpecker Sends a Town Running for Its Chain Saws." *New York Times*, September 24.

Baumol, William J. 1990. "Entrepreneurship: Productive, Unproductive and Destructive." *Journal of Political Economy* 98 (5): 893-921.

Buchanan, James M. and Gordon Tullock. 1962. *The Calculus of Consent: Logical Foundations of Constitutional Democracy.* Ann Arbor: University of Michigan Press.

Corey, Joab N. and Nicholas A. Curott. 2007. "Lower Business Regulation: Costs and Unintended Consequences." In *Unleashing Capitalism: Why Prosperity Stops at the West Virginia Border and How to Fix It*, edited by Russell S. Sobel, 131-43. Morgantown, WV: Center for Economic Growth, The Public Policy Foundation of West Virginia.

DeLeire, Thomas. 1997. "The Wage and Employment Effects of the Americans with Disabilities Act." PhD diss., Stanford University.

———. 2000. "The Unintended Consequences of the Americans with Disabilities Act." *Regulation* 23 (1): 21-24.

FollowTheMoney.org. 2010. "State Overview: Tennessee 2010." Helena, MT: National Institute on Money in State Politics. http://followthemoney.org/database/state_overview.phtml?y=2010&s=TN.

Friedman, Milton, and Rose Friedman. 1980. *Free to Choose: A Personal Statement*. New York, NY: Harcourt Brace Jovanovich.

Gwartney, James, Richard L. Stroup, and Dwight R. Lee. 2005. *Common Sense Economics: What Everyone Should Know about Wealth and Prosperity*. New York, NY: St. Martin's Press.

Hayek, F.A. 1945. "The Use of Knowledge in Society." *American Economic Review* 35 (4): 519-530.

———. 1967. *Studies in Philosophy, Politics, and Economics*. Chicago: University of Chicago Press.

Karabegovic, Amela, and Fred McMahon. 2008. *Economic Freedom of North America: 2008 Annual Report*. Vancouver, BC: Fraser Institute.

OpenSecrets.org. 2011. *Historical Elections: Contributions by State*. Washington, DC: The Center for Responsive Politics. www.opensecrets.org/bigpicture/statetotals.php?cycle=2010.

Read, Leonard E. 1958. "I, Pencil: My Family Tree as Told to Leonard E. Read." Irvington-on-Hudson: Foundation for Economic Education.

Schumpeter, Joseph A. (1911) 1934. *The Theory of Economic Development*. Cambridge: Harvard University Press.

Smith, Adam. (1776) 1998. *An Inquiry into the Nature and Causes of the Wealth of Nations*. Washington, DC: Regnery Publishing.

Sobel, Russell S. 2008. "Testing Baumol: Institutional Quality and the Productivity of Entrepreneurship." *Journal of Business Venturing* 23 (6): 641-655.

Sobel, Russell S., and Peter T. Leeson. 2007. "Why Capitalism Works." In *Unleashing Capitalism: Why Prosperity Stops at the West Virginia Border and How to Fix It*, edited by Russell S. Sobel, 37-54. Morgantown, WV: Center for Economic Growth, The Public Policy Foundation of West Virginia.

———. 2009. "Why Capitalism Works." In *Unleashing Capitalism: A Prescription for Economic Prosperity in South Carolina*, edited by Peter T. Calcagno, 49-70. Columbia, SC: South Carolina Policy Council.

Tennessee Ethics Commission, Bureau of Ethics and Campaign Finance. 2011. *Lobbyists, Employer, and Expenditure Reports*. Nashville, TN: Tennessee Ethics Commission. https://apps.tn.gov/ilobbysearch-app/search.htm.

Tollison, Robert D. 1982. "Rent Seeking: A Survey." *Kyklos* 35 (4): 575-602.

Tullock, Gordon. 1967. "The Welfare Cost of Tariffs, Monopolies, and Theft." *Western Economic Journal* 5 (3): 224-232.

U.S. Census Bureau. 2009. *The Statistical Abstract of the United States*. Table 395. Washington, DC: U.S. Census Bureau. http://www.census.gov/compendia/statab/cats /elections/gubernatorial_and_state_legislatures.html.

United States Elections Project. 2011. *2010 General Election Turnout Rates*. Fairfax, VA: George Mason University. http://elections.gmu.edu/Turnout_2010G.html.

CHAPTER 4

WHEN IT COMES TO TAXES IN TENNESSEE: FOCUS ON COMPETITIVE ADVANTAGE

by Joshua C. Hall and Adam J. Hoffer

Freedom and Prosperity in Tennessee

4

WHEN IT COMES TO TAXES IN TENNESSEE: FOCUS ON COMPETITIVE ADVANTAGE

Joshua C. Hall and Adam J. Hoffer

A common misperception is that the burden of taxes on an economy is simply equal to the tax revenue generated. In reality, taxes cost society much more than is generated in revenue. The additional costs come in many forms, including: administrative costs, enforcement costs, compliance costs, "excess burdens," and costs associated with resources spent by individuals and groups to avoid the tax, both before the tax is implemented (lobbying) and afterwards (evasion). High taxes are extremely costly to a state's economy. Countless studies find that higher taxes lead to significant reductions in economic growth. The purpose of this chapter is to explain the true costs of taxation, review the empirical literature on taxation and economic growth, and to examine Tennessee's overall tax burden relative to other states.[1]

WHY TAXES COST MORE THAN THEY TAKE

Just because a tax is levied on one specific group of individuals does not mean they will be the ones who bear the eventual burden of the tax. This concept is known in the economics literature as "tax shifting." A tax imposed on business assets, for example, might lead to higher prices for consumers, shifting some of the burden forward to consumers. Similarly, a tax imposed directly on consumers of a product will lead to reduced demand, shifting some of the burden backward onto the companies producing the good or service that is taxed.[2]

One thing is certain, however, and that is: all taxes are borne by *individuals*. A "business" cannot bear taxes. Instead, business taxes fall on the owners, employees, suppliers, or customers of the business.

According to the U.S. Census Bureau (2011), state and local governments around the nation took in more than $2.1 trillion in combined tax revenue for the 2009 fiscal year. State

---

[1] This chapter is based on Ross and Hall (2007) and Ross, Hall, and Calcagno (2009).
[2] For additional information on where the actual burdens of different taxes fall, see Pechman (1985); Fullerton and Rogers (1993).

and local government vary tremendously in their methods of raising revenue. The tools that are used to raise the most revenue are property taxes, sales taxes, selective sales taxes, and individual income taxes. Combined, these four sources totaled 88.8 percent of state and local tax revenues in 2009. States and local governments use these four taxes' sources in a variety of combinations to raise a majority of their revenue.

On average, individual income taxes averaged 21.3 percent of combined state and local tax revenues. Tennessee, however, is one of nine U.S. states to impose little or no state income tax. Specifically, Tennessee imposed a 6 percent flat tax exclusively on dividend and interest income and thus does not tax what is typically referred to as "ordinary income." All other personal income earned is free from taxation. Tennessee's tax revenues for 2009 are summarized by source in Figure 4.1. Combined state and local government tax revenue in Tennessee was nearly $18 billion, with over $10 billion levied at the state level.

Figure 4.1: Tennessee's Tax Revenue (in thousands) by Source 2009 Fiscal Year

	State	Local	Total
Tax Revenue	$10,433,133	$7,453,710	$17,886,843
Property	-	$4,697,932	$4,697,932
Sales and gross receipts	$8,000,471	$2,373,466	$10,373,937
General sales	$6,356,962	$1,942,228	$8,299,190
Selective sales	$1,643,509	$431,238	$2,074,747
Motor fuel	$815,611	-	$815,611
Alcoholic beverage	$116,056	$144,746	$260,802
Tobacco products	$301,219	-	$301,219
Public utilities	$8,071	$91,852	$99,923
Other selective sales	$402,552	$194,640	$597,192
Individual income	$221,685	-	$221,685
Corporate income	$816,261	-	$816,261
Motor vehicle license	$251,335	$147,510	$398,845
Other taxes	$1,143,381	$234,803	$1,378,184

Source: U.S. Census Bureau (2011).

What these revenue numbers exclude, however, are the many distortions in economic activity, and in the behavior of individuals, that occur in response to these taxes. Figure 4.2 helps to illustrate these costs. The direct cost of taxation is the obvious accounting cost—individuals who pay the tax will have less money to spend on other goods and services. The tax revenue generated does measure this reduction in private economic spending resulting from the tax. However, there are other significant costs.

Figure 4.2: The Cost of Taxation

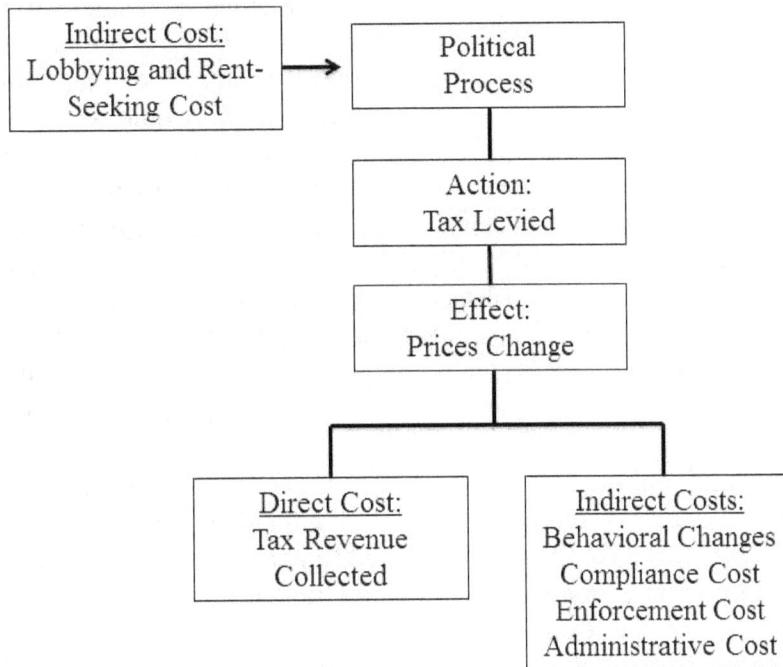

```
┌─────────────────┐        ┌─────────────────┐
│ Indirect Cost:  │   →    │   Political     │
│ Lobbying and Rent-      │   Process       │
│ Seeking Cost    │        │                 │
└─────────────────┘        └─────────────────┘
                                    │
                           ┌─────────────────┐
                           │    Action:      │
                           │   Tax Levied    │
                           └─────────────────┘
                                    │
                           ┌─────────────────┐
                           │    Effect:      │
                           │  Prices Change  │
                           └─────────────────┘
                    ┌───────────────┴───────────────┐
          ┌─────────────────┐           ┌─────────────────────┐
          │  Direct Cost:   │           │   Indirect Costs:   │
          │  Tax Revenue    │           │ Behavioral Changes  │
          │  Collected      │           │  Compliance Cost    │
          │                 │           │  Enforcement Cost   │
          │                 │           │  Administrative Cost│
          └─────────────────┘           └─────────────────────┘
```

Source: Ross and Hall (2007).

The first hidden cost of taxation comes from the political process itself. The indirect costs of lobbying and rent-seeking[3] (upper left box) reflect the resources devoted by individuals attempting to alter tax policy decisions within the political process. Interest groups will devote substantial time and effort into fighting against the imposition of a tax (or an increase in tax rates), as well as to secure reductions in tax rates, or their repeal.

To illustrate, suppose the legislature is considering a proposal to levy a new tax on unhealthy fast food. Further suppose that Hardee's estimates this new tax will cost the company $2 million. At this point, Hardee's would be willing to spend up to $2 million to prevent the imposition of the tax. They may hire lobbyists, make campaign contributions, attempt to secure media attention, or fight the legality of the tax in court. Once the tax is imposed, they will continue to devote resources to get the tax repealed, the rate lowered, or to secure an exemption from the tax. Resources spent in this manner are wasteful for precisely the reasons discussed in Chapter 3—they are taken away from other productive activities (which includes investments in capital equipment, buildings, or hiring more workers). In the terminology of Chapter 3, this is "unproductive entrepreneurship." It is important to note that

---

[3] Rent-seeking is "actions by individuals and groups designed to restructure public policy in a manner that will either directly or indirectly redistribute more income to themselves or the projects they promote" (Gwartney et al. 2013, 122).

these costs are present even if the tax is not enacted by the legislature. Simply the threat of imposing a new tax creates these costs.

To see the magnitude of these exemptions in practice, one only needs to skim the tax expenditure portion of the State of Tennessee's 2011-2012 Fiscal Year Budget (A-77 to A-79). Roughly speaking, tax expenditures are exemptions to specific taxes. For example, most states tax agricultural property at a lower rate than commercial or residential property. This differential rate is called a tax expenditure, since the deviation from the normal rate can be viewed as analogous to spending through the tax code.[4] Chapter 5 of this volume discusses these tax expenditures in more detail. At this point, however, we would like to focus attention on the rent-seeking costs associated with lobbying for such exemptions more generally.

Sobel and Garrett (2002) estimate the level of rent-seeking to be somewhere between 3.8 to 5.4 percent of a state's total tax revenue, implying an additional indirect cost of $679 to $965 million in wasted resources in Tennessee devoted to altering policy. To reduce these costs, many economists advocate broad-based uniform taxes rather than allowing rates and exemptions to vary across different goods and services (Holcombe 2001). Without the ability to individually reduce their own tax rate, any one particular industry is less likely to expend effort to lobby for changes. A tax that targets one specific industry, such as Tennessee's tax on beer, tends to generate larger indirect rent-seeking costs.[5]

Furthermore, unlike private markets in which you must pay prices for the things you purchase, with government it is often possible to receive the benefits of government programs while making *others* pay. Thus, there will be additional lobbying and rent-seeking costs associated with the fight over which programs will be funded, or who will obtain the benefits, when the revenue is spent. For example, the National Alliance on Mental Illness (NAMI) Tennessee (2012) successfully lobbied state government during the last legislative session to restore $24 million in community health services to the state budget. To restore that funding they had to compete against other groups who also wanted the same $24 million. While the restoration of that funding certainly matters for NAMI Tennessee and the individuals it represents, from society's standpoint the resources devoted to lobbying by NAMI Tennessee and others represents wasted resources.[6] The existence of opportunities for rent-seeking in the tax code winds up allocating state resources to those with the most political power, and not necessarily to welfare enhancing programs or to those most in need (Holcombe 2001).

Returning to Figure 4.2, the tax itself will cause additional indirect costs, highlighted in the lower right box in the figure. The first of these costs, the behavioral changes, is associated with distortions in the behavior of producers and consumers in response to the tax. To economists these costs are known as the "deadweight cost" or "excess burden" of taxation. Whenever a tax is imposed, individuals will substitute away from the activity that is taxed to other activities that are now comparatively cheaper. As an illustrative example, suppose Tennessee imposes a new $100 tax on each candy bar sold in the state. Further assume this would drive the price so high that candy bar sales would fall to zero. The tax would collect no revenue, but it clearly would still have a cost to society. Consumers who like to eat candy bars

---

[4] For more on some of the conceptual difficulties with the comparison between spending directly and through the tax code, see Hall (1999).

[5] For more on how high Tennessee's beer tax is relative to other states, see the *Commercial Appeal* (2012).

[6] In some cases it is not just private individuals lobbying, but state governments using tax money to lobby for more tax money (Owen, LeForge, and Turbeville 2009).

are now worse off because they are not consuming them, and the producers of candy bars are worse off as well due to the lower number of candy bars sold.

Consumers may also change where they make their purchases to avoid the tax, or if possible, where they live. Tennesseans living on the Georgia border might now drive to Georgia to buy candy bars, or chocolate lovers might even decide to move to another state. These are all costs of taxation that must be considered, and the easier it is for consumers to find substitute goods, shop, or move across the border, the larger these indirect costs.[7]

It is also important not to forget that business firms will also have an incentive to change their behavior in response to taxes. When a tax reduces the profitability of any one use of a business' resources, it means that other uses become *more profitable by comparison*, and the firm will make adjustments as a result, further increasing the behavioral costs of the tax. Like the consumer, firms can also move to areas that impose lower taxes. Again, the easier it is for firms to change their behavior in response to a tax, the larger will be the indirect behavioral costs of taxation.

The other indirect costs in Figure 4.2 are the compliance, enforcement, and administrative costs. Every tax must be administered and enforced by a taxing authority, and there will be costs associated with these activities. These are the least expensive indirect costs as a share of tax revenue, generally amounting to less than three percent (Payne 1993). Compliance costs, however, are considerable. While estimates vary, they have ranged from around 7 percent of total revenue raised (Slemrod and Sorum 1984) to 22.2 percent (Moody, Warcholik, and Hodge 2005). This cost includes the hours of bookkeeping, the time spent filling out tax forms, the hiring of accountants to address changes in tax laws, etc.[8]

When these direct and indirect costs are added up, they almost certainly constitute over half of every dollar in revenue raised. In other words, $1.00 of taxes costs the Tennessee economy upwards of $1.50. This has significant implications for the cost/benefit analysis of government projects funded through taxation. For example, a project with benefits of $150 million that requires $125 million in taxes to fund is not efficient to undertake once these additional costs of taxation are considered. While total state and local tax revenue in Tennessee amounts to almost $18 billion, the true cost of these taxes on the Tennessee economy is much higher. This is especially true when we consider the influence of taxation on economic growth.

TENNESSEE'S TAX BURDEN: A COMPARISON

In 2009, the per capita income in Tennessee was $36,157. The combined state and local taxes paid per capita was $2,752 during the same year (Prante and Robyn 2011). Using these two numbers, we can calculate the tax burden for Tennessee of 7.6 percent: (per capita total taxes paid $2,752) / (per capita income $36,157).

---

[7] Note that it is not just taxes that have this effect. Regulations create deadweight loss as well. In 2010, for example, Costco located in Catoosa County, Georgia, a mile and a half from the Tennessee state line. A deciding factor in their decision, according to some reports, was that they could sell wine in Georgia but not in Tennessee (Johns 2010).

[8] Evans (2003) provides a good overview and summary of these compliance cost studies.

How does Tennessee's tax burden compare to other states? The U.S. average tax burden was 9.8 percent during fiscal year 2010. These tax burdens and those of Tennessee's neighbors are listed in Figure 4.3. All 50 states are ranked according to their tax burden, with the state whose residents pay the greatest percentage of their income to state and local taxes ranked 1st (New Jersey) and the state whose residents have the lowest tax burden ranked 50th (Alaska).

Figure 4.3: Tax Burden for Tennessee and Its Neighbors, 2010 Fiscal Year

State	Taxes Paid by Residents as a Percent of Income	Rank	Taxes Collected by Governments as a Percent of Residents' Income	Rank
U.S. Average	9.80%	-	10.40%	-
Tennessee	**7.60%**	**47**	**8.30%**	**50**
Alabama	8.50%	40	8.40%	49
Arkansas	9.90%	14	10.10%	29
Georgia	9.10%	32	9.50%	36
Kentucky	9.30%	30	9.60%	33
Mississippi	8.70%	36	10.10%	28
Missouri	9.00%	34	8.80%	46
North Carolina	9.80%	16	9.70%	32
Virginia	9.10%	33	8.90%	45

Source: Robyn (2011).

Among all U.S. states, the tax burden of Tennessee's residents ranked 47th. At 7.6 percent, it is nearly a full percentage point less than Alabama, the neighbor with the closest ranking to Tennessee, and 2.3 percentage points less than Arkansas, the lowest ranking neighbor state, making Tennessee an attractive place to locate. The tax burden rankings stem largely from the friendly tax rate structure in the state and the competition Tennessee faces from its neighbors and the other U.S. states. We discuss both of these more in depth later in this chapter.

Columns four and five in Figure 4.3 present a similar measure of tax burden, but from a slightly different perspective. These data show where Tennessee's government ranks in collecting revenue compared to other states. While taxes paid by residents and taxes collected by the government are similar, they are not identical. Government tax revenue collected though special revenue sources, such as natural resource taxes, tourism, and all other taxes paid by non-state residents, are not counted toward taxes paid by residents. Thus, Alaska citizens have the 50th ranked tax burden, while the Alaskan government is ranked 1st among revenue collected as a percentage of residents' income.

Tennessee's government, on the other hand, had the lowest ratio of taxes collected compared to residents' income. At 8.3 percent, Tennessee's government collected more than two percentage points less than the U.S. average of 10.4 percent. Compared to some of its neighbors, however, Tennessee has only a slight margin. Alabama ranked 49th with a ratio of tax collections to income of 8.4 percent and Missouri ranked 46th with a ratio of 8.8 percent.

Tennessee has maintained a substantially lower tax burden than the U.S. average for as long as the statistic has been recorded. In 1977, Tennessee's was 8.2 percent and it has not been above 8.0 percent since 1978. The U.S. average state tax burden, however, has not been less than 9.0 percent since 1977, meaning that Tennessee's tax burden has been substantially lower than the U.S. average over the past 35 years. This is important for two reasons: economic growth and migration.

TAXATION AND ECONOMIC GROWTH: THE EMPIRICAL EVIDENCE

Over the past thirty years a considerable amount of economic research has been undertaken in an effort to understand the relationship between taxes and economic growth. While some minimal level of government is necessary to support the institutions of a free society, governments generally grow way beyond this optimal level. The reason why this is so and what can be done about it is an issue explored in more detail in Chapter 14.

Taxation is important, however, because it is the primary source of government spending. When government is small, its expenditures tend to be on economically productive activities such as highways. As state and local governments grow larger, however, new spending tends to become devoted to economically unproductive activities, such as transfer payments. From this perspective, it is clear that taxes *per se* are not bad, just as salt on food is not bad in small amounts. At higher levels, however, rising taxes not only have greater deadweight costs, but they depress the net return to private capital (Bania, Gray, and Stone 2007). This means that spending on normally productive activities (such as highways) can have a negative economic return when taxes are high. The theory behind this finding is that a rising tax share—even when spent on previously economically productive activities such as highways—leads to a crowding out of private investment because of the lower after-tax return on investment. In addition, more productive projects are likely to be pursued first, thus marginal infrastructure spending is likely going to have a lower return, regardless of the effect of higher taxes on private capital investment.

Looking specifically at taxes, there is extensive literature showing a strong negative relationship between taxes and economic growth. Mullen and Williams (1994) find that higher marginal income tax rates hurt economic growth. Jay Helms (1985) finds that taxation used to fund transfer payments significantly retards economic growth. Bartik (1992) provides an excellent summary of the research on state and local taxes and economic growth and concludes that state and local taxes have a consistently negative effect on state and city economic growth. In terms of business location decisions, it is not surprising that he finds tax decisions play a much larger role in studies that look across suburban jurisdictions than across states. Taxes are one part of the package that determines business location, including climate, local amenities, workforce quality, and public infrastructure. Once firms decide on a region, however, taxes can play a much larger role in their location choice. This point is especially important for Tennessee, given that three of its biggest metropolitan statistical areas straddle state lines. An individual or company can easily move across state borders to take advantage of favorable tax treatment without having to find a new job or new employees, respectively.

A study by Holcombe and Lacombe (2004) provides strong evidence of the cross-border effect of taxes. By comparing counties located across state borders from one another, Holcombe and Lacombe are able to effectively control for geographic similarities such as climate, workforce, and proximity to markets leaving only differences in state policy. Looking at the 30-year period from 1960 to 1990, they find that states raising their income tax rates faster than their neighbors had slower economic growth, leading to an average decline in per capita income of 3.4 percent. Reed (2008) also looks at the relationship between taxation and income growth at the state level from 1970-1999 using several different methodological approaches. He finds "robust" evidence that taxes used to fund general fund expenditures are negatively related to growth.

Plaut and Pluta (1983) find that high taxes have a negative effect on employment growth. Interestingly, they find a positive relationship between property taxes and industrial growth. They hypothesize that firms prefer locally-dominated tax systems to state-dominated tax systems, which are more prevalent in the South because the benefits related to the high local property taxes are likely to accrue locally.[9] Conversely, firms may avoid states where most taxes are levied at the state level because there is not as clear of a link between taxes paid and benefits received from the firm's perspective.

Writing for the Federal Reserve Bank of Atlanta, Becsi (1996) examines how state and local taxes affect relative state economic growth. He finds a significant negative relationship between relative state marginal tax rates and relative state growth from 1961 to 1992. The effect of differences in marginal tax rates across states helps to explain not only short-run differences in growth across states, but also the persistence of growth differentials among states over time.

Poulson and Kaplan (2008, 67) also look at the effect of taxes on state economic growth. They find the following:

> The analysis reveals that higher marginal tax rates had a negative impact on economic growth in the states. . . The analysis underscores the negative impact of income taxes on economic growth in the states. Most states introduced an income tax and came to rely on the income tax as the primary source of revenue. Jurisdictions that imposed an income tax to generate a given level of revenue experienced lower rates of economic growth relative to jurisdictions that relied on alternative taxes to generate the same revenue.

A low tax burden and avoidance of a tax on ordinary income is not a sufficient condition for economic growth; however, the evidence clearly points to it being a necessary condition as taxes influence individual behavior and the actions of individuals that drive economic prosperity. States that let people keep more of what they earn have greater incentives for people to earn more. In addition, people change their behavior to avoid taxes,

---

[9] In 2009, 52.3 percent of Tennessee's general revenue from own sources came from state taxes. This places the state 38th out of the 50 states in terms of the percentage of revenue coming from state sources. Tennessee thus has a comparative advantage when evaluated against its neighbors. Alabama (57.1 percent), Arkansas (74.7 percent), Kentucky (66.0 percent), Mississippi (58.4 percent), North Carolina (56.5 percent), and Virginia (57.0 percent) are all above Tennessee with only Georgia (46.0 percent) and Missouri (51.4 percent) falling below it on this measure.

including deciding where to live, and that is where Tennessee's tax system puts it at an advantage compared to other states.

TAXATION AND MIGRATION: THE EVIDENCE

Taxes not only impact where businesses locate, but also where people locate. If taxes get too high relative to the benefits received from government spending, people will move elsewhere. An early paper by Cebula (1974) found that migrants tended to move to areas with low property tax levels. Cebula's work has been replicated by many others such as Niskanen (1992). Conway and Houtenville (2001) look at migration by elderly Americans and find that elderly migration is motivated in part by low personal income taxes and estate taxes. Conway and Houtenville (2003) followed up their earlier study by looking at the difference between the so-called "young" elderly and older elderly. They find that both the young and the old elderly tend to migrate towards a temperate climate and lower taxes on income and property, but the older elderly in particular avoid states with high estate, inheritance, and gift taxes. Bakija and Slemrod (2004) also conclude that elderly individuals are responsive to state tax rates when making relocation decisions.

Cebula (2009) updated his earlier work to look specifically at the 2000-2005 period, and he finds similar results, namely that individuals during this period "voted with their feet" and were more likely to move to areas with lower tax burdens. Fox, Herzog, and Schlottmann (1989) find that an increase in income tax rates leads to a decrease in the likelihood of in-migration to metropolitan areas. Similarly, Coomes and Hoyt (2008) find that increases in state tax rates are associated with less in-migration. A recent study by Gius (2011) looks at interstate migration by age and race and finds that state income taxes play a large role for most age cohorts and racial groups. He finds that interstate migrants tend to move from states with high income taxes to states with lower income taxes.

This research is important for Tennessee because Tennessee does not have a tax on ordinary income which makes it appealing to individuals looking to migrate for climate, economic opportunity, or to escape high tax burdens relative to government benefits. Regardless of migrants' reasons for moving, Tennessee has at its advantage a more temperate climate than the average U.S. state as well as no tax on ordinary income. While it would be preferable in terms of permanency for the lack of an ordinary income tax to be codified in the state constitution, potential migrants know from history that it is much easier to raise rates on existing taxes than it is to raise taxes by enacting a tax on a completely new base.

In a recent paper, Davies and Pulito (2011) examine tax rate structures and migration at the state and county level. At the county level, they find that the lower the cutoff a county has for its highest income tax bracket, the lower the county's share of high-income households. They similarly show that there is a positive relationship between differences in tax rates and the ratio of in-migration to out-migration between states. In other words, the higher the income tax rate of other states, compared to Tennessee, the more residents that each state could be expected to lose to Tennessee.

We collect similar data from the Internal Revenue Service detailing state in-migration and out-migration to Tennessee for 2009-2010. Examining net migration (in-migration minus out-migration), Figure 4.4 presents the top ten states which had the most people relocate to Tennessee and the bottom ten states to which Tennessee lost the most people on net. Columns two and three present the tax burden of these states and their relative rank among the 50 U.S. states. Recall that Tennessee's tax burden in 2009 was 7.6 percent, the fourth lowest among all U.S. states (47th out of 50). Of the ten states which lost the most residents to Tennessee, four (New York, Wisconsin, California, and Pennsylvania) were among the ten states with the highest overall tax burden, all over 10.0 percent. Most of the states to which Tennessee was a net loser of residents had very similar tax burdens. This is consistent with taxes being an important, although not the only, factor influencing migration.

Figure 4.4: Net Migration to Tennessee

State	State Tax Burden	Tax Burden Rank	Net Migration	Adjusted Gross Income Change (Thousands of $)
Tennessee	7.6%	47	-	-
Top Ten States				
Michigan	9.7%	21	1148	$52,843
Florida	9.2%	31	1128	$48,350
Ohio	9.7%	18	764	$48,827
Illinois	10.0%	13	663	$57,220
New York	12.1%	2	424	$33,153
Indiana	9.5%	25	352	$23,092
Wisconsin	11.0%	4	348	$18,191
California	10.6%	6	327	$48,609
Pennsylvania	10.1%	10	305	$11,154
Georgia	9.1%	32	256	$28,644
Bottom Ten States				
Nebraska	9.8%	15	-20	$2,971
Alaska	6.3%	50	-22	$408
New Mexico	8.4%	41	-38	$1,061
Kansas	9.7%	19	-46	-$2,135
Missouri	9.0%	34	-48	$3,118
Arkansas	9.9%	14	-123	-$1,407
Oklahoma	8.7%	37	-146	-$1,855
Louisiana	8.2%	42	-192	-$773
Colorado	8.6%	39	-193	-$4,348
Texas	7.9%	45	-715	-$18,158

Source: Internal Revenue Service (2012).

The state which lost the most residents to Tennessee was Michigan. While Michigan is above the median mark of tax burden, economic decline, highlighted by that in Detroit and the auto industry, lead Michigan to lose more residents to migration than any other state in 2010 according to the Census Bureau. It is not surprising that many of those residents relocated to Tennessee, considering the opening of the new Volkswagen plant in Chattanooga.

These migration changes obviously can come with many benefits or losses to a state. The income data provided by the IRS allow us to measure the change in income resulting from migration. The 1,148 tax filers migrating to Tennessee from Michigan in 2009, for example, had adjusted gross incomes that totaled over $52.8 million. Adding up the incomes of in-migrants and subtracting out the incomes of out-migrants, we conclude that net migration into Tennessee lead to an additional $463 million in income in Tennessee in 2009. This is another important way that a sensible tax system contributes to economic progress.

TENNESSEE'S TAX STRUCTURE: A COMPARISON

Many studies of migration focus on people moving to the South in search of milder climates and lower taxes. But people also move within the South. For example, a person can move from Georgia into Tennessee to take advantage of its zero tax rate on ordinary income while still working the same job in Georgia. Because it is less costly to move shorter distances, it is important for states like Tennessee, which shares a border with the greatest number of U.S. states, to always keep an eye as to where they stand with respect to their neighbors.[10]

Figure 4.5 describes the composition of Tennessee's tax revenue and compares that with its neighboring states. State revenue collections are broken up into six categories: property taxes, sales taxes, selective sales taxes, individual income taxes, corporate income taxes, and other. The percentage of a state's total tax collections are listed under each category, with the six columns horizontally summing to 100 percent.

The most striking difference between Tennessee and its neighbors lies in the tax revenue collected from individual income taxes. By taxing only interest and dividend income, Tennessee's $221 million in income taxes comprised of only 1.2 percent of their total tax collections. The income tax brought in less revenue than the state tax on tobacco and was therefore a rather insignificant source of revenue for the state. This stands in stark contrast to Tennessee's neighbors and the U.S. average. The average state collected 21.3 percent of its revenue from individual income taxes, while Tennessee's neighbors collected between 16.5 percent (Mississippi) and 30.2 percent (North Carolina) of their revenue this way. In terms of interstate competition for mobile taxpayers, the lack of a tax on ordinary income favorably sets Tennessee apart from its neighbors.

Like many economic phenomena, however, this state of affairs comes with a tradeoff. Since Tennessee collects so little of its revenue from individual income tax, tax revenues from other sources will comprise a larger percentage of their total tax collections. The clearest example of this is illustrated by the percentage of Tennessee's revenue that comes from sales taxes. Sales tax collections make up 46.4 percent of all Tennessee's tax revenues. This is substantially higher than the U.S. average and the percentages of its neighbors. Just as the low percentage of revenues coming from individual income taxes is a benefit because it reflects the absence of a tax on ordinary income, a large percentage of Tennessee's revenue coming from sales taxes could be a bad sign if it is a symptom of really high sales tax rates.[11]

---

[10] Missouri also shares a border with eight U.S. states.

[11] As percentages, these numbers ignore the total amount of tax revenue collected by the government. Thus, any particular category could be high since all columns must sum to 100 percent, but the state still will not be "high tax" if overall spending (and thus taxation) is kept low.

Figure 4.5: Where Tennessee and Its Neighbors Collect Their Tax Revenue, 2009

	Property Taxes	Sales Taxes	Selective Sales Taxes	Individual Income Taxes	Corporate Income Taxes	Other
U.S Average	33.4	22.9	11.2	21.3	3.6	7.7
Tennessee	**26.3**	**46.4**	**11.6**	**1.2**	**4.6**	**9.9**
Alabama	17.9	29.0	18.1	20.9	3.7	10.4
Arkansas	16.8	39.0	12.2	23.8	3.7	4.6
Georgia	33.1	28.5	8.6	24.8	2.2	2.8
Kentucky	20.6	20.6	16.9	31.3	3.6	6.9
Mississippi	26.0	33.6	13.5	16.5	3.6	6.7
Missouri	28.7	25.0	11.9	26.4	1.7	6.3
North Carolina	25.7	23.3	11.8	30.2	2.8	6.2
Virginia	35.8	14.0	11.5	29.2	2.0	7.4

Source: U.S. Census Bureau (2011).

Interestingly, however, while compensating for the lack of income tax collections, Tennessee does not impose a sales tax rate that is substantially higher than its neighbors. This is illustrated in Figure 4.6, along with the tax rates levied on five of the popular selective sales tax items: gasoline, cigarettes, spirits, wine, and beer. Tennessee's sales tax rate of 7 percent was the same as Mississippi's and only one percent higher than the sales tax rate in Arkansas and Kentucky. None of Tennessee's selective sales tax rates are out of line with their neighbor's rates either.

So how does Tennessee manage to stay solvent despite collecting a minimalistic amount from individual income taxes and not escalating rates on other items? Tennessee manages to do so through a combination of three factors: an income effect, the structure of the state and local government system in Tennessee, and the overall size of Tennessee's government.

Because Tennessee does not implement an income tax, Tennessee residents will have more of their own money to spend. Likely, they will spend a large percentage of that extra income on taxable consumption, increasing sales tax collections. Compared to its neighbors, Tennessee had the third highest total taxable sales, behind only the larger populous states of North Carolina and Virginia. Per capita, Tennessee was behind only Arkansas in total taxable sales.[12] The increase in taxable sales, thus increasing sales tax revenue, translates into the state being more equipped to deal with less revenue from income taxes.

The second way Tennessee maintains a solvent government while not inflating their supplemental tax rates deals with the structure of the state and local government taxation system in Tennessee. Figure 4.1 highlights that over 40 percent of Tennessee's combined state and local sales tax revenue comes from local government sales tax collection. Additional local sales tax rates are not accounted for in the across-state analysis, implying that Tennessee's sales tax rates are certainly higher than 7 percent in various regions of the state.

---

[12] Author calculations.

Figure 4.6: State Sales and Excise Tax Rates: Tennessee and Its Neighbors, 2011

	Sales Tax	Gas Tax[a]	Cigarette Tax[b]	Spirits Tax[a]	Wine Tax[a]	Beer Tax[a]
Tennessee	**7.00%**	**$0.214**	**$0.62**	**$4.46**	**$1.27**	**$0.14**
Alabama	4.00%	$0.209	$0.43	$18.61	$1.70	$0.53
Arkansas	6.00%	$0.218	$1.15	$6.52	$1.39	$0.31
Georgia	4.00%	$0.294	$0.37	$3.79	$1.51	$1.01
Kentucky	6.00%	$0.278	$0.60	$6.85	$0.50	$0.08
Mississippi	7.00%	$0.188	$0.68	$8.43	$0.35	$0.43
Missouri	4.23%	$0.173	$0.17	$2.00	$0.42	$0.06
North Carolina	4.75%	$0.392	$0.45	$13.03	$0.79	$0.53
Virginia	5.00%	$0.198	$0.30	$20.91	$1.51	$0.26

Sources: Tax Foundation (2012); Federation of Tax Administrators (2012). Note: a: per gallon; b: per pack. The above numbers are excise tax rates and do not necessarily include all taxes on an item. For example, Tennessee also levies a 17 percent wholesale tax on beer. In addition, these numbers do not include local taxes.

Finally, perhaps the strongest reason for the maintained success of Tennessee's no income tax policy is due to the fact that Tennessee maintains a relatively small state government. Figure 4.3 showed that Tennessee collected the lowest amount of tax relative to income of all U.S. states. Tennessee is able to avoid an income tax and keep their other tax rates in line because they keep their overall government relatively small.

CONCLUSION

The aim of this chapter has been to clarify the true costs of taxation on the Tennessee economy, explore how Tennessee's taxes compare to its neighbors and the nation, and describe the relationship between taxation and economic growth and migration.

Tennessee has one of the most friendly tax systems in the entire country. This is highlighted by Tennessee's personal income tax being applied only to interest and dividend income, so that all other income earned is tax free at the state level. This helps Tennessee have one of the lowest tax burdens in all of the U.S. In fact, of all U.S. states, Tennessee's state and local governments collected the least amount of revenue relative to its residents' incomes.

This amenable tax system has helped Tennessee prosper. Recently, Tennessee has seen a major surge of in-migration, while losing far fewer residents to out-migration. This influx of new workers has come primarily from states with a far less friendly tax system and a much larger tax burden. These new workers have helped bring hundreds of millions of dollars in new income to Tennessee.

Empirical studies have a long history of consistently finding that state taxation hinders development and economic growth by constraining the entrepreneurial forces of free individuals. To continue to promote economic growth and remain a place where people want to live and work, Tennessee must find ways to keep its overall tax burden low while not letting its sales tax rate or other taxes become too much greater than its neighbors. The next chapter will explore several specific tax reforms that can help to accomplish this goal.

REFERENCES

Bakija, Jon, and Joel Slemrod. 2004. "Do the Rich Flee from High State Taxes? Evidence from Federal Estate Tax Returns." NBER Working Paper No. 10645.

Bania, Neil, Jo A. Gray, and Joe Stone. 2007. "Growth, Taxes, and Government Expenditures: Growth Hills for U.S. States." *National Tax Journal* 60 (2): 193-204.

Bartik, Timothy J. 1992. "The Effects of State and Local Taxes on Economic Development: A Review of Recent Research." *Economic Development Quarterly* 6 (1): 102-111.

Becsi, Zsolt. 1996. "Do State and Local Taxes Affect Relative State Growth?" *Federal Reserve Bank of Atlanta Economic Review* 81 (2): 18-36.

Cebula, Richard J. 1974. "Local Government Policies and Migration: An Analysis for SMSAs in the United States, 1965-1970." *Public Choice* 19 (l): 85-93.

———. 2009. "Migration and the Tiebout-Tullock Hypothesis Revisited." *American Journal of Economics and Sociology* 68 (2): 541-551.

Commercial Appeal PolitiFact Tennessee. 2012. "The Truth-O-Meter Says: Tax Foundation Says Tennessee Has Some of the Lowest Beer Excise Tax Rates in the Country." http://www.politifact.com/tennessee/statements/2012/mar/20/tax-foundation /taxfoundation-map-shows-tennessee-has-low-beer-ex/.

Conway, Karen S., and Andrew J. Houtenville. 2001. "Elderly Migration and State Fiscal Policy: Evidence from the 1990 Census Migration Flows." *National Tax Journal* 54 (1): 103-123.

———. 2003. "Out with the Old, In with the Old: A Closer Look at Younger versus Older Elderly Migration." *Social Science Quarterly* 84 (2): 309-328.

Coomes, Paul, and William Hoyt. 2008. "Income Taxes and the Destination of Movers to Multistate MSAs." *Journal of Urban Economics* 63 (3): 920–937.

Davies, Antony, and John Pulito. 2011. "Tax Rates and Migration." Mercatus Center Working Paper No. 11-31.

Evans, Chris. 2003. "Studying the Studies: An Overview of Recent Research into Taxation Operating Costs." *eJournal of Tax Research* 1 (1): 64-92.

Federation of Tax Administrators. 2012. *Tax Rates.* Washington, DC: Federation of Tax Administrators. http://www.taxadmin.org/fta/rate/tax_stru.html.

Fox, William, Henry Herzog, and Alan Schlottmann. 1989. "Metropolitan Fiscal Structure and Migration." *Journal of Regional Science* 29 (4): 523-536.

Fullerton, Don, and Diane Lim Rogers. 1993. *Who Bears the Lifetime Tax Burden?* Washington: The Brookings Institution.

Gius, Mark. 2011. "The Effect of Income Taxes on Interstate Migration: An Analysis by Age and Race." *Annals of Regional Science* 46 (1): 205-218.

Gwartney, James D., Richard L. Stroup, Russell S. Sobel, and David A. MacPherson. 2013. *Economics: Private and Public Choice*. 14th ed. Mason, OH: South-Western, Cengage Learning.

Hall, Joshua C. 1999. *Tax Expenditures: A Review and Analysis*. Washington, DC: Joint Economic Committee.

Helms, L. Jay. 1985. "The Effect of State and Local Taxes on Economic Growth: A Time Series-Cross-Section Approach." *The Review of Economics and Statistics* 67 (4): 574-582.

Holcombe, Randall G. 2001. "Public Choice and Public Finance." In *The Elgar Companion to Public Choice*, edited by William F. Shughart II and Laura Razzolini, 396-421. Cheltenham: Edward Elgar.

Holcombe, Randall G., and Donald J. Lacombe. 2004. "The Effect of State Income Taxation on Per Capita Income Growth." *Public Finance Review* 32 (3): 292-312.

Internal Revenue Service. 2012. *SOI Tax Stats—State-to-State Migration Database Files*. Washington: Internal Revenue Service. http://www.irs.gov/taxstats/article/0,,id =212702,00.html.

Johns, Andy. 2010. "Wine Laws May Have Lured Costco." *Times Free Press*, January 17.

Moody, J. Scott, Wendy P. Warcholik, and Scott A. Hodge. 2005. "The Rising Cost of Complying with the Federal Income Tax." *Tax Foundation Special Report No. 138*. Washington, DC: Tax Foundation.

Mullen, John K., and Martin Williams. 1994. "Marginal Tax Rates and State Economic Growth." *Regional Science and Urban Economics* 24 (6): 687-705.

National Alliance on Mental Illness Tennessee. 2012. "Mental Health Funding: Your Voice, Your Vote." *NAMI Tennessee Newsletter*. Nashville: National Alliance on Mental Illness Tennessee. http://www.namitn.org/documents/NAMITNFebNewsletter20122.5 .2012.pdf.

Niskanen, William A. 1992. "The Case for a New Fiscal Constitution." *Journal of Economic Perspectives* 6 (2): 13-24.

Owen, Justin, Emily LeForge, and Ryan Turbeville. 2009. *The Dangerous Cycle of Taxpayer Funded Lobbying*. Nashville: Tennessee Center for Policy Research.

Payne, James L. 1993. *Costly Returns: The Burdens of the U.S. Tax System*. San Francisco: ICS Press.

Pechman, Joseph A. 1985. *Who Paid the Taxes: 1966-1985?* Washington: The Brookings Institution.

Plaut, Thomas R., and Joseph E. Pluta. 1983. "Business Climate, Taxes and Expenditures, and State Industrial Growth in the United States." *Southern Economic Journal* 50 (1): 99-119.

Poulson, Barry W., and Jules Gordon Kaplan. 2008. "State Income Taxes and Economic Growth." *Cato Journal* 28 (1): 53-71.

Prante, Gerald, and Mark Robyn. 2011. "State-Local Tax Burdens Fall in 2009 as Tax Revenues Shrink Faster than Income." *Tax Foundation Special Report No. 189*. Washington: Tax Foundation. http://taxfoundation.org/article/state-local-tax-burdens-fall-2009-tax-revenues-shrink-faster-income.

Reed, W. Robert. 2008. "The Robust Relationship between Taxes and U.S. State Income Growth." *National Tax Journal* 61 (1): 57-80.

Robyn, Mark. 2011. "Census Bureau Releases 2010 State Tax Collection Data." *Tax Foundation Fiscal Fact No. 266.* Washington, DC: Tax Foundation. http:// taxfoundation .org/article/census-bureau-releases-2010-state-tax-collection-data.

Ross, Justin M. and Joshua C. Hall. 2007. "When It Comes to Taxes: Focus on Being Competitive." In *Unleashing Capitalism: Why Prosperity Stops at the West Virginia Border and How to Fix It,* edited by Russell S. Sobel, 69-79. Morgantown: The Public Policy Foundation of West Virginia.

Ross, Justin M., Joshua C. Hall, and Peter T. Calcagno. 2009. "When It Comes to Taxes in South Carolina: Focus on Remaining Competitive." In *Unleashing Capitalism: A Prescription for Economic Prosperity in South Carolina,* edited by Peter T. Calcagno, 73-85. Columbia: South Carolina Policy Council.

Slemrod, Joel, and Nikki Sorum. 1984. "The Compliance Cost of the U.S. Individual Income Tax System." *National Tax Journal* 37 (4): 461-474.

Sobel, Russell S., and Thomas A. Garrett. 2002. "On the Measurement of Rent Seeking and Its Social Opportunity Cost." *Public Choice* 112 (1-2): 115-136.

State of Tennessee, Office of Governor Bill Haslam. 2011. *The Budget: Fiscal Year 2011-2012.* Nashville: State of Tennessee. http://tennessee.gov/finance/bud/documents/11 -12BudgetVol1.pdf.

Tax Foundation. 2012. *Data.* http://taxfoundation.org/data.

U.S. Census Bureau. 2011. *State and Local Government Finances: 2009.* Washington: U.S. Census Bureau. http://www.census.gov/govs/estimate/.

CHAPTER 5

SPECIFIC TAX AND SUBSIDY REFORMS TO PROMOTE ECONOMIC PROGRESS IN TENNESSEE

by Art Carden and Joshua C. Hall

Freedom and Prosperity in Tennessee

5

SPECIFIC TAX AND SUBSIDY REFORMS TO PROMOTE ECONOMIC PROGRESS IN TENNESSEE

Art Carden and Joshua C. Hall

Chapter 4 outlined the importance to Tennessee of remaining competitive in terms of its overall tax system and the distribution of taxes among the various bases including property, sales, and income. Much of that discussion focused on the role the overall tax burden plays in attracting and retaining residents as well as how certain types of taxes have different effects on economic growth. In this chapter, we turn our attention to looking more closely at smaller elements of Tennessee's tax system to see how well they align with basic principles of tax policy.

There are many different ways for governments to command resources in order to undertake activities, and not all ways are equal in terms of promoting economic progress. For example, Tennessee collects as much revenue as a percentage of residents' incomes as does Alabama, even though Alabama levies a tax on ordinary income and Tennessee does not. While the dollars raised as a percentage of residents' income may be the same, there is at least some evidence that levying an income tax lowers a state's economic growth (Poulson and Kaplan 2008).

In considering basic principles of tax policy, it is important to note how Tennessee differs in comparison to the average state. Forty-one states tax ordinary income (wages and salaries) through a state income tax. Sobel and Lawson (2003) point out that states with more progressivity in their state income tax systems had lower growth over the previous decade. More recently, Walker and Arsenault (2009) highlight the problem of "bracket creep" with state income tax systems, where inflation pushes individuals into higher income tax brackets because the brackets are not indexed for inflation. Tennessee is fortunate to avoid the issues of slower growth and bracket creep because it only levies a tax on dividend and interest income.

Tennessee's overall tax environment is relatively favorable compared to other states. This, however, does not mean that there is not room for improvement, especially if the policy goal is to ensure a strong environment for economic development and growth. Widely-held principles of tax policy will be applied to several state and local tax policies in Tennessee that have been the subject of recent discussion. In addition, we discuss the growing use of targeted taxes and tax breaks to subsidize professional sports teams.

PRINCIPLES OF TAX POLICY

State and local governments undertake economic activity for a variety of reasons. For example, economic theory provides several important cases of market failure where government intervention might help markets become more efficient.[1] The field of public choice economics shows, however, that government often acts to further private interests rather than the public interest.[2] Regardless of the reasons why state and local governments undertake certain activities, they still have to raise money for the activities they undertake.

There are three primary ways that governments can take command over resources to directly undertake activities: borrowing, printing money, or taxation (Vedder and Gallaway 1998).[3] In the United States, state and local governments do not have the ability to print currency so it is of little concern in analyzing how effectively Tennessee raises revenue. Borrowing by states and localities, while it occurs, is also more heavily circumscribed than at the federal level, especially given that nearly all states, including Tennessee, have some form of a balanced budget requirement. Thus for many states, taxation is the primary way that the state is able to take control over resources to finance its activities.

Before considering what makes one form or structure of taxation better than another, however, it is important to remember that in the real world all taxes distort behavior and lower economic welfare. Basically, taxation reduces the gains from exchange of goods and services that are traded in markets. Consider an exchange occurring in a completely private market with no government taxation. In making the exchange, both the buyer and the seller expect to profit from the deal. The buyer values the good that she is purchasing more than the currency she is handing over. If this were not the case, she would not be part of the exchange. Economists call the difference between what she would have paid for the good and what she did pay for the good her "consumer surplus." Likewise, the producer will not undertake the trade unless she expects to profit from it. The difference between what she is willing to sell the product for and the price she is able to sell the good for is her "producer surplus." Consumer and producer surplus combined equal the gains from private exchange.

Taxation reduces these gains from exchange. Exactly how taxation does so varies from one type of tax to another, but the key to understanding how taxes reduce the gains from exchange is to see how they change consumer and producer behavior. Consider what happens if a corporate income tax were placed on the supplier of a good. This would raise the cost of supplying the good and reduce the willingness of the supplier to provide the good at the previous price. In fact, if the increase in cost was greater than the producer surplus was prior to the tax, then the exchange will no longer occur. The exchanges that no longer exist because of the tax lead to reduced consumer and producer surplus and thus make society worse off.[4] Economists use the term "deadweight loss" or "excess burden" of taxation to refer to the reductions in producer and consumer surplus associated with taxation.[5] Some estimates of the

---

[1] For a list of these reasons see any introductory economics textbook such as the one by Gwartney et al. (2011).

[2] For a brief introduction to public choice economics, see Shughart (2008).

[3] Government can also indirectly take command over resources through regulation. For more on the negative relationship between regulation at the state level and economic development, see Campbell, Heriot, and Jauregui (2010).

[4] Note that our analysis here focuses solely on the efficiency of the tax and does not take into account what is done with the tax revenue.

[5] For a thorough discussion of the excess burden of taxation and how it is measured, see Hines (2008).

cost of raising one dollar of revenue at the federal level put the deadweight loss at 75 percent (Hines 2007). It should be noted that the upper end of these estimates of deadweight loss tend to be for income or capital taxes at the federal level, and that the excess burden of taxation at the state level tends to be lower, but still often over 30 percent.[6]

While all taxes reduce economic welfare, not all taxes are created equal. For example, some taxes impose a greater administrative burden than other taxes. Other taxes distort behavior more per dollar raised than other taxes and thus have a greater excess burden. Finally, two taxes might have the same administrative burdens and excess burden but differ in terms of *which* citizens they impact. Good public policy should be directed toward minimizing the cost to society of raising a dollar of revenue. What criteria should be used to think about the costs a tax imposes on members of society? Vedder and Gallaway (1998) argue that there is broad agreement among public finance scholars regarding three broad principles of tax policy.

According to Vedder and Gallaway (1998, 4), "a good tax is:

1. Not costly for either government or taxpayers to calculate or administer; on the other hand tax avoidance is difficult and risky.
2. Neutral in its impact on resource allocation decisions, minimizing negative effects on economic growth; it does not lead to unproductive economic activity that is tax-induced.
3. Fair; people believe that the tax burden is equitably distributed amongst the tax-paying population."

Given that the focus of this book is on freedom and prosperity in Tennessee, we will primarily focus on the first two criteria in evaluating various Tennessee taxes. These two criteria also have the advantage of being relatively straightforward unlike the third criteria which is highly subjective. Fairness, like beauty, is in the eye of the beholder. For example, a sales tax rate of 7 percent on all purchases of goods and services might seem extremely fair to one person as every person pays the same rate on all of their consumption. The exact same sales tax rate might strike another person as extremely unfair given that the poor consume a greater portion of their income than the rich do.

At the core of all equity discussions involving taxation is the normative view that individuals with a greater ability to pay should pay more. This leads to the principle of "horizontal equity," which states that individuals in the same economic circumstances should pay the same amount in taxes. While seemingly straightforward, in practice this principle is difficult to apply. For example, what should we use to measure whether individuals have the same economic circumstances? Typically, annual income is used, but that is problematic (Cordes 1999). If annual income is used then we end up comparing people in very different life circumstances, such as college students who have summer jobs with elderly individuals on fixed incomes. Even if we could all agree that annual income was the correct standard for trying to measure economic circumstances, we would then likely disagree on how individuals' circumstances beyond income affected their ability to pay. For example, very few people would argue that a person making $20,000 in New York City has the same ability-to-pay as someone making the same income in Cumberland County, Tennessee.

---

[6] See, for example, Hawkins (2002).

Another principle often applied to issues of tax fairness is "vertical equity." Where horizontal equity looks at whether people of similar economic circumstances pay the same amount, vertical equity argues that people with higher incomes should have a greater ability-to-pay, thus taxes should rise with revenue. Even vertical equity, however, is an extremely subjective principle in practice. The principle states that individuals with higher income should pay more in taxes than individuals with lower incomes. But this just begs the question of how much more? More in total dollars? More in percentage terms? In practice, it often means more as a percentage of income, but that is just a normative statement on the part of the majority of economists (Walker and Arsenault 2009).

EVALUATING TENNESSEE'S TAX SYSTEM: THE SALES TAX

Tennessee has a very competitive overall tax system. The fact that it does not have an income tax is attractive to many individuals looking to migrate south from colder climates. While the Tennessee sales tax rate is higher than some states, once it is taken into account that Tennessee does not tax ordinary income, the higher rate seems more reasonable. In Tennessee, the basic sales tax rate is 7 percent, with a local option tax that varies from 1 percent to 2.75 percent. Memphis and Nashville, for example, both have local option taxes of 2.25 percent, causing the overall sales tax rate in both those cities to reach a rate of 9.25 percent (Drenkard, Raut, and Duncan 2012).

According to a recent study of sales tax rates in major U.S. cities by the non-partisan Tax Foundation, Memphis and Nashville are tied for seventh highest, beaten only by Birmingham, Montgomery, Chicago, Glendale (AZ), Seattle, and Phoenix (Drenkard, Raut, and Duncan 2012). While the fact that Tennessee does not levy a tax on ordinary income understandably explains this high rate, it should be a cause of concern given the opportunity to engage in tax avoidance through cross-border shopping and online purchases. To the extent that individuals expend resources to avoid the Tennessee sales taxes or do not engage in economic activity because the high rate produces economic inefficiency, higher sales tax rates create greater distortions. Thus, for any given amount of revenue raised, it is good tax policy to have an expansive tax base in order to have the lowest rate possible.

One reason that Tennessee may have higher sales tax rates is sales tax expenditures. Tax expenditures are deviations from what is considered a "normal" sales tax rate and base. While often thought of as "spending through the tax code," in many cases these exemptions are bad tax policy because they narrow the tax base and necessitate higher rates in order to raise a given amount of revenue. For example, aviation fuel used in the operation of aircraft engines is taxed at only 4.5 percent (Tennessee Department of Revenue 2011). According to the state's tax expenditure budget, that reduced rate cost state and local governments over $70 million in revenue during fiscal year 2011-2012 (Tennessee Department of Finance and Administration 2011). Regardless of the political or economic reasoning behind sales tax expenditures, such exemptions slowly erode the sales tax base, necessitating higher sales tax rates.

One of the most egregious sales tax expenditures is the reduced rate for food sales. While perhaps being good politics, having differential rates for food is bad tax policy. According to *State Tax Notes* columnist David Brunori (2012):

There are no economic or tax reasons for it. Sound tax policy requires groceries to be treated like any other personal consumption. And those of you who think that by exempting groceries, you're closing the gap on regressivity, take note: Rich people eat—and they eat better and more expensive food than you. We all would be better off with a broader base and lower rates. If food is exempt, the tax rate on everything else must be higher. If food is exempt, administering and complying with the tax becomes more difficult. And exempting groceries creates market distortions (favoring supermarkets over 7-Elevens) that have no place in the tax code.

According to the most recent tax expenditure budget, this exemption cost state and local governments over $130 million during the 2011-2012 fiscal year (Tennessee Department of Finance and Administration 2011).

Failure to tax food purchased for home consumption (or to tax it at a lower rate) is part of a continued narrowing of the sales tax base that necessitates even higher sales tax rates. Consider that in 1970 over 29 states fully taxed food purchased for home consumption. That was at a time when the average household was far poorer than they are today. In addition, only 7.75 percent of personal consumption expenditure today is on food, whereas in 1970 it was 16 percent (Mikesell 2012). If the concern is the cost of food for the poor, a blanket exemption for all taxpayers is a poor way to address that concern, especially when it leads to the continual erosion of the tax base. Brunori (2011) also highlights the administrative difficulty of deciding which foods are exempt from the sales tax on food because some are inputs into home food preparation, but others are taxable because they are to be consumed before arriving home.

In addition to narrowing the tax base, sales tax expenditures are poor tax policy because of their administrative burden and how they distort consumption patterns. Consider the case of sales tax holidays, which have occurred annually in Tennessee in recent years. Williams, Dubay, and Mausolf (2006) and Mikesell (2006) provide an overview of why sales tax holidays are "poor tax policy." Basically, there are two ways sales tax exemptions violate basic tax policy. First, they privilege some products at the expense of others as only certain items such as clothing and school supplies are exempt. This creates large distortions in consumption behavior, encouraging the purchase of more clothing and school supplies than families would otherwise purchase. A recent working paper by two economists at the Chicago Federal Reserve Bank provides empirical evidence of the distortions surrounding sales tax holidays (Marwell and McGranahan 2010). Using household level data, they find that households increase their spending on shoes and clothing by over 40 percent relative to what is normal. Second, exemptions increase the administrative burdens of tax collection by focusing on some items and not others. For example, belt buckles sold separately are not exempt from the sales tax during Tennessee's sales tax holiday, but belt buckles sold with a belt are exempt (Tennessee Department of Revenue 2012).

EVALUATING TENNESSEE'S TAX SYSTEM: THE ESTATE AND GIFT TAX

Tennessee's estate tax and its gift tax have been the subject of considerable debate in Tennessee in the past year (Humphrey 2012). During the recent legislative session, legislation was passed that will phase out Tennessee's estate tax over time and that immediately eliminated its gift tax (Sisk 2012b). Prior to its repeal, the state of Tennessee collected roughly $100 million per year from its estate tax and $15 million per year from its gift tax (Sisk 2012a). While not trivial sums, these two taxes represent a very small part of the over $12 billion in state revenue collected every year. Recognizing that the amount of revenue collected by these taxes is small and can easily be made up through the elimination of sales tax expenditures is important because of the large administrative costs and distortions associated with both taxes.

Estate and gift taxes are bad tax policy because they raise little revenue compared to the costs they impose on taxpayers. The administrative costs associated with complying with the estate tax, for example, have been known to be high for quite some time. In analyzing the federal estate tax, for example, a former member of President Clinton's Council of Economic Advisors estimated that the costs associated with estate tax compliance were equal to the amount of revenue raised (Munnell 1988). Turbeville and Cobb (2012) provide a first-hand account of a Tennessee farmer who spent countless hours of his valuable time and hired numerous estate planners and lawyers in order to minimize his estate tax bill. From the standpoint of society, the resources expended to avoid this tax are wasted as they could have been spent on improving his farm or other productive activities.

The size of the growth effects of repealing Tennessee's estate and gift taxes have been hotly debated. In a report by Arthur B. Laffer and Wayne H. Winegarden (2012, 3) for the Beacon Center of Tennessee, the authors estimate that "[h]ad Tennessee eliminated its gift and estate tax 10 years ago, Tennessee's economy would have been over 14% larger in 2010 and there would have been 200,000 to 220,000 more jobs in the state." In contrast, a recent study by the Institute on Taxation and Economic Policy (2012, 4) disagrees with their claims and concludes that "lawmakers seeking a clear-eyed assessment of the estate tax will have to look elsewhere."

Regardless of where one stands on the empirics of the stimulative effects of estate tax repeal, the large amount of unproductive and distortionary economic activity that occurred in response to Tennessee's estate and gift tax is obvious. High income and high wealth individuals, in particular, have been found to be very responsive to differences across states in estate and inheritance taxes (Bakija and Slemrod 2004). It does not take a large number of distortions of residency or estate-planning decisions of the wealthy for the costs of the estate and gift tax to exceed revenue raised.

TAXATION TO SUBSIDIZE PROFESSIONAL SPORTS

There have been a number of stadium-oriented development projects in Tennessee over the last two decades. Memphis is home to two state-of-the-art basketball arenas: the Pyramid and the FedEx Forum. Nashville is home to the Gaylord Center, where the Nashville Predators play, and LP field, home of the Tennessee Titans. Like many stadiums around the country, these professional sports arenas received numerous direct and indirect subsidies from taxpayers. FedEx Forum, for example, was almost entirely publicly funded through a variety of taxes and fees, including a surcharge on rental cars and higher hotel and rental fee taxes. This seems to be consistent with nationwide trends in professional sports team stadium financing (Matheson and Baade 2006).

These taxes are bad tax policy for at least three reasons. First, they can be relatively easy to avoid by not staying within the city while attending games or sporting events. Second, not all hotel and rental car users are in the city to see an athletic event or show, and thus there is a subsidization of sports fans by non-sports fans. Third, the higher taxes raise the price of hotels and car rentals, reducing consumption of both and resulting in reduced gains from exchange.

Local boosters vigorously support these new taxes for stadiums because it is argued that the stadiums will help revitalize the areas where they are located by drawing in new businesses. However, there are two problems with this argument. The first is related to the fact that the higher hotel and car rental fees discourage tourists from coming to the city on the margin. This has the effect of reducing demand for these ancillary businesses. Second, to the extent that economic activity increases in and around these stadiums, it is usually just redirected economic activity from elsewhere in the metropolitan area. Prominent sports economists Coates and Humphries (2008, 298) find in their survey of the literature on sports franchises and sports stadiums that "[m]uch of the consumer spending associated with professional sports comes out of the entertainment budgets of local residents."

It is not that professional sports are not beneficial. Clearly, a naive look at the taxes paid by team employees and the sales taxes generated by fans (both directly and indirectly related to the game) would show that sports teams have a positive benefit. But economists are trained to look at the costs as well as the benefits of an activity. Once both the costs and the benefits are considered, one almost always finds that subsidies for professional sports make cities poorer. Coates and Humphreys (2000) find, for example, that professional sports actually have a *negative* impact on the level of income across metropolitan areas. This finding is consistent with professional sports both deterring and shuffling around economic activity.

The damage is done with the stadiums that have already been built. It is hard to argue that the Memphis Pyramid was not a mistake overall, let alone how it was financed. Policymakers should learn from these mistakes and make sure that subsidization of these facilities through preferential tax treatment or passage of new taxes does not reoccur.

CONCLUSION

Tennessee already has the advantage of a relatively business-friendly tax system. However, there remains much room for improvement. Eliminating the state's estate and gift tax was a step in the right direction. Lowering the sales tax on food was a step in the wrong direction. Each and every sales tax exemption and preferential rate needs to be examined in order to ensure that Tennessee is able to maintain the broadest sales tax base possible. A broad sales tax base is necessary to ensure that Tennessee has a simple and efficient tax system moving forward. The ability of the sales tax system to raise revenue with low rates is crucial to improvements in the tax system as is evidenced by the important role that current tax receipts had to play in the repeal of the estate tax.

REFERENCES

Bakija, Jon, and Joel Slemrod. 2004. "Do the Rich Flee from High State Taxes? Evidence from Federal Estate Tax Returns." NBER Working Paper No. 10645.

Brunori, David. 2011. "After 80 Years, Still Trying to Figure out the Sales Tax." *State Tax Notes*, February 7.

———. 2012. "Exempting Groceries: Feel-Good, Bad Policy." *State Tax Notes*, February 20.

Campbell, Noel D., Kirk C. Heriot, and Andres Jauregui. 2010. "State Regulatory Spending: Boon or Brake for New Enterprise Creation and Income?" *Economic Development Quarterly* 24 (3): 243-250.

Coates, Dennis, and Brad R. Humphreys. 2000. "The Stadium Gambit and Local Economic Development." *Regulation* 23 (2): 15-20.

———. 2008. "Do Economists Reach a Conclusion on Subsidies for Sports Franchises, Stadiums, and Mega-Events?" *Econ Journal Watch* 5 (3): 294-315.

Cordes, Joseph. 1999. "Horizontal Equity." In *The Encyclopedia of Taxation and Tax Policy*, edited by Joseph J. Cordes, Robert D. Ebel, and Jane G. Gravelle, 195-6. Washington, DC: Urban Institute Press.

Drenkard, Scott, Alex Raut, and Kevin Duncan. 2012. "Sales Tax Rates in Major U.S. Cities." *Tax Foundation Fiscal Fact No. 296*.

Gwartney, James, Richard Stroup, Russell Sobel, and David Macpherson. 2011. *Economics: Private and Public Choice*. 13th ed. Mason, OH: South-Western Cengage Learning.

Hawkins, Richard. 2002. "Popular Substitution Effects: Excess Burden Estimates for General Sales Taxes." *National Tax Journal* 55 (4): 755-770.

Hines, James, Jr. 2007. "Taxing Consumption and Other Sins." *Journal of Economic Perspectives* 21 (1): 49-68.

———. 2008. "Excess Burden of Taxation." In *The New Palgrave Dictionary of Economics*. 2nd ed., edited by Steven N. Durlauf and Lawrence Blume. New York, NY: Palgrave Macmillan.

Humphrey, Tom. 2012. "Legislature Juggles Hot Topics in Final Week of Active Session." *The Tennessean*, April 22.

Institute on Taxation and Economic Policy. 2012. *Repealing Estate Tax Will Not Create an Economic Boom*. http://www.itepnet.org/pdf/lafferestate0412.pdf.

Laffer, Arthur B., and Wayne H. Winegarden. 2012. *The Economic Consequences of Tennessee's Gift and Estate Tax*. Nashville, TN: Beacon Center of Tennessee.

Marwell, Nathan, and Leslie McGranahan. 2010. "The Effect of Sales Tax Holidays on Household Consumption Patterns." Federal Reserve Bank of Chicago Working Paper WP-2010-06.

Matheson, Victor, and Robert Baade. 2006. "Have Public Finance Principles Been Shut Out in Financing New Stadiums for the NFL?" *Public Finance and Management* 6 (3): 284-320.

Mikesell, John L. 2006. State "Sales Tax Holidays: The Continuing Triumph of Politics over Policy." *State Tax Notes*, July 10.

———. 2012. The Disappearing Retail Sales Tax. *State Tax Notes*, March 5.

Munnell, Alicia. H. 1988. "Wealth Transfer Taxation: The Relative Role for Estate and Income Taxes." *New England Economic Review*, November, 3-28.

Poulson, Barry W., and Jules Gordon Kaplan. 2008. "State Income Taxes and Economic Growth." *Cato Journal* 28 (1): 53-71.

Shughart, William F., II. 2008. "Public Choice." In *The Concise Encyclopedia of Economics*, edited by David R. Henderson. Indianapolis, IN: Liberty Fund.

Sisk, Chas. 2012a. "Cut to TN Gift Tax Urged: Economist Laffer Tells Lawmakers Levy Drives Rich Retirees from State." *The Tennessean*, April 17.

———. 2012b. "Legislature Wraps Up Active Year." *The Tennessean*, May 2.

Sobel, Russell S., and Robert A. Lawson. 2003. *Income Tax Progressivity in Ohio*. Columbus, OH: The Buckeye Institute for Public Policy Solutions.

Tennessee Department of Finance and Administration. 2011. *2011-2012 Budget for the State of Tennessee*. Nashville, TN: Tennessee Department of Finance and Administration.

Tennessee Department of Revenue. 2011. *Sales and Use Tax Guide*. Nashville, TN: Tennessee Department of Revenue.

———. 2012. *Tennessee's Sales Tax Holiday*. http://www.tn.gov/revenue/salestaxholiday/One%20Pager%20Overview.pdf.

Turberville, Ryan, and Stephen Cobb. 2012. *Splitting the Farm: How the Death Tax Harms Our Economy and May Drive Farmers to Extinction*. Nashville, TN: The Beacon Center of Tennessee.

Vedder, Richard K., and Lowell E. Gallaway. 1998. *Some Underlying Principles of Tax Policy*. Washington, DC: Government Printing Office.

Walker, Douglas M., and Steven J. Arsenault. 2009. "Specific Tax Reforms to Increase Growth in South Carolina." In *Unleashing Capitalism: A Prescription for Economic Prosperity in South Carolina*, edited by Peter T. Calcagno, 89-107. Columbia, SC: South Carolina Policy Council.

Williams, Jonathan, Curtis S. Dubay, and Johanna Mausolf. 2006. "Sales Tax Holidays: Politically Expedient but Poor Tax Policy." *Tax Foundation Fiscal Fact No. 63*.

MAKING PROPERTY RIGHTS MORE SECURE IN TENNESSEE: LIMITING DISCRETIONARY POWERS OF EMINENT DOMAIN

by Edward J. López

Freedom and Prosperity in Tennessee

6

MAKING PROPERTY RIGHTS MORE SECURE IN TENNESSEE: LIMITING DISCRETIONARY POWERS OF EMINENT DOMAIN

Edward J. López

Part I of this book explained the combination of factors needed to support economic growth and prosperity. Those factors are shaped by the legal system, and its set of public policies, which either supports or retards economic growth depending upon how well it protects and enforces property rights. Where sound property rights interact with relatively light government regulation and taxation, economies tend to grow in a sustainable fashion. Yet, as many of the chapters in this volume show, where property rights are curtailed or violated by public policies, economic activity declines and peoples' well-being suffers. In this chapter, we focus on the area of public policy referred to as eminent domain, also known as "takings." In particular, we show how eminent domain is a key policy area in which the state of Tennessee can shift to a more pro-growth legal structure and set of public policies.

To define the term carefully at the outset, the Tennessee Code (2010) defines eminent domain as:

> the authority conferred upon the government, and those entities to whom the government delegates such authority, to condemn and take, in whole or in part, the private property of another so long as such property is taken for a legitimate public use and is accompanied by the payment of just compensation.
> (§ 27-17-102a)

If someone owns a home or business in Tennessee, no one can lawfully take, use, or occupy their property without their consent. However, if one of Tennessee's 930 government entities decides that some or all of that property is needed to serve a public use, and if that government is prepared to compensate them at the going market rate, then the owner's consent is removed from the decision. In other words, when governments exercise the power of eminent domain, they reduce the property owners' rights by removing the right *not* to sell (also known as the right of alienation).

Strong powers to curtail property rights through eminent domain can harm economic growth. Because maintenance and investment decisions in real property tend to require a long-term perspective, these decisions depend on the owner's expectations about the future returns on such expenditures. If the property owner perceives some threat of eminent domain in the future, then the return on property investment takes on greater uncertainty. Under greater uncertainty due to the threat of eminent domain, property owners are likely to reduce the extent of maintenance and investment, and this in turn pushes property values down. This outcome works against the stated objectives of using eminent domain for economic development purposes.

As we will see in this chapter, Tennessee law provides relatively broad latitude to local governments in choosing how to use eminent domain. This is true by comparison to the other 49 states, and even more so when compared to Tennessee's eight contiguous states. The next section of this chapter discusses the current state of eminent domain policy nationally. An important 2005 Supreme Court case, *Kelo v. City of New London, Conn.,*[1] provides the basis for the discussion. That ruling upheld a local government's decision to take nearly 20 homes in order to make land available for a new pharmaceutical plant and related development. The decision provoked a massive public outcry that was followed by widespread change of legislation among the states—including Tennessee. The legal and political background of the landmark *Kelo* case is important because it illustrates the manner in which state legislatures responded to the *Kelo* ruling. In particular, an issue at the center of these new state laws was a distinction between "traditional" uses of eminent domain—such as government buildings, power lines, or roads—versus more recent uses of eminent domain to promote economic development, job growth, and larger tax bases. Since this distinction appeared in the law in a 1954 Supreme Court case,[2] virtually no state or court has questioned local governments' authorities to use eminent domain for traditional purposes. However, after *Kelo* nearly all the state legislatures at least debated amending their laws governing takings for economic development purposes, and 43 of the 50 states have made statutory or constitutional changes designed to limit those takings.

Against this background, this chapter then focuses on Tennessee, drawing on recent scholarship in social sciences that analyzes the substance of these legislative responses. Several peer-reviewed studies have compared the strictness of these new laws across the 50 states. This section of the chapter illustrates how the academic literature can be used to quantitatively rank the new laws according to how strongly they protect property rights against the potential for eminent domain overreach. In addition, the rankings allow us to compare each state's protection of property rights legislation. Tennessee ranks near the very bottom, both nationally and when compared to neighboring states. In other words, Tennessee law provides relatively weak protection of private property against eminent domain for economic development. This puts Tennessee at a disadvantage in terms of sending property owners the message that their property investments and improvements are secure from being taken and sold to another private party simply because local officials might think it will be used more productively that way. By reforming the law in this area of public policy, Tennessee can situate itself as a more attractive environment for property owners, investors, and developers, to the benefit of the public as a whole.

---

[1] *Kelo et al. v. City of New London, Connecticut,* 545 U.S. 469 (2005).
[2] *Berman et al. v. Parker et al.,* 348 U.S. 26 (1954).

A NATIONAL VIEW OF PROPERTY RIGHTS, PROSPERITY, AND *KELO V. CITY OF NEW LONDON*

Kelo v. City of New London was a highly controversial Supreme Court case. When this ruling was issued on June 23, 2005, it fomented a widespread public outcry, which resulted in a wave of new legislation across the states. Although the Supreme Court ruled on other controversial topics in its 2004-2005 term (including the public display of the Ten Commandments, the federal government's authority to regulate medicinal marijuana, and a ban on peer-to-peer file sharing of copyrighted movies), none of these hot-button issues generated a fraction of the public outcry as that of *Kelo*. Looking at the case in historical context, we see that *Kelo* overpowered the historical competition as well. According to the legal scholar Ilya Somin (2008), the next most significant case affecting state legislation was in 1972 when the Supreme Court struck down state death penalty laws, prompting 35 states to pass new capital punishment legislation. In contrast, *Kelo* prompted changes in 43 state laws. Thus, Professor Somin (2008, 2012) argues by comparison that "a strong case can be made that *Kelo* has drawn more extensive legislative reaction than any other single court decision in American history."

The ruling was also extremely unpopular across the nation. The reigning sentiment running throughout the public's response seemed to be "if they can take Susette Kelo's house, they can take mine." This popular opposition was reflected in national opinion polls. In a July 2005 poll, for example, 68 percent of respondents said yes when asked "Do you favor legislative limits on the government's ability to take private property away from owners?" Also in 2005, The Saint Consulting Group (which focuses on the politics of land use) found that 81 percent of survey respondents disagreed with the *Kelo* Court. A separate national survey conducted by Zogby International reported that 95 percent of Americans either moderately or strongly disagreed with the ruling. Dozens of similar polls were taken in states and localities around the country, and they all consistently reveal super-majority opposition to takings for private development.[3]

Kelo's unpopularity swelled into organized political opposition. Neighborhood groups joined forces to march in protest. Public interest law firms like the Institute for Justice and small business associations like the National Federation of Independent Businesses came to the defense of property owners in high profile cases. Busloads of citizens hauled themselves to state capitols demanding action. Film makers released documentaries like "Battle for Brooklyn," which tells the story of local homeowners and shopkeepers in New York fighting to prevent their neighborhood from being replaced via eminent domain with a professional basketball arena, and ultimately losing that fight. And, increased media attention coincided with it all. A search for keywords "eminent domain" and "property rights" in the Lexis/Nexis™ database returns just 81 major newspaper stories in the year before *Kelo*, but 393 in the year after.

In the meantime, as voters were mounting the *Kelo* backlash, organized interests were lining up on either side of the issue. Local governments and the urban planning profession came out in support of *Kelo* style takings. For example, the National League of Cities filed a friend of the court brief in support of New London. Similarly, the urban planning community

---

[3] For national, state, and local poll results, see Somin (2008); Castle Coalition (n.d.).

broadly supported *Kelo* style takings, and the International Economic Development Council issued an eminent domain toolkit to its member organizations with the following endorsement:

> The 5-4 decision in Kelo v. New London affirms that eminent domain is an important tool for local governments in the redevelopment and revitalization of economically distressed areas...Judicious use of eminent domain is *critical* to the economic growth and development of cities and towns throughout the country. (2006, 4)

Favoring stronger property rights protections were public interest groups advocating for individual rights, for low-income property owners and tenants, and for minorities— including the Institute for Justice, the Cato Institute, the Becket Fund for Religious Liberty, and the National Association for the Advancement of Colored People. Joining these public interest organizations were organized economic interests, most significantly real estate agents and new homebuilders. For example, the National Association of Home Builders (NAHB) joined forces with the National Association of Realtors in submitting a friend of the court brief. Their reasoning was revealingly astute:

> The NAHB recognizes that housing will almost never afford a community with the economic development benefits that a commercial application will. If economic development as a sole justification for public use is decided using a rational basis test with deference to local legislative bodies, then the door is left open for local governments to abuse their eminent domain powers and take developable land from NAHB members as they could from any other property owner. (Pickel 2004, 2)

These same organized groups lobbied many of the state legislatures when considering how to amend their states' laws after *Kelo*. Therefore, state legislators across the nation had to strike a balance when it came time to answer the public outcry. They had to assuage an agitated electorate while also respecting the balance of important political interests aligned on either side of this issue. In many states, this proved to be a recipe for a form of symbolic legislation that *seemed* to restrict eminent domain powers for economic development, but actually did very little. Tennessee was one of these states.

Although there is some variation in the substance of the new state laws, virtually all of the new legislation starts out with a statement that prohibits takings for economic development. For example, a typical bill will say that "public use" does not include job creation, expansion of the tax base, or other measures of economic development. About two-thirds of the new laws essentially leave it at that. But others include *exemptions* for a variety of conditions. One broad category of exemptions is large, individual projects that were underway at the time. For example, when the state of Texas revised its eminent domain law in September of 2005, the new stadium being planned for the Dallas Cowboys was exempted. When construction on the stadium began eight months later, the city of Arlington, Texas had used eminent domain to remove half a dozen home and small business owners who did not want to sell.

However, it was not just special projects that were exempted. For example, of the 43 states that did enact new legislation, 14 of them included an exemption for "blighted" areas or properties. The argument for exempting blight starts out as a reasonable one. Legislators want to preserve local government's flexibility in dealing with extreme conditions of decline where property owners may be uncooperative or absent. If there is truly no alternative, then it can be important to public safety, health, morals, and welfare to have eminent domain available as a last resort. And indeed, many governments across the country have a record of responsible, careful, and very rare use of their takings power. Unfortunately, all too often the reverse is true and officials become too eager to take properties not as a last resort, but as an expedient measure to generate more tax revenue (Staley and Blair 2005). A blight exemption makes this all too easy. To see why, consider that another word for exemption is *loophole*.

In the context of blight, the magnitude of the initial loophole is determined by how narrowly or broadly the legislature defines "blight." If the definition features any vague or sufficiently general language, it can be very easy to argue that any area or property fits the definition. The effect of the loophole would be to nullify the legislature's intended restrictions. A development takings case out of Ohio illustrates this problem. Here, the local redevelopment agency had deemed a residential area to be blighted so the city could use eminent domain. Among the criteria listed by the agency were homes lacking two-car attached garages, homes with fewer than two full bathrooms or three proper bedrooms, and homes that had too few square feet.[4] A lawsuit later found that under these standards, most of the City Council members' homes would be blighted.

It is not always so easy to detect whether governments are acting in an expedient or principled manner. But the negative consequences of over-reaching with eminent domain can be seen in areas and times when eminent domain has been used most aggressively in attempts to redevelop. After the Supreme Court upheld Washington, DC's authority to raze and start over with a neighborhood in its southwest quadrant, the area never recovered (Gelinas 2005). In Poletown, Michigan, following a similar 1981 case that razed a working-class neighborhood to make way for a General Motors assembly plant, the facility never came close to delivering on the promised economic benefits (Somin 2010). When the state of Hawaii used eminent domain to help control rising housing costs by transferring title from land owners to residential tenants, the area became a more active real estate market and prices increased substantially (Stark 2007). And although the city of New London spent tens of millions of dollars assembling a tract where Susette Kelo's house formerly sat, no development has ever occurred there. The trend is not coincidence: where eminent domain has been used for economic development projects, peoples' incentives have become distorted and the economic outcomes suffer as a consequence.

In summary, it is helpful to characterize the new state laws as either having bark-*with*-bite (little to no exemptions) or bark-*no*-bite (blight or other broad exemptions). The intention behind a bark-no-bite approach may be noble. However, the costs of bark-no-bite soon emerge because it effectively removes limitations on takings for economic development, and this plays into the hands of expedient, over-reaching uses of the takings power. When local authorities are effectively unconstrained in their abilities to take properties, this sends the wrong signal to developers and property owners, and distorts their planning horizons by adding uncertainty to their long-term investment plans.

---

[4] The case is from the Ohio Supreme Court, *Norwood v. Horney,* 110 Ohio St.3d 353 (2006). For additional background, also see Institute for Justice (n.d.).

THE TENNESSEE CASE

Although it was the fifteenth state to change its eminent domain laws after *Kelo*, the Tennessee General Assembly did not act in haste. Near the end of its 2005 session, the legislature appointed a blue ribbon commission to study the impact of eminent domain and economic development in Tennessee. In the meantime, dozens of bills were introduced in both the House and Senate. Finally, in May of 2006, HB 3450/SB 3296 was approved and signed into law by Governor Phil Bredesen.

Unlike most of the new state laws, Tennessee's begins with an express statement of how the legislature intends the law to be applied: "It is the intent of the General Assembly that the power of eminent domain be used sparingly, and that laws permitting the use of eminent domain shall be narrowly construed so as not to enlarge by inference or inadvertently the power of eminent domain."[5] After this preamble affirming private property rights and the desire to protect them, HB 3450/SB 3296 proceeds along the lines of most of the other state laws. Namely, the bill defines "eminent domain" as this chapter reported above, and the bill more narrowly defines "public use" in the State as follows:

> "Public use" shall not include either private use or benefit or the indirect public benefits resulting from private economic development and private commercial enterprise, including increased tax revenue and increased employment opportunity, except as follows...[6]

The last three words of the quoted passage obviously tip the reality that Tennessee was one of the states to include exemptions. But the first point to recognize is that the bill came out with a loud bark: it strongly defends the philosophy of private property and in particular it excludes economic development from its definition of "public use." The bill also includes some additional notification and procedural requirements designed as added layers of protection to property owners.

However, this loud bark has comparatively little bite to it because of the exemptions that follow. Most importantly, the bill exempts blight, meaning Tennessee law expressly allows local governments to take properties in order to redevelop "blighted" properties or areas. The bill also exempts industrial parks, public utilities, and all "private uses" that are "merely incidental to a public use."[7] There is more than meets the eye when evaluating the intentions versus the effects of these exemptions, in particular the one for removal of blight. The purpose of exempting blight is certainly understandable. The General Assembly sought to reserve eminent domain as an option when conditions truly call for it. If the choice is between a new development project proceeding versus allowing a blighted neighborhood to continue its decline, the choice that serves the public benefit is clear to the legislature. However, the problem with this approach is that there is effectively no way to restrain authorities from

---

[5] General Assembly of the State of Tennessee, Senate Bill 3296 (Feb. 16, 2006), "An Act to amend the Tennessee Code relative to the power and use of eminent domain and property acquired through eminent domain," §29-17-101.

[6] *Ibid*, §29-17-102(b).

[7] *Ibid*, §29-17-102(b)(3). The complete wording of the bill exempts "Private use that is merely incidental to a public use, so as no land is condemned or taken solely for the purpose of conveying or permitting such incidental private use."

using the blight exemption as a loophole to condemn properties or areas that aren't *truly* blighted yet still fit the statutory definition of "blight." Recalling from above that broader definitions of blight act as more inviting loopholes to local officials, we locate the State's definition of blight in §13-20-2 of the Tennessee Code:

> (a) Blighted areas are areas, including slum areas, with buildings or improvements that, by reason of dilapidation, obsolescence, overcrowding, lack of ventilation, light and sanitary facilities, deleterious land use, or any combination of these or other factors, are detrimental to the safety, health, morals, or welfare of the community. Welfare of the community does not include solely a loss of property value to surrounding properties, nor does it include the need for increased tax revenues. Under no circumstance shall land used predominantly in the production of agriculture, as defined by § 1-3-105, be considered a blighted area.
>
> (b) As used in this chapter, dilapidation means extreme deterioration and decay due to lack of repairs to and care of the area.

This definition of blight has two opposing effects on whether local officials promote the legislature's stated intent to use eminent domain sparingly. On the one hand, paragraph (b) provides a clear and restrictive definition of "dilapidation" that pertains *only* to decisions by the property owner to maintain and care so poorly for the property that others in the area suffer harm. There is little interpretive discretion for officials to apply "extreme" conditions that are "due to a lack of repairs and care" in expedient ways. Furthermore, the definition of blight in paragraph (a) is beholden to this clear, restrictive definition of dilapidation. Both these features protect property owners from the potential of eminent domain over-reach.

On the other hand, paragraph (a) goes on to define "blight" more broadly than merely "dilapidation," to include other conditions that appear under scrutiny to be far more prone to misinterpretation and expedient, over-reaching uses of eminent domain. Wording such as "lack of ventilation" has been used to argue that properties are blighted because they lacked central air conditioning.[8] Similarly, "lack of sanitary facilities" has been construed as having too few bathrooms relative to some arbitrary standard. Reinforcing these potential loopholes, the new law also includes vague, all-encompassing language in the phrase "or any combination of these or other factors," which does little to dissuade regulators from using their discretion in clever, expedient ways. Suppose for example that certain local officials become persuaded that their budgetary stress could be relieved by forcing out some homeowners to build a tax revenue-generating development like a shopping mall or stadium. The bar in this scenario for establishing "public use" is low: an official who is eager to condemn a property simply has to identify one feature of the property that arguably meets the express criteria in the blight definition, and then complement this identified feature with "some combination of other factors" that the regulator believes are important to the public. Property owners may fight for more compensation, and a court may even overturn the official's public use argument. Yet the inviting language still invites misinterpretation and expedient rather than principled use of eminent domain.

Therefore, while defining blight as "dilapidation" has the effect of curtailing potential eminent domain abuse, these beneficial effects are dominated by the adverse effects of

---

[8] See Institute for Justice (n.d.) for discussion of *Norwood v. Horney,* 110 Ohio St.3d 353 (2006).

defining blight more broadly to include vague and all-encompassing criteria. The wording of these two exemptions may seem innocuous, but their actual effects in practice are to nullify almost entirely the protections that the General Assembly intended. At the end of the day, when property owners in Tennessee *most* need the law to protect them from eminent domain (i.e. when local officials are using eminent domain as an expedient) is when HB 3450 / SB 3492 is the weakest. Thus, the law in Tennessee confirms that the adage "if they can take Susette Kelo's house, they can take yours" applies to property owners in Tennessee.

RANKING TENNESSEE'S EMINENT DOMAIN LAWS

Recent academic literature can be used to construct a systematic ranking of the states according to how strongly their laws protect property against eminent domain. In particular, four recent studies evaluate whether states define public use to include economic development, whether states exempt blight, and other more detailed criteria. Each study then assigns an alphanumerical score to each state. In this chapter, we combine the four rankings into an overall score that can rank states according to how strongly their laws restrict eminent domain for economic development. With the overall ranking in hand, it is then a straightforward exercise to compare Tennessee with other states.

The first of the four rankings to consider is the Castle Coalition's (2007) *50-State Report Card: Tracking Eminent Domain Reform Legislation Since Kelo*. This report has been cited in a number of academic studies in the fields of law, economics, and political science.[9] The authors of this study painstakingly review whether and how each state responded with legislation in the two years following *Kelo* (June 2005 to June 2007). States score higher grades on this report for enacting legislation that prohibits eminent domain for private development, or for defining public use to exclude *Kelo*-style takings. States get lower grades for failing to enact any reform, or for enacting reform that allows exemptions for blight or special projects. Vaguely worded laws, or all-encompassing definitions of blight, also detract from a state's grade on this report. The letter grades range from "A+" to "F" and were converted to numerical scores in order to make this ranking comparable with the other three.

The second ranking comes from a study by the legal scholar Ilya Somin, "The Limits of Backlash: Assessing the Political Response to *Kelo*," published in 2009 in the *Minnesota Law Review*. Professor Somin analyzes each state's court precedent, as well as updates to legislation since *Kelo*, and finds that the states fall into three categories: first is *no reform*, meaning the state effectively adopts the federal baseline as established by *Kelo*; second is *ineffective reform*, which means that the state may have put some limitations on takings for economic development but there are exemptions for blight; and third is *effective reform*, meaning a state limited takings for economic development without exemption or otherwise meaningful loopholes. States are assigned a score of 0 for no reform, 1 for ineffective reform, and 2 for effective reform.

The third study is by López, Jewell, and Campbell, entitled "Pass a Law, Any Law, Fast! State Legislative Responses to the *Kelo* Backlash" and published in 2009 in the *Review of Law & Economics*. In this paper, the authors conducted a survey analysis of each new law using 18 separate criteria. For example, one of the criteria was "Does the law prohibit the use of eminent domain for promoting tax base, jobs, or economic development?" A "yes" answer

---

[9] Morriss (2009); Lopez, Jewell, and Campbell (2009); Somin (2008); Kerekes (2011).

to this would indicate that the law has bite to it, and the survey would then add a value of 1 to the state's score. In contrast, another of the criteria was "Does the law exempt eminent domain for blighted conditions while not defining blight narrowly?" A "yes" answer to this question would take some bite out of the law's restrictions on eminent domain, and the analysis would *subtract* a value of 1 from the state's score. After tallying each state on all 18 criteria, this study then assigns a numerical score, with higher scores indicating stronger protections of property rights.

The fourth study is an "eminent domain reform index" written by two political scientists, Jason Sorens of the University at Buffalo and Will Ruger of Texas State University (2011). The index elicits information on four criteria: did the state enact any reform, if so did the reform prohibit development takings, and if so did the reform prohibit takings even for the elimination of blight? Each of these criteria counts for plus 1 on their index. Furthermore, if a state's reforms were also written into the state's constitution, Sorens and Ruger assign an additional 1.5 points to the state's score. Therefore, the minimum score a state can receive on this index is 0 (no reform at all) and the maximum is 4.5. Finally, as with the other three studies, a greater score indicates greater protection of property against eminent domain.

How does Tennessee score on these four studies? Unfortunately, the answer is *not very well*. The 50-State Report Card assigns Tennessee a grade of "D-minus." Only four states received this dubious grade, and only nine got a worse grade (an outright "F" for enacting no reform). The study by Somin (2008) categorizes Tennessee as "ineffective reform," tying for middle place along with 22 other states. Similarly, the López, Jewell, and Campbell (2009) study finds that Tennessee ties for the third-lowest score on the survey instrument, ahead only of the handful of states that enacted no reform. And finally, on the index by Sorens and Ruger (2011), Tennessee achieves a score of 1.5 out of 3.5 possible points, again placing Tennessee at a tie for second-to-last place along with nine other states.

Figure 6.1: Ranking Tennessee and Neighboring States on Strength of Property Rights Protection against Eminent Domain

Regional Rank	State	Somin (2008)	Castle Coalition (2007)	Lopez, Jewell & Campbell (2009)	Sorens & Ruger (2008)	Average Rank
1	Georgia	2 (1)	11 (2)	5 (1)	3.125 (3)	1.75
2	Alabama	2 (1)	10 (3)	3 (3)	3.75 (2)	2.25
4	Virginia	2 (1)	10 (3)	(9)	1 (8)	5.25
5	North Carolina	1 (2)	5 (8)	1 (5)	1.5 (7)	5.5
6	Kentucky	1 (2)	4 (9)	1 (5)	1.5 (7)	5.75
7	Missouri	1 (2)	3 (10)	2 (4)	1 (8)	6
8	Tennessee	1 (2)	2 (11)	-1 (7)	1.5 (7)	6.75
9	Arkansas	0 (3)	1 (12)	-- (9)	0 (10)	8.5
10	Mississippi	0 (3)	1 (12)	-- (9)	0 (10)	8.5

Note: Raw scores appear on the first line. Rank among states appears on second line in parentheses. Average Rank is the unweighted mean of the rank on all four studies. Therefore, a lesser Average Rank score indicates stronger restrictions on eminent domain for economic development purposes or, equivalently, stronger property rights protections.

To show how Tennessee compares to neighboring states, Figure 6.1 converts each state's score on the above four studies into a ranking of Tennessee and its eight contiguous states. The rightmost column of Figure 6.1 is the average ranking of all the rankings on the four individual studies. A lower number on this ranking indicates stronger property protections against the potential for eminent domain over-reach. Tennessee's average ranking is 6.75, placing it third-to-last among neighboring states. Only Arkansas and Mississippi have a worse environment for property rights on this metric.

In similar fashion, Figure 6.2 presents the overall ranking for all 50 States. With its score of 6.75, Tennessee is tied with California for the thirty-seventh ranked environment for eminent domain over-reach. Only 12 states rank lower (again, for enacting no reform), and eight of these 12 states have notorious histories of frequent and controversial over-reach of eminent domain for economic development. By contrast, the top of the rankings in Figure 6.2 include several of Tennessee's contiguous neighbors, including Georgia and Alabama as seen

Figure 6.2: Ranking 50 States on Strength of Property Rights Protection against Eminent Domain Laws

National Rank	State	Somin (2008)	Castle Coalition (2007)	Lopez, Jewell & Campbell (2009)	Sorens & Ruger (2008)	Average Rank
1	Florida	2 (1)	12 (1)	5 (1)	4.5 (1)	1
2	Georgia	2 (1)	11 (2)	5 (1)	3.125 (3)	1.75
3	Alabama	2 (1)	10 (3)	3 (3)	3.75 (2)	2.25
4	South Dakota	2 (1)	12 (1)	3 (3)	3 (4)	2.25
5	Indiana	2 (1)	10 (3)	4 (2)	2.5 (5)	2.75
6	New Hampshire	2 (1)	10 (3)	1 (5)	3.75 (2)	2.75
7	Arizona	2 (1)	10 (3)	4 (2)	2 (6)	3
8	North Dakota	2 (1)	12 (1)	-- (9)	4.5 (1)	3
9	Louisiana	2 (1)	9 (4)	0 (6)	3.75 (2)	3.25
10	Michigan	2 (1)	11 (2)	-- (9)	4.5 (1)	3.25
11	South Carolina	1 (2)	10 (3)	0 (6)	3.75 (2)	3.25
12	Minnesota	2 (1)	8 (5)	2 (4)	2.5 (5)	3.75
13	Iowa	1 (2)	8 (5)	3 (3)	2 (6)	4
14	Colorado	1 (2)	6 (7)	4 (2)	2 (6)	4.25
15	Kansas	2 (1)	9 (4)	-1 (7)	2.5 (5)	4.25
16	Utah	1 (2)	9 (4)	0 (6)	2.5 (5)	4.25
17	New Mexico	2 (1)	11 (2)	1 (5)	0 (10)	4.5
18	Oregon	2 (1)	10 (3)	-- (9)	2.5 (5)	4.5
19	Pennsylvania	2 (1)	8 (5)	-2 (8)	3 (4)	4.5
20	Wisconsin	1 (2)	7 (6)	0 (6)	2 (6)	5

National Rank	State	Somin (2008)	Castle Coalition (2007)	Lopez, Jewell & Campbell (2009)	Sorens & Ruger (2008)	Average Rank
21	Idaho	2	4	2	1.5	5.25
		(1)	(9)	(4)	(7)	
22	Virginia	2	10	--	1	5.25
		(1)	(3)	(9)	(8)	
23	Alaska	1	3	3	1.5	5.5
		(2)	(10)	(3)	(7)	
24	North Carolina	1	5	1	1.5	5.5
		(2)	(8)	(5)	(7)	
25	West Virginia	1	5	0	2	5.5
		(2)	(8)	(6)	(6)	
26	Kentucky	1	4	1	1.5	5.75
		(2)	(9)	(5)	(7)	
27	Maine	1	4	1	1.5	5.75
		(2)	(9)	(5)	(7)	
28	Nevada	2	10	--	0	5.75
		(1)	(3)	(9)	(10)	
29	Missouri	1	3	2	1	6
		(2)	(10)	(4)	(8)	
30	Texas	1	5	-1	1.5	6
		(2)	(8)	(7)	(7)	
31	Wyoming	2	9	--	0	6
		(1)	(4)	(9)	(10)	
32	Illinois	1	4	-1	1.5	6.25
		(2)	(9)	(7)	(7)	
33	Montana	1	3	3	0	6.25
		(2)	(10)	(3)	(10)	
34	Nebraska	1	4	0	1	6.25
		(2)	(9)	(6)	(8)	
35	Delaware	1	2	1	1	6.5
		(2)	(11)	(5)	(8)	
36	Vermont	1	2	0	1.5	6.5
		(2)	(11)	(6)	(7)	
37	California	1	2	0	1	6.75
		(2)	(11)	(6)	(8)	
38	Tennessee	1	2	-1	1.5	6.75
		(2)	(11)	(7)	(7)	
39	Maryland	1	3	0	0	7
		(2)	(10)	(6)	(10)	
40	Ohio	1	3	-2	0.75	7.25
		(2)	(10)	(8)	(9)	
41	Connecticut	1	1	0	0	7.5
		(2)	(12)	(6)	(10)	
42	Washington	0	5	--	0	7.5
		(3)	(8)	(9)	(10)	
43	Oklahoma	0	1	--	0.75	8.25
		(3)	(12)	(9)	(9)	
44	Arkansas	0	1	--	0	8.5
		(3)	(12)	(9)	(10)	
45	Hawaii	0	1	--	0	8.5
		(3)	(12)	(9)	(10)	
46	Massachusetts	0	1	--	0	8.5
		(3)	(12)	(9)	(10)	
47	Mississippi	0	1	--	0	8.5
		(3)	(12)	(9)	(10)	
48	New Jersey	0	1	--	0	8.5
		(3)	(12)	(9)	(10)	
49	New York	0	1	--	0	8.5
		(3)	(12)	(9)	(10)	
50	Rhode Island	0	1	--	0	8.5
		(3)	(12)	(9)	(10)	

in Figure 6.1, in addition to other southeastern states such as Florida, Louisiana, and South Carolina. In terms of the legal system creating a sound environment for property rights against the potential for eminent domain abuse, Tennessee lags far behind the other states.

Of course, numerical rankings are but one lens through which to view the public policy problem. Tennessee's eminent domain problem is about more than just rankings. To see this, we now turn to the important case of Nashville and Mrs. Joy Ford.

JOY FORD AND COUNTRY INTERNATIONAL RECORDS

While Tennessee's legislature was reforming its eminent domain laws, a case in Nashville was unfolding that would soon and dramatically put the new laws to the test. In 2005, a Texas-based developer began assembling a tract out of parcels surrounding the property of Mrs. Joy Ford, who for decades had owned and operated Country International Records along the city's famed Music Row. The developer had plans to build a $100 million office building. Nashville officials were pushing new development at the time, and welcomed the idea of an expanded tax base. The development also promised construction jobs and ongoing business activity. The only problem was Joy Ford didn't want to sell.

After making repeated attractive offers, each of which was spurned by the holdout Mrs. Ford, the Texas developer grew frustrated. Nashville's Metropolitan Development and Housing Authority (MDHA) finally intervened in 2008, filing eminent domain papers on Mrs. Ford. The MDHA offered Mrs. Ford fair market value and reasoned that she had no right to refuse because the development—in particular, the jobs and richer tax bases it would create—qualified under Tennessee law as "public use." The outlook on the development brightened, as it appeared that the holdout was going to be forced out.

But Mrs. Ford had public opinion on her side, and she also attracted the attention of the National Federation of Independent Businesses and the Institute for Justice, a non-profit law firm that specializes in defending people's economic rights. Both organizations were soon at Mrs. Ford's side, organizing press releases and filing countersuits. Ford's attorneys argued that the MDHA's condemnation violated federal and state laws against eminent domain for transfer to private parties. Choosing to avoid the fight, the MDHA soon revoked the eminent domain proceedings on Mrs. Ford's property, and the Texas developer was sent back to the bargaining table.

Now with eminent domain off the table, Joy Ford still didn't want to sell. All she wanted was to continue running her business on Music Row. But by sitting back down at the bargaining table, the two sides were able to find another way. After intensive negotiations, the two parties agreed to a land swap. The Texas developer got the parking lot behind Joy Ford's building, and she in turn received a slightly larger lot on the side of her building. The developer had to redesign a parking structure to accommodate the land swap, but otherwise the deal introduced no obstructions to the development. And in the midst of a depressed economy, the construction project went forward and the city has reaped the public economic benefits that come along with it ("To Push Development" 2008).

THE CASE FOR REFORM IN TENNESSEE

Regardless of the MDHA's reasons for initially invoking and later revoking eminent domain powers, the public interest certainly is not served by using eminent domain in situations where private parties can achieve an agreement through continued negotiations. The public benefit is served *even more* when developments go through without infringing on property rights.

The Joy Ford case is instructive because the MDHA presumably exercised eminent domain because it believed there was no other way to get the development through. Aware of HB 3450/SB 3296, the MDHA also must have believed that it was acting within the General Assembly's stated intent of using eminent domain sparingly and only as necessary. But they were wrong. Infringing on Ford's property rights was not what the development needed to get through—instead, voluntary negotiations were. In fact, the case shows that the development could have gone through even if the MDHA were never vested with the powers to take properties in the first place.

Statistical analysis suggests that this anecdote is not a coincidence. A 2008 study of eminent domain reforms in all states found where states enacted meaningful reform they suffered no negative trend changes in construction jobs, building permits, or property tax revenues (Carpenter and Ross 2008). In other words, states that strongly protect property owners from eminent domain do not forfeit economic development.

Therefore, Tennesseans can confidently reform their laws to increase property rights protections, *without* a tradeoff of foregone economic development. Furthermore, Tennessee's low ranking relative to neighboring states demonstrates the need to reform in order to stay regionally competitive in attracting developments.

PROPOSED REFORMS

If the General Assembly wishes to promote economic development without infringing on property rights and, therefore, remaining regionally competitive, it could take three specific steps.

First, the General Assembly could amend §29-17-102(b) of the Tennessee Code to eliminate the exemption for blighted areas and properties. If this step is deemed impossible or infeasible, a compromise step would be to amend §13-20-2 to more narrowly define blight to be solely restricted to genuinely extreme conditions that are created by lack of care and maintenance.

Second, §29-17-102(b)(3) could be amended to eliminate the exemption for private transfers that are merely incidental to an otherwise traditional public use. Closing this loophole is important in the same manner as is closing the blight exemption. It would put Tennessee in the category of meaningful reform that has bite to go with its bark in protecting property owners from eminent domain over-reach.

Third, the General Assembly could begin the process of introducing these protections into the Tennessee Constitution. Taking these three steps would send a clear message to developers, property owners, and the entire world that Tennessee is a secure environment in which to build and invest in job-creating and tax-base-growing properties.

CONCLUSION

High and rising standards of living depend entirely on the ability to achieve economic growth, which in turn depends on how the State's legal system and its set of public policies structure the incentives of local governments and private parties. Economic theory and history have shown that stronger property rights enhance and support economic growth. In the specific context of eminent domain, it can be tempting for state legislators to want to preserve the powers of local governments to deal with "blight." But this highly reasonable intent is not as simple as what meets the eye. Scholars in economics, political science, and law have scratched the surface of this problem and analyzed its deeper currents. Too often a blight exemption is used to distort the effect of the law away from the legislature's stated intent for that law, and eminent domain becomes an expedient option rather than a last resort. The blight exemption should be eliminated or restricted to extreme conditions.

Critics will say that local officials' discretion is vital to getting economic development projects through. But the facts speak otherwise. It is a fact that economic development can and does proceed without resorting to eminent domain. It is a fact that Tennessee lags behind most other states, especially its regional competitors, in protecting property rights against the potential for eminent domain over-reach. And it is a fact that where eminent domain has been used most aggressively is also where it has failed most miserably. Tennessee can confidently eliminate its exemptions to its eminent domain law and expect to see economic developments begin to flourish from the bottom up as investment and maintenance decisions of individual property owners respond.

REFERENCES

Carpenter, Dick M., II, and John K. Ross. 2008. *Doomsday? No Way: Economic Trends and Post-Kelo Eminent Domain Reform*. Arlington, VA: Institute for Justice. http://www.ij .org /economic-trends-and-post-kelo-eminent-domain-reform.

Castle Coalition. (n.d). *The Polls Are In: Americans Overwhelmingly Oppose Use of Eminent Domain for Private Gain*. http://www.castlecoalition.org/polls.

Castle Coalition. 2007. *50-State Report Card Tracking Eminent Domain Legislation Since Kelo*. http://www.castlecoalition.org/pdf/publications/report_card/50_State_ Report .pdf.

Gelinas, Nicole. 2005. "They're Taking Away Your Property for What?" *City Journal,* Autumn. http://www.city-journal.org/html/15_4_eminent_domain.html.

Institute for Justice. (n.d). "Ohio's 'City of Homes' Faces Wrecking Ball of Eminent Domain Abuse." *Litigation Backgrounder*. http://www.ij.org/index.php?Option =com_content &task=view&id=1053&Itemid=16.

International Economic Development Council. 2006. *Eminent Domain Resource Kit*. June 20. www.iedconline.org.

Kerekes, Carrie B. 2011. "Government Takings: Determinants of Eminent Domain." *American Law and Economics Review* 13 (1): 201-219.

López, Edward J., R. Rodd Jewell, and Noel D. Campbell. 2009. "Pass a Law, Any Law, Fast! State Legislative Responses to the *Kelo* Backlash." *Review of Law & Economics* 5 (1): 101-135.

Morriss, Andrew P. 2009. "Symbol or Substance? An Empirical Assessment of State Responses to *Kelo*." *Supreme Court Economic Review* 17 (1): 237–278.

Pickel, Mary Lynn (Counsel of Record). 2004. "Brief of *Amici Curiae*: The National Association of Home Builders and the National Association of Realtors in Support of the Petitioners." *Kelo v. City of New London* 04-108. http://supreme.lp.findlaw.com /supreme_court/briefs/04-108/04-108.mer.ami.nahb.pdf.

Somin, Ilya. 2008. "Controlling the Grasping Hand: Economic Development Takings after *Kelo*." *Supreme Court Economic Review* 15: 183-271.

———. 2009. "The Limits of Backlash: Assessing the Political Response to *Kelo*." *Minnesota Law Review* 93 (6): 2100-2178.

———. 2010. "Economic Development Takings as Government Failure." In *The Pursuit of Justice: Law and Economics of Legal Systems*, edited by Edward J. López. New York, NY: Palgrave Macmillan.

Sorens, Jason, and William Ruger. 2011. *Freedom in the 50 States: An Index of Personal and Economic Freedom*. Arlington, VA: Mercatus Center. http://mercatus.org /freedom-50-states-2011.

Staley, Samuel R. and John P. Blair. 2005. "Eminent Domain, Private Property, and Redevelopment: An Economic Development Analysis." *Reason Foundation Policy Study* 331 (February): 1-44.

Stark, Debra Pogrund. 2007. "How Do You Solve a Problem Like in *Kelo*?" *John Marshall Law Review* 40: 609.

Tennessee Code. 2010. http://law.justia.com/codes/tennessee/2010/title-47/chapter-18/part-51/.

"To Push Development, Cities Turn to Eminent Domain as a Last Resort." 2008. *The City Paper: Nashville's Online Source for Daily News*, May 27. http://nashvillecitypaper. com/content/city-business/push-development-cities-turn-eminent-domain-last-resort.

CASES CITED

Berman et al. v. Parker et al., 348 U.S. 26 (1954).

City of Norwood v. Horney, 110 Ohio St.3d 353 (2006).

Kelo et al. v. City of New London, Connecticut, 545 U.S. 469 (2005).

CHAPTER 7

REDUCE LABOR RESTRICTIONS: FROM RIGHT-TO-WORK TO SCHOOL CHOICE

by Joshua C. Hall, Ashley S. Harrison, Nathan J. Ashby, and Susan S. Douglass

Freedom and Prosperity in Tennessee

7

REDUCE LABOR RESTRICTIONS: FROM RIGHT-TO-WORK TO SCHOOL CHOICE

Joshua C. Hall, Ashley S. Harrison, Nathan J. Ashby, and Susan S. Douglass

Public opinion polls report that the most important issues facing the nation today are the economy, job growth, and employment (Pew Research Center 2012). In addition to employment, individuals also desire higher wages. While nearly all Americans share these goals, opinion on how public policy can achieve them varies significantly across the general population. At their core, however, these issues represent fundamental economic questions and thus an analysis of both economic theory and evidence point toward a few clear solutions.

This chapter begins with a brief presentation of the economic principles of wage and employment determination which are then applied to a number of labor-market policies. This helps to identify effective policies that encourage job growth and employment and explains why well-intentioned policies are often counter-productive. Finally, the chapter addresses policy reforms on a broad range of topics related to labor and human capital, from occupational licensing and right-to-work legislation to school choice and lottery scholarships.

THE TRUTH ABOUT WAGES

Why do workers earn more today on average than they did 50 years ago? Why does a logger operating a feller-buncher earn more than a logger operating a chainsaw? The answer is productivity. Productivity refers to the quantity of goods and services an individual is capable of producing with his/her skills and abilities. The fact that wages are driven by productivity is indisputable among economists.

Figures 7.1 and 7.2 illustrate the relationship between productivity and wages and productivity and unemployment by tracing the movement of real per capita income growth, unemployment, and productivity growth for the United States from 1950 to 2010. When productivity increases, per capita income grows; when productivity growth is low, as it was in the 1970s and 1980s, unemployment rates are higher.

Figure 7.1: Productivity and Real Income Growth

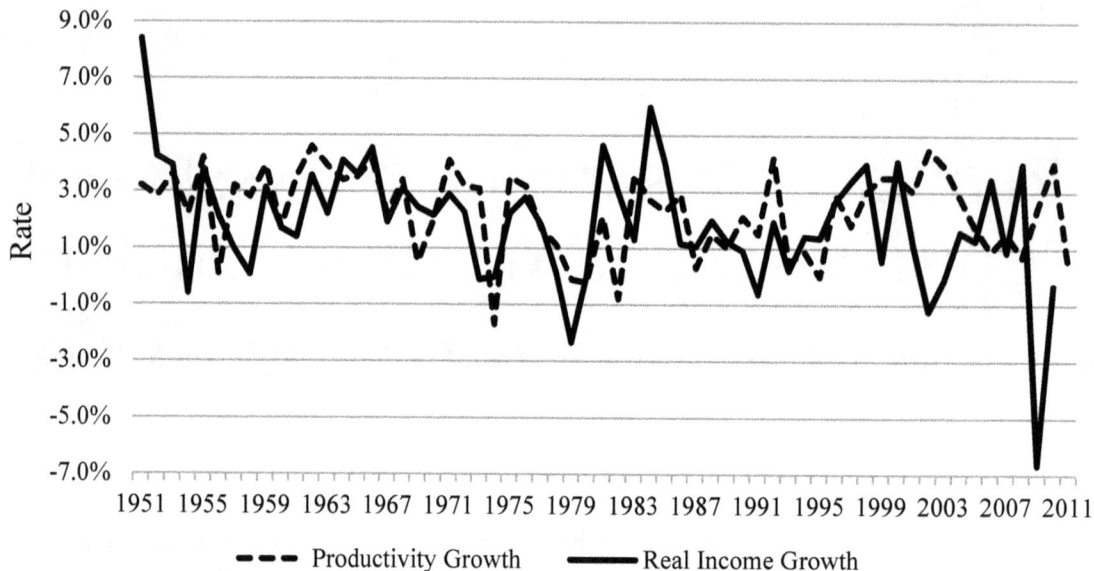

Sources: Bureau of Economic Analysis (2012)[1]; Bureau of Labor Statistics (2012c); Federal Reserve Bank (2012).

For example, in 1974, the rate of productivity growth began to slow, bottoming out in 1980. Following the decline in productivity growth, the rate of income growth declined, eventually turning negative. A similar close relationship between productivity growth and real income growth can be seen during the 1980s. This relationship seems to have changed in 2007, but Mandel (2012) argues that post-2007 productivity measures are inaccurate.[2]

Income and employment are derived from the value that workers provide others in terms of goods and services. The more goods and services a worker is willing and able to supply per hour, the more value she provides to customers per hour of her time. Employers might not like paying more productive workers more, but competition for productive workers forces them to do so. Sports fans observe this in action with free agents. Players whose statistics help the team win the most receive larger and longer contracts than do players who were not good enough to see regular playing time.

An extensive amount of research demonstrates the link between labor productivity and wages. Physical capital—tools and machinery—and human capital—skills, abilities, and education—contribute to a worker's productivity. For example, when a logger uses a feller-buncher in place of a chain saw, he is able to harvest significantly more trees. Enhancing human capital can also lead to increased productivity. For example, a doctor can learn a new procedure that provides better service to her patients, or an administrative assistant takes a computer skills class and is thus able to produce reports faster.

Historical evidence, as well as logical reasoning, establishes the definitive relationship between productivity, wages, and employment. Policies designed to increase incomes, wages, and employment should also target increasing productivity. Restrictive policies that limit wages or the entry of workers and entrepreneurs into industries reduce labor productivity and

---

[1] Includes Mid-Year Population estimates from the U.S. Census Bureau.

[2] The correlation between productivity growth and income growth is 0.219 (Figure 7.1). The correlation between productivity growth lagged one year and the unemployment rate (Figure 7.2) is -0.117 (Figure 7.2).

affect wages adversely. States such as Mississippi, Michigan, New York, and Alaska have not prospered in recent decades due to the heavy influence of labor market restrictions and constraints. However, in the same time period, states such as Texas, North Carolina, Georgia, and Virginia have realized stronger economic growth.

Figure 7.2: Productivity and Unemployment

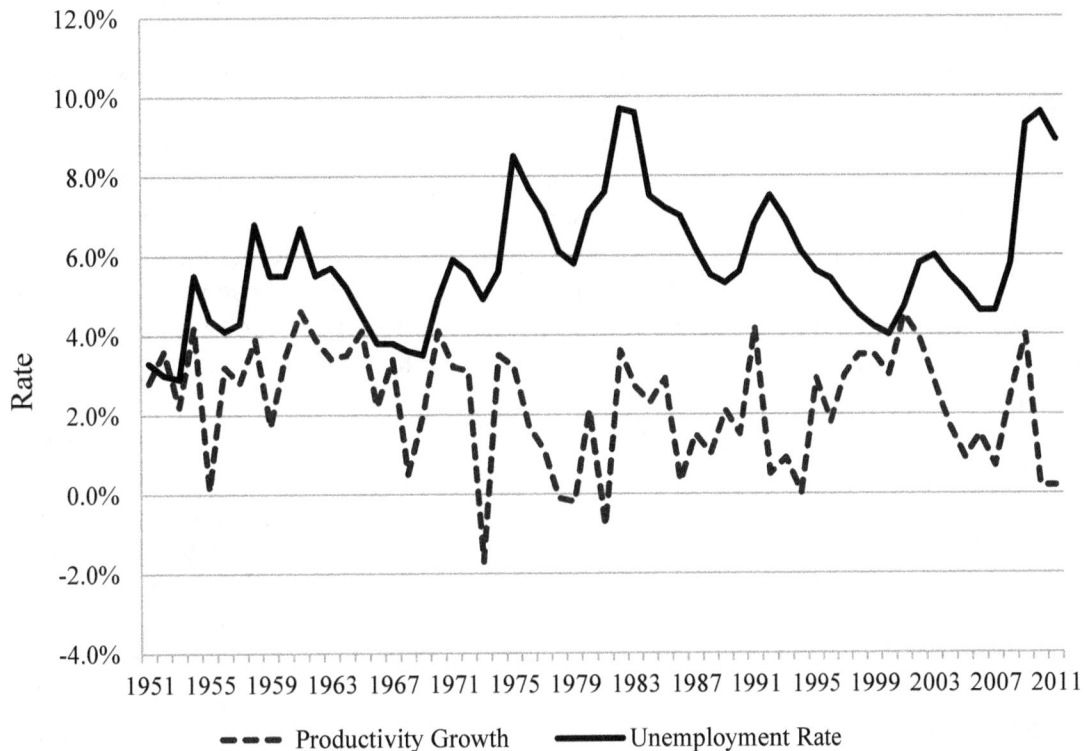

Sources: Bureau of Labor Statistics (2012a); Bureau of Labor Statistics (2012c).

The remainder of this chapter will address the policies and regulations that restrict the labor markets in Tennessee and suggest policy solutions to improve labor market conditions. The policies and regulations analyzed in this chapter should not be viewed as an exhaustive list. Instead, they are intended to exemplify the economic thinking behind how labor regulations and policies in general should be examined when attempting to predict the likely economic consequences.

TRYING TO DEFY THE LAWS OF NATURE

The well-intentioned desire of Congress to help the poor apparently will not be restrained by the rules and principles of the free market that otherwise do restrain American businesses and workers. Apparently, Congress can change the rules that would otherwise affect the affairs of mankind. So, Mr. Speaker, I have asked my staff to draft a measure I call the Obesity Reduction and Health Promotion Act. Since Congress will apparently not be restrained by the laws and principles that naturally exist, I propose that the force of gravity, by the force of Congress, be reduced by 10 percent. Mr. Speaker, that will result in immediate weight loss for every American.

Representative Bill Sali (*Idaho Statesman* 2007)

It is impossible to change the laws of gravity with legislation. What is true for scientific laws is also true for economic ones. The law of demand states that when the price of a good rises, consumers reduce the quantity demanded of it. In the market for labor, anything that raises the price of labor will reduce the quantity of it that is demanded. One important factor raising the price of labor is regulations.

Imagine living in a town where you were responsible for ensuring that each purchase you made conformed to hundreds of regulations. Any item purchased requires a significant amount of your time and resources researching the applicable regulations prior to executing the transaction. As a result, you and all other town residents would purchase fewer items due to the limited time available to examine all regulations germane to each specific purchase. If the same items could be purchased in a bordering town without such regulations, however, then we would expect consumers to begin making purchases in the neighboring city because their time and dollars would go farther.

This is the process that businesses undergo when deciding where to locate. Businesses are consumers of labor. The greater the number of labor regulations imposed on businesses, the higher their labor costs and the less labor they will use, other things being equal. Lower labor use predicates decreased competition for workers and lower wages in the long run. In addition, when bordering states have fewer labor regulations, many firms can "shop" for their workers in less costly states while remaining close to their customer base.

In many cases, labor regulations do not contribute to higher pay or safer workplace environments (Viscusi 1992). Most individuals work in environments that are significantly safer and receive greater compensation than the required minimums established by law. While employers prefer to maximize profits, they also must compete with other potential employers for workers. In order to compete for new workers and retain existing workers, firms must provide a compensation package and satisfactory workplace environment relative to other employers. Theory and research indicates that market competition is what results in higher wages and safer working environments in the long run, not regulation (Cowen and Tabarrok 2012; Yakovlev and Sobel 2010).

Policies that burden employers with costly rules, regulations, and mandates reduce the demand for workers leading to fewer workers being hired and generally making workers worse off. As discussed in Chapter 3, the American with Disabilities Act (ADA) example illustrates this point. The ADA was promoted and passed to increase employment opportunities for disabled citizens. However, the actual results indicate a significant decline in the employment rate for disabled citizens. As with any labor regulation, the ADA increased the costs of hiring a disabled person, and as a result, reduced the demand for their labor services.

Figure 7.3: Average Labor Market Freedom, Income Growth, and Unemployment (1981-2009)

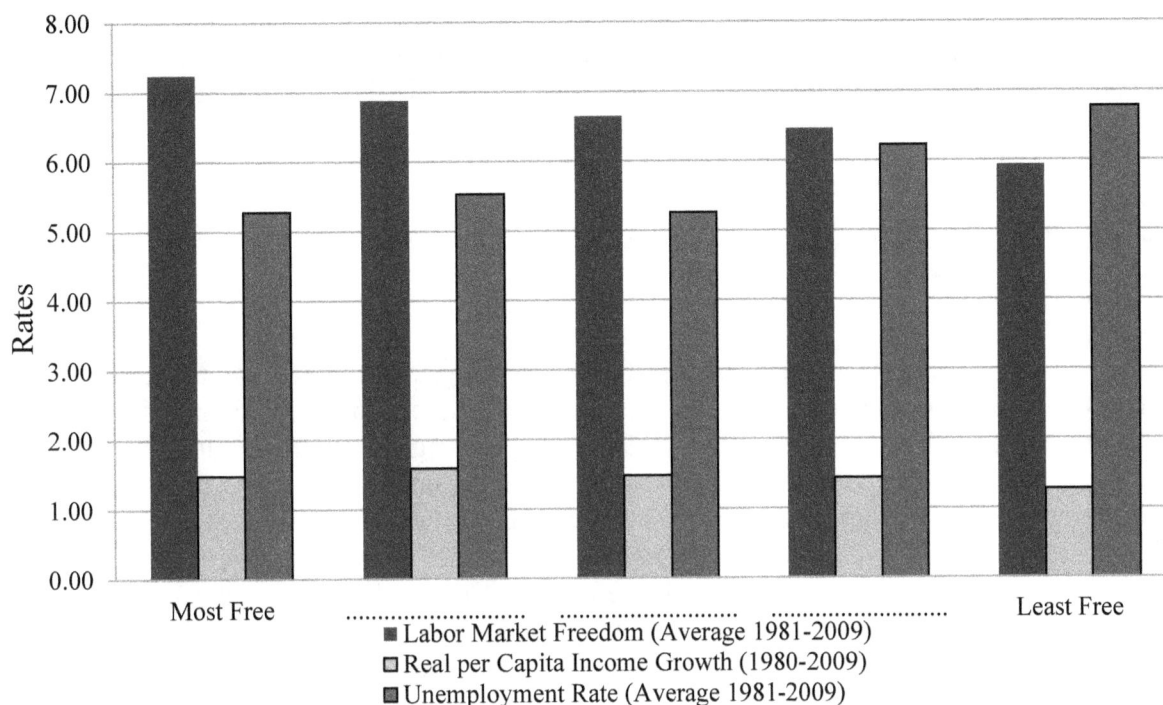

Labor Market Freedom (Average 1981-2009)
Real per Capita Income Growth (1980-2009)
Unemployment Rate (Average 1981-2009)

Sources: Bureau of Economic Analysis (2012); Bureau of Labor Statistics (2012c); Ashby, Bueno, and McMahon (2011).

In *Economic Freedom of North America 2011*, a subcategory measuring labor market freedom is included in the overall freedom index (Ashby, Bueno, and McMahon 2011). The labor market freedom variable provides a relative measure of a state's effort to avoid passing restrictive legislation on employment practices. Figure 7.3 provides a comparative analysis of labor market freedom, income growth, and unemployment rates from 1981 to 2009. The states have been divided into quintiles (groups of 10) and ordered from states with the most free labor market conditions to the least free. The data indicate that most states with greater labor market freedom also experienced higher income growth rates and lower unemployment numbers relative to states with the least free labor markets.

On average, Tennessee ranked in the 2nd quintile and 14th most free. However, North Carolina, Georgia, and Virginia, three of Tennessee's neighboring states, ranked in the 1st quintile. North Carolina was ranked the 2nd freest state in the nation. The remaining border states all ranked below Tennessee, beginning with Arkansas at 20th and, the least free, Mississippi at 41st. Compared to all states, Tennessee's current policies have produced an environment more conducive to increasing labor market competition by attracting businesses to the state. As a result, Tennessee workers have greater employment options, better compensation packages, as well as safer work environments than otherwise would be the case.

Contrary to popular belief about public policy, businesses are not opposed to all regulations. Some types of regulation—like restricting competition in an industry—can benefit businesses by allowing them to charge higher prices to consumers. Often times, businesses advocate these types of regulations. However, the regulations that businesses typically advocate for provide them with an advantage over their competition or restrict entry into the industry. As indicated in Chapter 2, an environment that encourages entrepreneurship and competition between existing firms is a vital component to economic freedom. The remainder of this chapter will address specific factors that Tennessee does well and recommend improvements to existing policies that historically have contributed to a decrease in labor market freedom.

RIGHT-TO-WORK LAWS: HIGHER EMPLOYMENT, FASTER GROWTH

While most economists oppose unions, their reasons are not based on the union itself. Individual freedom and personal choice are fundamental to economic freedom and capitalism, as acknowledged by Friedman ([1980] 1990), and the right for individuals to voluntarily organize is a personal choice. The problems arising from unions stem from their activities as the largest and most influential special interest group in the United States. Similar to occupational licensing, the special interest activities of unions obtain substantial benefits for a small, specific group at the expense of the general population. Due to the size and prowess of unions, politicians frequently serve their own best interests by catering to them. Friedman acknowledged "[t]he gains that strong unions win for their members are primarily at the expense of other workers" (233).

As a capitalistic society, individual laborers should have the right of choice to form and join unions. However, many states, as a result of union lobbying activities, have passed legislation requiring union membership as a condition for employment or requiring businesses to only hire union labor. In addition to using the political process to further the union cause, some unions have also resorted to using violent force against non-union employees and managers. These types of activities violate the key components necessary to nurture economic freedom. To ensure voluntary choice and competition for laborers and overcome the restrictions imposed by union activities, states can implement Right-to-Work legislation. Right-to-Work legislation legally protects the employee's right to personally choose whether or not to join the union by barring unions from requiring membership as a condition of employment at any time during the employment process. In so doing, Right-to-Work legislation encourages greater labor market competition and creates a more attractive environment for new businesses. Currently, 24 states have Right-to-Work laws (National Right to Work Legal Defense Foundation 2012).

A 1998 survey by economist William Moore investigating the effect of Right-to-Work legislation on state industrial growth found a significant and positive relationship. Right-to-Work states enjoyed higher industrial growth. In terms of reducing the unions' ability to persuade and commandeer state legislatures, economist Morgan Reynolds (1998) ranks Right-to-Work legislation as a 9 on a 10 point scale. Evidence suggests that states with Right-to-Work laws tend to experience lower unemployment rates and higher rates of income growth.

These differences are highlighted in Figures 7.4 and 7.5.[3] Figure 7.4 shows states with Right-to-Work legislation on average experience unemployment rates 0.5 percent lower than Non-Right-to-Work states. In addition, Figure 7.5 displays the differences in average income growth between Right-to-Work and Non-Right-to-Work states over the 30 year period 1980-2010; 20 year period from 1990-2010; 7 year period of 2000-2007; and the most recent decade 2000-2010. Right-to-Work states have experienced higher growth in per capita personal income rate during each time period reported.

Figure 7.4: Unemployment Rates and Right-to-Work Legislation

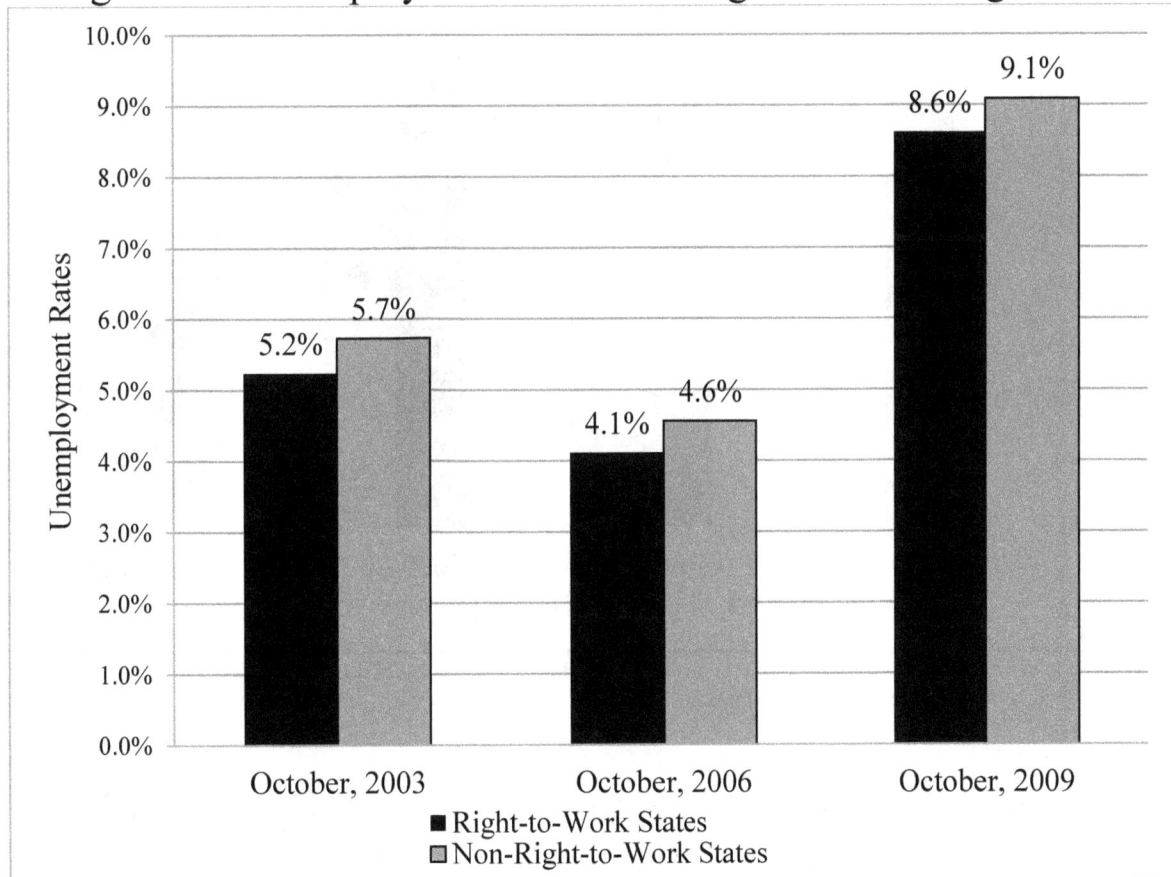

Sources: Bureau of Labor Statistics (2012b); National Right-to-Work Legal Defense Foundation (2012).

Opponents to Right-to-Work laws commonly attest that states without Right-to-Work legislation have higher average incomes as shown in Figure 7.6. However, the argument obscures the fact that the first states to enact Right-to-Work legislation were predominately southern states, beginning in the post-World War II era, and at a significantly lower income level. However, the disparity has declined from 12.31 percent in 1980 to 10.27 percent in

---

[3] In 2012, Indiana adopted Right-to-Work legislation, but was outside the time period included in Figure 7.6 calculations. In addition, Oklahoma, Texas, and Idaho adopted Right-to-Work legislation during the time periods reported. These states were included in the appropriate column, based on the year the Right-to-Work legislation went in effect.

2010. Due to the higher growth rates Right-to-Work states have experienced over Non-Right-to-Work states, we anticipate the disparity in average income to continue to decline.

Figure 7.5: Real Income Growth Rates in Right-to-Work States and Non-Right-to-Work States

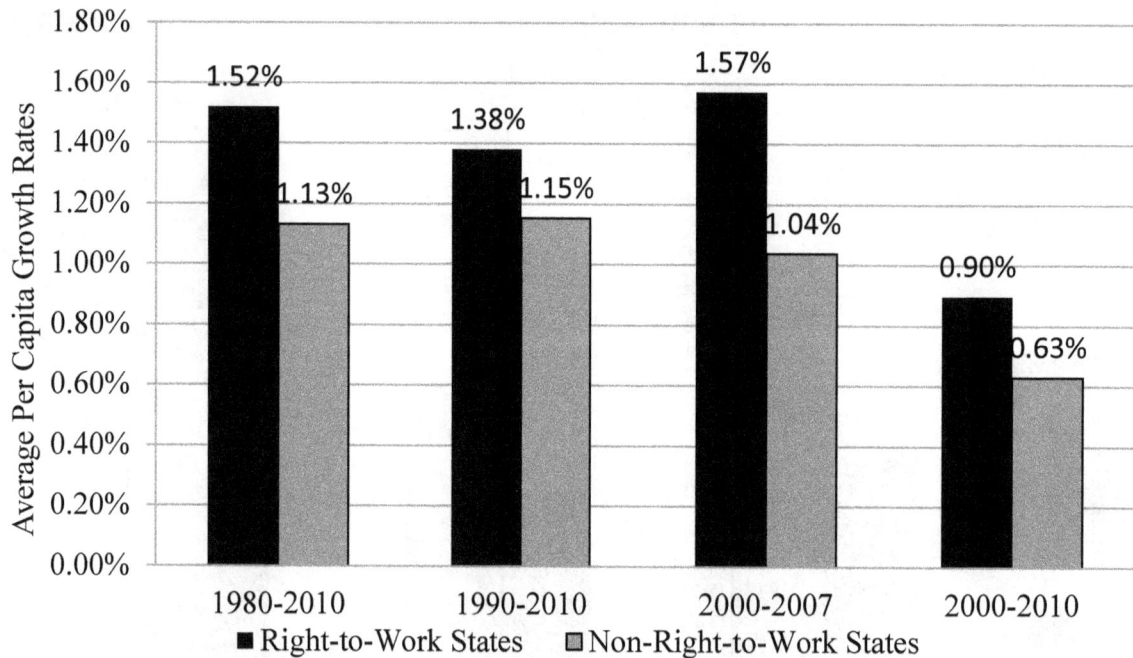

Sources: Bureau of Economic Analysis (2012); Federal Reserve Bank of St. Louis (2012); National Right-to-Work Legal Defense Foundations (2012); authors' calculations.[4]

Figure 7.6 Average Real per Capita Income in Right-to-Work and Non-Right-to-Work States

State Type	1980	1990	2000	2010
Right-to-Work States	$19,941	$23,639	$28,560	$30,948
Non-Right-to-Work States	$22,740	$27,331	$32,476	$34,488
Difference	12.31%	13.51%	12.06%	10.27%

Sources: Bureau of Economic Analysis (2012); Federal Reserve Bank of St. Louis (2012); National Right-to-Work Legal Defense Foundation (2012); authors' calculations. Note: Income data are adjusted for inflation to constant 2003 dollars using the Consumer Price Index.

---

[4] Income Growth Rates adjusted for inflation using the Consumer Price Index to constant 2003 dollars.

In 1947, Tennessee was among the earliest adopters of Right-to-Work legislation and has been successful in attracting many new businesses such as Volkswagen, FedEx, Amazon.com, Nissan, and Family Dollar. By continuing to support Right-to-Work legislation, Tennessee legislators reduce the influence of labor unions in the legislative process. In addition, support of Right-to-Work legislation also provides a more competitive work force, which is beneficial to the entire society through lower prices and greater job opportunities.

OCCUPATIONAL LICENSING

Occupational licensing legislation limits entry into specific fields by requiring practitioners of certain occupations to obtain state licenses to work in their fields. Legislation that limits entry or competition in specific occupations may increase wages for a select few, but causes

Figure 7.7 Occupational Licensing and Cost of Living by State

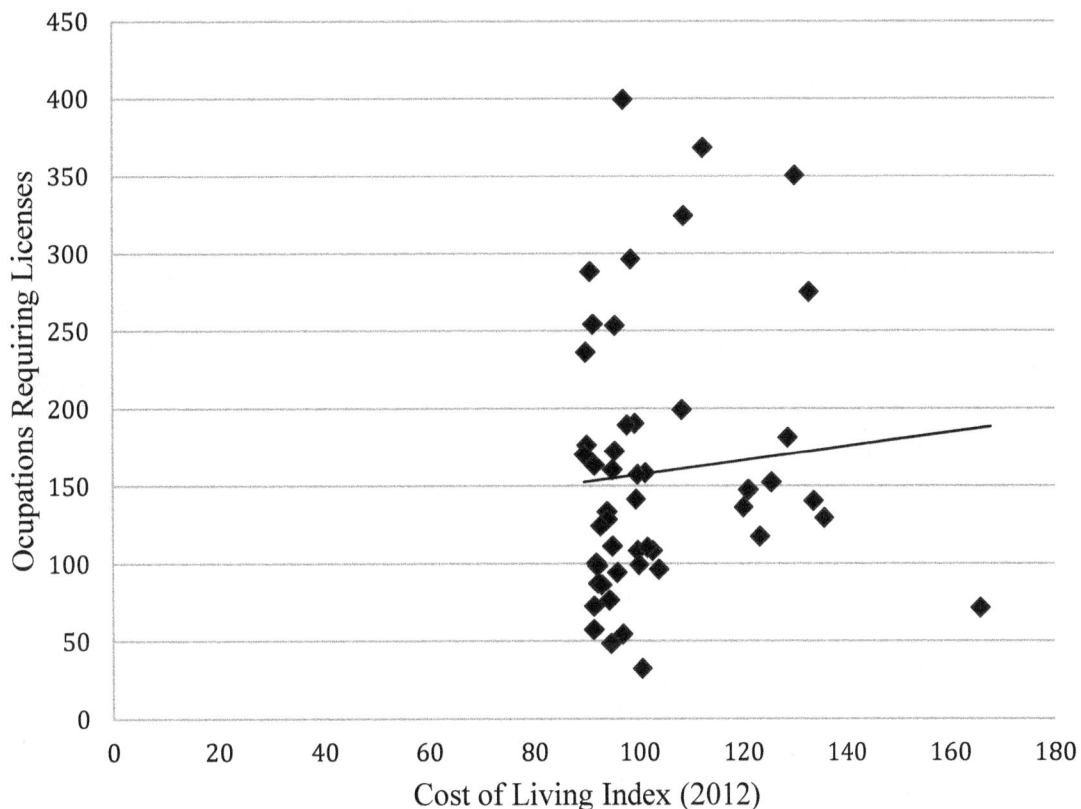

Sources: America's Career Info Net (2012); Missouri Economic Research and Information Center (2012).

significant cost of living increases making society worse off. The social costs created by occupational licensing, higher prices and reduced quantity of goods and services, significantly increase the cost of living for citizens. Figure 7.7 illustrates the positive relationship between the number of occupations licensed and cost of living increases caused by higher prices for goods and services.

Proponents of occupational licensing often contend that licensing regulations protect society from receiving poor services from unqualified providers. However, several studies have found that state licensing does not provide higher quality goods and services and may even result in a decline in quality (Leef 2007; Hood 1992; Kleiner 2000). Numerous alternative resources—CNet.com, *Consumer Reports*, and Angie's List—provide consumers with information on various goods and services without the societal costs imposed by occupational licensing. The effects of occupational licensing as well as the status of occupational licensing in Tennessee will be addressed in depth in Chapter 8.

THE HIGH COST OF MINIMUM WAGE

Minimum wage advocates allege that minimum wage legislation aids low-skilled workers in earning higher incomes. Unfortunately, similar to the ADA laws discussed earlier in the chapter, minimum wage legislation actually causes the most harm to those it is purportedly helping.

Many citizens understand the negative effects associated with minimum wage laws. If minimum wages were as simple as passing legislation then why not set the minimum hourly rate at $1,000? A minimum hourly rate of $1,000 per hour for a college professor would have adverse effects such as tuition increases for students, professor benefit packages would be reduced to offset the salary increase, and class sizes would be increased to minimize the number of professors on staff. In addition, fewer professors would be hired and a reduction in the number of professors employed would result.

Minimum wage increases result in greater unemployment of lower-skilled workers. Recent studies have estimated that employment of lower-skilled workers declines approximately 3 percent for every 10 percent increase in the minimum wage (Gwartney et. al 2009; Sobel 1999). In a June 12, 2009 *Wall Street Journal* article, David Neumark predicted that the 11 percent minimum wage increase in 2009 would cost over 300,000 jobs, commonly occupied by teens and young adults. The teenage unemployment rate actually reached its highest peak since World War II in September 2009 at 25.9 percent. An increase in unemployment rates for young workers also imposes long-run costs by reducing on-the-job training experiences that lead to higher future wages (Moore 2003).

It is important to note, however, the previously reported effects of minimum wage increases only estimate the negative consequences of a federal minimum wage increase that affects all states. State level minimum wage increases above the federal rate produce additional losses in addition to those observed at the federal level. States with a minimum wage above the federal level are likely to experience greater unemployment as businesses relocate to alternate states that do not impose state level minimum wages. In addition, state-level minimum wages above the federal level discourage businesses from establishing new operations in those states relative to other states. Finally, businesses that choose to remain in states with minimum wage rates greater than the federal rate operate at a competitive disadvantage due to relatively higher labor costs, thus increasing the prices of their goods and services relative to their national competitors.

Advocates of minimum wage legislation contend that the unemployment increases are justified because it helps low-income workers who remain employed receive higher wages that can push them out of poverty. However, research indicates the majority of individuals earning minimum wage are not impoverished. A recent study by Burkhauser and Sabia (2007) found that 87 percent of all minimum wage earners live in non-poor households. In addition, productivity is positively related to wages; therefore, workers with fewer skills and lower productivity levels are among the first to lose their jobs as a result of minimum wage increases (Neumark and Wascher 2002). Low skilled laborers have very limited employment opportunities. Their job options consist of a low paying job, no job at all, or a significantly less alluring position in the underground economy (Norberg 2004).

While numerous publications have reported the negative relationship between minimum wage and employment, one article by David Card and Alan Kruger published in 1994 found that an increase in the minimum wage did not decrease employment in the fast food industry in New Jersey and eastern Pennsylvania. Minimum wage proponents cite this article frequently. However, multiple follow up studies have discredited their reports citing problematic data (Neumark and Wascher 2000; Burkhauser, Couch, and Wittenburg 2000a, 2000b; Couch and Wittenburg 2001).[5]

MINIMUM WAGE AND POVERTY

Economic theory and the established literature have demonstrated minimum wage legislation is an ineffective antipoverty policy (Burkhauser and Sabia 2007). Figure 7.8 illustrates the positive relationship between high minimum wages relative to annual average income and poverty rates. States with highly restrictive minimum wage laws, such as Mississippi, West Virginia, Arkansas, and Alabama, also have the highest poverty rates. Alternatively, Wyoming, Connecticut, and New Jersey are examples of states that have the least restrictive minimum wage legislation and the lowest poverty rates. Simply stated, high relative minimum wages cause individuals to lose jobs and become impoverished.

Business growth and opportunities are typically unaffected for states with no minimum wage policy or whose minimum wage policy is to accept the federal minimum wage rate if the minimum wage rate is low relative to average income. However, states where the minimum wage rate is a greater percentage of annual income are negatively affected by outbound migration of productive resources—labor and capital (Ashby 2007). In Tennessee, the minimum wage rate is 39 percent of the average annual income and is the 18th highest in the nation. Compared with its neighbors, the minimum wage rate percentage of annual income in Tennessee is higher than Virginia, Georgia, North Carolina, and Missouri. In addition, Tennessee's rate is lower than Kentucky at 41.7 percent, Alabama at 43.8 percent, Arkansas at 45.9 percent, and Mississippi at 49.9 percent.

Decades of data have proven minimum wage laws decrease employment and increase poverty. Other negative effects of higher minimum wage rates relative to market wage rates include outward migration of existing productive resources in addition to reduced growth opportunities. Legislators should understand the negative effects on *freedom and prosperity* when considering any potential minimum wage legislation.

---

[5] Neumark and Wascher (2000) conducted a second study utilizing actual payroll data from the firms whose employees were surveyed in the Card and Kruger (1994) study and found employment was in fact negatively affected. For a comprehensive review of the effects of minimum wage legislation, please see Neumark and Wascher (2000).

Figure 7.8: Minimum Wage and Poverty Rates

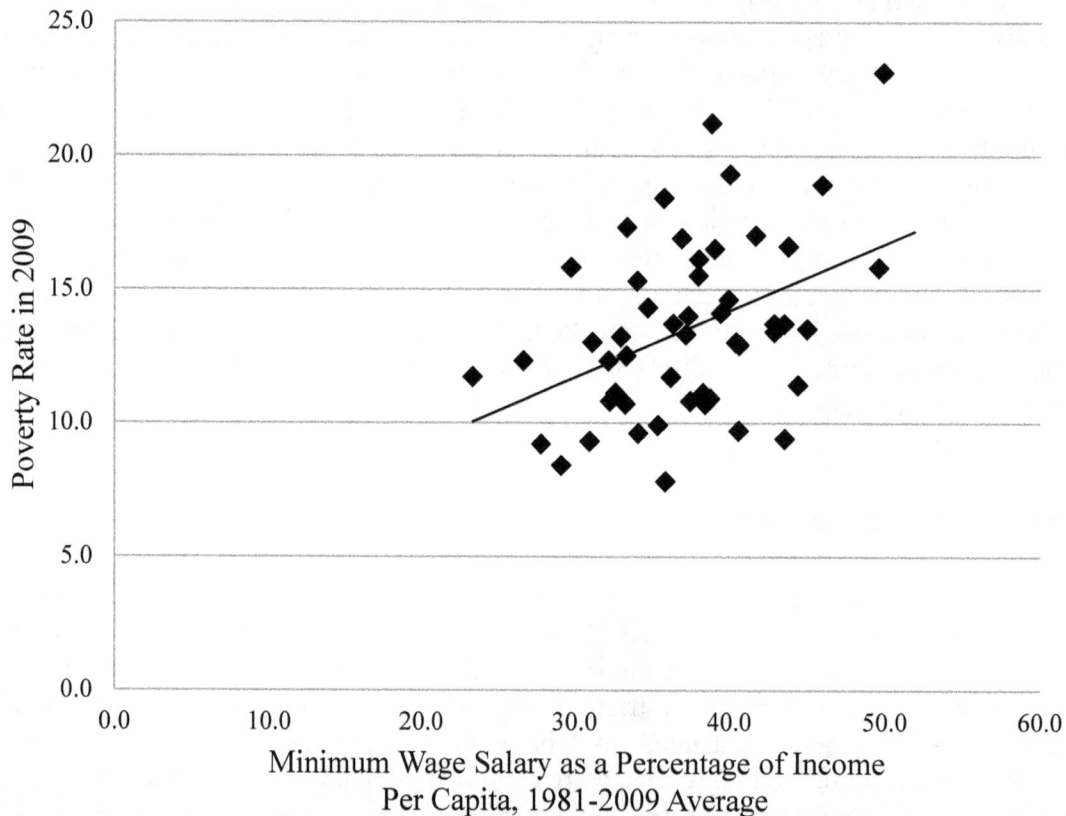

Sources: Ashby, Bueno, McMahon (2011); Bureau of the Census (2012).

PREVAILING WAGE RATES: PREVAILING WHERE?

Prevailing wages rates were enacted in 1931 with the Davis-Bacon Act in an effort to ensure quality work as well as protect workers from being unfairly paid. At present, 32 states including Tennessee have instituted prevailing wage laws for state-funded projects. Prevailing wages, similar to occupational licensing, restricts competition in the labor market and provides higher than market wages to laborers working on state-funded projects through the political process. In Tennessee, prevailing wage rates are set by the five members of the Prevailing Wage Committee.[6] Special interest groups benefit significantly from prevailing wage legislation and spend valuable resources to obtain beneficial policies from legislators that provide higher than market wages and limited competition.

Several articles have shown that nationwide prevailing wage rates do not correspond with the actual market rate. A study conducted in Oregon found that prevailing wages were on average 25 percent higher than market-established wages. In addition, the auditing agency for the United States Congress, the General Accounting Office, found that 57 percent of the

---

[6] For more information on the Tennessee Prevailing Wage Committee, see TN Acts 1975, ch. 368, § 1; T.C.A., §12-436.

prevailing wage rates were established based on union wage rates without conducting a true wage survey (Public Service Research Foundation 2001).

The prevailing wage rates in Tennessee are dependent upon the location of the county in which the project is being completed as well as the type of work performed. Some prevailing wages in Shelby County, Tennessee are $19.23 per hour for bricklayers, $25.82 per hour for plumbers, and $27.13 per hour for sheet-metal workers. Translated into annual incomes—40 hours per week for 50 weeks—bricklayers earn $38,460; plumbers earn $51,640; and sheet-metal workers earn $54,260. It is important to note that these figures only represent the primary base rate and are exclusive of the plentiful fringe benefits. In Tennessee, there are a total of 47 job classifications subject to prevailing rate regulation.

In addition to inhibiting competition in the labor market and providing significant benefits for only a few through higher than market wages, prevailing wages increase the costs of public projects adding to the tax burden of all citizens. Market regulation of wages on private projects produces profitable results, and could also provide similar results in government-funded projects as well. Furthering the interests of a well-organized few workers at the expense of other workers and the citizens of Tennessee reduces the *freedom and prosperity* of Tennesseans. Legislators should consider abolishing the state-wide prevailing wage law as well as prohibit local municipalities from enacting local prevailing wage legislation.

IMPROVING HUMAN CAPITAL THROUGH SCHOOL CHOICE

Labor productivity is positively related to quality education, which can significantly increase an individual's income. According to international test scores, the quality of education in United States primary and secondary schools has fallen substantially relative to other developed nations. One proposed factor contributing to the rising test scores in other developed nations is school choice. In many of these other countries, including most of Europe, parents are allowed to choose which school they wish to enroll their child, creating intense competitive pressures in the education market.

Milton Friedman (1962), in his book *Capitalism and Freedom*, used the U.S. education system as a fundamental example of a near perfect monopoly. In a monopolistic system, market pressures for schools to provide high quality services and high levels of customer satisfaction are absent. Primary and secondary students in the U.S. have very few choices regarding which school to attend. If a student has a poor experience at one school, in most cases, it is very difficult to enroll the student in a different school without changing residences. Essentially, regardless of how a school performs, their customers are compelled to continue subscribing to their services. In addition, schools are rewarded with extra funds for poor performance. As we report in Chapter 9, additional funds rarely provide higher test scores.

As Friedman proposed, one solution to alleviate the monopolistic situation is to institute a school voucher program. School vouchers would provide students with the funds needed to attend school and would allow parents and students the ability to choose which school they believe would provide the greatest benefit. One common concern is whether school vouchers would be limited to public schools or would be valid at private schools as well. The actual cost of a private school education is far less than a comparable public school education, sometimes estimated to be half the cost (Wenders 2005). If the vouchers applied to all schools—public and private—then parents would have significantly greater choices and control. Theoretically, all but the most exclusive private schools would be attainable by all students. A voucher program encourages competition among all schools, and as with other goods, increased competition provides higher quality and greater customer satisfaction.

Similar to school vouchers, charter schools also provide educational alternatives to parents. However, they do not provide the same level of entrepreneurial incentives that school vouchers allow. Typically, charter school programs are publically funded, but run by a private group. Charter schools operate under a written contract with the state government that includes the details of how the school will be organized and managed as well as the educational curriculum. In 2010, there were 40 charter schools operating in Tennessee with four additional schools scheduled to open in 2012. In 2011, the Tennessee legislature removed the cap on the number of charter schools that could operate in the state. Removing the cap on charter schools will increase competition among existing schools.

The established research on existing school voucher programs and charter schools indicates that these programs successfully increase the quality of education for students as well as provide students with the skills and knowledge needed to increase their lifetime earning potential (Hoxby 1994, 2003a, 2003b; Hoxby and Rockoff 2005; Greene 2001; Metcalf 1999; Rouse 1998). Successful school voucher programs currently exist in Florida, Indiana, Maine, Ohio (Cleveland only), Vermont, Utah, Wisconsin (Milwaukee only), and the District of Columbia. In the first year of operation, Indiana's school choice program attracted nearly 4,000 students (Sheffield 2011). Hoxby (2003a) found that public school performance in the areas where school choice programs were implemented also experienced massive improvements almost immediately. In some cases, educational quality improved more in the first few years after school choice programs were enacted than it had in the previous 30 years.

In 2011, the Tennessee Senate approved a bill that would provide school vouchers for low-income students or those attending failing schools (Sheffield 2011). However, the bill was unsuccessful in passing the Tennessee House and was returned to subcommittee for further study (Roberts 2011). The evidence clearly indicates that school choice programs offer significant increases in educational quality in all schools by providing students with vast benefits both in the short and long run. Improving the quality of primary and secondary education should be a priority for all Tennessee legislators. Enacting a school choice program could increase the quality of education available to all Tennessee children, increase the productivity of future laborers, and provide substantial growth potential for the Tennessee economy.

TENNESSEE EDUCATIONAL LOTTERY SCHOLARSHIP: AN INVESTMENT IN HUMAN CAPITAL

In 2004, Tennessee introduced the Tennessee Education Lottery Scholarship Program (TELS). Similar to the goals of all lottery-funded scholarship programs, the TELS was created to increase investment in higher education. The TELS provides various scholarship programs and subcategories among individual programs. Academic requirements are assessed from high school grade point averages and/or ACT scores. Minimum academic standards range from a high school GPA of 2.75 to 3.75 or an ACT score of 21 or greater. In addition, monetary awards vary from $1,750 to $3,500 for students attending a two-year college or $2,750 to $5,500 for students attending a four-year institution. Two programs are reserved solely for students with a maximum household income of $36,000 or less. As previously discussed, educational investments are significantly important to increasing human capital and productivity (Tennessee Student Assistance Corporation 2012). However, as we explain in Chapter 9, not all investments are always effective. One way the TELS could be considered a program that positively contributes to growing the Tennessee economy would be if it was shown to increase the number of low-income students attending college.

According to a case study at one Tennessee institution, overall college enrollment was found to be slightly elevated as a result of the TELS (Penn and Kyle 2007). Similar to studies evaluating other lottery-funded scholarship programs, Penn and Kyle also found that students from low-income households and non-white students were underrepresented in scholarship recipients. The findings were consistent with the widely established positive correlation between parent's income and children's educational attainment. Similar results were reported in the *Tennessee Education Lottery Scholarship Program Special Report* (Tennessee Higher Education Commission 2011). Their extensive evaluation of the TELS program found that approximately one-third of all scholarship recipients are from families with sufficient resources to pay for their college education. In addition, the report found that 45,500 students eligible for need-based awards did not receive them due to inadequate funding. Thus, the TELS appears to be mostly transferring income from all citizens to the higher income households in the form of tuition dollars.

To evaluate the TELS, one must ask if the program is providing a net benefit to Tennessee. According to the available research, it appears that the program is primarily providing benefits to non-low-income families that likely would have used their own resources to attend college. Although more information is needed to know if Tennessee's economy could be improved by eliminating the TELS program (such as whether it makes it more likely for Tennesseans to remain in-state following graduation), at the very least the program should undergo an overhaul to a means-based model. Doing so would reduce the likelihood of income transfers to individuals who are able to pay their college tuition costs and increase the number of scholarships available to those who could not attend college without assistance.

CONCLUSION

This chapter provided an in-depth review of the relationship between labor productivity and higher wages. Labor policies that encourage increased productivity and greater competition in labor markets increase the *freedom and prosperity* for all Tennesseans. Economic growth stems from policies that promote capital investment, which provides better wages and employment opportunities and benefits all citizens.

Market regulations are often imposed with the best of intentions, such as the protection of citizens. Unfortunately, most regulations provide benefits only to special interest groups and impose significant costs on the rest of society. Often the regulations, such as the immense training and fees required of a professional hair shampooer in Tennessee, are farcical and do not contribute to increased quality of services, only to increased costs through reduced competition. Labor is like any other good in that price increases will lead to less being used. That is true whether the cause is minimum wage laws, occupational licensure, or prevailing wage laws.

Finally, various studies have shown significant improvement in public education systems by enacting legislation to increase school choice through school vouchers and charter schools. In 2011, the Tennessee Legislature enacted a law that removed the previous cap on charter schools and took steps toward increasing school choice. However, much work remains to be done in order to improve the quality of education and thus the labor force in Tennessee. Implementation of a school voucher program would greatly increase the competition among schools and provide significantly higher quality education for all Tennessee children. Improvements are also needed at the college level to transform the TELS program to ensure that it increases the acquisition of human capital instead of merely subsidizing households who could afford college attendance anyway. High quality educational opportunities and a competitive labor market will provide the environment needed to attract new business opportunities to Tennessee.

REFERENCES

America's Career InfoNet. 2012. *Occupational Licensing*. Minnesota: CareerOneStop. http://www.careerinfonet.org/licensedoccupations/.

Ashby, Nathan J. 2007. "Economic Freedom and Migration Flows Between U.S. States." *Southern Economic Journal* 73 (3): 677-697.

Ashby, Nathan J., Avilia Bueno, and Fred McMahon. 2011. *Economic Freedom of North America 2011*. Vancouver, BC: Fraser Institute.

Bureau of Census, U. S. Department of Commerce. 2012. *Annual Social and Economic Supplement (ASEC) from the Current Population Survey*. Washington: U.S. Department of Commerce. http://www.census.gov/did/www/saipe/data/model/info/cpsasec.html.

Bureau of Economic Analysis, U.S. Department of Commerce. 2012. *Annual State Personal Income*. Washington: U.S. Department of Commerce. http://www.bea.gov/iTable/iTable.cfm?ReqID=70&step=1.

Bureau of Labor Statistics, U. S. Department of Labor. 2012a. *Labor Force Statistics from the Current Population Survey*. Washington: U.S. Department of Labor. http://www.bls.gov/cps/prev_yrs.htm/.

———. 2012b. *Local Area Unemployment Statistics*. Washington: U.S. Department of Labor. http://data.bls.gov/cgi-bin/dsrv?la.

———. 2012c. *Productivity and Costs, Business Output per Hour of All Persons*. Washington: U.S. Department of Labor. http://data.bls.gov/cgi-bin/surveymost?pr.

Burkhauser, Richard V., Kenneth A. Couch, and David C. Wittenburg. 2000a. "A Reassessment of the New Economics of the Minimum Wage Literature with Month Data from the Current Population Survey." *Journal of Labor Economics* 18 (4): 653-680.

————. 2000b. "Who Minimum Wage Increases Bite: An Analysis Using Monthly Data from the SIPP and the CPS." *Southern Economic Journal* 67 (1): 16-40.

Burkhauser, Richard V., and Joseph J. Sabia. 2007. "The Effectiveness of Minimum Wage Increases in Reducing Poverty: Past, Present, and Future." *Contemporary Economic Policy* 25 (2): 262-281.

Card, David, and Alan Krueger. 1994. "Minimum Wages and Employment: A Case Study of the Fast-Food Industry in New Jersey and Pennsylvania." *American Economic Review* 84 (4): 772-793.

Couch, Kenneth A. and David C. Wittenburg. 2001. "The Response of Hours of Work to Increases in the Minimum Wage." *Southern Economic Journal* 68 (1): 171-177.

Cowen, Tyler and Alexander Tabarrok. 2012. *Modern Principles: Microeconomics.* 2nd edition. New York: Worth Publishers.

Federal Reserve Bank of St. Louis, Economic Research. 2012. *Consumer Price Index for All Urban Consumers: All Items (CPIAUCSL).* St. Louis, Missouri: Federal Reserve Bank. http://research.stlouisfed.org/fred2/series/CPIAUCSL/.

Friedman, Milton. 1962 [1982]. *Capitalism and Freedom.* Chicago and London: University of Chicago Press.

Friedman, Milton and Rose Friedman. 1990 [1980]. *Free to Choose: A Personal Statement.* Orlando: Harcourt, Inc.

Greene, Jay P. 2001. *An Evaluation of the Florida A-Plus Accountability and School Choice Program.* New York: Manhattan Institute for Policy Research.

Gwartney, James D., Richard L. Stroup, Russell S. Sobel, and David A. MacPherson. 2009. *Economics: Private and Public Choice.* 12th edition. Mason, Ohio: Southwestern /Cengage Learning.

Hood, John. 1992. "Does Occupational Licensing Protect Consumers?" *The Freeman* 42 (11) 418-422.

Hoxby, Caroline M. 1994. "Do Private Schools Provide Competition for Public Schools. NBER Working Paper No. 4978. Cambridge: National Bureau of Economic Research.

————. 2003a. "School Choice and School Competition: Evidence from the United States." *Swedish Economic Policy Review* 10 (2): 9-65.

————. 2003b. "School Choice and School Productivity (Or, Could School Choice Be a Rising Tide That Lifts All Boats)." In *The Economics of School Choice,* edited by Caroline M. Hoxby, 287-341. Chicago: The University of Chicago Press.

Idaho Statesman. 2007. "Sali Makes Symbolic Bid to Abolish Gravity." January 13.

Kleiner, Morris M. 2000. "Occupational Licensing." *Journal of Economic Perspectives* 14 (4): 198-202.

Leef, George C. 2007. Review of *Licensing Occupations: Ensuring Quality or Restricting Competition?* by Morris M. Kleiner. *The Freeman* 57 (5): 42-43.

Mandel, Michael. 2012. The Myth of American Productivity. *Washington Monthly.* http://www.washingtonmonthly.com/magazine/january_february_2012/features/the _myth_of_american_productiv034576.php.

Metcalf, Kim K. 2001. *Evaluation of the Cleveland Scholarship Program, 1998-2000: Technical Report.* Bloomington: Indiana Center for Evaluation.

Missouri Economic Research and Information Center, Missouri Department of Economic Development. 2012. Cost of Living Data Series. Jefferson City, MO: Missouri Department of Economic Development. http://www.missourieconomy.org/indicators /cost_of_living/index.stm.

Moore, Jack. 2003. "Long-Term Consequences of Youth Unemployment." Stanford University working paper. Stanford University, Stanford, CA. http://economics .stanford.edu /files/Theses/Theses_2003/Moore.pdf.

Moore, William. 1998. "The Determinants and Effects of Right-to-Work Laws: A Review of the Recent Literature." *Journal of Labor Research* 19 (3): 445-469.

National Right to Work Legal Defense Foundation, Inc. 2012. *Right to Work States.* Springfield, Virginia: National Right to Work Legal Defense Foundation. http://www.nrtw.org/en/print/1052.

Neumark, David. 2009. "Delay the Minimum-Wage Hike." *Wall Street Journal,* June 12. http://online.wsj.com/article/SB124476823767508619.html.

Neumark, David and William Wascher. 2000. "Minimum Wage and Employment: A Case Study of the Fast-Food Industry in New Jersey and Pennsylvania: Comment" *American Economic Review* 98 (8): 1362-1396.

———. 2002. "Do Minimum Wages Fight Poverty?" *Economic Inquiry* 40 (3): 315-333.

Norberg, Johan. 2004. *In Defense of Global Capitalism.* Washington: Cato Institute.

Penn, David A. and Reuben Kyle. 2007. "The Tennessee Education Lottery Scholarship: A Reward for Past Achievement or Motivator for Future Performance." Department of Economics and Finance Working Paper Series. Middle Tennessee State University, Murfreesboro, TN.

Pew Research Center. 2012. "Problems and Priorities." PollingReport.com, June 7-17. http://pollingreport.com/prioriti.htm.

Public Service Research Foundation. 2001. *Do Prevailing Wages Really Prevail? Should Prevailing Wage Laws Be Repealed?* Vienna: Public Service Research Foundation. http://www.psrf.org/issues/prevailing.jsp.

Reynolds, Morgan O. 1998. "The Prospects for Right to Work." *Journal of Labor Research* 19 (3): 519-528.

Roberts, Jane. 2011. "Tennessee House Education Subcommittee Sends School Voucher Bill Back for More Study." *Commercial Appeal*, April 27. http://www .commercialappeal.com /news/2011/apr/27/tennessee-house-education-subcommittee-sends-schoo/.

Rouse, Cecilia E. 1998. "Private School Vouchers and Student Achievement: An Evaluation of the Milwaukee Parental Choice Program." *Quarterly Journal of Economics* 113 (2): 553-602.

Sheffield, Rachel. 2011. "School Choice Could Become a Reality for Tennessee School Children. http://blog.heritage.org/2011/12/01/school-choice-could-become-a-reality-for-tennessee-school-children/.

Sobel, Russell S. 1999. "Theory and Evidence on the Political Economy of the Minimum Wage." *Journal of Political Economy* 107 (4): 761-785.

Tennessee Higher Education Commission. 2011. *Tennessee Education Lottery Scholarship Program Special Report.*

Tennessee Student Assistance Corporation. 2012. "Money for College." http://www.tn.gov /CollegePays/mon_college/lottery_scholars.htm.

Viscusi, W. Kip. 1992. *Fatal Tradeoffs: Private and Public Responsibility Toward Risk*. New York: Oxford University Press.

Wenders, John T. 2005. "The Extent and Nature of Rent Dissipation in U.S. Public Education." *Cato Journal* 25 (2): 217-244.

Yakovlev, Pavel, and Russell S. Sobel. 2010. "Occupational Safety and Profit Maximization: Friends or Foes?" *Journal of Socio-Economics* 39 (3): 429-435.

CHAPTER 8

REGULATORY REFORMS AND PROSPECTS FOR GROWTH

by Art Carden

Freedom and Prosperity in Tennessee

8

REGULATORY REFORMS AND PROSPECTS FOR GROWTH

Art Carden

Tennessee has a long history of cultural, culinary, and commercial innovation. Memphis prides itself on being "the birthplace of Rock-n-Roll," and Nashville is the world's center for both country and contemporary Christian music. Memphis has a long tradition as one of the world's barbecue capitals. Any discussion of the history of Memphis would be incomplete without a reference to its stature as one of the legendary territories in the history of professional wrestling. Several Memphis-based firms are responsible for innovations that change the way we shop. Piggly Wiggly made self-service shopping successful. AutoZone has been an innovator in auto parts retail. Holiday Inn helped change the way people travel, and FedEx revolutionized shipping.[1] None of these innovations were planned; rather, they emerged in the context of an institutional environment that rewards entrepreneurship and allows people to take risks. This decentralized, and unpredictable, process of entrepreneurship and innovation that is fostered by the "invisible hand" of the marketplace when an economy has economic freedom was discussed at length in Chapter 3.

The state's two largest metropolitan areas are important, but entrepreneurial innovation is certainly not limited to Memphis and Nashville. Mayfield Dairy, a prominent innovator in the dairy industry, is now owned by Dallas-based Dean Foods but is headquartered in Athens, Tennessee. Magazines.com is headquartered just south of Nashville in Franklin, Tennessee. Averitt Express, one of the country's largest shipping companies, is headquartered in Cookeville. Nine firms in the 2012 Fortune 500 are headquartered in Tennessee: FedEx, HCA Holdings, International Paper, Dollar General, Community Health Systems, Unum Group, AutoZone, Eastman Chemical, and Vanguard Health Systems (Fortune 500).

Large companies play an important role in economic development, but small businesses play an even larger role as innovators and job creators. Pro-growth policy in Tennessee would include a regulatory environment that makes the state an attractive target for outside investors, but it would also include a regulatory environment that rewards and encourages indigenous entrepreneurs. The history of cultural, culinary, and commercial innovation in Memphis alone

---

[1] See Carden (2011) for a more detailed discussion of Piggly Wiggly, AutoZone, Holiday Inn, and FedEx.

suggests that Tennessee is blessed with entrepreneurial talent. One key to the development of the next FedEx, the next Holiday Inn, or the next AutoZone in Tennessee is a regulatory environment that provides people with maximum freedom to experiment and innovate—especially inexperienced new small-scale entrepreneurs. According to a 2012 survey of small business owners conducted by Thumbtack.com and the Ewing Marion Kauffman Foundation, "(s)mall businesses said licensing requirements were nearly twice as important as tax-related regulations in determining their state or city government's overall business-friendliness" (Thumbtack.com 2012b).[2] While large companies have legal and tax departments with experienced staff that navigate the regulatory, licensing, and permitting processes, new small businesses and first-time entrepreneurs are especially handicapped by a heavy regulatory burden.

Economists who have studied the relationship between government policies and economic development have shown that economic freedom is an essential element of a pro-growth business environment.[3] Tennessee does reasonably well in this regard; the state was ranked sixth for its regulatory environment in the 2011 Forbes "Best States for Business and Careers" rankings (methods are described by Badenhausen 2011). The states ranked first, second, and third—North Carolina, Virginia, and Georgia—border Tennessee, however. Thus while a regulatory ranking of sixth may seem sufficient, Tennessee has strong competition and room for improvement given three of its neighboring states—with whom Tennessee directly competes for businesses—rank even higher. In this chapter, we will consider several aspects of Tennessee's regulatory environment that restrict economic freedom, burden Tennessee businesses, and reduce growth. Specifically, we will consider occupational licensing and Tennessee's "price gouging" law. We will also consider interventions Tennessee policymakers have not adopted, but if adopted would reduce growth: a higher minimum wage, employment protection laws, and restrictions on large-scale retailers.

DOES REGULATION PROTECT CONSUMERS OR SPECIAL INTERESTS?

Scholars have developed two different theories of regulation. The first is what might be called the *public interest* theory of regulation, and it holds that governments regulate goods and services in order to protect members of the public from fraud, deception, shoddy products, and unscrupulous businesspeople. These theories are based on the idea that policy makers have the information and incentive to simply know the best responses and enact them—benevolent and omniscient central planning. But as we discussed in Chapter 3, knowledge in an economy is decentralized. Policy makers often do not know the full ramifications of new policies, and political incentives to get re-elected and secure political support often lead policy makers to support the policies that benefit these special interest groups.

The second is what might be called the *special interest* theory of regulation. It builds on an interesting empirical oddity that, at first glance, appears to be inconsistent with the public

---

[2] The Thumbtack.com survey is summarized in Allen and Daniels (2012). Over the course of two months, the two organizations offered Thumbtack.com members the option of filling out a survey on their state and local governments' friendliness to small business. They received approximately six thousand responses. It is important to note that the survey provides an under-estimate of the importance of regulation as it only surveys existing businesses, not businesses that do not exist because of regulation.

[3] See Gwartney, Lawson, and Hall (2011) for country-level data on economic freedom and Ashby et al. (2011) for state- and province-level data on economic freedom.

interest theory of regulation. It is often the dominant businesses within an industry or occupation who push government to adopt regulations like occupational licensing (Stigler 1971). The *special interest* theory of regulation holds that government regulation is primarily an anticompetitive device. Dominant firms lobby for regulations like occupational licensing in order to prevent entry by potential new competitors. This reduces output in the regulated industry and raises the incomes of those who are subject to the regulations—protecting existing businesses from competition at the expense of new businesses and consumers.

One of the clearest examples of government regulation is occupational licensing, which is a regulatory system in which someone needs a license from the government in order to enter a profession like law, dentistry, medicine, or cosmetology. Restrictions on entry in the form of regulations like occupational licensing requirements impose two kinds of costs on society. The first is called "deadweight loss," which is the gains from trade, societies are unable to enjoy because less of the regulated service is being produced. The second cost is subtler, but no less real. It is the wasted resources devoted to lobbying the government for special privileges. In a path-breaking contribution, Tullock (1967) described these costs of using the political system to obtain monopoly privileges or protective tariffs. Krueger (1974) referred to this as *rent-seeking*, but Henderson (2008) argues that a better term would be "privilege seeking." When people spend their time, talent, and resources privilege seeking, these resources are taken away from other productive areas. This concept of the tradeoff between productive and unproductive entrepreneurship was discussed in Chapter 3. When there is more unproductive entrepreneurship in a society it is poorer because there is an equivalent loss in the amount of productive entrepreneurship being undertaken. The social cost of regulation therefore includes not just the reduction in production and trade, but also the loss in productive activities that results from resources being re-allocated toward the political process through interest groups, lobbyists, and other ways of seeking government privileges.

OCCUPATIONAL LICENSING

Occupational licensing is one of the most prevalent ways governments intervene in the labor market. Approximately one in three American workers now needs a government license in order to work (Kleiner and Krueger 2008, 2009). This is up from approximately one in twenty during the 1950s, and it is a much larger fraction of the labor force than is affected by labor unions (Stephenson and Wendt 2009). It is difficult for an occupation to return to being unlicensed, but workplaces can (and do) often decertify labor unions (Kleiner 2006). Licensing might be a market-making solution to information problems, and there is evidence that this was the case for some professions in the Progressive Era (Law and Kim 2005). Nonetheless, Kleiner (2006) points out that research on occupational licensing shows that while there may be short-run benefits from improved quality, there are long-run costs as competition and innovation are restricted and consumers face higher prices.

Regulation creates winners and losers, and occupational licensing benefits the rich at the expense of the poor. Kleiner (2006) points out that the main beneficiaries of occupational licensing are high-income individuals who care about and can spend for higher-quality services, but licensing hurts low-income individuals who do not have the resources to pay for high-quality services and must do without the licensed service or resort to "do-it-yourself remedies" (43). Licensing—and regulation more generally—might raise the average quality of the services in question, but to borrow an analogy from Milton Friedman (1962), forms of occupational licensing are akin to regulations stating that people are not allowed to buy cars of lower quality than a Cadillac. Such regulations would raise the average quality of cars on the road, but they would mean that many people without the money to spend on a Cadillac would have to do without cars.[4]

Licensing requirements limit access to the labor market. In the words of Kleiner and Krueger (2009, 5), licensing of a service leads to "higher quality outcomes for those who are able to obtain the service, but fewer practitioners and less access to the service." Even still, there is some evidence that licensing does not improve quality in all cases. Kleiner and Kudrle (2000) found that there was little difference in dental quality for Air Force recruits from states with heavy licensing requirements and states with easier requirements.[5] With information on insurance rates for occupational therapists, practical and vocational nurses, or clinical psychologists, Kleiner (2006, 57) suggests that malpractice insurance markets do not reward licensees or punish the unlicensed, which suggests that licensing does not improve quality.

Teaching is an occupation where licensing has become more burdensome. Ostensibly, these requirements are there in order to ensure that only high-quality teachers enter the profession. Studies of student outcomes tell a different story. Kleiner (2006) summarizes the findings of several studies of licensing on quality, including studies of teachers by Kleiner and Petree (1988), Angrist and Guryan (2008), Kane, Rockoff, and Staiger (2005), and Kane and Staiger (2005). The consensus among these studies found the effect of teacher licensing on student achievement was either uncertain, nonexistent, or small. Kane, Rockoff, and Staiger (2008) support this finding with data from New York City suggesting that certification has small effects on student performance, if any. Further, people who are highly qualified and who would be good teachers have other opportunities. Citing Ballou and Podgursky (1998), Kleiner (2006, 44) notes that licensing requirements that lengthen the amount of time required to become a teacher means "that lower-qualified individuals with fewer labor market opportunities become teachers."

Ruger and Sorens (2011, 38) write that "[o]ccupational licensing has gone way too far" in Tennessee. Pro-growth policy with respect to occupational licensing will require a reversal of general historical patterns. Kleiner (2006, 5) notes that "[t]he path toward licensing usually includes initially becoming either certified or registered, but hardly ever does an occupation move from licensing to certification where others legally can do the work of certified practitioners." One Tennessee respondent to the Thumbtack.com/Kauffman survey, a beautician from Hamilton County, offered an insightful comment: "They should make having a license easy for my type of business so that I can expand [my business] and create more jobs" (Thumbtack.com 2012a, Beautician, Hamilton mouse-over text).

Indeed, Carpenter et al. (2012, 33) point out how this happened in Mississippi: "When Mississippi replaced its cosmetology-license requirement for African hair braiders with a modest registration requirement, 300 new braiders registered with the state." When licensing requirements are relaxed, entrepreneurs like the prospective Hamilton County beautician will be able to "expand and create more jobs."

[4] Friedman's analogy is also discussed in Stephenson and Wendt (2009, 187).
[5] Discussed in Kleiner (2006, 9).

LICENSING IN TENNESSEE

A 2012 study by the Institute for Justice evaluates occupational licensing for relatively low- to moderate-income jobs, and it ranks states on the number of occupations (out of 102 that they survey) that require licenses, the burdensomeness of the requirements, and the degree to which the state's requirements are "broad and onerous." The 102 occupations were chosen based on the fact that they "are recognized by the BLS [Bureau of Labor Statistics] in which practitioners make less than the national average income and where the occupation is licensed in at least one state" (Carpenter et al. 2012, 6). The survey's rankings for Tennessee and surrounding states are reported in Figure 8.1.

Figure 8.1 Ranking of Occupational Licensing, 2012

	Occupations Licensed (out of 102)	Burdensome Requirements Rank	Broad and Onerous Rank
Tennessee	53	34	13
Alabama	47	38	24
Arkansas	52	2	5
Georgia	33	18	37
Kentucky	27	15	45
Mississippi	55	45	18
Missouri	31	35	47
North Carolina	48	29	21
Virginia	46	8	11

Source: Carpenter et al. (2012).

Tennessee requires licenses for 53 out of the 102 occupations analyzed. Of Tennessee's neighboring states, only Mississippi (with 55) requires more occupations be licensed. Tennessee ranks thirty-fourth on the list of states ranked for having the most "burdensome requirements," but the state's "broad and onerous" ranking is much higher as Tennessee ranks thirteenth. As Carpenter et al. (2012) note, Tennessee is part of a group of states that licenses a large number of occupations but imposes "relatively light burdens." Tennessee fares well relative to neighboring states in terms of "burdensome requirements" as it imposes lighter burdens on licensed occupations than Arkansas, Georgia, Kentucky, North Carolina, and Virginia (but heavier burdens than Alabama, Mississippi, and Missouri). When the breadth of Tennessee licensing is considered, however, things change somewhat. Among Tennessee's neighbors, the only states that impose more "broad and onerous" restrictions on the occupations studied by Carpenter et al. (2012, 24) are Arkansas and Virginia.

Tennesseans face barriers to entry into a number of occupations that require licenses, examinations, or specific education. Tennesseans seeking to enter these occupations will pay an average of $218 and spend 222 days in training. On average, they will also take one exam (Carpenter et al. 2012). Tennessee's most strictly licensed occupations are preschool teacher, pest control applicator, vegetation pesticide handler, athletic trainer, and auctioneer. The pest control applicator and vegetation pesticide handlers in Tennessee require four years of education, but "32 and 39 states, respectively, find no need for any education requirement." Carpenter et al. also note that "[a]spiring manicurists lose 140 days to training, while the national average is 87 days" (120). To coach school sports in Tennessee requires a $285 fee and a day of education/experience, while to be a bartender requires $55 in fees, an exam, and a day of education/experience.

PRICE GOUGING LAWS

"The logic of supply and demand, so clear to economists, has had little effect on price gouging policies." Giberson (2011, 49)

The analysis of legally-imposed maximum prices using supply and demand analysis is a standard example in introductory economics classes. Price controls create unintended consequences (a concept discussed in Chapter 3). Specifically, they lead to shortages of the goods and services subject to the controls. Many states and localities have price regulations that are intended to protect consumers from large price increases after natural disasters, but the regulations themselves create shortages and the vagueness of laws against price gouging creates uncertainty for business owners (Carden 2008, 2009).

Tennessee's Price-Gouging Act of 2002, which was inspired by the threat of terrorism after September 11, creates uncertainty for businesses that now have to fear the threat of prosecution after natural disasters. In the law itself, one can read that

> [t]he intent of the general assembly...is to protect citizens from excessive and unjustified increases in the prices charged during or shortly after a declared state of emergency for goods and services that are vital or necessary for the consumer. Further, it is the intent of the general assembly that this part be liberally construed so that its beneficial purposes may be served. (Tennessee Code 2010)

At 47-18-5103 of the Tennessee Code, we read of "Prohibited acts during state of emergency." The text of the code is as follows:

> Upon the proclamation of a state of emergency and continuing until the state of emergency is terminated, it is unlawful, in any county or municipality covered by the state of emergency, for any person to charge any other person a price for any consumer food item; repair or construction services; emergency supplies; medical supplies; building materials; gasoline; transportation, freight, and storage services; or housing, that is grossly in excess of the price generally charged for the same or similar goods or services in the usual course of business immediately prior to the events giving rise to the state of emergency. An otherwise grossly excessive price increase shall not be unlawful if the person charging such higher price establishes by prima facie evidence that the increase was directly attributable to additional costs imposed on it by the supplier of the goods or services, or was directly attributable to additional costs for labor or materials used to provide the goods or services.

The text of the law is sufficiently imprecise as to create what Higgs (2006) called "regime uncertainty," which is a type of uncertainty about what the rules are and how they will be enforced. Higgs blamed regime uncertainty for the duration of the Great Depression, and it is another cost of doing business that Tennessee businesspeople must confront.

Giberson (2011) discusses the prosecution of several Tennessee firms like Weigle's, a Knoxville-area convenience store chain, in the wake of Hurricane Ike. According to Giberson, small firms like Weigle's are able to keep their prices low by purchasing on wholesale spot markets. This is risky, however, because tightening supplies (like supply disruptions resulting from natural disasters) can lead to large price increases. This is precisely what happened just before Hurricane Ike, and "[d]uring Hurricane Ike's weekend, the Knoxville area had the highest gasoline prices in the United States," and "Tennessee received more than 4,000 price complaints during the emergency period" (48). This led to prosecutions of seventeen firms, all of which denied that they had done anything wrong, but that ultimately agreed to settle with the state and with consumers. Weigle's, which settled a year after the other sixteen firms, did so "only to avoid the costs and risks inherent in protracted litigation with the state" (49). Giberson notes that "vague price gouging laws add to the uncertainty faced by merchants operating in disaster-affected areas" (53). Not only does this additional uncertainty reduce growth, it helps to exacerbate shortages and prolong recoveries after natural disasters. As Zwolinski (2008) argues, there is no compelling reason to have price gouging laws—they do more harm than good to the consumers the laws are intended to help. In the absence of price controls, supply and demand work to set the market prices of goods and services, and everyone willing and able to pay these market prices can obtain them. In the presence of price controls, there are widespread shortages, long waiting lines, and fewer of the needed goods and services available. In addition, the uncertainty regarding when and how the laws will be enforced directly stifles business activity as it increases the risks associated with doing business.

REGULATING LABOR MARKETS AND RETAIL: UNINTENDED CONSEQUENCES

Pro-growth policy involves examining regulations that are already in place. It also involves a commitment to avoid enacting policies that would compromise growth and place an unnecessary burden on the economy. Licensing is not the only way governments intervene in labor markets. Governments also pass laws to protect disadvantaged groups, to protect workers as a whole, and to raise the incomes of low-income workers. These interventions have unintended consequences that can actually work to the detriment of the laws' intended beneficiaries. As we discussed in Chapter 3, the Americans with Disabilities Act, for example, reduced employment opportunities for disabled Americans by making them more expensive to hire (Acemoglu and Angrist 2001). Regulatory cures can be worse than the diseases they seek to address.

THE LABOR MARKET: MINIMUM WAGES AND EMPLOYMENT PROTECTION

Minimum wages and employment protection legislation provide two examples of policies that have negative unintended consequences. Neumark and Wascher (2008) offer a detailed summary of research across a number of contexts in which scholars argue that minimum wages reduce employment.[6]

Employment protection might sound worker-friendly, but it isn't. Skedinger (2010) summarizes the literature and argues that the evidence on the employment effects of employment protection legislation is mixed; however, such laws strengthen the positions of the already-employed at the expense of "vulnerable groups, especially the youth" (7). According to Skedinger (2010, 7) "Employment protection therefore works as a regressive redistribution mechanism on the labour market, that is, those who are better off are favoured at the expense of those who are in a more precarious economic situation." He continues:

> Vulnerable groups in the labour force are put at a disadvantage. Above all, employment prospects deteriorate for youth, while middle-aged men benefit the most. Increased use of temporary job contracts in countries where regulations for permanent employment are stricter contribute to increased labour market segmentation. (129)

Finally, Skedinger points out that the additional security offered by employment protection legislation reduces productivity, "probably due to slower structural change and decreased work intensity among the employed, for example, through increased worker absenteeism" (7).

RETAIL: CHAIN STORES AND "WAL-MART TAXES"

States also regulate the retail environment. In the early twentieth century, the anti-chain store movement sought punitive taxes and special regulations on chain stores.[7] The modern incarnation of the anti-chain store movement is the public and political backlash against Big Box retailers like Wal-Mart. A large body of scholarly literature has grown up around the analysis of Big Box retailers—Wal-Mart, specifically.[8] While Big Box retailers are sometimes the beneficiaries of subsidies and other assistance from state and local governments, several state and local governments have enacted laws designed to disadvantage Big Box retailers. In his survey of the economic effects of Wal-Mart, Michael J. Hicks (2007) suggests that policymakers should avoid "activist policy targeting Wal-Mart, for or against" (266). Pro-growth policies would avoid "activist policy targeting" any firm, and the evidence on Big Box stores' effects on prices, incomes, and the labor market suggests that fears of these firms are misplaced.

Several scholars have studied the effect of Wal-Mart on employment. At the county level, Basker (2005) found that a new Wal-Mart created fifty new retail jobs and reduced wholesale employment by about twenty jobs. In contrast, Neumark, Zhang, and Ciccarella (2008) found that each new Wal-Mart employee took the place of 1.4 retail employees but suggested that the net employment effect was likely zero because people would find new jobs. Sobel and Dean (2008) examined the effect of Wal-Mart on the small business environment and found that Wal-Mart did not affect the number of small businesses on net.

While Goetz and Rupasingha (2006) argued that Wal-Mart reduces a community's "social capital," Carden, Courtemanche, and Meiners (2009a) found that a reduction in "social

---

[6] A comprehensive review of the effects of minimum wages on the low-income workers and economic prosperity is discussed in Chapter 7.

[7] See Hicks (2007, 7-26) for a discussion of the anti-chain movement.

[8] Carden (2012) discusses this literature in greater detail.

capital" was not supported by more comprehensive, individual-level data. Further, Carden Courtemanche, and Meiners (2009b) concluded that Wal-Mart does not affect individual values in the communities it enters. Carden and Courtemanche (2009) found that Wal-Mart influences participation in leisure activities for which the inputs can be purchased at Wal-Mart; further, there is some evidence that Wal-Mart increases the frequency with which people participate in "high culture" activities like visits to art galleries and classical music concerts. Presumably, this would be due to an income effect from Wal-Mart's low prices: people save money because of Wal-Mart's low prices and because of the company's effect on competitors' prices. They can then use these savings in a number of different ways including leisure and cultural activities such as visiting museums or attending concerts.

Hausman and Leibtag (2007, 2009) argue that stores like Wal-Mart, Sam's Club, Costco, Target, and K-Mart have had a pronounced impact on prices. Borrowing from Hausman and Leibtag's work, Furman (2005) called Wal-Mart "a progressive success story" based on the company's effect on food prices and, therefore, the purchasing power of the poor. Basker and Noel (2009) show that Wal-Mart Supercenters reduce prices, particularly at low-end stores (which presumably serve low-income consumers). Courtemanche and Carden (2011) found that Wal-Mart Supercenters increase obesity slightly, while health costs associated with the additional Wal-Mart Supercenter-related obesity only offset about 5.6 percent of the $177 Wal-Mart Supercenters saved the average household in 2002. Matsa (2011) argues that incumbents improve their inventory management after Wal-Mart enters. Pope and Pope (2012) estimate that, contrary to popular belief, Wal-Mart actually slightly raises housing values. Houses within 0.5 miles of Wal-Mart increase in value by 2-3 percent, and houses located 0.5-1 mile from Wal-Mart increase in value by 1-2 percent.

The academic literature on Big Box stores like Wal-Mart suggests that they have positive effects on the economy, largely through the money they save for consumers, but also through other channels like real estate values. Why, then, the opposition? Hicks (2007) offers some evidence that enactment of "Wal-Mart taxes"—taxes that are aimed primarily at large firms employing large numbers of low-wage workers—is consistent with the special interest theory of regulation as states with less exposure to Wal-Mart are more likely to introduce Wal-Mart taxes. When existing firms use the political process to block out new competitors they may be better off, but consumers in Tennessee are made worse off. In light of the evidence on the effects of Wal-Mart and other Big Box retailers, a "Wal-Mart tax" or a similar piece of legislation would be at odds with pro-growth policies.

CONCLUSION

Tennessee has a long and venerable history of innovation on a number of fronts. Pro-growth policy in Tennessee should be focused on establishing a regulatory environment that provides entrepreneurs with the freedom, the flexibility, and the certainty they need to focus on their core business and innovate. While Tennessee's regulatory environment ranks sixth in the 2011 Forbes "The Best States for Business and Careers" rankings, there is definitely room and need for improvement given that three of Tennessee's neighboring states rank even higher—giving them an advantage in attracting and supporting new entrepreneurial businesses.

This chapter presents several ways Tennessee policy makers can improve growth. By scaling back occupational licensing, Tennessee can create an environment in which entrepreneurs can flourish and in which consumers can have access to a wider array of goods and services at lower prices. Research suggests that occupational licensing restricts participation in the labor market, and to the degree it benefits anyone, it benefits the wealthy at the expense of the poor. Reducing occupational licensing requirements would create a more vibrant Tennessee economy without compromising the quality of the services people are able to enjoy.

Tennessee's price gouging law exemplifies statutory vagueness that creates uncertainty and increases the cost of doing business in Tennessee. As price controls and gouging statutes create shortages and increase uncertainty, if the current statues were repealed Tennesseans could enjoy a more vibrant economy and more rapid recoveries from disasters that happen from time to time. Repealing Tennessee's law against price gouging would provide Tennessee entrepreneurs with the flexibility they need to respond to emergencies, expedite recovery, and make a larger quantity of needed goods and services available to consumers. The lower probability of prosecution for violating a vague price-gouging statute will also encourage people to enter industries that supply the kinds of goods and services needed in emergencies.

A pro-growth regulatory environment also requires a hard look at policies Tennessee has not adopted yet but that might be on the horizon someday. Examples include a higher minimum wage, expanded employment protection legislation, and new taxes and regulations that target Big Box retailers like Wal-Mart. The evidence suggests that a higher minimum wage would reduce employment opportunities, especially for poor Tennesseans. Employment protection laws would likely reduce productivity and advantage relatively well-off Tennesseans at the expense of the poor and the young. In light of the evidence on the effects of Big Box stores like Wal-Mart on prices and incomes, legislation attempting to protect incumbent retailers from competition would hurt all Tennessee consumers, but especially the poor.

According to the special interest theory of regulation, firms seek regulation from the government in order to create barriers to entry that protects them from competition. This reduces output and raises their incomes, but their higher incomes come at the expense of consumers who pay higher prices, consumers who are unable to enjoy the newly-limited services, and potential competitors who are shut out of the market by regulation. The evidence suggests that regulation benefits special interests at the expense of everyone else.

In addition to targeting specific regulations like the ones detailed in this chapter for repeal, there is also a need for reforms to Tennessee's overall process of regulatory review as we discussed in Chapter 2. These broader changes to the process by which all regulations are reviewed would help to eliminate not only some of the specific regulations mentioned in this chapter, but also many other regulations in the Tennessee code that hamper economic growth. As Chapter 2 discussed, changes to the method and length of Tennessee's sunset requirement, and a more meaningful requirement for an independent, non-governmental, body to undertake serious and transparent cost-benefit and efficiency analysis, with public input, would help to improve Tennessee's regulatory code more broadly. Eliminating these burdensome regulations is an important step toward a more prosperous economy for Tennessee.

REFERENCES

Acemoglu, Daron, and Joshua D. Angrist. 2001. "Consequences of Employment Protection? The Case of the Americans with Disabilities Act." *Journal of Political Economy* 109 (5): 915-957.

Allen, Nathan, and Sander Daniels. 2012. "Thumbtack.com Small Business Survey: Methodology and Analysis." http://cdn-1.thumbtackstatic.com/media/_survey/2011/v5/ThumbtackSurveyMethodology.pdf.

Angrist, Joshua, and Jonathan Guryan. 2008. "Does Teacher Testing Raise Teacher Quality? Evidence from State Certification Requirements." *Economics of Education Review* 27: 483-503.

Ashby, Nathan J., Avilia Bueno, and Fred McMahon. 2011. *Economic Freedom of North America 2011*. Vancouver, BC: Fraser Institute.

Badenhausen, Kurt. 2011. "Best States for Business Methodology." *Forbes*, November 22. http://www.forbes.com/special-report/2011/best-states-11_rank.html.

Ballou, Dale, and Michael Podgursky. 1998. "Teacher Recruitment and Retention in Public and Private Schools." *Journal of Policy Analysis and Management* 17 (3): 393-417.

Basker, Emek. 2005. "Job Creation or Destruction? Labor-Market Effects of Wal-Mart Expansion." *Review of Economics and Statistics* 87 (1): 174-183.

Basker, Emek, and Michael Noel. 2009. "The Evolving Food Chain: Competitive Effects of Wal-Mart's Entry into the Supermarket Industry." *Journal of Economics and Management Strategy* 18 (4): 977-1009.

"Best States for Business and Careers, The." 2011. *Forbes*, November 22. http://www.forbes.com /special-report/2011/best-states-11_rank.html.

Carden, Art. 2008. "Beliefs, Bias, and Regime Uncertainty after Hurricane Katrina." *International Journal of Social Economics* 35 (7): 531-545.

———. 2009. "Sound and Fury: Rhetoric and Rebound after Katrina." *Journal of Business Valuation and Economic Loss Analysis* 4 (2): Article 2.

———. 2011. "Economic Progress and Entrepreneurial Innovation: Case Studies from Memphis." *Southern Journal of Entrepreneurship* 4 (1): 36-48.

———. 2012. "Retail Innovations in American Economic History: The Rise of Mass-Market Merchandisers." *Routledge Handbook of Major Events in American Economic History*. Forthcoming.

Carden, Art, and Charles Courtemanche. 2009. "Wal-Mart, Leisure, and Culture." *Contemporary Economic Policy* 27: 450-461.

Carden, Art, Charles Courtemanche, and Jeremy Meiners. 2009a. "Does Wal-Mart Reduce Social Capital?" *Public Choice* 138: 109-136.

———. 2009b. "Painting the Town Red? Wal-Mart and Values." *Business and Politics* 11: Article 5.

Carpenter, Dick M. II, Lisa Knepper, Angela C. Erickson, and John K. Ross. 2012. *License to Work: A National Study of Burdens from Occupational Licensing*. Arlington, VA: Institute for Justice. http://ij.org/licensetowork.

Courtemanche, Charles, and Art Carden. 2011. "Supersizing Supercenters? The Impact of Wal-Mart Supercenters on Body Mass Index and Obesity." *Journal of Urban Economics* 69: 165-181.

Fortune 500. 2012. CNNMoney/*Fortune*. http://money.cnn.com/magazines/fortune/fortune500 /2012./states/TN.html.

Friedman, Milton. 1962. *Capitalism and Freedom*. Chicago: University of Chicago Press.

Furman, Jason. 2005. "Wal-Mart: A Progressive Success Story." Center for American Progress, November 28. http://www.americanprogress.org/kf/walmart_progressive.pdf.

Giberson, Michael. 2011. "The Problem with Price Gouging Laws: Is Optimal Pricing during an Emergency Unethical?" *Regulation* 34 (1): 48-53.

Goetz, Stephan J., and Anil Rupasingha. 2006. "Wal-Mart and Social Capital." *American Journal of Agricultural Economics* 88 (5): 1304-1310.

Gwartney, James, Robert Lawson, and Joshua Hall. 2011. *Economic Freedom of the World: 2011 Report*. Vancouver, BC: Fraser Institute.

Hausman, Jerry, and Ephraim Leibtag. 2007. "Consumer Benefits from Increased Competition in Shopping Outlets: Measuring the Effect of Wal-Mart." *Journal of Applied Econometrics* 22 (7): 1157-77.

———. 2009. "CPI Bias from Supercenters: Does the BLS Know that Wal-Mart Exists?" In *Price Index Concepts and Measurement*, edited by W.E. Diewert, J.S. Greenlees, and C.R. Hulten, 203-31. Chicago, IL: University of Chicago Press.

Henderson, David R. 2008. "Rent Seeking." In *The Concise Encyclopedia of Economics*. Library of Economics and Liberty. http://www.econlib.org/library/Enc/ RentSeeking.html.

Hicks, Michael J. 2007. *The Local Economic Impact of Wal-Mart*. Youngstown, NY: Cambria Press.

Higgs, Robert. 2006. *Depression, War, and Cold War: Studies in Political Economy*. New York, NY: Oxford University Press.

Kane, Thomas J., Jonah E. Rockoff, and Douglas O. Staiger. 2005. "Identifying Effective Teachers in New York City." Paper presented at NBER Summer Institute, Cambridge, MA, July 28.

———. 2008. "What Does Certification Tell Us about Teacher Effectiveness? Evidence from New York City." *Economics of Education Review* 27 (6): 615-631.

Kane, Thomas J., and Douglas O. Staiger. 2005. "Using Imperfect Information to Identify Effective Teachers." Unpublished manuscript.

Kleiner, Morris M. 2006. *Licensing Occupations: Ensuring Quality or Restricting Competition?* Kalamazoo, MI: W.E. Upjohn Institute for Employment Research.

Kleiner, Morris M., and Alan B. Krueger. 2008. "The Prevalence and Effects of Occupational Licensing." NBER Working Paper 14308.

———. 2009. "Analyzing the Extent and Influence of Occupational Licensing on the Labor Market." NBER Working Paper 14979.

Kleiner, Morris M. and Robert T. Kudrle. 2000. "Does Regulation Affect Economic Outcomes? The Case of Dentistry." *Journal of Law and Economics* 43 (2): 547-582.

Kleiner, Morris M. and Daniel L. Petree. 1988. "Unionism and Licensing of Public School Teachers: Impact on Wages and Educational Output." In *When Public Sector Workers Unionize*, edited by Richard B. Freeman and Casey Ichniowski, 305-19. Chicago, IL: University of Chicago Press.

Krueger, Anne. 1974. "The Political Economy of the Rent-Seeking Society." *American Economic Review* 64: 291-303.

Law, Marc T. and Sukkoo Kim. 2005. "Specialization and Regulation: The Rise of Professionals and the Emergence of Occupational Licensing Regulation." *Journal of Economic History* 65 (3): 723-756.

Matsa, David. 2011. "Competition and Product Quality in the Supermarket Industry." *Quarterly Journal of Economics* 126: 1539-1591.

Neumark, David and William Wascher. 2008. *Minimum Wages*. Cambridge, MA: MIT Press.

Neumark, David, Junfu Zhang, and Stephen Ciccarella. 2008. "The Effects of Wal-Mart on Local Labor Markets." *Journal of Urban Economics* 63: 405-430.

Pope, Devin G., and Jaren C. Pope. 2012. "When Wal-Mart Comes to Town: Always Low Housing Prices? Always?" NBER Working Paper 18111.

Ruger, William P. and Jason Sorens. 2011. *Freedom in the 50 States: An Index of Personal and Economic Freedom*. Arlington, VA: Mercatus Center. http://mercatus.org/sites/default /files/publication/Freedom_in_the_50_States.pdf.

Skedinger, Per. 2010. *Employment Protection Legislation: Evolution, Effects, Winners and Losers*. Translated by Laura A. Wideburg. Cheltenham, UK: Edward Elgar.

Sobel, Russell S., and Andrea Dean. 2008. "Has Wal-Mart Buried Mom and Pop? The Impact of Wal-Mart on Self Employment and Small Establishments in the United States." *Economic Inquiry* 46: 676-695.

Stephenson, E. Frank, and Erin E. Wendt. 2009. "Occupational Licensing: Scant Treatment in Labor Texts." *Econ Journal Watch* 6 (2): 181-194.

Stigler, George J. 1971. "The Theory of Economic Regulation." *Bell Journal of Economics and Management Science* 2 (1): 3-21.

Tennessee Code. 2010. http://law.justia.com/codes/tennessee/2010/title-47/chapter-18/part-51/.

Thumbtack.com with Ewing Marion Kaffuman Memorial Foundation. 2012a. *Tennessee Small Business Friendliness*. http://www.thumbtack.com/tn/.

Thumbtack.com with Ewing Marion Kauffman Memorial Foundation. 2012b. *United States Small Business Friendliness*. http://www.thumbtack.com/survey#states.

Tullock, Gordon. 1967. "The Welfare Costs of Tariffs, Monopolies, and Theft." *Western Economic Journal* 5 (3): 224-232.

Zwolinski, Matthew. 2008. "The Ethics of Price Gouging." *Business Ethics Quarterly* 18 (3): 347-378.

CHAPTER 9

EDUCATION REFORM IN TENNESSEE: SPENDING MONEY ON WHAT MATTERS

by Joshua C. Hall and Ashley S. Harrison

Freedom and Prosperity in Tennessee

9

EDUCATION REFORM IN TENNESSEE: SPENDING MONEY ON WHAT MATTERS

Joshua C. Hall and Ashley S. Harrison

Education policy is very important to a prosperous economy. Educational funding is at the center of the prevailing debate regarding education policy and is often portrayed as an investment in future prosperity. Investment in education can produce positive returns. For example, a recent research study found that Tennessee taxpayers received $1.64 for each $1.00 invested in The University of Tennessee at Chattanooga (UTC) students, equivalent to an 8.92 percent rate of return (Probasco Chair of Free Enterprise 2010). However, funding alone, especially in K-12 education, does not always yield better results (Hanushek 1986, 1997).

According to recent National Center for Education Statistics (NCES) data, Tennessee spent over $8.6 billion on K-12 education, or just under $9,000 per pupil, during the 2008-09 school year (2012a). That amounts to over $1,300 a year from every man, woman, and child in Tennessee in taxpayer support for K-12 education. As tax dollars have alternative uses both in the public sector or remaining in private hands, it is important to ensure that each dollar spent in elementary and secondary education is being used efficiently.

In recent decades, economists have taken the tools they use to study production in other parts of the economy and applied them to the production of education. These "education production functions" have provided insight into the "black box" that is the educational process. While the results from these studies are not always satisfying in that they often do not point to simple solutions, they have highlighted factors that education policy *cannot* influence, as well as identified a few that seem to matter (Hall 2006).

The purpose of this chapter is to provide a summary of this research to increase general understanding of current educational debates in Tennessee. The literature review is also used to identify the school district level factors influencing test scores in Tennessee. As we will see, the factors that matter for school district performance are not those that are frequently the source of public debate.

THE ROLE OF MONEY IN EDUCATION

Tennessee spends nearly $9,000 annually for every elementary and secondary education student. While $9,000 may appear to be a significant amount, it is relatively low when compared to other states. According to the National Center for Education Statistics (2012a), the average state, Virginia for example, spent over $12,000 per pupil during the 2008-2009 school year. The variance expands when comparing Tennessee to other individual states. At the upper level, some states like Connecticut, New York, New Jersey, and Rhode Island spent over $15,000 a student.[1] Tennessee has the fourth lowest spending among all 50 states. The only states with lower spending per pupil are Utah ($8,494), Idaho ($8,618), and Oklahoma ($8,716). Compared to its neighboring states, Tennessee is therefore clearly at the bottom, as can be seen in Figure 9.1.

Figure 9.1: Tennessee's Education Spending Compared to Its Neighbors, 2008-09 School Year

State	Spending Per Pupil	National Rank
Alabama	$10,550	39
Arkansas	$10,152	42
Georgia	$11,468	27
Kentucky	$10,208	41
Mississippi	$8,948	46
Missouri	$11,403	30
North Carolina	$9,567	45
Tennessee	**$8,895**	**47**
Virginia	$12,264	19

Sources: NCES (2012a) and authors' calculations.

Tennessee's low ranking on spending per pupil is often taken as a prima facie case of poor education.[2] Is this really the case? At the most basic level, the goal of K-12 education should be the successful completion of high school. The NCES produces comparable data across the 50 states each year on the percentage of 18-24 year olds who completed high school. A three-year average from 2007-2009 is provided in the most recent edition (2012a) to minimize the variation that might occur in any one-year period.

As depicted in Figure 9.2, Tennessee fares quite well compared to its neighbors in terms of high school completion. From 2007-2009, 83.3 percent of 18-24 year olds in Tennessee were high school completers, ranking the state 30th among the 50 states. In fact, Tennessee had a higher completion rate than all of its neighbors except for Virginia. Georgia spent over $2,500 per pupil more than Tennessee and had a high school completion rate that was 4.3 percentage points lower. Missouri also spent over $2,500 per pupil more than Tennessee and experienced a result slightly worse than Tennessee's on this measure.

---

[1] The NCES (2012a) data shows that spending per-pupil in the District of Columbia schools exceeded $27,000 per pupil during the 2008-2009 school year.

[2] See, for example, the 2008 Today show episode that picks Clarksville Tennessee as the worst place to raise a family in the United States primarily because education spending is low! (BestLife Magazine/Today Show 2008) http://today.msnbc.msn.com/id/24713234/ns/today-today_101/t/best-places-raise-family/#.T-InrByBVbQ.

Figure 9.2: Tennessee's High School Completion Rate Compared to Its Neighbors, 2007-2009

State	Percent of 18-24 Year Olds Who Were High School Completers, 3-Year Average	National Rank
Alabama	80.3	43
Arkansas	81.6	39
Georgia	79.0	47
Kentucky	82.9	32
Mississippi	79.4	45
Missouri	82.7	34
North Carolina	82.9	33
Tennessee	**83.3**	**30**
Virginia	86.9	11

Sources: NCES (2012a) and authors' calculations.

This data, of course, does not mean that money does not matter. It merely means that money is not the *only* thing that matters. It is clear evidence against naive arguments that favor increasing education spending without specifying what it should be spent on. Tennessee policymakers could raise taxes to accommodate an increase in per pupil spending equivalent to Missouri or Georgia, but if the additional funds are not spent on productive activities, the large increase in spending could produce little to no improvement.

Clearly, a wide variety of factors contributes to measures of school outcomes such as graduation rates or test scores. Family influences, peer influences, school environment, school resources, and innate ability are all determinants in advancing students from kindergarten to graduation. In a simple table or graph, it is impossible to control for all of these other factors, which is why economists and other social scientists turn to larger-scale statistical analysis in an attempt to account for these components simultaneously. The goal is to isolate the effect of one factor–such as school spending–while holding all other factors constant. Consequently, we can be more confident that school spending is having an effect on the outcome variable and not something related to school spending, for example teacher salaries.

Empirical studies relating school, family, and peer inputs into the production of education outputs (graduation rates, test scores, college enrollment, life outcomes, etc.) can be traced back to 1966 and the so-called "Coleman Report" (Coleman et al. 1966). The study, resulting from an explicit directive included in the Civil Rights Act of 1964, examined over 800,000 public school students across the United States and produced numerous findings. Perhaps the most revolutionary result found that variations among schools' inputs and resources explained very little of the differences between student outcomes (Hanushek 1986). Coleman et al. (1966) instead found that family background and peers played a large role.

The somewhat counterintuitive result, spending does not matter, generated considerable controversy and fostered subsequent research into the relationship between school inputs and school performance. In 1986, economist Eric Hanushek of the University of Rochester summarized the results of 147 published educational production function studies. Sixty-five studies examined the effect of per pupil expenditures on various measures of educational outcomes such as graduation rates or test scores. Only 13 studies of the 65 found a statistically significant relationship between expenditures and school outcomes. Three studies found a statistically significant negative relationship. The vast majority, however, found no statistically significant relationship between spending per pupil and outcomes.

Similar to the Coleman Report, Hanushek's research has generated considerable new inquiries examining his results and methodology employed to evaluate the literature (Greenwald, Hedges, and Laine 1996; Hanushek 1996; Krueger 1998). By the time Hanushek (1997) published a follow-up review a decade later, 376 published education production function studies had been published. As Hanushek (2003) reports, 163 of these studies controlled for expenditure per pupil and only 27 found a positive and statistically significant relationship between spending and outcome variables. Again, a large number of these 163 studies found no clear relationship between spending per pupil and school outcomes.

The message to be derived from this literature is not that money *never* matters. Certainly it does matter in many places and circumstances. However, aggregate analyses indicate that no clear systematic relationship has been found between spending per pupil and school outcomes. Accordingly, simplistic solutions to school improvement problems, such as increased school spending, are likely to prove ineffective. Instead, factors affecting school improvement are likely either outside the direct control of policymakers (family and peer effects) or related to how schools are structured, financed, and operated. To improve school performance, the legislature should explore policies that change the other variables, holding spending constant.

AN EDUCATION PRODUCTION FUNCTION MODEL FOR TENNESSEE

To provide additional insight into possible avenues for education reform in Tennessee, we estimated an education production function for Tennessee school districts. We used individual school districts as the unit of analysis for two primary reasons. First and foremost, a considerable amount of state education policy is implemented via school districts. Second, many decisions made at the district level significantly influence educational outcomes, such as school financing (Fischel 2001; Hall 2007) or teacher pay and allocation decisions (Podgursky and Springer 2011). For these reasons, many empirical studies of education production, as well as lawsuits concerning school finance, also focus on the school district and its efficiency (Ruggerio 2001).

We constructed our data set primarily from the annual Tennessee Department of Education (2012) report cards. To adequately control for important demographic factors, the data obtained from the Tennessee Department of Education was matched with data from the special school district tabulation from the 2000 census conducted by the U.S. Census Bureau and published by the National Center for Education Statistics (2012b). We, therefore, focus on the 1999-2000 school year since that is the time frame for which all the necessary family demographic controls can be obtained.

The sample was limited to K-12 school districts and districts with missing data were excluded. Data from 121 school districts for the 1999-2000 school year comprised the sample. A list of the variables examined and their descriptive statistics are displayed in Figure 9.3. Before proceeding with our empirical analysis, we will discuss the variables chosen for our analysis.

Figure 9.3: Summary Statistics of Tennessee School District Data

Variable	Min	Max	Mean	St. Dev.
High School Math Competency Scores	51.0	96.0	73.23	9.42
Districts Collectively Bargaining With Teachers	0	1	0.69	0.46
% White Students	11.6	100.0	87.98	16.21
% Students Receiving Free or Reduced Price Meals	5.7	85.1	43.11	14.28
% Students Title 1	1.3	100.0	31.77	25.77
District Per Pupil Expenditure	$4,281	$7,872	$5,446.79	$642.88
Average Teacher Salary in District	$29,774	$44,318	$33,636.43	$3,347.91
% Funding from Local Sources	12.5	64.7	32.20	11.78
Median Household Income	$10,794	$32,495	$16,889.20	$3,055.70
% District Residents with B.A. or Higher	4.1	44.4	12.84	6.91
% District Students Enrolled Non-Public Schools	0.0	35.98	6.27	5.28
Degree of Racial Fractionalization	0.0	0.56	0.16	0.15
Teacher-Student Ratio	12.9	18.7	15.70	1.10
District Attendance Rate	87.9	97.5	93.53	1.78

Sources: Tennessee Department of Education (2012); NCES (2012b).

The outcome variable selected to measure school district performance was their scores on the grade 9 Tennessee Comprehensive Assessment Program (TCAP) Competency Test in mathematics. We chose this measure of school outcomes for two reasons. First, exams in high school tend to be more representative of the long-run performance of a school district because the ability to do well on a ninth grade exam is indicative of persistent school quality. Second, math scores tend to be a superior measure of school district performance because there is less subjectivity in grading and, thus, less statistical noise in the measure.

The next variable is a binary variable that takes a value of one if the school district engaged in collective bargaining with its teachers and a zero otherwise. The issue of collective bargaining for teachers has been a serious policy issue in Tennessee for some time. Most recently, in the winter of 2011, a bill was introduced in the Tennessee House of Representatives that would eliminate the requirement that Tennessee school districts engage in contract negotiations with teachers' unions (Schelzig 2011). In June of 2011, Governor Bill Haslam signed into law legislation repealing an earlier law which mandated collective bargaining for elementary and secondary school teachers in Tennessee public schools

(Ghianni 2011).[3] Thus, while in our sample nearly 70 percent of Tennessee school districts collectively bargained with their teachers, that percentage is expected to decline in the future.

A recent Associated Press analysis reported that Tennessee school districts that did not engage in collective bargaining had higher test scores than those that did (Schelzig 2012). The same study showed that collective bargaining districts achieved larger gains during the previous year, according to news reports. While, the study did not, to our knowledge, control for other factors that might explain test scores across school districts, larger gains on state exams could be the result of starting from a lower base, not necessarily the result of collective bargaining directly.

The intent of this study is to control for collective bargaining to discern if districts that engage in collective bargaining have lower test scores, other things being equal, than districts that do not collectively bargain. The results would be consistent with the Associated Press study (Schelzig 2012) as well as much of the economics literature on the effects of teacher unions on educational achievement. Hoxby's (1996) study is widely considered the best of the empirical studies on the relationship between collective bargaining and student performance. She finds that increases in collective bargaining by teachers have led to an increase in school spending, primarily on teacher salaries. This increase in spending has been accompanied by a decline in teacher productivity, leading to an overall decline in student performance as measured by dropout rates. Peltzman (1993, 1996) and Moe (2009) find similar results. Proposed explanations for this decline in productivity are numerous, but typically target the effect of collective bargaining on the ability to reward effective teachers and replace ineffective teachers.

At the same time, some other empirical studies have shown that teachers unions raise achievement (Eberts and Stone 1984; Kleiner and Petree 1988). This could be for a variety of reasons, but typically attributed to empirical evidence that unionized teachers have higher salaries and their districts have more standardized curriculum and instruction (Baugh and Stone 1982; Johnson 1984; Eberts and Stone 1986). Finally, a recent study by Lindy (2011) found collective bargaining by teachers leads to higher SAT scores, but lower graduation rates, suggesting that the effects of unionization on student performance are not uniform across students. While our measure cannot show the effect of collective bargaining on different types of students, it does summarize the general relationship between collective bargaining and student achievement in Tennessee.

The remainder of our control variables can be separated into one of two categories. The first broad category—family and peer effects—has been widely used in similar studies to aid in the explanation of student performance across various time periods and contexts (Coleman et al. 1966; Hanushek 1986, 1997, 2003; Hanushek et al. 2003; Hall 2006, 2007; Houtenville and Conway 2008; Chakraborty 2009). While these effects are actually different influences, at our level of analysis it is often difficult, if not impossible, to disentangle empirically whether a particular variable is measuring a peer or family effect. The variables used as proxy for these family and peer effects have, according to scholarly literature, been identified as significant contributors to school district performance.

The two most obvious socioeconomic variables are ones that directly influence demand for high quality public schools. For example, parents with a bachelor's degree or more are likely to demand better test scores in addition to expending their own time and resources to ensure that the local schools are run efficiently. Similarly, families in school

---

[3] For a good scholarly overview of the legal and policy issues surrounding this change, see Gibbons (2012).

districts with higher median incomes will also have a higher demand for school quality. Other socioeconomic controls include the racial diversity of the district (percent white students and degree of racial fractionalization), percentage of students receiving free or reduced price meals, and the percentage of students eligible for funding under Title 1 of the Elementary and Secondary Education Act.[4] By controlling for the level of school resources in our analysis, these socioeconomic factors should not be thought of as occurring through school funding, but instead through direct family and peer effects.

The remaining variables are directly or indirectly related to state and school district policy. The most obvious of these is the district expenditure per pupil. As discussed earlier, a large body of literature finds no relationship in the aggregate between expenditure per pupil and school performance. Including the variable in our model allows us to confirm if similar results are observed for Tennessee, as well as ensure that all other factors that could reasonably influence student performance are being held constant.

How much schools spend is important, but how funds are spent is significant as well. The largest expense of any school district is teacher salaries, but differences do exist across districts in this regard. As can be seen in Figure 9.3, during the 1999-2000 school year the average teacher salary across Tennessee school districts ranged from over $29,774 to a high of $44,318. Higher teacher spending could be the result of the deliberate decision to pay teachers more, or it could reflect the decision to have more experienced teachers that are higher up on the teacher salary schedule. Unfortunately, no comprehensive data on teacher experience across school districts exists for Tennessee so we were unable to make strong inferences from the teacher salary variable in addition to being unable to control for teacher experience.

Research by Hoxby (1999) and Hall (2007) has pointed to the efficiency of locally financed public schools for many of the same reasons as pointed out by Glaeser (1996) about the efficiency of local property taxation. The basic reasoning behind the importance of local financing is that in a system of locally financed schools, the capitalization of school quality in housing prices helps to ensure that all local taxpayers are concerned about whether the local schools have enough money and how efficiently it is being spent.[5]

The ratio of teachers to students is also included as a proxy for class size, which has been one of the most debated topics in the literature in recent decades (Hanushek 1999a, 1999b; Hoxby 2000b; Krueger 2003; Rivkin, Hanushek, and Kain 2005; Cho, Glewwe, and Whitler 2012). In Tennessee, this topic has experienced immense discussion largely due to the famous Tennessee Project STAR experiment where some students in K-3 grades were randomly assigned into classrooms with 13-17 students and others were randomly assigned into rooms with 22 to 25 students (Mosteller 1995). According to Chingos and Whitehurst's (2011) review of the Tennessee Project STAR experiment, "large class-size reductions, on the order of magnitude of 7-10 fewer students per class, can have significant long-term effects on student achievement and other meaningful outcomes" (1). While, the evidence appears to indicate that class size reductions matter, policy relevance of this literature is not always

---

[4] While many studies include just one measure of racial diversity in the regression, we include two for reasons laid out in Hall and Leeson (2010a, 2010b). The basic reasoning is that many empirical studies include a variable like % white students as a crude proxy of diversity when in fact they should be measuring the degree of diversity using something like a Hirschman-Herfinahl Index. See Hall and Leeson (2010a) for more detail on how the racial fractionalization variable is calculated.

[5] This is also why taxpayers often vote for more money for schools even though a majority of voters do not have children in the public schools (Hilber and Mayer 2009).

straightforward, primarily, because *how* lower class sizes are achieved is vital to policy effectiveness. For example, one way to lower class sizes is to hire more teachers. If school districts are already employing the best teachers available, then the newly hired teachers may lower the quality of the average teacher in a district.

So the question of whether class size reductions enhance student achievement depends largely upon a variety of tradeoffs that are difficult to evaluate. Is a student better off in a large classroom with an above-average teacher or a small classroom with an average teacher? Recent research tries to answer this question, but its general applicability is unclear, although it does highlight how strong these offsetting effects can be. Consider Jepsen and Rivkin (2009), who analyzed California's expenditure of over $1 billion on class size reductions. Their results denote that while smaller classes improved learning, they also caused a large increase in the number of teachers without prior experience or full certification. Jepsen and Rivkin estimate the $1 billion expenditure actually led to small gains in student achievement. Other examples of offsetting behavior include increases in class size in upper grades to minimize the cost of class size reductions in lower grades (Sims 2009).

Unsurprisingly, research has shown that student performance is higher in school districts with higher attendance rates (Lamdin 1996). To account for this, we include the attendance rate in the district. Finally, we include the percentage of students in the district enrolled in non-public schools. In doing so, we followed Hall and Vedder (2003-04) who used this variable to control for the degree of competition and found areas with greater competition from private schools also have higher public school performance, other things being equal.[6] Hoxby (2000a) finds a similar competition effect for public schools, although Rothstein (2007) disputes this finding. It is also possible for private schools to lead to lower student achievement in public schools if the market is such that many of the high-achieving students attend private schools.[7] Note that in order to evaluate whether this is good or bad from society's viewpoint we would have to examine the net effect on private and public school students.

THE EMPIRICAL RESULTS

To verify the extent to which the above relationships hold in Tennessee, we estimated the full model using regression analysis.[8] Our analysis uses the variables described in Table 9.3 to explain school district math competency scores. Column 1 of Table 9.4 provides the name of each variable, with column 2 giving the estimated coefficients. Standard errors are presented in column 3. The stars next to the coefficients represent the extent to which the estimated relationship is statistically significant at conventional levels.

---

[6] Ponzo (2011) finds similar results for Italian public schools. Vedder and Hall (2000) also find that public school teachers make more when more competition from private schools is present.

[7] This argument is in the same vein as the "cream skimming" arguments regarding private and charter schools. The answer as to whether or not cream skimming exists depends on the place and characteristics of the local market (Epple and Romano 1998, 2008; Figlio and Stone 2001).

[8] For a clear and concise background into regression analysis and empirical work in economics, we recommend Chapter 2 of Hicks (2007).

Figure 9.4: Determinants of Tennessee School District 9th Grade Math Test Scores

Variable	Coefficient		Standard Error
Constant	-30.480		47.299
Districts Collectively Bargaining With Teachers	-2.544	*	1.526
% White Students	.167		.101
% Students Receiving Free or Reduced Price Meals	-.234	**	.098
% Students Title 1	.029		.037
District Per Pupil Expenditure	-.004		.003
Average Teacher Salary in District	.001	**	.001
% Funding from Local Sources	-.044		.125
Median Household Income	.000		.001
% District Residents with B.A. or Higher	.335		.229
% District Students Enrolled Non-Public Schools	-.131		.189
Degree of Racial Fractionalization	8.332		10.294
Teacher-Student Ratio	-2.028	**	.967
District Attendance Rate	1.242	***	.437
Number of Observations	121		
R squared	0.478		

Sources: Tennessee Department of Education (2012); NCES (2012b).
Note: Dependent variable is High School Math Competency Scores. All data is for the 1999-2000 school year. * represents significance at the 10 percent level; ** represents significance at the 5 percent level; and *** represents significance at the 1 percent level.

In this basic specification, the first thing to note is the negative relationship between school district collective bargaining and test scores on the TCAP exam. Statistically significant at the ten percent level, the coefficient in column 2 suggests that districts that collectively bargain have math test scores that are 2.54 percent lower than districts that do not collectively bargain. This seems to confirm at least a portion of the Associated Press analysis mentioned earlier, showing that districts that collectively bargain had lower test scores than those that did not.

In terms of family and peer variables, the only one that is statistically significant is the percentage of students receiving free or reduced price meals, which is negatively related to student achievement as expected. Contrary to Hall and Leeson (2010a), racial fractionalization does not negatively influence educational performance in Tennessee as it did in their Ohio sample. The lack of a relationship between median household income and math scores or college attainment and test scores is likely the result of a strong relationship between these two variables.[9]

---

[9] A high correlation between two independent variables is called multicollinearity. After reviewing the options of dealing with multicollinearity as presented by Kennedy (2003, 210-11), we decided to keep both variables in the model as dropping one of the variables would not reduce the variance of the remaining variables enough to overcome the bias introduced by the specification error.

Turning our attention to policy-relevant variables, we note that, consistent with the previous literature, spending per pupil is not positively related to math scores in a statistically significant manner. (In fact, the relationship is negative.) Average teacher salaries are positively related to math scores at the 5 percent level of significance. The coefficient, 0.001, indicates that if average teacher salaries increased $1,000, then the student achievement variable, TCAP score, would experience a one point increase. District expenditures would increase substantially to realize a relatively modest gain, for example $2.6 million would be required to fund a $1,000 increase in average teacher salaries in Hamilton County. However, this finding provides insight regarding education policy. First, expenditure per pupil is held constant, thus the positive relationship likely reflects that classroom teachers contribute more to student achievement than other non-instructional school activities. Secondly, due to the absence of a teacher experience variable, teacher salaries may be reflecting teacher experience instead of teacher salaries since school districts with higher average teacher salaries are likely to have more experienced teachers.

Higher teacher-student ratios—again holding expenditure per pupil constant—are negatively related to high school math competency scores. As noted earlier, this relationship is consistent with much of the literature. However, for effective classroom reduction policy, legislators should cautiously examine how class sizes are reduced to ensure that 1) the benefits are actually realized, and 2) that they are valued more than alternative uses of the tax dollars required to fund classroom reduction policies.

Finally, we found an extremely strong positive relationship between the student attendance rate in a school district and their scores on the math competency test. In all likelihood, this variable represents a combination of district policy as well as parental influence. A growing body of literature at the student level has begun highlighting the negative effects of missing even a few days of school has on student performance (Gottfried 2010, 2011). Attention focused on maximizing student attendance through frequent reminders to family about student absenteeism and celebration of good attendance seems like a cost-effective way to improve educational attainment in Tennessee (Sheldon and Epstein 2004).

OTHER EDUCATIONAL POLICY ISSUES: SCHOOL CONSOLIDATION

While district-level analysis has highlighted many of the important relationships in education policy, the methodological approach does not address an additional educational issue facing Tennessee: school consolidation. In February 2011, Tennessee Governor Bill Haslam signed Senate Bill 25/House Bill 51, a bill that delays the planned consolidation of the Memphis and Shelby County Schools until further study can be conducted. A thorough study is important as the issues driving the current consolidation may cause policymakers to miss the bigger picture of the entire state education system in the long run.

Economists speak of people "voting with their feet" in choosing where to live. One of the primary factors in choosing where to live is the quality of the local public school district. A large number of local school districts allow the public school system to accommodate a variety of different household demands for education. Shopping for schools is in many ways no different than shopping for groceries. It is a much more critical and *costly* decision because it involves children and moving. Providing families with a large number of school districts to choose among without considering private schools or leaving the city is an important component of Tennessee's economic growth.

Typically, the benefits of school consolidation are predicated on the individuals in the affected area not having their own goals and plans. Families want choice not for its intrinsic value, but because it allows them to attain desired benefits for their children. Perhaps they want their children to attend a school, not because of smaller class sizes, but because everyone knows everyone and there is a sense of community.[10] A district of 150,000 students cannot and will not be able to provide that and thus some parents will opt-out of the public system.

The history of recent school consolidation in Tennessee shows that consolidation has increased private school enrollment. A 2001 study conducted by the Memphis City Schools on school consolidation found that private school enrollment increased in Chattanooga, Knoxville, and Nashville following consolidation. Over time, school district enrollments change as people decide to live outside the county or send their children to private schools. Even when enrollment increases because more people are moving to the metropolitan area because of job or family reasons, it often rises slower in the consolidated county schools than in the metropolitan area as a whole, as was the case in Knoxville (Pohlmann, Clay, and Goings 2001).

Beyond these enrollment issues, more school districts are beneficial not only because it creates choice, but because it creates competition. Areas with more school districts have been found to have higher test scores than areas with fewer school districts (Staley and Blair 1997; Hoxby 2000a). Competition also helps keep costs in line. While there is some evidence of cost savings from rural school consolidation (Duncombe and Yinger 2010), few studies have systematically investigated consolidation of large school districts similar to the district consolidation being proposed in Memphis. One recent study conducted by two education professors from The University of Tennessee at Martin reviewed the decade following the consolidation of the Chattanooga City School district with the county system (Cox and Cox 2010). They found a 50 percent increase in school district expenditures the decade following consolidation, with little corresponding benefit in terms of student performance.

CONCLUSION

Effective public policies distribute tax dollars to programs that produce positive gains to the state economy or benefit citizens more than the next best alternative use of those funds. As evidenced by The Economic Impact of UTC study, an investment of tax dollars in education can generate favorable results (Probasco Chair of Free Enterprise 2010). However, all investments are not equal. The educational output measured in this chapter, high school student achievement, was found, in aggregate, to have no clear systematic relationship with per pupil expenditures. One significant policy implication derived from this study is that more money does not always produce greater results. The cost of reducing class sizes or pupil-teacher ratio demonstrates this principle. While lower class sizes appear to raise average student achievement, the costs of systematically lowering class sizes are substantial

---

[10] There are public school districts that are small enough (less than 1000 students K-12) to provide such a learning environment, but they are in states like Ohio that have many more school districts (over 600 in Ohio's case).

and could potentially produce greater results if spent elsewhere in schools, such as in efforts to increase attendance rates.

The education production model for Tennessee also highlighted several areas where non-funding related policies could positively affect educational output, such as the elimination of collective bargaining requirements for school districts. However, policymakers should also be cognizant of the many factors influencing schools and educational outcomes of students that may not be responsive to education policy reform. The prime drivers of school district achievement are factors relating to family and socioeconomic status. This is not to suggest that socioeconomic status is the only thing that matters, but that policymakers should be realistic with their expectations of policy effects.

In terms of day-to-day impact on the lives of the average Tennessean, education is probably the most important activity undertaken by Tennessee government at any level. For state policymakers to create effective legislation, it is critical that they possess a good understanding of the dynamics of education. By focusing attention on sensible policy changes that will either raise achievement at low cost or lower cost at no risk to student achievement, the productivity of Tennessee schools will be improved.

REFERENCES

Baugh, William H., and Joe A. Stone. 1982. "Teachers, Unions and Wages in the 1970s: Unionism Now Pays." *Industrial and Labor Relations Review* 35 (3): 368-376.

BestLife Magazine/Today Show. 2008. *The 100 Best Places to Raise A Family.* http://today.msnbc.msn.com/id/24713234/ns/today-today_101/t/best-places-raise-family/#.T-InrByBVbQ.

Chakraborty, Kalyan. 2009. "Efficiency in Public Education: The Role of Socio-Economic Variables." *Research in Applied Economics* 1 (1): 1-18.

Chingos, Matthew, and Grover Whitehurst. 2011. *Class Size: What Research Says and What It Means for State Policy*. Washington, D.C.: Brookings Institution.

Cho, Hyunkuk, Paul Glewwe, and Melissa Whitler. 2012. "Do Reductions in Class Size Raise Students' Test Scores? Evidence from Population Variation in Minnesota's Elementary Schools." *Economics of Education Review* 31 (3): 77-95.

Coleman, James S., Ernest Q. Campbell, Carol J. Hobson, James McPartland, Alexander M. Mood, Frederic D. Weinfeld, and Robert L. York. 1966. *Equality of Educational Opportunity*. Washington, D.C.: Government Printing Office.

Cox, Betty, and Becky Cox. 2010. "A Decade of Results? A Case for School District Consolidation?" *Education* 131 (1): 83-92.

Duncombe, William D., and John M. Yinger. 2010. "School District Consolidation: The Benefits and Costs." *School Administrator* 67 (5): 10-17.

Eberts, Randall W., and Joe A. Stone. 1984. *Unions and Public Schools: The Effect of Collective Bargaining on American Education*. Lexington, MA: Lexington Books.

———. 1986. "Teacher Unions and the Cost of Public Education." *Economic Inquiry* 24 (4): 631-643.

Epple, Dennis, and Richard E. Romano. 1998. "Competition between Private and Public Schools, Vouchers, and Peer-Group Effects." *American Economic Review* 88 (1): 33-62.

————. 2008. "Educational Vouchers and Cream Skimming." *International Economic Review* 49 (4): 1395-1435.

Figlio, David N., and Joe A. Stone. 2001. "Can Public Policy Affect Private School Cream Skimming?" *Journal of Urban Economics* 49 (2): 240-266.

Fischel, William. 2001. "Homevoters, Municipal Corporate Governance, and the Benefit View of the Property Tax." *National Tax Journal* 54 (1): 157-173.

Ghianni, Tim. 2011. "Tennessee Limits Collective Bargaining Rights for Teachers." *Reuters*, June 1. http://www.reuters.com/article/2011/06/01/us-unions-states-tennessee-idUSTRE75071I20110601.

Gibbons, William. 2012. "Comment: Tennessee Tussle: The Struggle over Tennessee's Collective Bargaining Curtailment and Its Potential Future Impact." *Tennessee Journal of Law and Policy* 8: 142-164.

Glaeser, Edward. 1996. "The Incentive Effects of Property Taxes on Local Governments." *Public Choice* 89 (1-2): 93-111.

Gottfried, Michael A. 2010. "Evaluating the Relationship between Student Attendance and Achievement in Urban Elementary and Middle Schools: An Instrumental Variables Approach." *American Educational Research Journal* 47 (2): 434-465.

————. 2011. "The Detrimental Effect of Missing School." *American Journal of Education* 117 (2): 147-182.

Greenwald, Rob, Larry V. Hedges, and Richard D. Laine. 1996. "The Effect of School Resources on Student Achievement." *Review of Educational Research* 66 (3): 361-396.

Hall, Joshua. 2006. "The Dilemma of School Finance Reform." *Journal of Social, Political, and Economic Studies* 31 (2): 175-190.

————. 2007. "Local School Finance and Productive Efficiency: Evidence from Ohio." *Atlantic Economic Journal* 35 (3): 289-301.

Hall, Joshua, and Peter T. Leeson. 2010a. "Racial Fractionalization and School Performance." *Journal of Economics and Sociology* 69 (2): 736-758.

————. 2010b. "The Unimportance of Spending: How Fractionalization Affects School Performance." *International Advances in Economic Research* 16 (1): 130-131.

Hall, Joshua, and Richard Vedder. 2003-04. "The Impact of Private Schools on Public School Performance: Evidence from Ohio." *Journal of Economics and Politics* 16 (1): 77-92.

Hanushek, Eric A. 1986. "The Economics of Schooling: Production and Efficiency in Public Schools." *Journal of Economic Literature* 24 (3): 1141-1177.

————. 1996. "A More Complete Picture of School Resource Policies." *Review of Educational Research* 66 (3): 397-409.

————. 1997. "Assessing the Effects of School Resources on Student Performance: An Update." *Education Evaluation and Policy Analysis* 19 (2): 141-164.

————. 1999a. "The Evidence on Class Size." In *Earning and Learning: How Schools Matter*, edited by Susan Mayer and Paul Peterson, 131-68. Washington, DC: Brookings Institution.

———. 1999b. "Some Findings from an Independent Investigation of the Tennessee Star Experiment and from Other Investigations of Class Size Effects." *Education Evaluation and Policy Analysis* 21 (2): 143-163.

———. 2003. "The Failure of Input-Based Schooling Policies." *Economic Journal* 113: F64-F98.

Hanushek, Eric A., John Kain, Jacob Markman, and Steven G. Rivkin. 2003. "Does Peer Ability Affect Student Achievement?" *Journal of Applied Econometrics* 18 (5): 527-544.

Hicks, Michael J. 2007. *The Local Economic Impact of Wal-Mart*. Youngstown, NY: Cambria Press.

Hilber, Christian, and Christopher Mayer. 2009. "Why Do Households without Children Support Local Public Schools? Linking House Price Capitalization to School Spending." *Journal of Urban Economics* 65 (1): 74-90.

Houtenville, Andrew, and Karen Conway. 2008. "Parental Effort, School Resources, and Student Achievement." *Journal of Human Resources* 43 (2): 437-453.

Hoxby, Caroline. 1996. "How Teachers' Unions Affect Education Production." *Quarterly Journal of Economics* 111 (3): 671-718.

———. 1999. "The Productivity of Schools and Other Public Good Producers." *Journal of Public Economics* 74 (1): 1-30.

———. 2000a. "Does Competition among Public Schools Benefit Students and Taxpayers?" *American Economic Review* 90 (5): 209-231.

———. 2000b. "The Effects of Class Size on Student Achievement: New Evidence from Population Variation." *Quarterly Journal of Economics* 115 (4): 1239-1285.

Jepsen, Christopher, and Steven Rivkin. 2009. "Class Size Reduction and Student Achievement: The Potential Tradeoff between Teacher Quality and Class Size." *Journal of Human Resources* 44 (1): 223-250.

Johnson, Susan M. 1984. *Teacher Unions in Schools*. Philadelphia, PA: Temple University Press.

Kennedy, Peter. 2003. *A Guide to Econometrics*. 5th ed. Cambridge, MA: MIT Press.

Kleiner, Morris M., and Daniel Petree. 1988. "Unionism and Licensing of Public Sector Teachers: Impact on Wages and Educational Output." In *When Public Sector Workers Unionize*, edited by Richard Freeman and Casey Ichiowski, 305-19. Chicago, IL: University of Chicago Press.

Krueger, Alan B. 1998. "Reassessing the View That American Schools Are Broken." *Federal Reserve Bank of New York Economic Policy Review* 4 (1): 29-43.

———. 2003. "Economic Considerations and Class Size." *Economic Journal* 113 (485): F34-F63.

Lamdin, Douglas. 1996. "Evidence of Student Attendance as an Independent Variable in Education Production Functions." *Journal of Educational Research* 89 (3): 115-162.

Lindy, Benjamin. 2011. "The Impact of Teacher Collective Bargaining Laws on Student Achievement: Evidence from a New Mexico Natural Experiment." *Yale Law Journal* 120: 1130-1191.

Moe, Terry. 2009. "Collective Bargaining and the Performance of the Public Schools." *American Journal of Political Science* 53 (1): 156-174.

Mosteller, Frederick. 1995. "The Tennessee Study of Class Size in the Early Grades." *The Future of Children* 5 (2): 113-127.

National Center for Education Statistics. 2012a. *Digest of Education Statistics, 2011*. Washington, DC: National Center for Education Statistics.

———. 2012b. *School District Demographics System Census 2000 School District Tabulation (STP2) Data*. http://nces.ed.gov/surveys/sdds/.

Peltzman, Sam. 1993. "The Political Economy of the Decline of American Education." *Journal of Law and Economics* 36 (1): 331-70.

———. 1996. "Political Economy of Public Education: Non-College Bound Students." *Journal of Law and Economics* 39 (1): 73-120.

Podgursky, Michael, and Matthew Springer. 2011. "Teacher Compensation Systems in the United States K-12 Public School System." *National Tax Journal* 64 (1): 165-192.

Pohlmann, Marcus, Joy Clay, and Kenneth Goings. 2001. *School Consolidation: State of Tennessee*. Memphis: Memphis City Schools.

Ponzo, Michela. 2011. "The Effects of School Competition on the Achievement of Italian Students." *Managerial and Decision Economics* 32 (1): 53-61.

Probasco Chair of Free Enterprise. 2010. *The Economic Impact and Return on Investment of UTC: What Tennessee Taxpayers Receive for Their Money 2009-2010*.

Rivkin, Steven G., Eric A. Hanushek, and John F. Kain. 2005. "Teachers, Schools, and Academic Achievement." *Econometrica* 73 (2): 417-458.

Rothstein, Jesse. 2007. "Does Competition among Public Schools Benefit Students and Taxpayers? A Comment on Hoxby (2000)." *American Economic Review* 97 (5): 2026-2037.

Ruggerio, John. 2001. "Determining the Base Cost of an Education: An Analysis of Ohio School Districts." *Contemporary Economic Policy* 19 (3): 268-279.

Schelzig, Erik. 2011. "TN Teachers' Collective Bargaining Rights Targeted." *Boston Globe*, January 25. http://www.boston.com/news/education/k_12/ articles/2011/01/25/tn_teachers_collective_bargaining_rights_targeted/.

———. 2012. "TN Schools With Collective Bargaining Have Better Gains, but Lower Scores." *Associated Press*, May 12. http://blogs.knoxnews.com/humphrey/2011/08/tn-schools-with-collective-bar.html.

Sheldon, Steven B., and Joyce L. Epstein. 2004. "Getting Students to School: Using Family and Community Involvement to Reduce Chronic Absenteeism." *School Community Journal* 14 (2): 39-56.

Sims, David. 2009. "Crowding Peter to Educate Paul: Lessons from a Class Size Reduction Externality." *Economics of Education Review* 28 (4): 465-473.

Staley, Samuel, and John Blair. 1997. "Institutions, Quality Competition, and Public Service Provision: The Case of Public Education." *Constitutional Political Economy* 6 (1): 21-33.

Tennessee Department of Education. 2012. *Report Card: 2000*. http://www.tn.gov/education/reportcard/index.shtml.

Vedder, Richard K., and Joshua Hall. 2000. "Private School Competition and Public School Teacher Salaries." *Journal of Labor Research* 21 (1): 161-168.

WELFARE REFORM AND INCENTIVES TO WORK IN TENNESSEE

by Art Carden

10

WELFARE REFORM AND INCENTIVES TO WORK IN TENNESSEE

Art Carden

Successful anti-poverty policies encourage growth when they include incentives that reward work effort and/or regaining employment. In 1996, Congress passed the Personal Responsibility and Work Reconciliation Act (PRWORA), which replaced Aid to Families with Dependent Children (AFDC) with Temporary Aid to Needy Families (TANF). Instead of being administered at the federal level, TANF was administered by the states using federal block grants. Research on welfare reform suggests that the TANF program increased employment and reduced dependency.[1] At the same time, however, policies adopted by federal and state lawmakers have provided disincentives to supply labor as well as disincentives to demand it.

This chapter considers two related themes—welfare reform and its effects, plus other incentives to work—and how they relate to economic growth. Specifically, it explores demand-side and supply-side factors affecting welfare participants and workers in the low-wage labor market. As we discussed in Chapters 1 and 2, economic growth not only expands people's range of possibilities, but is also associated with higher standards of living on virtually every margin. Economic growth allows workers and their families to be better fed, clothed, and sheltered in exchange for less (and less strenuous) labor. Economic history provides ample evidence.[2] Here is an oft-quoted passage from Joseph Schumpeter ([1942] 1975, 67) on what he calls "the capitalist achievement":

> There are no doubt some things available to the modern workman that Louis XIV himself would have been delighted to have yet was unable to have—modern dentistry, for instance. On the whole, however, a budget on that level had little that really mattered to gain from capitalist achievement. Even speed of traveling may be assumed to have been a minor consideration for so very dignified a gentleman. Electric lighting is no great boon to anyone who has

---

[1] See Blank (2002; 2006; 2009) and Grogger (2003; 2009) for surveys of this research.
[2] See McCloskey (2006; 2010) for detailed examinations and a broad historical perspective.

money enough to buy a sufficient number of candles and to pay servants to attend to them. It is the cheap cloth, the cheap cotton and rayon fabric, boots, motorcars, and so on that are the typical achievements of capitalist production, and not as a rule improvements that would mean much to the rich man. Queen Elizabeth owned silk stockings. The capitalist achievement does not typically consist in providing more silk stockings for queens but in bringing them within the reach of factory girls in return for steadily decreasing amounts of effort.

The capitalist achievement has done more to improve the wellbeing of the poor than government anti-poverty programs and income redistribution. Nobel Laureate Robert Lucas (2004) addressed the distributional consequences of economic growth:

> Of the tendencies that are harmful to sound economics, the most seductive, and in my opinion the most poisonous, is to focus on questions of distribution. In this very minute, a child is being born to an American family and another child, equally valued by God, is being born to a family in India. The resources of all kinds that will be at the disposal of this new American will be on the order of 15 times the resources available to his Indian brother. This seems to us a terrible wrong, justifying direct corrective action, and perhaps some actions of this kind can and should be taken. But of the vast increase in the well-being of hundreds of millions of people that has occurred in the 200-year course of the industrial revolution to date, virtually none of it can be attributed to the direct redistribution of resources from rich to poor. The potential for improving the lives of poor people by finding different ways of distributing current production is *nothing* compared to the apparently limitless potential of increasing production. (last paragraph)

Theory and evidence suggest that poverty alleviation policies should be aimed at encouraging economic growth, not redistributing resources. Research on welfare reform suggests that reform policies have been successful in reducing welfare rolls and increasing employment. Employment enables workers to obtain skills that will increase their future earnings, and government funds that would have otherwise been spent on welfare programs can be used to reduce tax burdens on Tennessee businesses and workers.

A growth-centered approach to Tennessee's future and to participants in Tennessee's TANF program requires attention to more than just the incentives inherent in welfare programs themselves. Several factors influence demand for welfare services. Education is highly correlated with earnings and welfare dependence, for example. So too are barriers to entry into the labor market. A holistic approach to the labor market considers how public policy affects the incentives for workers and employers. The welfare reform of 1996 was successful on many margins, but there are still supply side factors, demand side factors, and institutional factors—such as certain characteristics of the criminal justice system—that burden participants in the labor market.

WELFARE, WELFARE REFORM, AND THE POOR

Tennessee's TANF plan, called Families First, was already being developed at the time of the 1996 welfare reform,[3] and welfare dependency in Tennessee dipped somewhat between 2005 and 2010. As of September 2010, Tennessee's Families First program was handling 63,661 cases as compared to 67,411 cases from 2005 (Fox, Cunningham, and Hamblen 2011). Of these, 53.8 percent of the cases were in Tennessee's urban counties (Davidson, Hamilton, Knox, and Shelby). Shelby County's 20,641 cases were "nearly one-third of the total caseload in the state" (xiii). The average Families First grant was smaller in 2010 than it has been through the 2000s:

> The average Families First monthly benefit has decreased, falling from $170 in 2000 and 2003 to $166 in 2005 to $158 currently. Over half of all AGs [assistance groups] (57.2 percent) receive grants of $150 or less per month, while only 1.3 percent receive monthly grants in excess of $300. (xvii)

This has been offset somewhat by more generous food stamp payments even though the percentage of assistance groups receiving food stamps fell from 86.5 percent in 2005 to 82.2 percent in 2010. In 2005, the average monthly food stamp allotment was $332, and it was $445 in 2010; adjusted for inflation, this was a 16.4 percent real increase.

Of caretakers receiving assistance, 60.8 percent of caretakers are single, never married. Fathers are largely absent in Families First assistance groups. The percentage of respondents answering "never" to "How often does the father of the youngest assistance-group child provide regular financial support?" was 60.8 percent. In addition, 68.4 percent responded "never" to "How often does the father of the youngest assistance-group child provide direct care (feeding, dressing, child care)?" and 49.5 percent to "How often does the father of the youngest assistance-group child show love and affection to the child?" For "How often does the father of the youngest assistance-group child serve as an authority figure and discipline the child?" the percentage reporting "never" was 63.7 percent (Fox, Cunningham, and Hamblen 2011, 44-45). Incidentally, the percentages were slightly higher for rural than urban assistance groups. The data suggest that paternal absence is one of the main reasons Tennessee children are deprived.

A growing body of research has been assessing the effects of the 1996 welfare reform.[4] Grogger and Karoly (2005) note that the Temporary Aid to Needy Families (TANF) reduced welfare caseloads by about 20 percent and increased employment by about 4 percent relative to Aid to Families with Dependent Children (AFDC). The 1996 reform was largely successful in reducing welfare caseloads and moving people off of the welfare rolls and into employment (Daly and Kwok 2009). They note that, for single mothers between the ages of 18 and 24, "increased attachment to the labor market has also given these young women increased access to an important safety net—unemployment insurance" (paragraph 3).

Discussing the incentives provided by AFDC and TANF, Blank (2006, 36-37) notes that "[u]nder the old AFDC program, for many women earnings gains were offset almost dollar-for-dollar by benefit declines once earnings rose above a (very low) disregard level.

---

[3] Rudolph and O'Hara (2002) summarize the history of welfare reform in Tennessee.
[4] See Blank (2002, 2009) for summaries and citations.

Under TANF, the majority of states provided for slower declines in benefits, allowing women to see greater income growth as their earnings grew." Higher welfare benefits increase welfare participation and reduce employment. According to Grogger (2003, 402), "[h]igher welfare benefits appear to decrease employment, at least among families whose youngest children are 14 or younger." Because welfare programs reduce benefits as individuals earn income, this functions as an implicit tax on earnings. If benefits are reduced at a high enough rate as income rises, it can severely reduce the incentive to work. At the extreme, if benefits were reduced by $1 for every $1 in earned income, there becomes no personal incentive for welfare recipients to work as their own income is no higher from working than not working and receiving benefits. Once one considers the cost of child-care, transportation, and clothing associated with working, in some cases welfare systems were structured so poorly that individuals were actually worse off if they worked than if they did not.

The effects of the 1996 welfare reform were concentrated on the largest welfare-receiving population: single mothers. Blank (2006) points out that the labor force participation rate for single mothers rose from 44 to 66 percent between 1994 and 2001. At the same time, their earnings increased by more than their welfare benefits fell, and "poverty rates among single-mother households fell to historically low levels by the late 1990s" (2). Measuring the effect of welfare reform as such is tricky because these reforms were occurring at the same time as expansions in the Earned Income Tax Credit, a booming economy, and expansion of Medicaid coverage.

Blank (2009, 53) summarizes the literature on welfare reform as follows: "Those who supported welfare reform because it promised greater work and less welfare usage should find their expectations more than met." She continues with a less-rosy picture of what welfare reform has meant to low-income mothers:

> Those who expected welfare reform to truly transform the lives of low-income mothers should be more disappointed. Despite dramatic changes in work behavior and welfare reliance, there is so far little evidence that marriage or fertility patterns have changed much as a result of welfare reform, nor is there evidence that the children of low-skilled working mothers are doing better than the children of welfare recipients a decade ago.

While welfare reform has been successful on some margins, some have slipped through the cracks. To address this, we turn to a discussion of the incentives present on both the supply side and the demand side of the labor market.

INCENTIVES TO WORK: THE SUPPLY SIDE

Recognition of the fact that programs like AFDC provided substantial incentives to stay out of the labor force helped drive the 1996 welfare reform.[5] All else equal, welfare makes work less attractive; for example, someone who loses $300 per week in welfare benefits by taking a job that pays $400 per week only nets $100 from working compared to welfare. When

---

[5] See Rudolph and O'Hara (2002) for a history of Tennessee's Families First program and a discussion of the incentive effects of AFDC. Leguizamon (2012) offers estimates of implicit marginal tax rates.

welfare policy effectively taxes work (by taking away benefits), people are less willing to work.

In addition to education, people can improve their productivity by gaining experience in the labor force. When people have incentives to work more today, it will presumably provide them with skills that will make them more valuable workers tomorrow. Grogger (2009) notes that one of the motivations for the welfare reform of the mid-1990s was the idea that by encouraging people to work, the government would encourage them to obtain valuable skills and training that would increase their future earnings. Consistent with this prediction, Grogger uses data from Florida's Family Transition Program to show that wages increased by approximately 4 percent, 4 years after the experimental reform of 1994 and 1995 (2009).

One of the major changes of the mid-1990s welfare reform was the introduction of time limits. The Florida program limited the amount of time people could earn benefits—to 24 months out of a 60-month period or 36 months out of 73 for those who were "more disadvantaged." The treatment and control groups faced different incentives, with the treatment group being allowed to "keep the first $200 they earned each month, as well as 50 percent of the amount over $200" while "control group members faced the tax schedule from the Aid to Families with Dependent Children program. After the first four months of work, [the control group's] marginal tax rate on earnings was 100 percent if they earned over $90 per month" (Grogger 2009, 491). In summary, participants were faced with a new set of incentives that encouraged work and that ultimately increased their future earnings.

AFFORDABLE CHILD CARE

Fox, Cunningham, and Hamblen (2011) summarize survey responses from Families First participants suggesting that lack of access to affordable child care is an important barrier to employment. When asked "Which of the following support services do you feel you need in order to work?" 26 percent of respondents to the Families First survey, said "child care" (27 percent in urban areas, 24.8 percent in rural areas) (172). Affordable child care is clearly a major obstacle to employment. The National Association of Child Care Resource and Referral Agencies reported in 2006 that child care is often one of a family's most important expenses, and they note that this is especially true for low-income families.

As we discussed in Chapter 8, regulation makes regulated activities, such as child care, more expensive. Tennessee and Florida require the highest frequency of annual inspections of child care facilities with four per year (Blau 2003). Blau recognizes explicitly that lax regulation of child care could be a pro-growth policy that makes it easier for women to find work. In his words, "[a]nother state might emphasize economic growth, leading to lax regulations in an effort to keep the cost of child care low to facilitate women's employment" (450).

Summarizing previous research on the role of child care regulations, Blau (2003) discusses prior studies showing that "stricter regulations reduce the number of child care slots available per child in licensed facilities;" he also points out that several pre-welfare reform studies of regulation and women's labor force participation have found that regulations have negative (albeit not statistically significant) effects on women's labor force participation.[6] In

---

[6] The effect of child care regulations on hours worked is, to the best of my knowledge, unstudied. Economic theory predicts that an increase in the cost of each hour of child care will increase the opportunity cost of each additional hour of labor and, therefore, reduce the number of hours worked.

his study of child care regulations, he determines that while regulations appear to matter, "it is difficult to detect any consistent pattern of regulation effects" (450).

Regulations may increase quality, but by so doing restrict the supply of regulated goods and services and increase their costs. Strict regulations reduce the supply of affordable child care by rendering illegal price/quality combinations that buyers and sellers might otherwise find agreeable. In response to the reduction in supply, people might resort to inferior "do-it-yourself" solutions (Kleiner 2006). Blau (2007) explores the consequences of group size, staff-child ratio, and staff qualification regulations on day care centers and preschools. He finds that they do not affect price or quality but that the increased costs are borne by day care workers. These findings have an important implication both for the availability of quality child care and the earnings of low-income workers at child care facilities. First, eliminating training regulations and child-staff ratio regulations on child care facilities would make more facilities available without compromising quality. Second, removing the regulations would raise the incomes of child care workers. Blau (2003) notes that there is a large informal "underground" market for child care that could be increased in size with tougher regulations. Under a regime of certification rather than licensing, more information would become readily available as people currently providing child care in the informal sector have incentives to seek certification from either the state or an independent organization like the National Association for the Education of Young Children.

According to Carpenter et al. (2012), preschool teachers face the most onerous licensing requirements of any of the occupations they study. Accordingly, potential preschool teachers in Tennessee face the greatest licensing requirements as well. To become a preschool teacher in Tennessee requires no fees, but people are barred from the field for 1,825 days while they accumulate education and experience. They also have to take an exam. In light of research on the effects of licensing and regulation, it is by no means clear that this is necessary. Deregulating child care and eliminating licensing for preschool teachers could remove a formidable barrier to labor force participation.

NEGATIVE INCOME TAXES

Changes to anti-poverty programs have included expansions of the Earned Income Tax Credit (EITC). Researchers have found that unlike other benefits, the EITC increased labor force participation by providing people with an incentive to work (Rosen 2005). Grogger (2003, 408) notes that "the EITC may be the single most important policy measure for explaining the decrease in welfare and the rise in work and earnings among female headed families in recent years."

Milton Friedman ([1962] 2002) discussed the case for a "negative income tax" like the EITC in his classic text *Capitalism and Freedom*. There are ways governments can redistribute wealth without penalizing work in the way that direct welfare transfer programs do. As Friedman notes:

> The advantages of this arrangement [a negative income tax] are clear. It is directed specifically at the problem of poverty. It gives help in the form most useful to the individual, namely, cash. It is general and could be substituted for the host of special measures now in effect. It makes explicit the cost borne by society. It operates outside the market. Like any other measures to alleviate

poverty, it reduces the incentives of those helped to help themselves, but it does not eliminate that incentive entirely, as a system of supplementing incomes up to some fixed minimum would. An extra dollar earned always means more money available for expenditure. (192)

In terms of providing incentives to work, negative income taxes like the Earned Income Tax Credit (EITC) are apparently superior to other forms of assistance. Grogger (2003) argued that time limits for receiving benefits in a consecutive period helped explain part of the increase in employment over the preceding decade, but did not affect either earnings or income. Meanwhile, Grogger credits the EITC for increases in employment, labor supply, and earnings. Research suggests that the EITC has increased labor force participation rates.[7] Relative to other welfare options, the EITC provides income support while maintaining incentives for people to work.

Determining how welfare benefits affect incentives to work is extremely tricky. Leguizamon (2012) shows that calculations of implicit marginal tax rates—meaning the rate one's income is reduced when she earns money in the labor market and consequently loses eligibility for some benefits—are sensitive to the assumptions one uses about the costs of housing, the age of children, and other factors. With assumptions about Tennessee's work requirements to stay eligible and Tennessee's cost of living, Leguizamon (2012, 418) calculates that the state had the lowest implicit marginal tax rate in the country of -32.3 percent (for a hypothetical minimum-wage earning mother of two children under age six). This suggests that earnings were actually subsidized.[8] Tennessee's welfare benefits are apparently already structured with strong incentives to work. They might also be strengthened if Tennessee were to join the ranks of states that offer their own versions of Earned Income Tax Credits. In particular, such a program might help to address the fact that state sales taxes tend to fall disproportionately on the poor.

INCENTIVES TO WORK: THE DEMAND SIDE

In addition to increasing people's incentives to supply labor, pro-growth policy would increase employers' incentives to demand labor. Laws that make labor more expensive will reduce opportunities for people who wish to enter the labor market. Chapter 8 explores the relationship between regulation—occupational licensing, in particular—and pro-growth policy. Reduction or removal of taxes and regulations that make labor more expensive would create employment opportunities for current welfare participants, provide positive incentives to work, and ultimately reduce the burden on the taxpayers who fund Families First and related programs.

LABOR MARKET FLEXIBILITY AND WELFARE PARTICIPATION: LICENSING

Chapters 7 and 8 discussed the effects of occupational licensing on labor markets and summarized research showing that the poor are hurt by licensing. Carpenter et al. (2012)

---

[7] See Rosen (2005, 177-178) for a textbook discussion.

[8] It is important to note that the Leguizamon (2012) does not include medical benefits in his analysis.

survey how licensing burdens people who wish to enter low- to middle-income occupations. Eliminating licensing increases workers' access to the licensed professions. It also creates additional employment opportunities through two other effects.

The first effect comes from higher incomes. In the absence of licensing, Tennesseans as a whole would enjoy higher incomes out of which they can spend and save. Additional spending would create employment opportunities in sectors that help consumers satisfy their desires for present consumption. Additional saving would create a larger pool of resources that can be used to finance longer-term projects and new businesses.

The second effect is an increase in demand for support services and investment goods. This is likely to be especially acute in occupations with entrepreneurial potential. Removing barriers to entry into currently-licensed occupations would remove an important obstacle for potential entrepreneurs who are considering starting their own businesses.

To construct an example, consider a prospective entrepreneur who wishes to open a health spa, but who finds it prohibitively costly because of licensing requirements for athletic trainers, skin care specialists, and massage therapists. These professions have the fourth, thirteenth, and sixteenth most onerous licensing requirements among low- to middle-income occupations for which licenses are required in Tennessee (Carpenter et al. 2012). If licensing requirements are eliminated, the prospective entrepreneur may now find it advantageous to open the spa. Not only would this create opportunities for prospective trainers and therapists who now have access to these professions, it would also create opportunities for other people who might be hired as the result of the new spa (janitors, administrative assistants, and others).[9] As participants in programs like Families First tend to be low-skilled, such a move would create new opportunities for low-income Tennesseans and their families.

EDUCATION AND PRODUCTIVITY

Blank (2007, 2009) points out that the least-educated single mothers might slip through the cracks created by welfare reform, and indeed education is an important correlate of earning opportunities. Education reforms (discussed in Chapters 7 and 9) may therefore reduce demand for anti-poverty programs like Families First.

MINIMUM WAGES AND EMPLOYMENT

Maintaining incentives to work requires the consideration of existing policies that affect those incentives. It also requires that policymakers avoid enacting future policies that will negatively affect incentives to work. Many people advocate higher minimum wages, for example, as a possible way to improve the living standards of the poor. However, as reported in Chapter 7, volumes of data found minimum wage legislation to be ineffective in reducing poverty.

---

[9] Evidence suggests that licensing requirements can be relaxed without compromising quality. See Kleiner (2006) for a discussion.

INCARCERATION, PARENTAL ABSENCE, AND WELFARE PARTICIPATION

Parental absence is one reason people participate in Families First, and incarceration is one cause of parental absence. Crime and violence are among the major issues affecting the poor, and according to the data provided by Fox, Cunningham, and Hamblen (2011), prison is a leading reason for fathers' absences. The absent parent of an assistance group child has "served time for a criminal conviction" for 39.4 percent of "assistance groups where deprivation is due to an absent parent" (Fox, Cunningham, and Hamblen 2011, 47). The percentage is slightly lower for urban assistance groups (36.6 percent) and slightly higher for rural assistance groups (42.9 percent). For 39 percent of "those assistance groups where deprivation is due to an absent parent and the absent parent has served time for a criminal conviction," the absent parent is currently in prison. Here, the percentage is higher for urban assistance groups (42 percent) and lower for rural assistance groups (36 percent) (Fox, Cunningham, and Hamblen 2011, 47).

In the absence of policy changes, incarceration-related parental absence will apparently increase over time. Citing data from Beck, Karberg, and Harrison (2002), Raphael (2006) points out that the probability of serving time in a state or federal prison for white males born in 2001 is 5.9 percent as compared to 2.2 percent for white males born in 1974. For black males, the increase has been dramatic: 13.4 percent for black males born in 1974 but 32.2 percent for black males born in 2001. There is a greater-than-fourfold increase in probabilities for Hispanic males. For Hispanic males born in 1974, the probability of jail time is 4 percent. While it increased to 17.2 percent in 2001. The effects are clear: "[p]rison time substantially interrupts the potential work careers in the legitimate labor market of imprisoned young men" (352).

Why has the probability of incarceration increased? Miron (2004) points out that the war on drugs is at the front of the increase in crime (both violent and non-violent). Drug demand is extremely inelastic, which means that reducing drug supply actually increases revenues for drug dealers. Since competition over these increased revenues is illegal, it turns violent.[10]

Minimum wages affect welfare dependency primarily because they reduce employment. However, they also likely affect welfare dependency by inadvertently encouraging crime. Hashimoto (1987) points out that higher minimum wages reduce labor market opportunities and lead young people into crime. Beauchamp and Chan (2012, 1) estimate that "a one-percent increase in the minimum wage increases juvenile drug crime by 1.4-2.8%, property crime by 1.8-2.3%, and violent crime by 2.1-2.4%." Crime increases are concentrated among young people, and the crime increases appear to be geared toward income production. Beauchamp and Chan note that "[v]iolent crime increases were concentrated among crimes with a clear monetary reward" (1). As Beauchamp and Chan (2012) note, raising the minimum wage makes it more difficult for someone to participate in the formal, licit labor market. This pushes people toward informal and illicit ways of earning income. In some cases, these can be relatively benign endeavors like off-the-books food preparation, child care, car care, or other services.[11] Crime is another way someone can use

---

[10] See Cowen and Tabarrok (2009, 59-60) for a literal textbook treatment.
[11] Venkatesh (2006) offers a fascinating survey of life in "the underground economy of the urban poor."

his or her time, and as Beauchamp and Chan show, this appears to be one of the unintended consequences of minimum wages.

The downstream and indirect consequences are even more subtle than they might at first appear. When people are forced out of the labor market by a minimum wage, they are denied the opportunity for current employment. This obviously reduces their current earnings, but it also reduces their future earnings because it denies them experience. It also makes crime a relatively more attractive option since participation in the licit, formal labor market has been closed off by legislation. Crime leads to incarceration, which might further reduce earnings. Furthermore, by encouraging more crime (and, therefore, more incarceration), minimum wages contribute to a burden on the Families First program through indirect channels as well.

Fortunately, Tennessee does not have a minimum wage above the federal minimum. In order to maintain "incentives to work," policymakers should resist efforts to increase the state's minimum wage. Furthermore, dialogue between state policymakers and the state's congressional delegation could emphasize that the elimination of anti-poor, anti-growth policies like the minimum wage should be a legislative priority. At the state level, regulations that make it difficult to hire people will likely have similar effects.

Incarceration is a problem with respect to parental absence among participants in Families First. To the extent that parental absence leads to welfare dependency and incarceration leads to parental absence, the causes of incarceration are worth studying. Drug prohibition is an important source of crime. As Miron (2004) notes, intense enforcement of drug laws puts many drug-related transactions outside the scope of legal dispute resolution channels. Thus, parties resort to extra-legal enforcement mechanisms.

One main reason why Tennessee has worse than average problems in the areas of both crime and divorce was illustrated in Chapter 1. When looking across all U.S. states, these (as well as other) measures of social conditions in the areas of health, crime, and family stability are clearly related to the average income levels in the states. Put simply, higher income states have better outcomes in these areas, and poorer states—like Tennessee—have worse outcomes in these areas. As we mentioned in Chapter 1, families living in the five states with the highest incomes experience significantly lower divorce rates than families in the five lowest income states (2.8 versus 4.8 on average). Richer families have fewer money problems destroying their marriages and more money to spend on family vacations and leisure activities. States with higher incomes also have significantly lower rates of violent crime (3.4 versus 4.8 on average). This is why reforming Tennessee's policies to embrace economic freedom, and create a better environment for economic growth are critical to helping to solve many of Tennessee's problems, in all areas including parental absence.

GROWTH, NEED, AND THE PRIVATE PROVISION OF WELFARE SERVICES

Critics of welfare point out that it creates perverse incentives and crowds out private charity. Brooks (2006) calculates that a 10 percent increase in TANF spending is associated with a 3 percent reduction in charitable giving. He then compares Tennessee and New Hampshire strictly for illustrative purposes, but his calculation is useful. Brooks claims "that were Tennessee to raise its average TANF payment to New Hampshire's level, it would, in the process, crowd out about 42% of charitable giving" (60). Even though this is an imprecise measure, it, nonetheless, suggests that public assistance crowds out private charity.

Others ask whether private charity will be sufficient to meet the needs. Americans have a long and rich history of social innovations that have solved problems related to insurance, poverty, and social safety nets. Beito (2000) chronicles the history of insurance societies, mutual aid societies, fraternal societies, and friendly societies that served their fellows (albeit not without fault), provided insurance, and helped to reduce people's costs of finding and obtaining gainful employment. American Federation of Labor president Samuel Gompers "frequently found that my affiliation to the Masonic order has been a protection to me" (59).

In 2009, Elinor Ostrom was awarded the Nobel Prize in economics for research including how rules and norms that allow for the management of natural resources evolve from the ground up (Ostrom 2009). In addition, the research of Beito (2000) and Murray (2007) offer historical treatments of how solutions to important problems evolve from the ground up.

Murray (2007) asks why Americans did not adopt some kind of universal health insurance and concludes that industrial sickness funds provided the kind of insurance people wanted and needed. In short, progressive reformers were unable to obtain the health reform they wanted because, for the most part, working people were satisfied with the arrangements they had made to provide for sickness and old age: participation in workplace-based or union-based industrial sickness funds, saving, and other channels. In particular, the funds improved over "passing the hat" because they allowed, in the words of one Colorado employer, workers to avoid "the stigma of charity" (69). In short, Murray provides a wide-ranging survey of one of the important ways in which ordinary people solved seemingly intractable problems. Industrial sickness funds were not perfect, but they were also not "obviously worse than the state-led alternative" (247). They provide just one example of people banding together through voluntary, decentralized channels to solve their own problems. Pro-growth policies in Tennessee could recognize the fact that people can and have solved the problems that face them without top-down encouragement or intervention.

In light of the insights of Lucas (2004) and the summary of modern economic growth offered by McCloskey (2006, 2010), economic growth is what ultimately alleviates the material needs of the poor. Over the long run, pro-growth policy will do more to alleviate genuine suffering than redistribution. Redistribution also has its drawbacks. If done incorrectly, redistribution reduces incentives to work and fosters dependency. Furthermore, welfare programs like TANF crowd out private charity. Most importantly, however, eliminating disincentives to work will ultimately reduce demand for welfare services by addressing people's needs through voluntary channels.

CONCLUSION

Economic growth is more effective than redistribution in fighting poverty over the long run. A pro-growth approach to policy will examine the sources of work incentives in Tennessee. These include factors that encourage or discourage potential workers, such as access to affordable child care and the implicit marginal tax rate from welfare benefits. It also includes factors that influence worker productivity and employers' incentives to hire labor. Such factors include the education system as well as restrictions on the operation of the labor market including licensing, regulation, and minimum wage laws.

Institutional and legal factors are also important determinants of participation in Tennessee's Families First program. Parental absence is particularly common among deprived children, and one of the causes of parental absence is incarceration. Minimum wage policies have also been shown to have the unintended consequence of increasing crime (Beauchamp and Chan 2012) and are another indirect channel through which the minimum wage policy might burden the poor. In addition, lower income states—like Tennessee—generally have higher rates of divorce and crime than higher income states, and therefore reforms that promote economic growth will help to solve many of these social problems by increasing average incomes among Tennesseans.

Finally, detailed historical studies by Beito (2000) and Murray (2007) illustrate some of the ways in which people organize to address the problems that periodically confront them. From charitable and fraternal organizations to industrial sickness funds, people innovated and devised risk-sharing and information-sharing arrangements that comprised effective ways of solving problems and addressing risks. Tennesseans have a long history of displaying entrepreneurial innovation and ingenuity. With pro-growth policies aimed at providing people better incentives to work, we should expect to see these entrepreneurial and innovative energies channeled into better, more prosperous lives for Tennesseans.

REFERENCES

Beauchamp, Andrew, and Stacey Chan. 2012. "Crime and the Minimum Wage." Working Paper, Boston College, Chestnut Hill, MA.

Beck, Allen J., Jennifer C. Karberg, and Paige M. Harrison. 2002. "Prison and Jail Inmates at Midyear 2001." *Bureau of Justice Statistics Bulletin*. http://www.bluelineradio.com /DOJPRISIONJAIL.pdf.

Beito, David. 2000. *From Mutual Aid to the Welfare State: Fraternal Societies and Social Services, 1890-1967*. Chapel Hill, NC: University of North Carolina Press.

Blank, Rebecca M. 2002. "Evaluating Welfare Reform in the United States." *Journal of Economic Literature* 40 (4): 1105-1166.

———. 2006. "What Did the 1990s Welfare Reforms Accomplish?" In *Public Policy and the Income Distribution*, edited by Alan J. Auerbach, David Card, and John M. Quigley, 33-79. New York: Russell Sage Foundation.

———. 2007. "Improving the Safety Net for Single Mothers Who Face Serious Barriers to Work." *The Future of Children* 17 (2): 183-197.

———. 2009. "What We Know, What We Don't Know, and What We Need to Know About Welfare Reform." In *Welfare Reform and Its Long-term Consequences for America's Poor*, edited by James P. Ziliak. Cambridge, UK: Cambridge University Press.

Blau, David M. 2003. "Do Child Care Regulations Affect the Child Care and Labor Markets?" *Journal of Policy Analysis and Management* 22 (3): 443-465.

———. 2007. "Unintended Consequences of Child Care Regulations." *Labour Economics* 14: 513-538.

Brooks, Arthur C. 2006. *Who Really Cares: The Surprising Truth about Compassionate Conservatism*. New York: Basic Books.

Carpenter, Dick M., II, Lisa Knepper, Angela C. Erickson, and John C. Ross. 2012. *License to Work: A National Study of Burdens from Occupational Licensing*. Arlington, VA: Institute for Justice. http://www.ij.org/licensetowork.

Cowen, Tyler, and Alex Tabarrok. 2009. *Modern Principles: Economics*. New York, NY: Worth Publishers.

Daly, Mary, and Joyce Kwok. 2009. "Did Welfare Reform Work for Everyone? A Look at Young Mothers." *Federal Reserve Bank of San Francisco*, August 3. http://www.frbsf .org/publications/economics/letter/2009/el2009-24.html.

Fox, William F., Vickie C. Cunningham, and William R. Hamblen. 2011. *Families First 2010 Case Characteristics Study*. Tennessee Department of Human Services. Knoxville, TN: Center for Business and Economic Research.

Friedman, Milton. (1962) 2002. *Capitalism and Freedom*. Chicago: University of Chicago Press.

Grogger, Jeffrey. 2003. "The Effects of Time Limits, the EITC, and Other Policy Changes on Welfare Use, Work, and Income among Female-Headed Families." *Review of Economics and Statistics* 85 (2): 394-408.

———. 2009. "Welfare Reform, Returns to Experience, and Wages: Using Reservation Wages to Account for Sample Selection Bias." *Review of Economics and Statistics* 91 (3): 490-502.

Grogger, Jeffrey and Lynn A. Karoly. 2005. *Welfare Reform: Effects of a Decade of Change*. Cambridge, MA: Harvard University Press.

Hashimoto, Masanori. 1987. "The Minimum Wage Law and Youth Crimes: Time-Series Evidence." *Journal of Law and Economics* 30: 443-464.

Kleiner, Morris M. 2006. *Licensing Occupations: Ensuring Quality or Restricting Competition?* Kalamazoo, MI: W.E. Upjohn Institute for Employment Research.

Leguizamon, J. Sebastian. 2012. "Estimating Implicit Marginal Tax Rates of Welfare Recipients across the US States." *Public Finance Review* 40 (3): 401-430.

Lucas, Robert E. 2004. "The Industrial Revolution: Past and Future." *The Region*, May. http://www.minneapolisfed.org/publications_papers/pub_display.cfm?id=3333.

McCloskey, Deirdre N. 2006. *Bourgeois Virtues: Ethics for an Age of Commerce*. Chicago: University of Chicago Press.

———. 2010. *Bourgeois Dignity: Why Economics Can't Explain the Modern World*. Chicago, IL: University of Chicago Press.

Miron, Jeffrey. 2004. *Drug War Crimes*. Oakland, CA: Independent Institute.

Murray, John E. 2007. *Origins of American Health Insurance: A History of Industrial Sickness Funds*. New Haven, CT: Yale University Press.

National Association of Child Care Resource and Referral Agencies. 2006. *Breaking the Piggy Bank: Parents and the High Price of Child Care*. http://www.naccrra.org/sites /default/files/news_room/press_releases/2010/breaking_the_piggy_bank.pdf.

Ostrom, Elinor. 2009. "Beyond Markets and States: Polycentric Governance of Complex Economic Systems." Nobel Prize Lecture. http://www.nobelprize.org/nobel_prizes /economics/laureates/2009/ostrom-lecture.html.

Raphael, Stephen. 2006. "The Socioeconomic Status of Black Males: The Increasing Importance of Incarceration." In *Public Policy and the Income Distribution*, edited by Alan J. Auerbach, David Card, and John M. Quigley. New York, NY: Russell Sage Foundation.

Rosen, Harvey S. 2005. *Public Finance*. 7th ed. New York, NY: McGraw-Hill.

Rudolph, Linda and Michael O'Hara. 2002. "Families First: Landmark Transition." Bureau of Business and Economic Research/Center for Manpower Studies, University of Memphis. http://state.tn.us/humanserv/adfam/ff-transition.pdf.

Schumpeter, Joseph A. (1942) 1975. *Capitalism, Socialism, and Democracy*. New York, NY: HarperPerennial.

Venkatesh, Sudhir. 2006. *Off the Books: The Underground Economy of the Urban Poor*. Cambridge, MA: Harvard University Press.

CHAPTER 11

GAMBLING ON LOTTERIES AND CASINOS IN TENNESSEE

by Douglas M. Walker

Freedom and Prosperity in Tennessee

11

GAMBLING ON LOTTERIES AND CASINOS IN TENNESSEE

*Douglas M. Walker**

Some industries face much more government regulation than others. The gambling industry can be considered to be an entertainment-type industry, like movies or professional sports, in which people pay to engage in an activity, but nothing tangible is produced. The gambling industry, generally defined, is one of the most regulated industries there is. Historically, the industry has been banned or strictly regulated by government, at both the federal and state levels.

Lotteries are operated in forty-three states and the District of Columbia and have become the most common form of gambling now allowed in the states. Since the late 1980s, however, casino gambling has seen enormous growth, and is currently a controversial public policy in many states. While casinos may promote employment and tax revenues, they may also cause economic and social ills. The next phase of the expansion of the gambling industry in the U.S. is going to be online gambling.

Tennessee is a relatively new entrant to the legal gambling world, only having introduced the lottery in 2004. Prior to that, Tennessee had been one of fewer than five states that did not allow its citizens to engage in some form of legal gambling. Now that Tennessee has opened the door to legal gambling, is the expansion of the gambling industry consistent with *freedom and prosperity* in the state? This chapter examines the likely economic and social impacts of expanded legal gambling options in Tennessee. We begin with a brief review of the Tennessee lottery and the typical concerns people have with state lotteries. Next, we examine how different gambling industries affect each other; which will provide insight into how the introduction of casinos or online gambling might affect Tennessee's lottery or businesses. Then, we examine the various benefits and costs to be expected with the introduction of casinos. The chapter concludes with a discussion of moral and philosophical issues related to legalized gambling.

---

* Thanks to Russell Sobel for helpful suggestions on the organization of this chapter.

The Tennessee Education Lottery

Forty-three states, plus Washington, DC, now operate a lottery. Tennessee voters approved a lottery in 2002, which began operation in early 2004. Tennessee was relatively late to join the lottery game, as most states introduced the lottery in the 1980s and 1990s. Numerous economic analyses of the lottery have been published in the literature. Some of the most important issues raised are examined in this section.

Like many state lotteries, Tennessee's lottery was promoted and passed by affiliating it with a good cause—education. According to the lottery's public information sheet, the lottery has raised more than $2.3 billion for education programs. The lottery subsidizes college students, after-school programs, and pre-K programs (Tennessee Lottery 2012). Figure 11.1, shows the lottery's gross nominal sales since its inception in January 2004. The 2004 fiscal year figure is low because the lottery was operating only about half of the 2003-04 fiscal year, which ended on June 30.

Figure 11.1: Tennessee Lottery Sales by Fiscal Year, 2004-2011

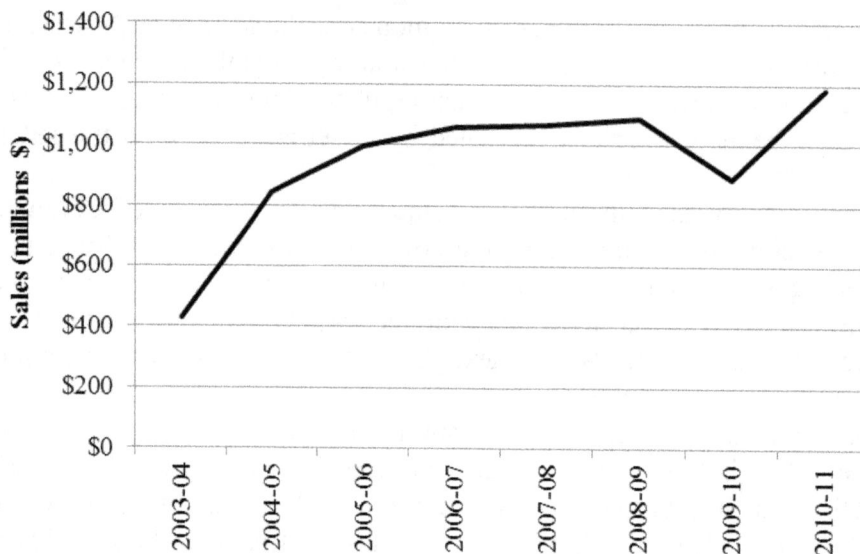

Source: Tennessee Lottery (2012).

Lottery Adoption

The primary reason state lotteries have become so popular is that they provide another source of government revenue (Jackson, Saurman, and Shughart 1994). However, during the 1990s and 2000s, it became more common for newly-adopting states to tie the lottery to some good cause, such as education. Tennessee's lottery is called the "Tennessee Education Lottery," and lotteries in Georgia, South Carolina, and other relatively recent adopters are also tied to education. If states that adopted lotteries later had more opposition to them from their citizens, then it makes sense as a matter of politics that the lottery needs to be tied to a good cause. Perhaps doing so helps to offset moral arguments people raise against the lottery or against the state leaders promoting gambling.

THE LOTTERY "TAX"

Most state lotteries are designed so that roughly 50 percent of sales are returned to players in the form of prizes, about 10 percent goes toward operating expenses, and 40 percent represents "tax" revenue (Clotfelter and Cook 1990). The typical lottery in the U.S. is designed to maximize revenues for the state (Garrett 2001). Until recently, the issue of cross-border shopping was a fairly important issue, as isolated states could attract out-of-state lottery ticket buyers, earn tax revenues from non-residents, and possibly increase state-level economic growth (Walker and Jackson 1999). However, since there are no longer "isolated" lottery states, cross-border shopping is generally not an important issue, as most lottery ticket purchases come from state residents.

Since the lottery is effectively a tax, several papers have examined who buys lottery tickets. That is, who ends up paying the lottery tax to government? The lottery is often characterized by its critics as being "a tax on the poor and stupid." Generally, empirical studies confirm that lottery purchases come disproportionately from lower-income individuals and the less educated. According to one study, about 49 percent of lottery players do not have a high school diploma, while only 30 percent of lotto players have a college degree (Clotfelter and Cook 1990). A variety of studies also confirm that individuals with lower incomes tend to spend a higher percentage of their income on lottery tickets than higher income individuals. The lottery is, therefore, considered to be a *regressive tax*.[1]

Aside from the fact that the lottery tax falls heavier on the relatively poor, it is also worth noting that how the state spends lottery revenue also contributes to the regressivity of the lottery as a public policy. For example, Rubenstein and Scafidi (2002) examine the incidence of the lottery tax for Georgia's HOPE Scholarship program, a program in which the lottery covers college students who had a "B" average (or better) in high school. The authors found that lower income, non-white households spend more on the lottery and receive lower benefits, in terms of financial support for college. This evidence is representative of much of the literature which indicates fairly strongly that the lottery is a regressive tax.

On the other hand, one could argue the regressivity issue may not be as serious a problem with the lottery as some observers think. Consider that the lottery represents a *voluntary tax*. That is, the tax is quite easy to avoid. Individuals do not have to pay the tax if they do not buy lottery tickets. Since economists generally believe that individuals can best decide the best way to spend their own money, the voluntary tax argument may offset the regressivity issue to some extent. (Additional information concerning Tennessee's lottery can be found in Chapter 7.)

POLITICS AND FUNGIBLE BUDGETS

As noted above, state fiscal stress is certainly one of the key factors that has lead so many states to adopt state lotteries. But, there is an important political explanation for this too. Politicians want to be popular, of course, and introducing a lottery, that many people like,

---

[1] For more information on the lottery, see Clotfelter and Cook (1991) and Borg, Mason, and Shapiro (1991).

may increase their popularity. Perhaps more importantly, if the lottery were not introduced, politicians may need to either cut spending or raise taxes in the state. So the lottery ends up being a politically easy way to raise revenues or to avoid having to cut spending.

Another way in which the lottery acts as a political tool can be seen when considering the fungibility of budgets. In Figure 11.1, one can see that the Tennessee lottery has had sales of around $1 billion each year since the 2005-06 fiscal year. Supposing that around 50 percent of these revenues have been given back to lottery players in the form of prizes, one might expect expenditures on Tennessee education has increased by roughly $500 million each year. This is clearly what the lottery officials would like people to believe, as they advertise the amount of money given to various education programs. However, when considering the ultimate effects of the lottery, it is important to recognize that *budgets are fungible*.

It may be the case that the Tennessee legislature and governor have maintained or even increased their expenditures on education in the state. But it may be more likely that, with the availability of lottery funding for education, the state has *decreased* its support of public education. Many states have been facing budget cuts, even before the 2007-2009 recession. Many public universities have seen their budgets shrinking. So even though the lottery may advertise how much it is doing for education, at the same time state politicians may be cutting their support for education. The net impact of the lottery on education probably varies by state. There has not been any empirical study of this particular issue since the most recent recession and, because Tennessee introduced the lottery only a few years earlier, there is no empirical evidence available to determine the net impact of the lottery on Tennessee education.

Finally, since one function of the lottery is to subsidize college students, a likely effect of lotteries being tied to college scholarships is that the tuition and fees charged by colleges increase. Since the students do not bear much of the cost of tuition increases, colleges can increase tuition and their revenues as lottery scholarships boost demand for college. This may be one explanation of why the cost of college increases at a rate much higher than the overall inflation rate.

CONSUMER SOVEREIGNTY

There are a variety of arguments given in opposition to state lotteries: lotteries represent a regressive tax; they may encourage people to gamble rather than work hard for a living; or, they may not end up increasing net funding for socially desirable ends. In addition, one could argue whether or not the state should be sponsoring legalized gambling.[2] But in terms of economics and consumer sovereignty, it seems clear that individuals should be allowed to spend their money as they wish. After all, each individual knows his own utility function best and can make consumption decisions in a way to maximize his own welfare.

People obviously enjoy playing the lottery. The recent $640 million Mega Millions jackpot proves this, as lottery ticket sales reached a record high rate leading up to the winning drawing. Although most people do not get any tangible benefit from playing the lottery, clearly people get some benefit or personal amusement from imagining what they could do with half a billion dollars. In the end, the lottery may just provide a daydream for people, but it's something for which people are willing to pay.

---

[2] A discussion of private lottery ownership is beyond the scope of this chapter.

The lottery in Tennessee is undoubtedly a successful program with an annual average of over $1 billion in sales for most of the life of the lottery. This chapter has examined some of the concerns that many people have over state-operated lotteries. However, since Tennessee only recently introduced the lottery, data are limited, and, thus, the economic impact of the lottery in Tennessee has not been examined. Clearly, the lottery provides some revenue to government. Aside from that, there are unlikely to be other major economic impacts from the lottery.

What is perhaps more important is the likely impacts on the Tennessee lottery if the state were to introduce other forms of legalized gambling such as casinos or online gambling. We examine these issues in the next section.

INTER-INDUSTRY RELATIONSHIPS[3]

Like most other states, Tennessee will be forced to consider whether or not it should expand its offering of legalized gambling beyond the lottery. One key consideration, given the Tennessee lottery is so new, is how any new gambling in the state would affect the lottery or other industries. In particular, the introduction of casinos and online gambling should be considered, as these are the most popular types of legalized gambling right now.

Figure 11.2: Studies on the Relationships among Gambling Industries

Paper	Years	States/Counties	Findings
Anders, Siegel, and Yacoub (1998)	1990-96	1 county (AZ)	Indian casinos cause a reduction in tax revenue
Borg, Mason, and Shapiro (1993)	1953-87	10 states	Lotteries cause a decline in some other tax revenue, but total tax revenue increases
Elliot and Navin (2002)	1989-95	All states	Casinos and pari-mutuels harm lotteries
Fink, Marco, and Rork (2004)	1967-99	All states	Net increase in lottery revenue causes a decrease in state aggregate tax revenue
Kearney (2005)	1982-98	All states	Lotteries do not harm other forms of gambling
Popp and Stehwien (2002)	1990-97	33 counties (NM)	Indian casinos reduce county tax revenue
Siegel and Anders (1999)	1994-96	1 state (MO)	A 10 percent increase in gambling tax revenue leads to a 4 percent decline in other tax revenue
Siegel and Anders (2001)	1993-98	1 state (AZ)	Slots harm lottery; horse and dog racing do not affect lottery

A variety of studies have examined the impacts of one gambling industry on another, but these studies tend to be limited, in terms of their scope and time period covered. The

---

[3] This section draws material from Walker and Jackson (2008).

findings are mixed, suggesting that gambling industries affect each other in varied ways. Figure 11.2 summarizes some recent studies on gambling inter-industry relationships.

Two studies of particular interest are those by Borg, Mason, and Shapiro (1993) and Kearney (2005). The Borg, Mason, and Shapiro study shows that, while lotteries may reduce revenues in other industries, the overall tax revenues to states tend to increase with the introduction of lotteries. The resulting increases in overall tax revenues are logical because states typically keep around 50 percent of all lottery ticket sales. The study by Kearney shows that lotteries do not reduce revenues in other gambling industries.

A more recent and comprehensive study examines the inter-industry relationships between casinos, lotteries, horse racing, and greyhound dog racing (Walker and Jackson 2008). The study uses panel data for all states from 1985-2000. The inter-industry relationships found are presented in Figure 11.3. Figure 11.3 indicates that the industries listed in the rows affect industries in the columns in a positive way (+) or negative way (-). Parentheses indicate that the results were not statistically significant. Generalizing from studies in other states, one would expect that Tennessee, which currently has only a lottery, would experience the following impacts on its lottery: commercial and tribal casinos would harm the lottery; horse or dog racing would have a positive impact on the lottery. In other words, based on the results from the Walker and Jackson (2008) study, casinos and lotteries are substitutes, while the lottery and racing are complementary. In any case, it is likely that the introduction of a new type of gambling, particularly casinos, would lead to an *increase* in overall tax revenues, even if casinos would cannibalize some of the lottery revenues.

Figure 11.3: Summary of Intrastate Industry Relationships[4]

Model and Variables	Casino	Dog Racing	Horse Racing	Lottery
Casino		–	+	–
Dog Racing	(–)		–	+
Horse Racing	+	–		+
Lottery	–	+	+	
Indian Casino	+	(+)	+	–

The Tennessee lottery may see a modest reduction in sales (or lower growth in sales) with the introduction of any new type of gambling in the state. Previous empirical studies suggest that some gambling industries act as substitutes and others act as complements. Depending on the goal of public policy, this consideration may be very important or irrelevant. If one is interested in allowing consumers to spend their money how they wish, then perhaps additional forms of gambling should be legalized, regardless of the net tax impacts on the state. After all, the introduction of a new good or service is likely to be beneficial to those consumers who choose to consume the good or service, as well as the industry providing it.

---

[4] The variable tested for each industry is revenue (or volume), except for Indian casinos. Since tribes are sovereign nations, they are not required to report or publicize revenue data. Indian casino square footage is a proxy for the volume/revenue at tribal casinos.

BORDERING STATE COMPETITION

Casino gambling is likely to become a serious public policy issue of debate sooner or later in Tennessee. There are several critical issues to consider with respect to the availability of casino gambling in neighboring states. As shown in Figure 11.4, Tennessee borders eight other states. Casino gambling (tribal or commercial) is already available in Missouri, North Carolina, and Mississippi.

Figure 11.4: Map of Tennessee and Bordering States

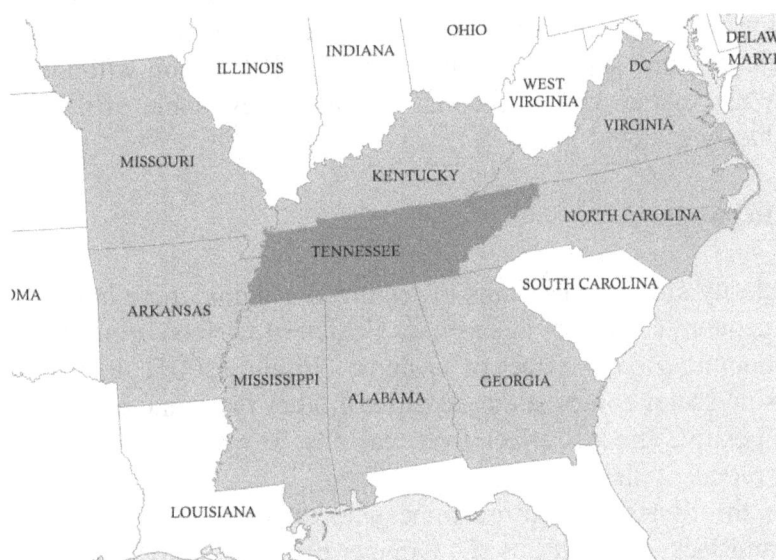

The ninth largest casino market in the U.S. during 2011 was Tunica, Mississippi (AGA 2011). This market is roughly 30 miles from Memphis and just 15 miles across the Tennessee-Mississippi state line. Data from the Mississippi Gaming Commission (2012) indicates that over 30 percent of patrons to Tunica casinos come from Tennessee. The Cherokee Casino in Cherokee, NC, is about 75 miles from Knoxville, TN. Again, this provides a casino opportunity for people living in a large Tennessee city. Finally, there is a small riverboat casino in Caruthersville, MO, right on the Missouri-Tennessee state line, which is convenient for the rural northwest part of the state (near Dyersburg, TN). Thus, many Tennessee citizens already have fairly easy access to casino gambling and both Kentucky and Arkansas are actively considering the legalization of casinos in the future. One argument typically given in support of introducing casinos in a state is that citizens of the state are already patronizing casinos in other nearby states. Subsequently, the state in question might as well introduce its own casinos to keep the tax revenue at home. This is a major consideration which finally resulted in legal casinos in Massachusetts. The argument makes sense from a fiscal perspective. If citizens are already gambling at casinos, perhaps the state could benefit by keeping the people in their home state.

A second argument is that the introduction of casinos will create a new tourist attraction and may increase the amount of tourism in the state. It is difficult to estimate the overall size and impact of this effect. Given the now widespread availability of commercial and tribal casinos (nearly 1,000 of them in the U.S. currently), it is unlikely that the introduction of casinos in Tennessee would generate a significant amount of new tourism for the state.

ECONOMIC BENEFITS OF CASINOS IN TENNESSEE

In previous sections, the Tennessee lottery, its likely relationship to other forms of legalized gambling, and how gambling in Tennessee would compete with gambling in neighboring states have been discussed. Now in anticipation that commercial casinos will be considered as a public policy issue, we discuss the likely impacts of casinos being introduced in Tennessee. Without exception, state governments consider legalizing casinos because they believe casinos will create jobs and supplement state coffers. This section will address the economic benefits typically associated with casinos as well as review some of the costs and negative impacts of introducing casinos.

ECONOMIC GROWTH

Despite the popularity among politicians of legalized casinos, there has been relatively little research on the economic impacts of casinos. Critics of casinos argue that there is little, if any, positive economic growth effect of casinos. Grinols (2004), for example, argues that growth in the casino sector comes at the expense of other firms and industries, so that there is little if any net positive growth effect from casinos. However, Grinols does not base his discussion on empirical evidence.

In one of the first studies to examine whether casinos are a catalyst for economic growth, Walker and Jackson (1998) used a Granger causality analysis modified for panel data to test the relationship between casino revenues and state-level per capita income. The analysis found that casinos cause economic growth. However, the sample period was relatively short, spanning from 1991-1996. The study was repeated in 2007 and no significant Granger causal relationship was found (Walker and Jackson 2007). The conflicting results from the two studies could be interpreted as showing that casinos appear to have at least a short-term positive impact on state-level economic growth. This conclusion was further supported when the impact of rebuilding the casino industry in the wake of Hurricane Katrina was examined (Walker and Jackson 2009). The study found that states in which there was a casino industry saw a statistically significant higher rate of economic growth in the aftermath of Katrina, compared to those states that were affected but did not have commercial casinos.

The intuition behind casinos having at least a short-term stimulus effect is straightforward. Building a casino, which may cost anywhere from several hundred million to billions of dollars, requires a large inflow of capital to a state or region. In addition, both the building and operation of a casino are relatively labor intensive. So the building and operation of a casino represents economic activity, as does the customers betting on casino games. In these respects, casinos act as economic engines just as do other firms in the economy that are producing goods or services.

One caveat regarding the research that shows the positive impact of casinos on state-level economic growth is that the empirical work has not been sophisticated enough to tell exactly *how much* economic growth can be attributed to casinos; the literature only shows that there is a positive correlation between the casino industry growth and state economic growth.

The empirical work does suggest that the direction of "causation" is from casino growth to economic growth. This suggests that the introduction of casinos in Tennessee would be helpful to the state economy.

EMPLOYMENT

If casinos were introduced in Tennessee, we can trace out what would be expected to happen with employment in the state. As of March 2012, Tennessee had an unemployment rate of 7.9 percent (Bureau of Labor Statistics 2012). To the extent that casino construction and operation jobs come from unemployed workers in the state, the casinos would clearly represent an economic stimulus for the state. The unemployed would be going back to work, transfer payments would decrease, and economic activity would increase.

To the extent that casino construction and operations jobs are filled by individuals already employed, this too is likely to have a positive economic impact. Consider that workers are rational and will choose the best job they can get, given their preferences, expected wage rate, and any other factors that are important to them.[5] If a worker chooses to leave a current job in favor of taking a job at the casino, it must be the case that the worker sees the choice as his or her best option, given the various characteristics of the job on which workers make their decision about which job to take.

Another consideration is that when a casino opens it represents a new firm on the demand side of the local labor market. This means there will be increased competition among employers for qualified and productive employees. The increased competition for workers should push wage rates, benefits, or other amenities of jobs higher, resulting in an improved situation for workers.

It is possible, of course, that through increased competition in the entertainment market, some firms will be unable to compete successfully with a casino. In this situation, jobs created by the casino come at the expense of firms that have failed. The net employment impact in this case is zero, and it may be the case that the casino job is less preferred than the job that was eliminated. However, this possibility does not represent a good economic justification for preventing a casino from opening in a market. If it did, then one could argue against any new firm opening in a market. Such a stance is clearly contrary to economic development and a free market economy.

There has not been much empirical economic analysis of the impacts of casinos on labor markets. Perhaps the most comprehensive study to be published on the subject is the paper by Cotti (2008).[6] Cotti studies all U.S. counties from 1990-96. This period includes much of the first wave of casino adoptions in the U.S. The analysis uses county level employment and average weekly earnings data to determine whether there is a statistical difference between counties with a casino and those without. Cotti finds that total casino employment in casino counties rises 8.2 percent relative to non-casino counties, and that county earnings in casino counties rise 0.79 percent faster in casino than in non-casino counties. In order to test the robustness of his results, Cotti adjusts the model to include

---

[5] Some casino critics have argued that jobs at casinos are inferior to other jobs. This logic is suspect when one considers that workers will try to choose the best job available to them.

[6] The discussion on Cotti's (2008) paper is taken from a report written on the "substitution effect" of casinos for Spectrum Gaming's 2008 report for the State of Massachusetts. We use that discussion here because it is the most comprehensive review of Cotti's paper that has been written.

county-level trends in employment. He still finds the same qualitative effects, but they are smaller in magnitude. An additional finding is that the results seem stronger in rural counties compared to large urban counties. This makes sense, as a casino represents a relatively large firm in a rural county but not in a large urban county.

Cotti also tests the employment effects on other sectors in the economy, particularly other entertainment industries. His results suggest that there is an insignificant effect on the sub-sectors tested, including museums, zoos, parks, golf courses, ski resorts, marinas, fitness centers, and bowling alleys. The results do show a negative coefficient on employment for bars and restaurants, but it is not statistically significant from zero. Finally, the paper examines whether there are employment and/or earnings effects observed in neighboring counties with casinos. He finds no negative impacts and even finds that employment in the entertainment sector in neighboring casino counties increases. Overall, the results of Cotti's study suggest that casinos will have a net positive impact on the local economy through employment and wages.

TAX REVENUES

Aside from the expected employment effects from casinos, the tax revenues are typically the most important political motivation for the legalization of casino gambling. Tennessee may eventually introduce commercial casinos, or it may sign an agreement (i.e., compact) to allow a tribal casino in the state.[7] If the state signs a compact with the Cherokee (or another tribe whose reservation lands are within Tennessee), the state can seek to receive payments in return for its consent for the tribe to open a casino. In some cases, such payments are given on the condition that the state guarantees a monopoly for the tribal casino. In general, however, commercial casinos represent a greater potential benefit for state budgets.

A variety of studies have examined the impacts on state revenue from the introduction of casinos. The most comprehensive study on the topic to date examined state government revenues, net of federal transfers, for 1985-2000 (Walker and Jackson 2011). When tested, the net impact of casino revenues, and implicitly, casino taxes, were found to have a modestly *negative* impact from the introduction of casinos. It should be emphasized that the model tested included all states, but a limited sample size. Therefore, it may very well be the case that Tennessee would see a positive net impact on state revenues if it were to introduce casinos. However, the available evidence suggests that a positive tax revenue impact from casinos is not guaranteed.

Whatever the empirical evidence suggests as likely effects of gambling on net state tax revenues, both lottery and casino revenues face very high relative tax rates. This implies that the introduction of casinos should lead to an increase in net tax revenues, even if 100 percent of the casinos' revenues come at the expense of other industries in the state, as long as the state sets the casino tax at a higher rate than the sales tax. Although the empirical evidence is mixed, it is clear that tax revenues are a primary catalyst for states to introduce casinos. If nothing else, the casinos represent an alternative for politicians to cutting spending or raising other types of taxes in the state.

---

[7] The introduction of a tribal casino typically requires that the tribe build a casino on its reservation land. The introduction of tribal casinos requires federal government approval as well as the state's consent. Because tribal casinos are generally not regulated by the state, a detailed discussion of tribal casinos is beyond the scope of this chapter.

SOCIAL COSTS OF CASINOS

The social costs of gambling, and particularly those affiliated with casinos, have received an enormous amount of attention in the literature. Here we discuss two specific areas of this research which will be enlightening for predicting the likely impact of introducing casinos in Tennessee. First, the sources of social costs and the empirical estimates of the social costs of gambling are presented. An analysis of the relationship between casinos and crime concludes this section.

SOCIAL COST ESTIMATES

When states first began legalizing commercial casinos (outside of Nevada and New Jersey) in the early 1990s, there was much debate about the alleged social costs of gambling that are attributed to "disordered gamblers." Among the different topics of research related to gambling, estimating the prevalence and treatment of disordered gambling has become the major area of research. Psychology research finds that roughly 1 percent of the adult population can be considered to have a gambling problem.[8]

Problem gamblers often exhibit a variety of unhealthy and anti-social behaviors. Researchers have attempted to put dollar values on some of these bad behaviors, the sum of which came to be known as the "social costs of gambling" in the literature. Walker and Barnett (1999, Table 1) list some of the commonly alleged social costs to be associated with disordered casino gambling:

- Income lost from missed work
- Decreased productivity on the job
- Depression and physical illness related to stress
- Increased suicide attempts
- Bailout costs
- Unrecovered loans to pathological gamblers
- Unpaid debts and bankruptcies
- Higher insurance premiums resulting from pathological gambler-caused fraud
- Corruption of public officials
- Crime
- Strain on public resources
- Industry cannibalization
- Divorces caused by gambling

---

[8] The American Psychiatric Association (2000) publishes the *Diagnostic and Statistical Manual* which provides disorder categories as well as diagnostic criteria. Discussing the prevalence and diagnosis of gambling problems is beyond the scope of this chapter; therefore, such problems that exist among a small proportion of the population will be taken for granted. The term used to describe gambling problems has evolved. In the 1990s, there was "problem" and "pathological" gambling. The newest term is "disordered gambling." These different labels are used interchangeably in this chapter.

Researchers have tried to estimate the monetary value of these and other social costs. Grinols (2004) estimates the social costs per year per pathological gambler is $10,330. This estimate is derived by averaging the estimates from several other studies that provided original estimates. However, none of the papers used by Grinols went through a peer review, and many arguably have serious methodological flaws. There are several major problems with the social costs of gambling literature and empirical estimates. Many of these issues were identified by Walker and Barnett (1999) and Walker (2007b).

The first problem with many of the social cost studies is that their authors fail to define what "social cost" means. Many of the cost estimates were performed by individuals from disciplines other than economics, such as public administration, law, and even landscape architecture! These disciplines do not have a rigorous definition of social costs. Walker and Barnett (1999) argue that from a welfare economics perspective, a social cost represents a decrease in societal wealth. This definition precludes wealth transfers from being considered as social costs. Thus, among the effects on the list above, bailouts, income lost from missed work, decreased productivity, and bad debts could not actually be classified as social costs. True social costs—those that do decrease the wealth of society—may include police enforcement costs, incarceration costs, and treatment costs. As a whole, however, the social cost estimates in the literature dramatically overestimate the true social costs of gambling.

Another problem with the social cost estimates in the literature is that many of them are based on surveys of *Gamblers Anonymous* members. Since these individuals are likely those with the worst gambling problems in society, they likely overestimate the social costs of gambling for society at large. Further, it is questionable whether problem gamblers are able to accurately estimate the costs they have incurred or caused as a result of their disordered gambling.

A key problem with estimating the social costs of gambling—the problem that makes it effectively impossible—is "comorbidity," or that more disorders are present simultaneously than just the primary disorder. Recent published studies in psychology have shown that around 70 percent of problem gamblers have other behavioral problems. For example, Petry, Stinson, and Grant (2005) find that 73.2 percent of U.S. pathological gamblers have an alcohol use disorder. The prevalence rate for drug use disorders is around 38 percent for pathological gamblers. Another study (Westphal and Johnson 2007) found that 77 percent of their subjects with a gambling problem had a co-occurring behavioral problem, and 56 percent had multiple problems. The problem that comorbidity creates is that it makes it impossible to partition the socially costly behaviors among an individual's various disorders. Yet, *all* social cost of gambling estimates have ignored this issue, simply attributing all of the costs to problem gambling. This clearly means that social cost estimates overstate the true cost of problem gambling.

CASINOS AND CRIME

Perhaps one of the greatest concerns voters and policymakers have about the introduction of casinos is that casinos may create or attract crime. The fact that casino customers often carry large amounts of cash may be a catalyst for criminals to flock to casinos. Alternatively, disordered gamblers may commit crimes to get money to continue gambling. There have been a number of studies that have examined the relationship between casinos and crime. However, the results of these studies are far from conclusive.

One of the most comprehensive studies published to date on the relationship between casinos and crime is by Grinols and Mustard (2006). This study uses a county-level analysis of crime rates in casino and non-casino counties from 1977 to 1996. The authors find that casinos are responsible for a significant amount of crime in casino counties four or five years after casinos are introduced in the county. Several other studies have found similar results. However, studies linking casinos to crime have been criticized.[9] It turns out that a key empirical issue that affects whether a study can link casinos to crime is how the crime rate is measured. The crime rate helps us to judge the relative safety (or danger) of different communities, or the risk of an individual becoming a victim of crime; it is usually expressed as a rate per 100,000 population:

$$\text{Crime rate} = \frac{\text{\# of crimes committed}}{\text{population at risk}}$$

A review of the casino-crime literature (Walker 2010) found several important caveats to consider when evaluating the alleged link between casinos and crime. A key finding is that most of the papers that conclude that casinos cause crime exclude casino visitors (i.e., tourists) from the crime rate calculation, whereas studies that find no link between casinos and crime include visitors in calculating the crime rate.

When the Grinols and Mustard (2006) analysis concludes that casinos cause an increase in the crime rate, it is because they include the crimes committed by casino county visitors in the numerator, but exclude the number of visitors from the population at risk measure (in the denominator). This overstates the crime rate in casino counties.

A more recent study by Reece (2010) helps alleviate some of the problems in the casino-crime literature. Although Reece studied only one state (Indiana), he was more careful than most other researchers in modeling the casino-crime relationship. First, he controls for casino volume by including casino turnstile count as an explanatory variable in his model. He also included a variable for hotel rooms to help control for tourism in general. Reece's results indicate that increased casino activity *reduces* crime rates, except for burglary.

There exists conflicting evidence on the link between casinos and crime. But the best empirical work indicates that, if Tennessee were to legalize casinos and tourism increased, the number of crimes committed would increase, but the crime *rate* accounting for tourism would likely fall. In short, crime tends to be a larger concern about casinos than is warranted based on the empirical evidence.

If casinos are eventually introduced in Tennessee, a variety of social impacts can be expected. A proportion of the population can be expected to exhibit disordered gambling behaviors. However, it is not clear that the number of people with this type of infliction in Tennessee depends on whether or not casinos exist in the state. This is because many Tennessee citizens are already within a short drive to a casino.

Nevertheless, psychologists and economists tend to agree that there are some socially harmful impacts from casinos. Monetary estimates of these social ills are unreliable, so concerned citizens and politicians should simply be aware of the potential problem some individuals will have with gambling. But the issue is not much different from tobacco, alcohol, or fast food. Some people consume too much of these products, but this typically is not a good argument for government to ban the product—at least in a free society.

---

[9] For a detailed critique of the Grinols and Mustard (2006) paper, see Walker (2008).

ONLINE GAMBLING

As computer technology and Internet speed have increased, so too has the availability and volume of online gambling. There has been little empirical analysis of the online gambling market, but everyone with a computer has had access to Internet gambling for at least the past decade.

The online gambling market changed somewhat in 2006 with the passage of the Unlawful Internet Gambling Enforcement Act (UIGEA) which sought to ban banking transactions that involved gambling via the Internet. The law did little to curb Internet poker and other gambling, but it did cause much of the industry to move offshore. In April 2011, the FBI and Department of Justice seized the domain names of three of the biggest online gambling websites in one of the largest and most publicized acts to enforce laws against online gambling in the U.S. Still, people in the U.S. can gamble online, as the laws are easy to skirt and are not consistently enforced against individual gamblers.

In December 2011, the U.S. Justice Department surprised everyone by issuing an opinion that clarified its position on Internet gambling with respect to the Wire Act. The opinion effectively gives the right to states to individually regulate online gambling.[10] Several states have already begun drafting legislation to begin offering online gambling and Illinois became the first state to introduce online lottery sales in March 2012.

Because legal, state-regulated online gambling is virtually new, there is almost no empirical evidence to indicate what the likely effects of online gambling would be on other types of gambling. For example, if Tennessee were to introduce casinos and online gambling, how would these industries affect each other and the lottery?

One study that examines online gambling and its impacts on casinos is by Philander (2011). This study finds that each dollar increase in online gambling leads to a 30 cent reduction in commercial casino revenues. Yet, even in this case, the introduction of online gambling is likely to lead to a net *increase* in overall state revenue. Another study (Philander and Fiedler 2012) finds that online poker and offline (casino) gambling are complementary, rather than substitutes.

Since Tennessee currently has neither casinos nor online gambling, if it were to introduce the two simultaneously, it would likely maximize its revenues from legalized gambling offerings. The new forms of gambling would likely have a negative impact on lottery sales as explained earlier in the chapter. However, the introduction of new forms of gambling would almost certainly increase the overall amount of tax revenues from legalized gambling.

In terms of employment and other effects on the Tennessee economy, the introduction of online gambling in the state may stimulate employment, but most likely only modestly. An Internet gambling industry that serves the state would not likely be a very labor intensive operation. However, as with other types of legalized gambling, it does represent an industry that would offer something that consumers want. In this sense, one would expect online gambling to contribute to the state economy.

---

[10] This exempts sports gambling, as the opinion specifies that the Wire Act applies specifically to sports betting. See Seitz (2011).

CONCLUSION

States that have introduced lotteries, casinos, and other forms of legalized gambling typically do so after attempting at least a simple cost-benefit analysis. State government may hire consultants to provide empirical estimates of the costs and benefits of introducing a certain number of casinos in the state. But such empirical estimates are often flawed and, to some extent, arbitrary.

Legislation to introduce casinos typically specifies that the casinos must include a minimum capital investment, pay relatively high taxes, or other requirements. The legislation attempts to guarantee the state a minimal amount of benefits. At the same time, legislation may include provisions that require the casino industry to fund treatment or hotlines for problem gamblers, fund infrastructure improvements, and otherwise attempt to offset any social costs that may be attributed to casinos.

Rarely is the casino question considered simply in the context of whether the supply and demand sides of the market can interact to create value for the individuals in society. The gambling industry is thought of as a public policy, not as a typical market. But what about the issues of property rights, freedom of choice, and the role of government in a free society? These issues, widely discussed previously in the research literature (Walker 2007a), are also applicable in considering legalized gambling in Tennessee.

If we believe in individual freedom and property rights, values that were the basis for founding the United States, then why should these values not apply in the case of legalized gambling? Why shouldn't property owners be allowed to build a casino if they view that as the highest-valued use of their property? Similarly, why shouldn't consumers be allowed to spend their money as they choose, so long as their choices do not harm other people?[11] A classical liberal perspective on government is that government is created by individuals to protect their freedom and property rights. Yet, in the case of gambling, the role of government appears to be to protect people from themselves.

As other chapters in this volume have argued, the best path toward increased prosperity in Tennessee is more freedom, the reliance on market forces, and limited government. The application of these principles with respect to legalized gambling suggests that government should allow but regulate these industries. And, other states have provided a number of examples for how the industry can be effectively regulated. A completely free market for gambling is not politically feasible, nor is it something that would win popular support from voters. But a ban on gambling (except the lottery) is a highly inefficient policy because it prevents willing buyers and sellers of a popular entertainment industry from operating in the state. As with other sectors of the economy, a more free market with respect to the gambling industry would increase economic development in Tennessee.

---

[11] Critics of legalized gambling argue that the potential social costs associated with gambling represent externalities and therefore justify government regulation of the industry.

REFERENCES

AGA (American Gaming Association). 2011. *State of the States, 2011: The AGA Survey of Casino Entertainment*. Washington, DC: American Gaming Association.

American Pshychiatric Assocation. 2000. *Diagnostic and Statistical Manual of Mental Disorders*. 4th ed. Washington, DC.

Anders, Gary C., Donald Siegel, and Munther Yacoub. 1998. "Does Indian Casino Gambling Reduce State Revenues? Evidence from Arizona." *Contemporary Economic Policy* 16: 347-355.

Borg, Mary O., Paul M. Mason, and Stephen L. Shapiro. 1991. *The Economic Consequences of State Lotteries*. New York, NY: Praeger.

———. 1993. "The Cross Effects of Lottery Taxes on Alternative State Tax Revenue." *Public Finance Quarterly* 21: 123-140.

Bureau of Labor Statistics, U.S. Department of Labor. 2012. *Economy at a Glance: Tennessee*. Washington, DC: U.S. Department of Labor. http://www.bls.gov/eag/eag.tn.htm.

Clotfelter, Charles T., and Philip J. Cook. 1990. "On the Economics of State Lotteries." *Journal of Economic Perspectives* 4: 105-119.

———. 1991. *Selling Hope: State Lotteries in America*. Cambridge, MA: Harvard University Press.

Cotti, Chad D. 2008. "The Effect of Casinos on Local Labor Markets: A County Level Analysis." *Journal of Gambling Business and Economics* 2 (2): 17-41.

Elliott, Donald S., and John C. Navin. 2002. "Has Riverboat Gambling Reduced State Lottery Revenue?" *Public Finance Review* 30 (3): 235-247.

Fink, Stephen C., Alan C. Marco, and Jonathan C. Rork. 2004. "Lotto Nothing? The Budgetary Impact of State Lotteries." *Applied Economics* 36: 2357-2367.

Garrett, Thomas A. 2001. "The Leviathan Lottery: Testing the Revenue Maximization Objective of State Lotteries as Evidence for Leviathan." *Public Choice* 109: 101-117.

Grinols, Earl L. 2004. *Gambling in America: Costs and Benefits*. New York: Cambridge University Press.

Grinols, Earl L., and David B. Mustard. 2006. "Casinos, Crime, and Community Costs." *The Review of Economics and Statistics* 88 (1): 28-45.

Jackson, John D., Davis S. Saurman, and William F. Shughart, II. 1994. "Instant Winners: Legal Change in Transition and the Diffusion of State Lotteries." *Public Choice* 80: 245-263.

Kearney, Melissa S. 2005. "State Lotteries and Consumer Behavior." *Journal of Public Economics* 89: 2269-2299.

Mississippi Gaming Commission. 2012. http://mgc.state.ms.us.

Petry, Nancy M., Frederick S. Stinson, and Bridget F. Grant. 2005. "Comorbidity of DSM-IV Pathological Gambling and Other Psychiatric Disorders: Results from the National Epidemiological Surveys on Alcohol and Related Conditions." *Journal of Clinical Psychiatry* 66: 564-574.

Philander, Kahlil. 2011. "The Effect of Online Gaming Revenue on Commercial Casino Revenue." *UNLV Gaming Research & Review Journal* 15 (2): 23-34.

Philander, Kahlil, and Ingo Fiedler. 2012. "Online Poker in North America: Empirical Evidence on Its Complementary Effect on the Offline Gambling Market." UNLV Working Paper.

Popp, Anthony V., and Charles Stehwien. 2002. "Indian Casino Gambling and State Revenue: Some Further Evidence." *Public Finance Review* 30 (4): 320-330.

Reece, William S. 2010. "Casinos, Hotels, and Crime." *Contemporary Economic Policy* 28 (2): 145-161.

Rubensetin, Ross, and Benjamin Scafidi. 2002. "Who Pays and Who Benefits? Examining the Distributional Consequences of the Georgia Lottery for Education." *National Tax Journal* 55 (2): 223-238.

Seitz, Virginia A. 2011. "Whether Proposals by Illinois and New York to Use the Internet and Out-of-State Transaction Processors to Sell Lottery Tickets to In-State Adults Violate the Wire Act." *Memorandum Opinion for the Assistant Attorney General, Criminal Division, U.S. Department of Justice*, September 20.

Siegel, Donald, and Gary Anders. 1999. "Public Policy and the Displacement Effects of Casinos: A Case Study of Riverboat Gambling in Missouri." *Journal of Gambling Studies* 15: 105-121.

———. 2001. "The Impact of Indian Casinos on State Lotteries: A Case Study of Arizona." *Public Finance Review* 29 : 139-147.

Spectrum Gaming Group. 2008. *Projecting and Preparing for Potential Impact of Expanded Gaming on Commonweath of Massachusetts.* http://www.mass.gov/hed/docs/eohed/ma-gaming-analysis-final.pdf.

Tennessee Lottery. 2012. *Lottery Reports.* http://www.tnlottery.com/aboutus/ reports.aspx.

Walker, Douglas M. 2007a. *The Economics of Casino Gambling.* New York, NY: Springer.

———. 2007b. "Problems with Quantifying the Social Costs and Benefits of Gambling." *American Journal of Economics and Sociology* 66 (3): 609-645.

———. 2008. "Evaluating Crime Attributable to Casinos in the U.S.: A Closer Look at Grinols and Mustard's 'Casinos, Crime, and Community Costs.'" *Journal of Gambling Business and Economics* 2 (3): 23-52.

———. 2010. "Casinos and Crime in the U.S.A." In *Handbook on the Economics of Crime*, edited by B.L. Benson and P.R. Zimmerman. Northampton, MA: Edward Elgar.

Walker, Douglas M., and Andy H. Barnett. 1999. "The Social Costs of Gambling: An Economic Perspective." *Journal of Gambling Studies* 15 (3): 181-212.

Walker, Douglas M., and John D. Jackson. 1998. "New Goods and Economic Growth: Evidence from Legalized Gambling." *Review of Regional Studies* 28 (2): 47-69.

———. 1999. "State Lotteries, Isolation, and Economic Growth in the U.S." *Review of Urban & Regional Development Studies* 11 (3): 187-192.

———. 2007. "Do Casinos Cause Economic Growth?" *American Journal of Economics and Sociology* 66 (3): 593-607.

———. 2008. "Do U.S. Gambling Industries Cannibalize Each Other?" *Public Finance Review* 36 (3): 308-333.

———. 2009. "Katrina and the Gulf States Casino Industry." *Journal of Business Valuation and Economic Loss Analysis* 4 (2): article 9.

———. 2011. "The Effect of Legalized Gambling on State Government Revenue." *Contemporary Economic Policy* 29 (1): 101-114.

Westphal, James R., and Lera Joyce Johnson. 2007. "Multiple Co-Occurring Behaviours among Gamblers in Treatment: Implications and Assessment." *International Gambling Studies* 7: 73-99.

CHAPTER 12

COURT REFORM:
"COMPETITION IN THE COURTROOM"

by Art Carden and Justin Owen

Freedom and Prosperity
in Tennessee

12

COURT REFORM: "COMPETITION IN THE COURTROOM"[1]

Art Carden and Justin Owen

"The assumption that there is a unique, correct resolution, which serves so well in empirical investigations, leads one astray when dealing with legal matters." (Hasnas [1995] 2007, 167)

A growing body of research emphasizes the importance of secure private property rights and a well-functioning legal system in achieving economic prosperity. Secure private property rights reduce the cost of transacting and, therefore, enable more trade, more innovation, and more wealth creation. Secure private property rights give people incentives to invest in long-term projects and valuable skills. With secure property rights, people know they will be able to keep the fruits of their labors. A well-functioning legal system is an essential element of a pro-growth institutional environment. In this chapter, we explore the relationship between the courts, methods of judicial selection, the rule of law, and economic performance. In addition, we summarize and evaluate law and economics research suggesting that a free market in legal institutions would be superior to state-created and state-operated legal institutions.

The rule of law is an essential element of a well-functioning capitalist economy; indeed, McCloskey (2006, 14), for example, defines "capitalism" as "private property and free labor without central planning, regulated by the rule of law and by an ethical consensus." Annual reports on economic freedom in different parts of the world have inspired a rich stream of empirical research showing that the institutions of a free society lead to prosperity (for example, Carden and Hall 2010).[2]

A well-functioning legal system is impartial. It dispenses justice blindly and efficiently. In light of the goals of a well-functioning judicial system, different states have adopted different methods of selecting judges. The empirical literature suggests that there are differences in judicial performance across different systems of judicial selection. Looking at evaluations of democratic decision-making by Caplan (2007) and Pincione and Teson (2006),

---

[1] Many insights in this chapter are drawn from various lectures given by John Hasnas.

[2] See Gwartney, Lawson, and Hall (2011) for data and analysis at the international level and Ashby, Bueno, and McMahon (2011) for data and analysis for North America.

it is clear that attempts to centrally plan legal systems sacrifice the essential information-generating characteristics of the market process. Democratic failure and the problems associated with central planning suggest that a free market in legal and judicial services is worthy of serious consideration. An obvious objection, of course, concerns the effect of such a system on the poor, but there are good reasons to think that a competitive, free market legal system would actually serve the poor better than a centrally planned legal system.

WELL-FUNCTIONING LEGAL SYSTEMS

Proposals for court reform, including proposals endorsing different methods of judicial selection, are generally aimed at implementing reforms thought to improve the performance of the system. It is generally accepted that a neutral and independent judiciary is necessary for a well-functioning legal system. Judicial independence is rooted in the notion that it is important to shield judges from bias and undue outside influence. Parties that appear before courts should be confident that the judge(s) will hear their arguments on their merits and issue a neutral, objective ruling. Those concerned with the processes of judicial selection tend to emphasize the importance of preventing special interests from interfering with the neutrality and objectivity of the system. Others tend to emphasize the importance of an independent judiciary beholden only to the people rather than the two other branches of government. The significance of a neutral and independent judiciary is commonplace in the debate over judicial selection, no matter what the specific process employed.

A well-functioning legal system also mitigates the degree to which partisanship is involved in the judicial selection process. By their very name, partisan elections tend to encourage partisanship, while merit selection processes tend not to do so. As long as the democratic process is used and free speech rights are upheld, partisanship will play a role in judicial selection. Thus, those decrying partisanship in the judicial system typically find judicial elections unappealing, while proponents of involving political parties in the process tend to repudiate merit selection.

Preventing politically motivated outcomes is another important issue. Some involved in the process decry "judicial activism," a term that has recently become prevalent. The concern is that judges will use their position of power to advocate particular policy positions that should be left to the legislature. Alexander Hamilton (1788, paragraph 16) even warned against this: "The courts must declare the sense of the law; and if they should be disposed to exercise *will* instead of *judgment*, the consequence would equally be the substitution of their pleasure to that of the legislative body." Some evidence suggests that states with direct elections usually have more instances of politically motivated court rulings (Choi, Mulati, and Posner 2008). This is somewhat ironic, as proponents of judicial elections often cite "judicial activism" as a reason to necessitate direct elections in an attempt to emphasize another goal: judicial accountability.

The specific approach taken by a given state varies depending on the level of concern for judicial accountability and the most effective means to achieve that accountability. Aside from the dispute over whether a direct election or some other procedure provides more judicial accountability, there are other factors related to this goal. Thus, the differences in terms (limited or life tenure), frequency of elections (if held at all), type of election (open ballot or retention), and impeachment mechanisms vary greatly from state to state based on different levels of concern with judicial accountability.

Another consideration involves the desire to place qualified persons on the bench. This is probably the most cited reason for the development of the merit selection process as an alternative to elections. Elections tend to give deference to the democratic process, which does not always translate into well-qualified judges.[3] Regardless of the approach taken, seeking to place the most qualified members of the bar on state benches is of tremendous importance.

These goals are not exhaustive, and discussions about improving the judicial selection process are certainly not limited to these few. These are, however, the most prominent and often referenced. While others may appear from time to time, the aforementioned goals will become most familiar to anyone who follows the judicial selection debate. Further, while states consider each of the above factors when choosing a selection process, the attention paid to each goal varies as much as the different processes themselves. Much of the emphasis in a given state depends strongly on the historical problems that state has encountered with its selection process. Some states emphasize the importance of preventing judges from taking an active role in a current hot-button issue such as same-sex marriage or tort reform. Others attempt to combat the corrupting influences of partisanship and campaign financing on the state judiciary. Still others seek to increase the level of judicial independence from influence by the legislature or executive branches. It is important to understand these various concerns and how they affect the development of different and ever-changing processes for selecting state judges.

JUDICIAL SELECTION: METHODS AND CONSEQUENCES

Dubois (1986) claimed that judicial selection was probably the most widely-discussed issue in law reviews over the previous five decades. It remains the subject of a substantial amount of literature. Judicial selection processes vary from state to state. They can be grouped into four distinct categories: election, direct appointment (gubernatorial nomination followed by legislative advice and consent), merit selection, or some combination of the above (Choi, Gulati, and Posner 2008).

The traditional approach to judicial selection is to hold free and open elections. Most states are moving away from partisan elections, but a few states still select their entire slate of judges in partisan elections (Alabama, Illinois, Louisiana, Pennsylvania, Texas, and West Virginia). Other states have either retained their original nonpartisan election process, or they have revised their elections to be nonpartisan. A very limited number of states select judges via direct appointment. Judicial selection in Maine, New Jersey, and Delaware closely resembles the federal approach of executive nomination followed by legislative advice and consent. In only two states, Virginia and South Carolina, is the legislature responsible for selecting judges (American Judicature n.d.).

About half the states have resorted to a process whereby an independent judicial selection commission submits judicial candidates to the governor, who then must make appointments from the submitted list. Because Missouri was the first state to adopt a merit

---

[3] Caplan (2007) discusses the likelihood of bias contaminating democratic outcomes.

selection approach in 1940, this process is generally referred to as the "Missouri Plan." Alaska, Colorado, Connecticut, Hawaii, Iowa, Maryland, Nebraska, Rhode Island, Utah, Vermont, and Wyoming are among the states that began emulating the Missouri Plan in the thirty years afterward (American Bar Association 2000). The District of Columbia also has a similar approach, where the president of the United States appoints candidates nominated by a selection commission, subject to confirmation by the U.S. Senate. Similarly, nine of the states that follow the Missouri Plan require eventual senate confirmation of the governor's appointment. (Rhode Island requires both houses to approve its supreme court nominees) (American Judicature n.d.). Judges appointed through this process typically face retention elections after a specified term.

Ten states have a combined approach to judicial selection. The most prevalent approach taken is merit selection for appellate courts and either partisan or nonpartisan elections for all lower-level judicial offices. The states implementing a combined approach are Arizona, Florida, Indiana, Kansas, Missouri, New Mexico, New York, Oklahoma, South Dakota, and Tennessee (American Judicature n.d.). Tennessee itself is in the middle of a process to reform how judges are selected. A proposal has passed the first step toward becoming a constitutional amendment, and will continue to be discussed by the next General Assembly in 2013 or 2014, before potentially being placed on the ballot for voters in the November 2014 election. The proposal would resemble the federal approach, whereby the governor appoints judges subject to the advice and consent of the state legislature.

IMPACT OF THE SELECTION PROCESSES

There are studies that compare the various selection methods to judicial quality. As noted by Hicks (2007), the legal system quality is lower in states whose citizens elect their Supreme Court justices. Partisan elections create even less quality than nonpartisan elections, according to the Institute for Legal Reform's State Liability Systems Ranking (Hicks 2007). This was validated by a similar study by Sobel and Hall (2007, 79), which found that

> judicial quality is lower in states that utilize elections to select their judges. Utilizing a new dataset measuring judicial quality across the 50 U.S. states, we also find it is the partisan nature of judicial elections that is the primary reason for lower judicial quality in elective states that utilize partisan elections.

Choi, Gulati, and Posner (2008, 290) take a different view, providing evidence that "(a)ppointed judges write higher-quality opinions than elected judges do, but elected judges write more opinions, and the evidence suggests that the large quantity difference makes up for the small quality difference." Meanwhile, they find no additional independence for appointed as opposed to elected judges. They interpret this as evidence "that elected judges focus on providing service to the voters, whereas appointed judges care more about their long-term legacy as creators of precedent" (293). Appointed judges write opinions that are cited more frequently, but elected judges make up for relatively lower quality by providing more opinions.

If the government is to continue to provide judicial services, the best method of selecting justices might depend on the context. Maskin and Tirole (2004) develop a model in which accountability is desirable when people know and understand the consequences of the policies that will be enacted. Specialization and hierarchy might be more appropriate when voters have bad information, when it is costly to acquire, and when feedback about the effects of a policy is slow to emerge. Whether this is the case in the market for judicial services remains to be seen. There are important differences between judicial services provided by a government and judicial services provided in the competitive marketplace. Regardless of the system of selection under consideration, the differences between incentives in the political arena and incentives in the marketplace have important implications for the efficacy of the legal system.

DEMOCRATIC FAILURE AND COMPETITION IN THE LEGAL SYSTEM

Posner (2005) notes that one of the obvious problems with judicial elections is that they limit the pool of potential judges by including only those who are good at campaigning. By the same token, we might say that the problem with judicial appointments and variations is that it reduces the potential pool of judges to those who are good at winning the favor of people who are good at campaigning. By forsaking the market in the selection of judicial services, governments create dysfunctional systems and discard the crucial information that markets provide. As Mises ([1920] 1990) and Hayek (1945) (among others) have shown, central planning is literally impossible in the absence of private ownership of the means of production and the prices, profits, and losses that will be generated by exchange. In short, we cannot centrally plan an economy. There is no compelling reason to think we can centrally plan a legal system, and indeed, socialized ownership of the means of the production of justice runs into many of the same problems.

With respect to selection of the judiciary, political means run into the difficulties that emerge from democratic systems. Caplan (2007) argues that one of the reasons governments make bad economic policies in democratic countries is because voters want them. He identifies four biases: anti-market bias, anti-foreign bias, make-work bias, and pessimistic bias, and he documents evidence for these biases using data from the Survey of Americans and Economists on the Economy. Carden and Hammock (2010, 71-76) discuss a fifth bias, which they call "stick-it-to-the-man bias" and note that this bias pervades some discussions of environmental policy. These biases are likely to influence the outcomes of judicial selection.

In both elected and appointed judicial systems, we can expect a degree of responsiveness to these biases. For elected judges, the way to stay in office will be to cater to the biases of the electorate. In an appointed system, those doing the appointing will be influenced by voter biases. Given the objectives of politicians (to get elected), voter biases are likely to bleed into judicial selection. The fundamental problem with politics is that voting is not particularly costly, nor is an individual vote likely to influence the outcome of an election. Votes, therefore, can be cheap signals of policy preferences, and voters have extremely weak incentives to update false information or correct their biases.

However, incentives are much stronger in competitive systems. In a free market for judicial services, competing firms would have powerful feedback mechanisms that provide them with information and incentives they need to provide appropriate services. Specifically, firms that do a bad job in the eyes of their customers (both actual and prospective) would lose money, while firms that do a good job would make money. In light of an emerging body of research on market provision of services we usually associate with governments, free markets in judicial services should be considered as a viable alternative.

FREE MARKETS IN LAW

"If human beings had the wisdom and knowledge-generating capacity to be able to describe how a free market would work, that would be the strongest possible argument for central planning. One advocates a free market not because of some moral imprimatur written across the heavens, but because it is impossible for human beings to amass the knowledge of local conditions and the predictive capacity to effectively organize economic relationships among millions of individuals." (Hasnas [1995] 2007, 185)

"Political economy has disapproved equally of monopoly and communism in the various branches of human activity, wherever it has found them. Is it not then strange and unreasonable that it accepts them in the industry of security?" (de Molinari 1849)

A growing body of research suggests that judicial services can be provided in the free market.[4] Further, these services can be provided in greater quantity, with greater efficiency, at lower cost, and to the benefit of the poor. Pro-growth policy in Tennessee should recognize and encourage trends toward the substitution of private arbitration for government-provided judicial services. As Benson ([1990] 2011), Hasnas ([1995] 2007), and Hayek (1973) have noted, law emerges through a trial-and-error process by which people seek to resolve conflicts. The law embodies not necessarily abstract principles of cosmic justice, but the practical principles that emerge as people seek solutions to the problems that confront them from day to day. There are arguments that judicial services are public goods that should be provided by the state; however, as Coase (1974) has argued for lighthouses and D'Amico (2010) has argued for prisons, markets can and do provide these services. D'Amico argues that "the rise of a government's system was more the result of private rather than public interest" (461). Moreover, market-provided law would most likely be oriented toward restitution and recovery rather than retribution and incarceration (Benson [1990] 2011).

Alternative Dispute Resolution (ADR) has risen as a free market solution to resolving private disputes. There are various types of ADR. First, mediation "is a method for settling disputes outside of a court setting" whereby a mediator is agreed upon by the parties in dispute who works to reach consensus among the parties (Black 1968). Another type of ADR is arbitration, where the parties agree to appoint a neutral, third party arbitrator to settle the dispute. In many cases, the parties agree to select arbitration far before a dispute ever arises, such as in contract situations where a provision will stipulate that if a dispute arises out of the agreement, it will be settled via arbitration.

These types of dispute resolution may be conducted at the direction of or with permission from a judge, thus they are often intertwined with the traditional court system. However, as noted above, there are situations where parties themselves select a method of ADR without ever entering into the traditional court system. ADR continues to become a preferred process for many because it is oftentimes less costly, less risky, and provides for a

---

[4] See, for example, the essays collected in Stringham (2007).

quicker resolution than an overburdened court system can afford. In fact, it is particularly popular in commercial disputes. A recent survey of 1,000 of the large U.S. companies showed that 79 percent had resolved their disputes via arbitration during the previous three years (National Arbitration Forum 2005).

Because ADR is voluntary and mutually agreed upon by the parties, it has market-driven elements that the traditional court system lacks. Its results, often quicker and cheaper, are thus preferred more and more by those who find themselves in a legal dispute. At the very least, ADR provides citizens with choice, allowing them to decide the best venue for resolving their conflicts: mediation, arbitration, or the traditional court system. As economists Bryan Caplan and Edward Stringham (2008, 503) have written

> Public courts lack both incentives to be customer oriented and pricing mechanisms, plus they face problems associated with the bureaucratic provision of services. When parties can choose their tribunals, in contrast, those tribunals must serve customers and be mindful about conserving resources.

Just as competition works to the benefit of consumers in other sectors, it does so in the legal system, unless of course the public courts exercise their monopoly over the service.

The government monopoly of the public court system is imposed in a variety of ways. First, the judiciary (or legislative branch via statutory law) often restricts the types of alternative dispute resolutions available to consumers. They also impose rules on these private tribunals or allow for appeal of an alternative resolution such as arbitration to a traditional court. Finally, courts frequently overrule contracts that spell out an alternative resolution plan voluntarily agreed upon by the parties (Caplan and Stringham 2008). Caplan and Stringham (2003) argue that without these restrictions private tribunals might become even more utilized to resolve disputes.

Markets in judicial services give potential providers incentives to develop reputations for honesty, integrity, and fair judgment. Chapter 8 discussed the effects of regulation and licensing, and Klein (2012) discusses how private certification mechanisms like credit ratings, Better Business Bureau membership, and other forms of evaluation and information transmission provide competitive checks on opportunism. Posner (2005) points out explicitly how the incentives of private arbitrators are affected by the possibility of losing business. Posner notes that a private arbitrator is chosen by both sides to a dispute, and an arbitrator who develops a reputation for always coming down on the side of one group (management, for example, as opposed to labor) will find itself unacceptable to one party in a dispute. Why, then, aren't they more prevalent? Posner (2005, 1261) notes that government subsidies to adjudication via the court system place private arbitration firms at a "cost disadvantage." Removing subsidies for government adjudication would encourage innovation in the private sector. In spite of fear that the interests of the wealthy would dominate a free market in dispute resolution and judicial services, there are sound reasons to think that such reforms would work to benefit the poor.

What About the Poor?

"In spite of popular myths about capitalism oppressing the poor, the poor are worst off in those things provided by government, such as schooling, police protection, and justice."
(Friedman [1989] 2007, 54)

One of the main concerns people have when confronted with the idea of a purely free market legal system is that such a system might allow the poor to slip through the cracks. Perhaps such a system would be prone to abuse, or alternatively it could best serve the interests of the already well-off. Scholars who have studied the practical issues related to free market law have addressed these issues, and there is at least a plausible case to be made that the poor will be better served by a competitive legal system rather than a government monopoly.[5]

Why? The poor are ill-served by a monopoly court system as things stand. When we are considering legal institutions, the relevant comparison is not "a perfect court system" versus a free market in law but "what we have now" versus a free market in law. There will be trouble, undoubtedly, in a purely free market system. However, it is a mistake to indulge what some economists have called "the Nirvana Fallacy," which is to assume that perfection is part of the range of institutional possibilities. Chapter 10 explored the role of incarceration in fostering participation in Tennessee's Families First welfare program. A system of privately provided law focused on restitution and recovery rather than retribution and incarceration would likely help to alleviate some of the problems of parental absence that are contributing to the size of Tennessee's welfare-receiving population.

As Friedman ([1989] 2007) notes in the quote above and as scholars like Deirdre McCloskey (2006, 2010) have documented, the poor have been the biggest winners from modern capitalism. The incentives provided by the market process are clear and easy to interpret. Profits and losses tell people whether they are using resources wisely or wastefully. Political incentives are much more difficult to interpret, and in light of the voter biases identified by Bryan Caplan (2007), it is not at all surprising that a politically operated court system would produce pathologies, injustice, and oppression. Through political systems and courts, people can impose large costs on others at minimal cost to themselves simply by voting for it. If the costs of oppression were privatized, we suspect that relatively few people would be willing to indulge (Friedman [1989] 2007).

We also suspect that most people would likely agree that the legal system as it currently operates does not serve the poor especially well. While it is possible that a purely private market for law will be worse, the claim that "the poor will be left behind" in a free market for law and law enforcement is a canard. If the poor are already being left behind, then it is perhaps reasonable to examine the incentives embedded in the institutions in place.

The current legal system is costly, and litigation is often very time-consuming. This is disadvantageous for the indigent more so than any other group. To the contrary, market-based systems, similar to the ADR approaches previously discussed, would be more efficient and less costly, thus offering greater access at a more affordable price for the poor. Rather than "eat their losses" as many indigent citizens may do in the current system, a free market in law would give them greater recourse, allowing the poor to resolve their disputes on a level

---

[5] See Rothbard ([1973] 2007) for a discussion of rogue private police forces.

playing field. Far from being left behind, the poor might be better served by a free market legal system than one that is centrally planned.

CONCLUSION

Encouraging economic growth in Tennessee requires a careful examination of the state's legal institutions. The process by which judges are selected influences judicial outcomes, and these in turn affect economic activity. There is no hierarchical, political way to determine which arrangement of judicial services best serves Tennesseans, and a growing body of research suggests that centrally planned, government provided and administered judicial services lack the information-generating characteristics of market provided and administered judicial services. In light of emerging research on the relationship between bias and inefficient outcomes, as well as research on the private provision of judicial services, Tennessee policymakers should consider ways to substitute more private solutions such as ADR for government planning within the state's legal system. In spite of objections to the contrary, such a system is likely to work for all Tennesseans in the long run, including the poor.

REFERENCES

American Bar Association. 2000. *Standards on State Judicial Selection: Report of the Commission on State Judicial Selection Standards*. July. http://www.lwvohio.org /assets/attachments/file/Standards%20on%20State%20Judicial%20Selction.pdf.

American Judicature Society. n.d. *Methods of Judicial Selection*. http://www .judicialselection.us /judicial_selection/methods/selection_of_judges.cfm.

Ashby, Nathan J., Avilia Bueno, and Fred McMahon. 2011. *Economic Freedom of North America: 2011 Annual Report*. Vancouver, BC: Fraser Institute.

Benson, Bruce. (1990) 2011. *The Enterprise of Law: Justice without the State*. Oakland, CA: Independent Institute.

Black, Henry Campbell. 1968. *Black's Law Dictionary*. 4th ed. St. Paul, MN: West.

Caplan, Bryan. 2007. *The Myth of the Rational Voter: Why Democracies Choose Bad Policies*. Princeton: Princeton University Press.

Caplan, Bryan, and Edward Peter Stringham. 2003. "Networks, Law, and the Paradox of Cooperation." *Review of Austrian Economics* 16 (4): 309-326.

———. 2008. "Privatizing the Adjudication of Disputes." *Theoretical Inquiries in Law* 9 (2): 503-528.

Carden, Art, and Josh Hall. 2010. "Why Are Some Places Rich and Others Poor? The Institutional Necessity of Economic Freedom." *Economic Affairs* 30 (1): 48-54.

Carden, Art, and Mike Hammock. 2010. "The Truthiness Hurts." *Economic Affairs* 30 (2): 71-76.

Choi, Stephen J., G. Mitu Gulati, and Eric A. Posner. 2008. "Professionals or Politicians: The Uncertain Empirical Case for an Elected Rather than Appointed Judiciary." *Journal of Law, Economics, and Organization* 26 (2): 290-336.

Coase, Ronald. 1974. "The Lighthouse in Economics." *Journal of Law and Economics* 17 (2): 357-376.

D'Amico, Daniel. 2010. "The Prison in Economics: Private and Public Incarceration in Ancient Greece." *Public Choice* 145: 461-482.

de Molinari, Gustave. 1849. "On the Production of Security." *Journal des Économistes*, February 15. http://www.panarchy.org/molinari/security.html.

Dubois, Phillip L. 1986. "Accountability, Independence, and the Selection of State Judges." *Southwestern Law Journal* 40: 31.

Friedman, David. (1989) 2007. "The Machinery of Freedom: Guide to a Radical Capitalism." In *Anarchy and the Law: The Political Economy of Choice*, edited by Edward P. Stringham, 40-56. Piscataway, NJ: Transaction Publishers and the Independent Institute.

Gwartney, James D., Robert A. Lawson, and Joshua C. Hall. 2011. *Economic Freedom of the World: 2011 Annual Report*. Vancouver, BC: Fraser Institute.

Hamilton, Alexander. 1788. "Federalist #78." In *The Federalist Papers*. Library of Congress. http://thomas.loc.gov/home/histdox/fed_78.html.

Hasnas, John. (1995) 2007. "The Myth of the Rule of Law." In *Anarchy and the Law: The Political Economy of Choice*, edited by Edward P. Stringham, 163-92. New Piscataway, NJ: Transaction Publishers and the Independent Institute.

Hayek, Friedrich A. 1945. "The Use of Knowledge in Society." *American Economic Review* 35 (4): 519-530.

———. 1973. *Law, Legislation, and Liberty, Volume I: Rules and Order*. Chicago: University of Chicago Press.

Hicks, Michael J. 2007. "Reduce the Cost of Civil Litigation and Depoliticize the Courts." In *Unleashing Capitalism: Why Prosperity Stops at the West Virginia Border and How to Fix It*, edited by Russell S. Sobel, 185-97. Morgantown, WV: Center for Economic Growth, The Public Policy Foundation of West Virginia.

Klein, Daniel B. 2012. *Knowledge and Coordination: A Liberal Interpretation*. Oxford, UK: Oxford University Press.

Maskin, Eric, and Jean Tirole. 2004. "The Politician and the Judge: Accountability in Government." *American Economic Review* 94 (4): 1034-1054.

McCloskey, Deirdre N. 2006. *The Bourgeois Virtues: Ethics for an Age of Commerce*. Chicago: University of Chicago Press.

———. 2010. *Bourgeois Dignity: Why Economics Can't Explain the Modern World*. Chicago: University of Chicago Press.

Mises, Ludwig von. (1920) 1990. *Economic Calculation in the Socialist Commonwealth*. Translated by S. Adler. Auburn, AL: Ludwig von Mises Institute.

National Arbitration Forum. 2005. *Business-to-Business Mediation/Arbitration vs. Litigation: What Courts, Statistics & Public Perceptions Show about How Commercial Mediation and Commercial Arbitration Compare to the Litigation System*. January. http://www.adrforum.com/users/naf/resources/GeneralCommercialWP.pdf.

Pincione, Guido and Fernando Teson. 2006. *Rational Choice and Democratic Deliberation: A Theory of Discourse Failure*. Cambridge, UK: Cambridge University Press.

Posner, Richard A. 2005. "Judicial Behavior and Performance: An Economic Approach." *Florida State University Law Review* 32: 1259-1280.

Rothbard, Murray N. (1973) 2007. "For a New Liberty: A Libertarian Manifesto." In *Anarchy and the Law: The Political Economy of Choice*, edited by Edward P. Stringham, 18-39. Piscataway, NJ: Transaction Publishers and the Independent Institute.

Sobel, Russell S. and Joshua C. Hall. 2007. "The Effect of Judicial Selection Processes on Judicial Quality: The Role of Partisan Politics." *Cato Journal* 27 (1): 69-82.

Stringham, Edward P., ed. 2007. *Anarchy and the Law: The Political Economy of Choice*. Piscataway, NJ: Independent Institute and Transaction Publishers.

CHAPTER 13

LEGAL REFORM: SPECIFIC CHANGES TO FOSTER ECONOMIC GROWTH

by Justin Owen

13

LEGAL REFORM: SPECIFIC CHANGES TO FOSTER ECONOMIC GROWTH[1]

Justin Owen

The term "tort" derives from the French word meaning "wrong." In the American legal system, tort law is designed to protect injured parties against tortfeasors, or wrongdoers. In a perfect or ideal tort system, a person who injures another—the defendant—would fully compensate the victim—the plaintiff—for all harm done. The plaintiff would be "made whole" by receiving full compensation from the defendant for his or her injuries.

In reality, however, the tort system has been expanded to include not only actual damages, but also non-economic damages as well as punitive damages. Economic damages compensate a victim for such expenses as medical bills, lost wages, and, if necessary, future care. Economic damages are based upon evidence provided by the plaintiff and are reasonable compensation for injury.

In addition to economic damages, plaintiffs may also be able to recover non-economic damages if the facts of the case support such awards. Unlike economic damages, which are based on tangible evidence such as bills and receipts, non-economic damages are awarded based on amorphous concepts like pain and suffering and loss of enjoyment of life. While non-economic damages are sometimes deserved, they can at other times be wildly disproportionate to economic damages.

The third type of damages, or punitive damages, are awarded not to make the victim whole, but to punish the defendant or attempt to defer future wrongful activity on his or her part.

Despite (or possibly as a result of) the growing definitions of damages, the U.S. tort system is rife with inefficiencies. The tort system of the United States has an annual direct cost of $180 billion, amounting to 1.8 percent of the gross domestic product (GDP), which makes it the most expensive tort system in the world. In 1960, tort costs amounted to just 0.6 percent of the GDP, rising to 1.3 percent of the GDP by 1970. Despite this high cost, plaintiffs receive an average of just 42 percent of the amount spent in the tort system, and only about 20 percent of the total costs directly compensate victims for economic losses. The

---

[1] Portions of this chapter were adapted from a study conducted by the author and published by Owen et al. (2011).

majority of direct tort costs, or 58 percent, goes toward administration, attorneys' fees, and defense costs (Council of Economic Advisors 2002).

Compare this to the U.S. workers' compensation system, which has been referred to by the White House Council of Economic Advisors as an ideal system for litigation cost-breakdown. According to the National Academy of Social Insurance, for every dollar paid to workers' compensation claimants, approximately 23 percent is paid in administrative costs (Mont et al. 2001). This represents less than half the per capita administrative costs eaten up by the current U.S. tort system.

Finally, the existing tort system leads to activity that would otherwise not occur in a natural world of voluntary transactions. For instance, doctors frequently practice defensive medicine, ordering tests and procedures not because they are necessary or prudent, but out of fear of subjecting themselves to legal liability if they did not. This leads to excess costs and drives up consumer prices for both healthcare and health insurance.

Using data from a PriceWaterhouseCoopers study, the nonprofit Pacific Research Institute has found that unnecessary spending on defensive medical procedures reaches $124 billion per year nationwide (McQuillan and Abramyan 2008). According to the study, defensive practices have made personal health insurance unaffordable for an estimated 3.4 million people nationally (McQuillan, Abramyan, and Archie 2007).

The ultimate burden of the tort system's current excess costs is borne by individuals through job loss, reduced wages, and increased consumer prices. Thus, an inefficient and abused tort system leads to less freedom and lower prosperity. In order to eradicate inefficiencies in their tort systems that have led to these consequences, several states have enacted various reform measures. Among the most prevalent reform measures include non-economic damages caps, punitive damages caps, the enactment of a loser pays system, collateral-source rule reform, and changes to class action lawsuits.

Tennessee has enacted several of these reforms over the past few years. First, the General Assembly enacted reforms that specifically impacted the medical community. In 2008, the Legislature passed legislation that, among other changes, requires plaintiffs' attorneys to provide notice to all medical providers who may be named in a medical malpractice lawsuit and file a "certificate of good faith" based on an evaluation by an independent medical expert that the claim has merit.

Second, in 2011, the Legislature undertook its most comprehensive reform steps to date. Lawmakers enacted the Civil Justice Act of 2011, which placed specific caps on non-economic and punitive damages and tweaked a host of other tort provisions in the state code. Third and most recently, the legislature enacted a type of loser pays system that will apply in certain cases after 2012.

There is some data available on the first round of reforms and their impact on medical liability cases. The 2011 reforms did not take effect until October of that year, and the 2012 reforms have yet to take full effect. Thus, an estimate of the economic benefit of these recent reforms to Tennessee can only be determined based on analyzing the impact similar reforms have had in other states. Multiple studies have been conducted in an effort to do just that.

FIRST ROUND: MEDICAL LIABILITY REFORMS OF 2008

In 2008, the Tennessee General Assembly embarked on the first changes to the state's medical malpractice liability act since 1975. After years of gridlock on the issue, a compromise bill was passed and signed by then governor, Phil Bredesen, in May 2008.

Among the changes, the law now requires plaintiffs' attorneys to provide 60 days notice to all medical providers who may be named in a medical malpractice lawsuit. They must also file a "certificate of good faith" that the claim has merit. The certificate must be based on an evaluation by an independent medical expert. Plaintiffs and their attorneys that act in bad faith according to the judge can be sanction for filing a frivolous suit. The law also requires that all parties in a suit be provided copies of a plaintiff's medical records within 30 days after they are requested (Locker 2008).

As of 2011, Tennessee Administrative Office of the Court records indicate that medical malpractice claims have decreased by 44 percent following the 2008 changes (Advisory Board Company 2011). In addition, lawmakers previously cited the state Department of Commerce and Insurance's Annual Report on Medical Malpractice as proof that reforms were necessary. According to the report, in 2008, more than 80 percent of medical malpractice claims resulted in no payout to the plaintiff, signaling that there were a significant number of frivolous lawsuits being filed (Farmer 2010). In 2011, the number of cases resulting in no payout had decreased to 62 percent (Tennessee Administrative 2010).

It appears the 2008 reforms have succeeded at reducing the number of medical malpractice claims filed, resulting in a reduction in frivolous lawsuits that drive up legal costs and lead to delays in the court system. By extension, this efficiency measure may prove to reduce healthcare costs, as similar reductions in claims have led to lower costs in other areas of the economy.

SECOND ROUND: COMPREHENSIVE REFORMS OF 2011

Notwithstanding the medical liability reforms made in 2008, Tennessee continued to fall in national tort liability rankings, promoting a call for more significant reforms. In 2006, Tennessee was ranked first nationally in the Pacific Research Institute's annual U.S. Tort Liability Index rating, but by 2010, the state had plunged to twenty-second place. Further, while the total number of tort cases disposed of between 2004 and 2009 decreased, the total monetary damages awarded actually increased place (Perryman Group 2011).

The reforms included in the Tennessee Civil Justice Act of 2011 were designed to eliminate inefficiencies, and create balance and predictability in the system. Unlike economic damages, which can easily be determined because they represent actual costs borne by the plaintiff, non-economic and punitive damages are more difficult to establish and quantify. The 2011 reforms capped non-economic damages such as pain and suffering, mental anguish, and loss of consortium at $750,000 per occurrence for medical liability actions and per plaintiff for non-medical actions. Punitive damages are now capped at $500,000 or twice all other damages, whichever is greater.

There are higher caps in place for catastrophic events such as spinal cord injuries, extensive burn injuries, intent to injure, and other specific circumstances. In those cases, the caps are $1 million for non-economic damages.

Further, unless directly involved in the design and/or manufacturing of a product, sellers are no longer liable for punitive damages. Unless the manufacturer withheld or omitted regulatory information, manufacturers are no longer liable for punitive damages as long as they were in regulatory compliance.[2]

Data suggest that the caps in particular lead to greater economic growth in states that enact them. This is true both within the medical field and for the general business climate. Two such states, Texas and Mississippi, have witnessed greater economic growth since the enactment of damages caps. According to one study, the average Texas household saves $1,078 per year as a result of its reforms. The state's employment rate has increased by 3.57 percent after its reforms were enacted in 1995 (Perryman Group 2000). Similarly, Mississippi saw an increase in jobs of about 4.6 percent after its 2004 enactment of damages caps (National Center 2008).

A preliminary study by The Perryman Group in March 2011 sought to quantify the potential economic impact of similar reforms in Tennessee. While this is a challenge due to alternative factors and differences among states, the study determined that at the very least, Tennessee could realize an additional $8.8 billion in gross state product and more than 66,000 permanent new jobs. Texas witnessed a significant increase in job growth after enacting caps in 2003. According to studies, these reforms have led to nearly half a million jobs in the state. If Tennessee experiences economic growth equal to that of Texas, this would lead to an additional $16.2 billion in annual economic output by the end of the next decade, and a total of 122,442 permanent jobs (Perryman 2011).

In addition to the general economic benefits linked to caps on damages, states have also experienced declines in medical malpractice costs, which have led to an increase in doctor populations and lower health insurance rates for consumers. In Mississippi, the number of medical malpractice lawsuits had decreased by 90 percent just four years after reform, resulting in a drop in malpractice insurance rates ranging from 30 to 45 percent (Moore 2008). Similarly, the five largest medical liability insurers in Texas lowered their rates after the state passed reform measures, saving doctors in the state approximately $50 million (Elliott 2005).

These lower insurance rates—and thus lower costs of practicing medicine—have a direct impact on physician supply, which in turn affects consumers' healthcare and health insurance costs and quality. One study found that states with damages caps similar to those recently enacted in Tennessee increased their physician supply by 2.2 percent relative to states without caps (Encinos and Hellinger 2005).

Specialized and emergency room physicians, who also happen to be those most susceptible to high malpractice insurance costs, are even more abundant in reform states, particularly in rural areas. The emergency physician supply is 11.5 percent higher in states with caps than those without. Rural counties in states with caps also have about 10 percent more surgical specialists than their counterparts without caps (Matsa 2007).

Increasing the physician supply will lead to direct prosperity for Tennesseans, particularly those in rural areas. Lower healthcare costs and greater access to quality care are essential to health and prosperity, and statistics show that caps on non-economic and punitive damages can create such an atmosphere in states.

---

[2] 2011 Tenn. Pub. Acts 510.

LOSER PAYS: 2012 CHANGES

In an effort to obtain further economic benefits and limit the negative impact of lawsuit abuse, proponents of tort reform have offered additional measures for state lawmakers to consider, some of which were passed into law during the 2012 legislative session. Among them include a system of loser pays in cases where the plaintiff fails to state a claim upon which relief can be granted.

The goals of a loser pays system are threefold. First, a loser pays system aims to reduce costs by controlling litigation expenses and caseloads. Second, the system aims to better compensate prevailing parties for costs incurred, such as attorney's fees. Finally, the loser pays system aims to deter frivolous suits while promoting meritorious ones.

Loser pays is a cost-effective measure imposed primarily in European countries. Currently, Alaska is the only state with a true loser pays system, maintaining this system since 1884. So has this complete loser pays system reduced the state's judicial costs? The most recent economic data for Alaska's court costs indicate that the state spent $75,093,700 on judicial expenses in fiscal year 2011 (Alaska Court 2009). In the same year, the U.S. Census Bureau estimated that Alaska's population was 722,718 (U.S. Census 2011a). Therefore, the cost per resident for Alaska's judicial system is approximately $103.91. On the other hand, Tennessee's budget for the same fiscal year was $119,586,800 (State of Tennessee 2012). The population in Tennessee for the same year was estimated at 6,403,353. Therefore, the cost per resident for Tennessee's judicial system is significantly lower at approximately $18.68 per person, and the court system in Tennessee only accounts for less than 0.4 percent of the state budget, well below the national average (U.S. Census 2011b).

Despite Tennessee's modest per capita court costs, awards given in tort suits rose sharply between 2008 and 2009. In 2009, total awards given for tort suits in Tennessee totaled $83.6 million, up $25.6 million from the previous year (Tennessee Administrative 2010). Advocates of the loser pays system posit that adopting it would increase the likelihood of settlement, and that those settlements will be more aligned with the true harm incurred by plaintiffs.

Research concerning settlements in a loser pays system, however, is deeply split on the validity of this claim.[3] Furthermore, while there is evidence to suggest that loser pays may cause litigants to weigh the merits of their claim more thoroughly, there is also evidence suggesting that a full-fledged loser pays system can result in a settlement in cases where a risk-averse defendant is worried about paying court costs even on a frivolous claim (McCabe and Inglis 2007).

Therefore, based on the evidence above, there is not clear proof that a comprehensive loser pays system either reduces the costs to the state or increases the likelihood of meritorious settlements. The most complete study of Alaska's loser pays system indicates that it has had no discernable effect on reducing the number of suits filed. According to the study, Alaska recorded 5,793 civil filings per 100,000 inhabitants in 1992. This number was only slightly below the national median of 6,610 per 100,000 that year and was very close to the filing rates of other relatively rural states (Di Pietro, Carns, and Kelley 1995).

---

[3] Studies suggesting that a loser pays rule would raise settlement rates include: Baye (2005); Snyder and Hughes (1990). Studies suggesting that a loser pays rule would lower settlement rates include: Bebchuk and Chang (1996); Hylton (2002); McCabe and Inglis (2007); Shavell (1982).

Seven states currently have some type of modified loser pays system.[4] While true loser pays systems are generally subject to heavy criticism, states that have selected specific types of suits for loser pays have seen greater success. For example, small claims cases are often cost prohibitive for poorer plaintiffs with meritorious claims; however, numerous studies have shown that loser pays systems targeted at small claims cases have been successful at encouraging meritorious suits among people who could not otherwise afford them (Bebchuk 1993; Hylton 1993; Katz 1987; Shavell 1982; Tullock 1980; Snyder and Hughes 1990).

The specific proposal recently passed by the Tennessee General Assembly stipulates that if a plaintiff's case is dismissed for failing to state a claim, the plaintiff would be responsible for all "costs and reasonable and necessary attorneys' fees incurred in the proceedings" up to $10,000.[5] This is designed to discourage frivolous lawsuits and encourage the expeditious resolution of cases. In essence, it penalizes parties for filing tenuous cases by placing the burden of paying the court costs on them.

Based on the preceding data collected from Alaska's experience with a true loser pays system, as well as a survey of several states with modified systems, evidence suggests that a modified loser pays system is more effective at meeting the goals of loser pays than a system like the one in Alaska. Tennessee's recently enacted loser pays applies to a limited subset of cases, and therefore may result in a greater degree of effectiveness at curbing frivolous lawsuits. However, this approach has not had time to run its course and be tested to determine its usefulness.

ADDITIONAL OPPORTUNITIES FOR REFORM

In addition to the changes already enacted by the Tennessee General Assembly, there are numerous other reforms states frequently debate when seeking to improve their tort systems. For instance, reforms to the collateral source rule and class action reform have been undertaken in a number of states.

COLLATERAL SOURCE RULE

The collateral source rule prohibits courts from admitting evidence that a plaintiff's costs after an accident will be paid by a collateral source such as an insurance company or worker's compensation. The theory behind the collateral source rule is that a defendant should not escape paying for an injury that he or she causes simply because the plaintiff has access to alternate forms of compensation. The collateral source rule has come under scrutiny from

---

[4] Oregon and Oklahoma have enacted statutes that apply loser pays principles to many areas of litigation. In Oklahoma, a defendant can choose an "offer of judgment" provision. Oregon has converted numerous one-way loser pays statutes into two-way loser pays statutes. Texas has an offer of settlement system in which the defendant must state that the case is subject to this system. If an offer is rejected and the ultimate judgment is significantly less favorable, the offering party can recover certain costs. However, in certain situations such provisions are not allowed, for example, in class action lawsuits, worker's compensation cases and family law cases. California and New York use a loser pays system when a plaintiff sues for unfair and deceptive business practices. Both states also have an offer of settlement system if the final outcome is worse than a settlement offer. Illinois has a loser pays system when suing for unfair and deceptive business practice. Florida has an offer-settlement system if the final outcome is worse than a settlement offer.

[5] 107th Tennessee General Assembly. HB3124/SB2638.

advocates of tort reform, however, who argue that the collateral source rule brings unnecessary and duplicate costs into the court system by making defendants pay for injuries that are already covered by third parties—after all, the goal of economic damages in particular is to make the plaintiff whole. These advocates call for disclosure of collateral compensation at trial, and for that compensation to offset the cost for which the defendant is liable. To understand what effect, if any, these reforms would have on Tennessee, it is instructive to compare Tennessee's existing collateral source rule reform with that of other states.

Tennessee's only collateral source rule reform relates to medical liability. Tennessee law allows economic damages to be offset in medical liability cases by collateral sources, except for sources including the assets of the plaintiff and the immediate family, or insurance purchased by the plaintiff.[6] Tennessee joins 37 other states that have some form of collateral source rule reform and is one of 13 states that have collateral source rule reform only in the field of medical liability (Schap and Feeley 2006).[7]

A recent survey of tort reform initiatives revealed that collateral source rule reform in medical liability cases—like the kind Tennessee has enacted—is a crucial part of reducing medical insurance premiums. The study found that collateral source rule reform in medical liability suits alone can lower premiums by as much as one to two percent, and when coupled with reforms such as non-economic damages caps and elimination of joint and several liability, can create even greater reductions (Avraham, Dafny, and Schanzenbach 2009). Furthermore, evidence suggests that instituting collateral source rule reform for medical liability reduces medical costs by five to nine percent within three to five years of adoption without substantially affecting mortality or medical complications (Kessler and McClellan 1996).

However, exploring alternate forms of collateral source rule reform is vital because of the prevalence of collateral source payments in our judicial system outside of medical liability claims. While the collateral source rule draws less attention than other reform measures, it is arguably of greater importance, as it potentially affects nearly every lawsuit in America to some extent (Kelly 2006). Imposition of the collateral source rule, or reforms that eliminate its application, have consequences for both plaintiffs and defendants.

Based on a recent study (Owen et al. 2011), 20 states permit consideration of collateral source payments offsetting a plaintiff's cost during trial, while 14 states require consideration of such offsets after the judgment or award. Six states require the offset to be taken after the jury's verdict but before entry of judgment by the court. New Hampshire has eliminated the collateral source rule altogether. In that state, the jury is allowed to consider evidence of insurance payments, as well as the cost of obtaining collateral source payments in medical liability cases. Evidence of government benefits such as Medicare, Medicaid, or Social Security may also be considered by the jury.

Research indicates that reforms to the collateral source rule, including outright elimination of the rule or using it to offset costs, decrease the number of lawsuits filed (Kelly 2006). Elimination of the rule would allow evidence of third party payments to be admitted at trial when determining damages owed by the defendant. These reforms result in a decreased caseload because, although introducing evidence of collateral source payments or post-verdict reductions of awards based on collateral payments do not completely eliminate a defendant's

---

[6] Tenn. Code Ann. § 29-26-119 (2009).

[7] States whose only collateral source rule reform concerns medical liability include Delaware, Massachusetts, Montana, Nebraska, Nevada, Oklahoma, Pennsylvania, South Dakota, Texas, Utah, Washington, and Wisconsin.

payment to an injured party, there is less motivation for a potential plaintiff to file a claim when the plaintiff's primary loss is economic and has already been substantially recovered through collateral sources, such as insurance (Kelly 2006).

Despite the potential for decreasing the number of tort suits as well as the costs associated with them, a major argument against reform to the collateral source rule involves the concept of subrogation. Subrogation occurs when an insurance company recoups funds that it paid to the insured after determining that those funds should have come from another source. Opponents argue that if the collateral source rule is eliminated or collateral payments are allowed to be introduced into evidence to offset costs, then plaintiffs will not be fully compensated in some situations. This would occur if an insurance company demanded that a plaintiff repay funds given to him because the costs were owed by the defendant, while the defendant was absolved of paying for the injury because he could use evidence of collateral payment to offset his costs to the plaintiff.

While subrogation issues are not particularly common, some state legislatures have reformed their collateral source rule laws and devised several remedies to deal with the subrogation issue (Wershbale 2008). Another suggestion to account for subrogation concerns modifying the concept of subrogation itself. Rather than have the plaintiff pay the costs of subrogation, if Tennessee adopted greater collateral source rule reform, Tennessee could craft a law that the defendant would have to pay the subrogation costs back to the plaintiff's insurer if an issue of subrogation arose (Rubin and Shepherd 2006). That way, the plaintiff would not lose out on full compensation, and the defendant would not run the risk of paying a plaintiff who was already fully compensated for his injuries by a third party. In the end, such reforms could lead to greater efficiency in the tort system by decreasing the number of lawsuits filed.

CLASS ACTION LAWSUITS

Another frequently considered reform is that surrounding class action lawsuits. Class action lawsuits represent mass tort claims, where a large number of plaintiffs collectively bring a claim in court, or where a plaintiff brings a claim against a large number of defendants. Class action lawsuits are more common in the United States than in other parts of the world. Before a class action lawsuit can proceed, the "class" must be certified by the court. This process requires the court to define the class, i.e., lay out the boundaries of who can be a plaintiff in the suit, approve the figurehead person or entity who represents all other plaintiffs, evaluate the initial plausibility of the claim, etc.

The majority of cases certified to proceed on a class-wide basis result in settlement, not trial (Willging, Hooper, and Niemic 1996). This is a recurring theme in civil litigation, where observations about the "vanishing trial" have become commonplace (Vanishing Trial 2004). One reason for this development lies in the rights of the opposing parties during the certification process. If the court does not certify the class, the plaintiff may appeal the decision of the court in hopes of obtaining a favorable judgment by a higher court. If a favorable judgment is indeed obtained, the suit would then proceed.

However, in many states, if the class is certified by the court, the defendant may not appeal the decision to certify the class to a higher court. This puts pressure on the defendant to settle the case with the plaintiff class rather than fight an enormously expensive class action suit in court which they cannot be certain they will win. The prevailing rule of trials is that only the final decision may be appealed to a higher court. However, in some limited instances, procedural decisions made by the court during a trial may be appealed. These procedural appeals are known as interlocutory appeals. Plaintiffs are able to appeal denials of class certification easily because the denial is essentially a final judgment on the case. An appeal of a class certification, though, would be an interlocutory appeal, and is only available in a limited number of states and situations. The current law in most states allows only the plaintiff the right to appeal a judge's denial of class certification. A defendant is denied the right of appeal if they believe the suit is being brought without just cause and must either settle or proceed to trial. With decreasing exception, class certification sets the litigation on a path towards settlement, not a full-fledged testing of the plaintiff's case by trial (Nagareda 2009).

Since 1997, 10 states have enacted some type of reform surrounding class action lawsuits, most often enabling interlocutory appeal of class action certification. This gives the defendants the same rights that plaintiffs already have—the ability to appeal a judge's decision to certify a class of plaintiffs and allow a lawsuit to proceed. Class action reform tends to make appellate review of class certification easier to obtain, the rules regarding the interlocutory appeal clearer, and attempts to accelerate the process so the suit may proceed if the appeal is denied. The ultimate effect is to increase fairness and efficiency.

The federal government took action in 2005 to reform class action procedures by passing the Class Action Fairness Act. Part of the effect of the act was to make appellate review of trial court certification decisions more readily available. The act did not address every detail of the relevant civil procedure, however, leaving many decisions to the courts. In the years since the act was passed, the courts have been unable to address every unanswered question. However, the presence of the act lends some support to states' attempts to enact their own versions of class action reform. Also, while many aspects of tort reform have faced legal challenges, class action reform has not been challenged in the states that have passed it (American Tort 2012).

CONCLUSION

Tennessee only recently began to tackle reforms in the medical malpractice and overall tort fields, thus most of the data for the state is prospective in nature. But based on the results from other states that have a lengthier experience with these reforms, numerous legal changes have proven to lead to a more balanced, fair, and efficient judicial system. Some proposals have also shown to boost economic performance, thereby leading to greater *freedom and prosperity*.

Some reforms, however, have failed to yield beneficial economic results. Others still lead to economic benefits if structured properly, but may cause unintended consequences if not. A continued attention to what works and what does not is imperative if the General Assembly seeks to improve our legal system and increase *freedom and prosperity* in Tennessee as a result.

REFERENCES

Advisory Board Company, The. 2011. "Tenn. Malpractice Lawsuits Drop 44% after Reforms." April 26. http://www.advisory.com/Daily-Briefing/2011/04/26/Tenn-malpractice-lawsuits-drop-44-percent-after-reforms.

Alaska Court System. 2009. *Annual Statistical Report 2009*. http://www.courts. alaska.gov /reports/annualrep-fy09.pdf.

American Tort Reform Association. 2012. "Class Action Reform." http://www.atra.org/issues /class-action-reform.

Avraham, Ronen, Leemore S. Dafny, and Max M. Schanzenbach. 2009. "The Impact of Tort Reform on Employer-Sponsored Health Insurance Premiums." NBER Working Paper No. 15371.

Baye, Michael R. 2005. "Comparative Analysis of Litigation Systems: An Auction-Theoretic Approach." *Economic Journal* 115: 583–601.

Bebchuk, Lucian A. 1993. "A New Theory Concerning the Credibility and Success of Threats to Sue." *Journal of Legal Studies* 25: 1-25.

Bebchuk, Lucian Arye and Howard F. Chang. 1996. "An Analysis of Fee Shifting Based on the Margin of Victory: On Frivolous Suits, Meritorious Suits, and the Role of Rule 11." *Journal of Legal Studies* 25 (2): 371–403.

Council of Economic Advisors. 2002. *Who Pays for Tort Liability Claims? An Economic Analysis of the US Tort Liability System*. April.

Di Pietro, Susanne, Teresa W. Carns, and Pamela Kelley. 1995. *Alaska's English Rule: Attorney's Fee Shifting in Civil Cases*. Alaska Judicial Council. October.

Elliott, Janet. 2005. "AMA Takes Texas off Its Liability Crisis List/Limits Credited for More Doctors and Fewer Claims." *Houston Chronicle*, May 17. http://www.chron.com /CDA /archives/archive.mpl?id=2005_3871129.

Encinosa, William E., and Fred J. Hellinger. 2005. "Have State Caps on Malpractice Awards Increased the Supply of Physicians?" *Health Affairs,* June 27, W5-317-W5-325.

Farmer, Blake. 2010. "Medical Malpractice Suits Drop with New Requirements." *WPLN, Nashville Public Radio*, January 4. http://wpln.org/?p=13393.

Hylton, Keith N. 1993. "Litigation Cost Allocation Rules and Compliance with the Negligence Standard." *Journal of Legal Studies* 22 (2): 457–76.

———. 2002. "An Asymmetric Model of Litigation." *International Review of Law and Economics* 22 (May): 153–75.

Katz, Avery. 1987. "Measuring the Demand for Litigation: Is the English Rule Really Cheaper?" *Journal of Law, Economics, & Organization.* 3 (2): 143-176.

Kelly, Michael B. 2006. "What Makes the Collateral Source Rule Different?" *Akron Law Review* 39: 1171-1180.

Kessler, Daniel, and Mark McClellan. 1996. "Do Doctors Practice Defensive Medicine?" *Quarterly Journal of Economics* 111 (2): 353-90.

Locker, Richard. 2008 "Tenn. Senate Sends Medical Malpractice Bill to Governor." *Commercial Appeal*, April 24. http://www.commercialappeal.com/news/2008/apr/24 /tenn-senate-sends-medical-malpractice-bill-governo/?print=1.

Matsa, David A. 2007. "Does Malpractice Liability Keep the Doctor Away? Evidence from Tort Reform Damage Caps." *Journal of Legal Studies* 36 (2): S143-S182.

McCabe, Kevin and Laura Inglis. 2007. "Using Neuroeconomics Experiments to Study Tort Reform." Mercatus Center at George Mason University. Policy Comment No. 16: 18.

McQuillan, Lawrence J. and Hovannes Abramyan. 2008. "U.S. Tort Liability Index: 2008 Report." Pacific Research Institute. http://www.pacificresearch.org/docLib /20080222_2008_US_Tort_Liability_Index.pdf.

McQuillan, Lawrence J., Hovannes Abramyan, and Anthony P. Archie. 2007. "Jackpot Justice: The True Cost of America's Tort System." *Pacific Research Institute*. http://www.pacificresearch.org/docLib/20070327_Jackpot_Justice.pdf.

Mont, Daniel, John F. Burton Jr., Virginia Reno, and Cecili Thompson. 2001. "Workers' Compensation: Benefits, Coverage and Costs, 1999 New Estimates, 1996-1998 Revisions." *National Academy of Social Insurance*. May.

Moore, Stephen. 2008. "Mississippi's Tort Reform Triumph." *The Wall Street Journal*, May 10. http://www.pacificresearch.org/press/mississippis-tort-reform-triumph.

Nagareda, Richard A. 2009. "Class Certification in the Age of Aggregate Proof." *New York University Law Review* 84 (97).

National Center for Policy Analysis. 2008. "Mississippi's Tort Reform Triumph." *Daily Policy Digest,* May 14. http://www.ncpa.org/sub/dpd/index.php?Article_ID =16547.

Owen, Justin, William Hines, Allyn Milojevich, and Jefferson Poole. 2011. "Lawsuit Abuse Reform in the Volunteer State: Evaluating the Legal and Economic Impact of Various Reform Measures." Tennessee Center for Policy Research, Policy Report No. 11-02. February 21. http://www.beacontn.org/wp-content/uploads/Lawsuit-Abuse-Reform-in-the-Volunteer-State.pdf.

Perryman Group, The. 2000. *The Impact of Judicial Reforms on Economic Activity in Texas Overall Economic Impact on State's Economy*. August.

———. 2011. *The Potential Impact of the Proposed Comprehensive Tort Reform Legislation on Business Activity in Tennessee*. March, 3.

Rubin, Paul H., and Joanna Shepherd. 2006. "Tort Reform and Accidental Deaths." Emory Law and Economics Research Paper No. 05-17; Emory Public Law Research Paper No. 05-29. February 20.

Schap, David, and Andrew Feeley. 2006. "(Much) More on the Collateral Source Rule." College of the Holy Cross, Department of Economics Faculty Research Series, Paper No. 06-05, June, Worcester, MA.

Shavell, Steven M. 1982. "Suit, Settlement, and Trial: A Theoretical Analysis under Alternative Methods for the Allocation of Legal Costs." *Journal of Legal Studies* 11 (1): 55-81.

Snyder, Edward A., and James W. Hughes. 1990. "The English Rule for Allocating Legal Costs: Evidence Confronts Theory." *The Journal of Law, Economics, & Organization* 6 (2): 345–80.

State of Tennessee. 2012. *The Budget: Fiscal Year 2012-2013*. A-42. http://www.tn.gov /finance/bud/documents/2012-2013BudgetDocumentVolume1.pdf.

Tennessee Administrative Office of the Courts. 2010. *Annual Report of the Tennessee Judiciary Fiscal Year 2008-2009*. 333. http://www.tncourts.gov/sites/default/files /docs/2008-2009_annual_report_02192010.pdf.

Tullock, Gordon. 1980. *Trials on Trial: The Pure Theory of Legal Procedure*. New York: Columbia University Press.

U.S. Census Bureau. 2011a. *State and County QuickFacts: Alaska*. http://quickfacts.census
    .gov/qfd/states/02000.html.

——. 2011b. *State and County QuickFacts: Tennessee*. http://quickfacts.census.gov/qfd
    /states/47000.html.

Vanishing Trial Symposium, The. 2004. *Journal of Empirical Legal Studies* 1: 459.

Wershbale, Jamie L. 2008. "Tort Reform in America: Abrogating the Collateral Source Rule
    across the States." *Defense Counsel Journal,* October 1.

Willging, Thomas E., Laura L. Hooper, and Robert J. Niemic. 1996. "An Empirical Analysis
    of Rule 23 to Address the Rulemaking Challenges." *New York University Law Review*
    71 (74).

CHAPTER 14

CONSTITUTIONALLY CONSTRAIN GOVERNMENT TO PROMOTE FREEDOM AND PROSPERITY

by George Crowley and Daniel Sutter

Freedom and Prosperity in Tennessee

14

CONSTITUTIONALLY CONSTRAIN GOVERNMENT TO PROMOTE FREEDOM AND PROSPERITY

George Crowley and Daniel Sutter

Society can either rely on the private or public sector to allocate resources. The chapters of this book have described the benefits of capitalism, or private sector decision-making. This chapter addresses the most direct way government can allocate resources, by taxing and spending. Economists have documented the benefits of limiting the size and scope of government, and we will begin by reviewing the evidence on how big government slows growth. Public choice economists argue that despite this cost, the interactions of self-interested politicians, bureaucrats, citizens, and interest groups result in excessive spending, or more spending than desired by the average citizen. Three ways to counter the spending bias of representative democracy—tax and expenditure limits, fiscal decentralization and competition between local governments, and separation of powers—will be examined and Tennessee will be evaluated on each measure. On the surface, Tennessee seems to have institutions in place to restrain government. For instance, Tennessee was one of the first states to adopt a constitutional fiscal constraint, has a line-item veto, and scores well in measures of fiscal decentralization. Closer examination reveals some fundamental problems with these constraints, and an unbalance in the separation of powers leaves Tennessee vulnerable to excessive state spending. Reducing the size of state and local government will be important in promoting *freedom and prosperity* in Tennessee.

MARKET INSTITUTIONS AND ECONOMIC PROSPERITY

Adam Smith, the founder of economics, was an early proponent of the role of institutions in generating wealth for nations. The last several decades have witnessed an explosion of research examining the link between institutions, and specifically the institutions of the market economy, to economic growth, both across nations and within nations. Humans have an inherent tendency to improve the quality of their lives, and the institutions of a market economy harness this self-interest in service to others through the profit incentive.

239

Much of the recent research on institutions and economic performance employs an index of economic freedom for more than 140 countries worldwide compiled by the Fraser Institute (Gwartney, Lawson, and Hall 2011). The international economic freedom index measures the quality of institutions based on five component areas: the size of government, the legal system and protection of property rights, the quality of the money supply, freedom to engage in international trade, and economic regulation (e.g., of credit and labor markets). The index is a score from 0 to 10, with 10 representing a high level of economic freedom. The index allows comparisons between countries, or a way to classify countries as having more or less economic freedom. A market economy requires a legal infrastructure protecting property rights and the freedom to trade. Internationally, many weak or predatory governments fail to supply the basic framework for market exchange, with terrible consequences for human well-being, as illustrated by Figure 14.1. The figure reports Gross Domestic Product (GDP) per capita, a measure of the standard of living across nations, averaged across quartiles of countries as ranked by their economic freedom score, as reported by Gwartney, Lawson, and Hall (2011). GDP per capita is roughly ten times higher in the top 25 percent of countries as ranked by economic freedom than in the bottom 25 percent of countries. These differences in standard of living did not occur overnight, and can reflect the cumulative impact over decades of an environment hospitable to a market economy. The difference between the top and bottom quartiles of nations reflects the effect of the lack of protection of property and the rule of law. But GDP per capita is still more than double in the freest 25 percent of countries than in the second 25 percent, so even among nations where the rule of law is reasonably well established, limiting government spending and regulation is critical for growth and a high

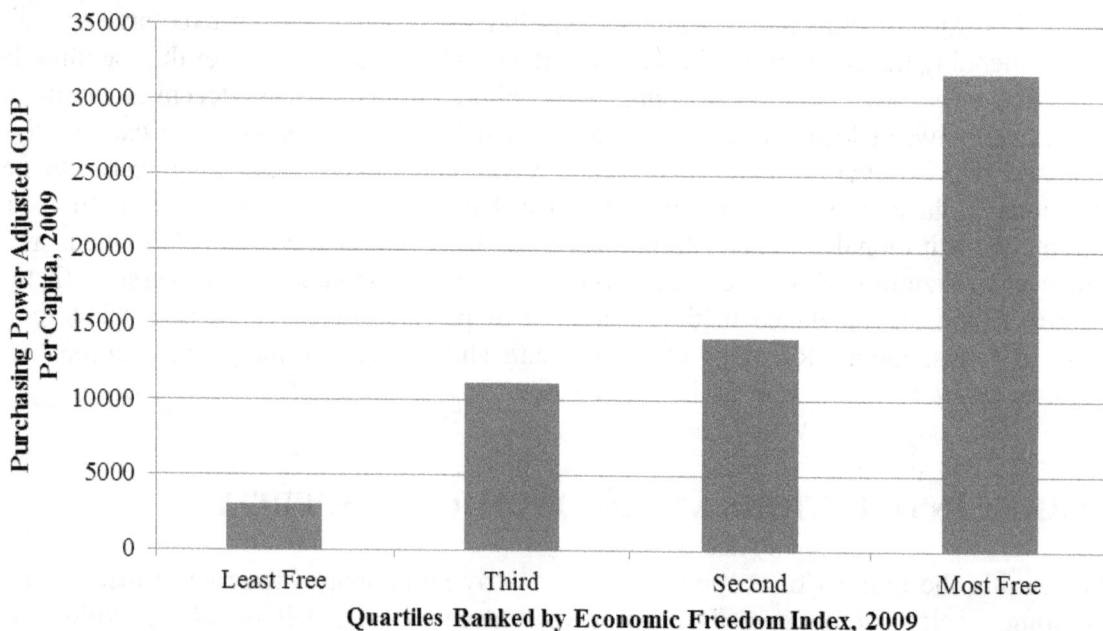

Figure 14.1 Economic Freedom and Prosperity

Sources: Heston, Summers, and Aten (2011); Gwartney, Lawson, and Hall (2011); Bureau of Labor Statistics (2006).

standard of living.[1] Economic freedom does not merely lead to the pursuit of a narrow measure of the standard of living, or produce growth for some at the expense of poverty for others. Norton and Gwartney (2008) show that economic freedom reduces extreme poverty and improves a nation's score on the United Nations' Human Poverty Index.

Figure 14.2: Per Capita Income (2010) vs. Size of State Government (1979)

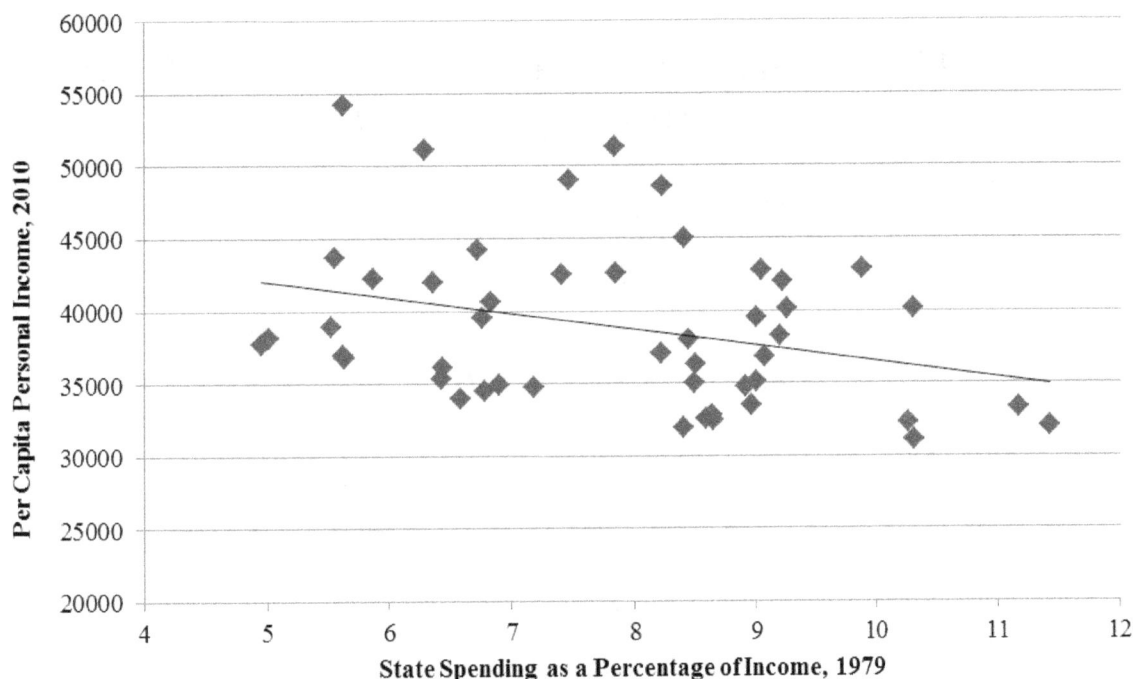

Sources: U.S. Census Bureau (1980); Bureau of Economic Analysis (2012); Bureau of Labor Statistics (2006).

The data clearly show a negative relationship between the size of state government and economic growth. The impact of state and local government on economic performance is surprising, given that all U.S. states share the same basic legal framework (the rule of law, an independent judiciary) and that federal government spending, taxation, and regulation are consistent across the states. Yet, differences in reliance on the private sector versus the public sector across states affect prosperity. Figure 14.2 provides evidence of the long-run relationship between government size and the economy. The figure plots state per capita personal income (PCPI) in 2010 against state direct expenditure as a percentage of personal income in 1979 for the 48 contiguous U.S. states. This figure provides insight into the effect of large state government in 1979 on standards of living three decades later. The negative slope of the trend line plotted through the scatter plot shows that states with larger governments in 1979 had lower incomes 30 years later. For the states with the largest

---

[1] Economists have extensively investigated the relationship between economic freedom and prosperity. For a discussion of some of the findings of these studies, see Gwartney, Holcombe, and Lawson (2004) and Lawson (2007).

governments in 1979 (those with spending making up about 11 percent), PCPI in 2010 was about $6,000 less than for those states with the smallest governments (making up about 5 percent of income). Figure 14.3 provides further evidence of the negative relationship between the size of state government and economic growth by plotting the relationship between growth of state direct expenditure and economic growth. The figure plots the growth in real PCPI between 1992 and 2010 for the contiguous United States against the growth in state direct expenditure as a percentage of income over the same period. As before, the trend line shows a clear negative relationship between fast growing governments and economic growth.[2]

Figure 14.3: Growth in Per Capita Personal Income vs. Growth in State Spending (1992-2006)

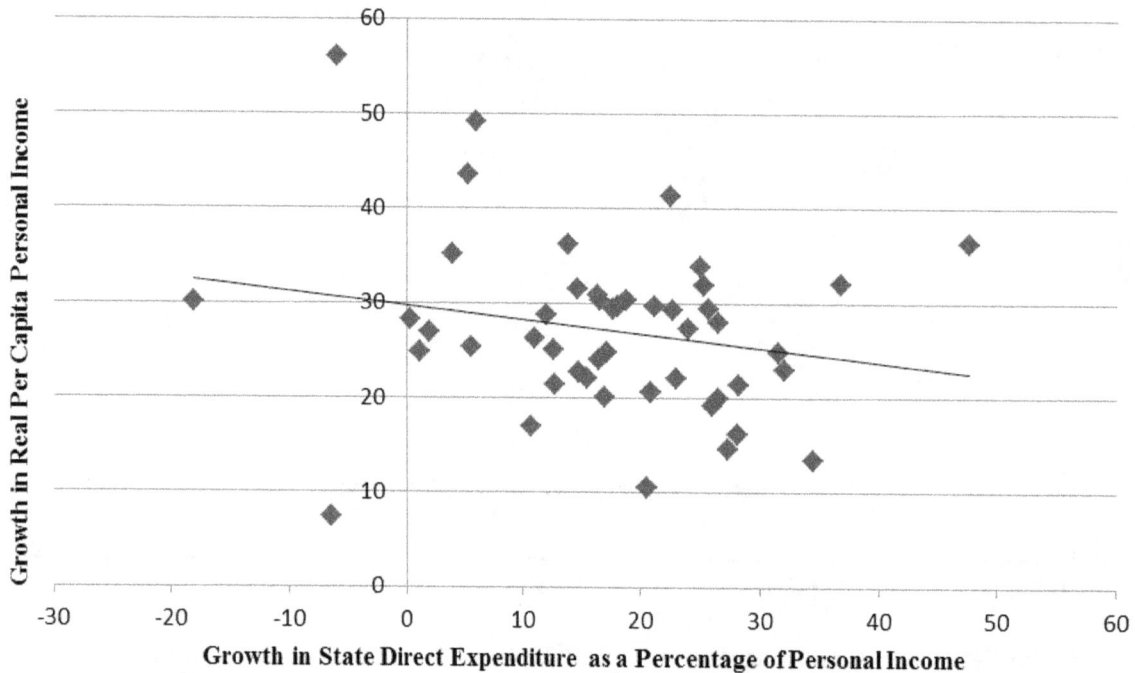

Sources: U.S. Census Bureau (2011b); Bureau of Economic Analysis (2012); Bureau of Labor Statistics (2006).

Regulations and mandates can substitute for government spending, so spending may paint an incomplete portrait of government allocation of resources. For example, government could protect coastal barrier islands by purchasing private lands at fair market value, which would involve a substantial expenditure, or simply prohibit owners from developing their property. Regulation affects the use of private property as surely as if the state government had purchased the lands. Lower economic freedom, even at the subnational level, reduces income and slows growth. Figure 14.4 plots the 2011 annual subnational economic freedom

---

[2] Vedder and Gallaway (1997, 1998) provide further evidence on the consequences for growth of excessive spending and references to other recent econometric studies.

scores (from 2009) of the 48 contiguous states against per capita personal income.[3] The positive relationship between the two is clear: states with a greater reliance on capitalism (and less of a reliance on government) are more prosperous. Tennessee's overall subnational score of 8.0 ranks 4th nationally, indicating a substantial amount of economic freedom within the state. Especially noteworthy are Tennessee's scores in Areas 2 and 3 of the index, which measure Takings and Discriminatory Taxation, and Labor Market Freedom. In these Areas, Tennessee truly stands out, ranking as the 5th and 1st most free state. Where Tennessee falters, however, is in Area 1, the portion of the index which measures the size of government. Here, Tennessee scores a 7.4, and ranks 18th among the states. Thus, while Tennessee is much more reliant on capitalism than other states in general, improvements with regards to the size and scope of government can still be made.

Figure 14.4: Economic Freedom and Per Capita Income

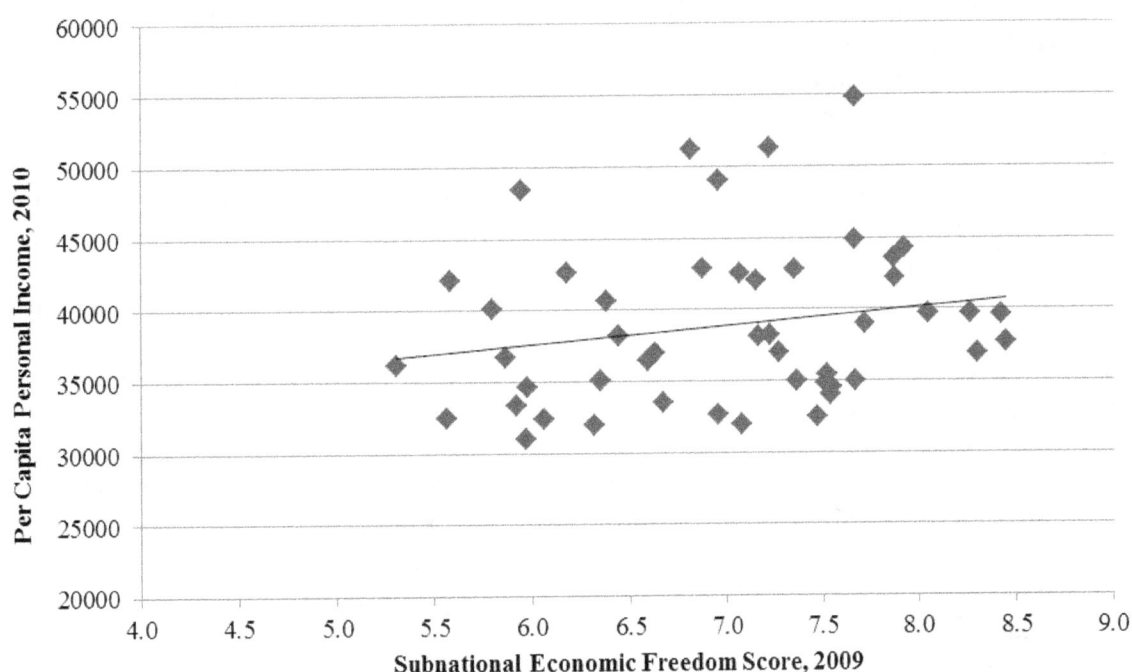

Sources: Bureau of Economic Analysis (2012); Ashby, Bueno, and McMahon (2011); Bureau of Labor Statistics (2006).

The importance of limiting the size of government for economic prosperity cannot be overstated. Economists Richard Vedder and Lowell Gallaway (1998) conclude, based on evidence at the state, federal, and international level, that a stable, hill-shaped relationship exists between income and the size of the public sector.[4]

As government grows from a very low level, the growth provides police, courts, and national defense which sustain the framework the market economy requires: stable property

---

[3] The full indices that accompany Ashby, Bueno, and McMahon's 2011 report are available on-line at www.freetheworld.com/efna.html.

[4] Vedder and Gallaway (1998) call this the "Armey curve" in honor of economist and former Congressman Richard Armey, who hypothesized the existence of such a relationship.

rights, enforcement of contracts, and protection from foreign invaders and marauders. Government provided infrastructure and services like roads and highways, schools, and fire protection also increase the productivity of the economy. However, as government expands past these core functions, the expansion of government reduces growth and income begins to fall.[5] Government growth hurts the economy in three ways. First, government increasingly makes resource allocation decisions, and these decisions are made for political reasons, not profit or loss considerations. Second, government must tax to fund spending. Taxes distort choices in the market, and the cost to the economy of this distortion exceeds the dollars collected for government to spend. Higher taxes reduce economic freedom, entrepreneurship (Garrett and Wall 2006), and growth (Poulson and Kaplan 2008). Marginal tax rates, the tax people pay if they earn an extra $1,000 or if a business earns an extra $1 million in profit, determine how much taxes reduce economic activity. The disruptive effect of taxes increases more than proportionally with the tax rate, so that the distortion from a 20 percent income tax rate is more than double that from a 10 percent. Vedder and Gallaway (1999) contend, based on the available evidence, that the cost of taxes may be 40 cents or more per dollar of revenue raised. Third, interest groups use resources to lobby politicians for increased spending, what Gordon Tullock (1967) labeled "rent seeking." Resources spent trying to secure favors from government cannot be used to produce things of value like cars, clothes, homes, and computers, making society poorer.

Economists have made considerable progress over the past several years establishing entrepreneurship as the link between economic *freedom and prosperity*. This is not surprising as, previously, economists like Joseph Schumpeter, Ludwig von Mises, and Israel Kirzner argued that the entrepreneur is the agent of creative destruction and progress in the market economy. The entrepreneur is the source of ideas for new or improved products, new uses for existing products, and new forms of economic organization. Entrepreneurship requires a free market, because we cannot know what new ideas will be discovered, or from where these ideas will come. Recent research documents how economic freedom increases entrepreneurship, using a variety of different measures of entrepreneurial activity, including the number of sole proprietorships, net business formation, patents, and venture capital.[6] On the other hand, politicization of the economy shifts entrepreneurship to socially unproductive forms, as William Baumol (1990) has argued, like litigation or the pursuit of government subsidies and favors. The same creativity, alertness, and intelligence which generate new wealth for the economy under good institutions become a drain on the productive economy. We see political entrepreneurship at work when companies exploit state development incentives and in the successful efforts of banks and automakers to obtain government bailouts.

---

[5] Olson (1982) examines democratic rent seeking and economic stagnation.
[6] For evidence on the relationship between economic freedom and entrepreneurship see Kreft and Sobel (2005); Garrett and Wall (2006); Campbell and Rodgers (2007); Sobel (2008).

The Imperfections of Politics and Excessive Government Spending

The economic analysis of institutions and growth demonstrates what government must do to facilitate growth: maintain secure property rights, provide an efficient court system, and supply important public goods like national defense or infrastructure. Then government must avoid politicizing the economy, by taxing, spending, and regulating too much. The question then becomes how to limit government and unleash capitalism. The obvious approach would be for Tennessee voters to elect politicians who will limit government and reduce spending. Voters across the nation took a step in this direction in 2010 by electing Tea Party candidates.

Yet, direct political action, paradoxically, is unlikely to attain this goal. To understand why, we must consider insights from public choice economics. The vision of democracy emerging from public choice scholarship contrasts sharply with high school civics class. Political decision making suffers from numerous serious deficiencies in comparison with market decision making. The maladies of politics, or what public choice economists call government failures, lead government to spend more than preferred by the average citizen. Representative government results in a budget which is not merely larger than fiscal conservatives desire, but larger than the majority of voters prefer. Democratic politics fails to deliver a government of the size citizens desire.[7]

The first cause of excessive spending is the considerable power to shape government decisions possessed by political agenda setters. Politics is like sports in that match ups matter. Some teams match up very well against some opponents, but very poorly against others. If you could set the matchups in the NCAA basketball tournament, you could set up a bracket to help your favorite team make the Final Four, even without blatantly cheating in your team's favor (e.g., making their opponents play with ankle weights or with four players). A similar dynamic prevails in politics. Legislators can limit what bills their colleagues get to vote on, or if their colleagues can offer amendments during floor debate. Legislative leaders can assign a bill they oppose to a hostile committee to ensure that the bill dies; agenda setting explains why the majority party in Congress or a state legislature has so much power. Politicians and bureaucrats can also manipulate the ballot propositions and tax measures which citizens get to vote on in elections. Voting and elections never pin down one outcome, allowing politicians to influence the eventual outcome. Given that politicians can benefit from spending money (providing benefits to grateful constituents or bureaucrats), they will take advantage of agenda power to increase government spending.

We live in a representative, not a direct, democracy, and this creates a second problem, the control of politicians. A legislator can pursue his or her interests at constituents' expense on some issues because voters have only relatively weak means to control politicians. Citizens control their representatives through reelection, while other types of political action, like making phone calls and sending emails, or working for and contributing to a candidate, affect reelection prospects. Yet legislators are elected once every two, four, or six years. Consequently, all the votes, committee work, bills sponsored, and hearings held over two (or more) years by an incumbent legislator must be reduced to one vote for or against, and

---

[7] The classic public choice analysis of democracy is Buchanan and Tullock (1962). Mueller (2003) provides a recent synthesis and overview, while Mitchell and Simmons (1994) provide a very readable treatment. For an analysis of the differences in the pathologies of politics at the level of the individual citizen, see Caplan (2007).

defeating the incumbent may mean electing a weak opponent. Citizens might have one or two issues which matter most to them, and vote for or against their legislator based on these issues. Beyond one's vote, the citizen has no further leverage to reward or punish any other actions by their representative. By contrast, firms can have their employees work for a salary, or on commission, or pay bonuses based on profit or team performance, offer promotions and raises, and terminate employment relatively quickly for unacceptable performance. Control mechanisms are much more nuanced in the private sector than in representative democracy. Legislators end up with comparatively broad discretion to pursue policies that either they or special interest groups prefer at the expense of constituents.

The third problem of politics is a lack of decisiveness for individual action, that is, individuals do not directly decide political outcomes. In the market, our choices or actions decide what happens to us, largely if not totally. For example, if you choose to buy soft drinks and not bottled water at the grocery store, you will come home with soft drinks. We can decide on a career or to start a business, even though we cannot guarantee ourselves success. In politics, citizens can vote or volunteer or contribute money to their favorite candidate or cause, yet still end up with the other outcome. In politics, an individual's actions rarely determine outcomes: an individual's vote only actually decides a tie election, which almost never occurs. The weak correlation between action and outcomes gives people little reason to participate in politics—why take time off work to go stand in line if your vote is unlikely to matter? This also reduces the incentive for people to become informed about politics—candidates in elections, ballot propositions, and bills under consideration. The lack of incentive to follow politics is known as rational ignorance. The lack of decisiveness also lowers the cost of voting to make a statement without regard to the actual consequences of a policy. Thus, people might vote to increase the minimum wage to show that they care about the working poor, even though a higher minimum wage increases unemployment for low wage workers.[8]

The maladies of politics result in excessive spending under representative democracy through the "law" of concentrated benefits and dispersed costs.[9] Agenda control creates the ability for politicians to pursue policies benefitting themselves or interest groups, and infrequent elections are a weak device to prevent such manipulation. Bureaucrats and government employees will favor increased spending which leads to higher salaries, larger staffs, greater prestige from controlling a larger budget, and additional resources to pursue their mission, and will support representatives who deliver larger budgets.[10] Politicians can take credit for government spending to address a problem, like say hiring more police officers to fight crime, building more prisons, or raising teacher salaries. Because of the weak connection between participation and outcomes in politics, only people with a lot at stake tend to follow the issue and get involved. Generally, these are the beneficiaries of government spending, as the costs of government spending—higher taxes and reduced disposable income for families—are widely dispersed, and rarely result in press conferences or photo opportunities. For example, there are about 65,000 full-time public school (K-12) teachers in Tennessee, and about 2.5 million households in the state. If the state government appropriated

---

[8] Brennan and Lomasky (1993) call this type of voting "expressive voting" and analyze such incentives in democracy. See also Caplan (2007) on how the lack of decisiveness can have far-ranging effects on voters' political world views.

[9] Buchanan and Wagner (1977) offer an excellent dissection of democratic politics' pro-spending bias.

[10] Niskanen (1971) analyzes the pro-spending bias of government bureaucracy.

funds to give each teacher a $5,000 per year raise, the cost per household would be about $130 per year. The average teacher has much more at stake than the average taxpayer. Consequently, teachers and not taxpayers rally at the state capitol when the legislature considers school funding. Powerful teachers unions will lobby and make campaign contributions to support legislators who vote to increase spending on public schools.[11] Politicians will find that voting for increased spending brings them benefits.

THE NEED FOR CONSTITUTIONAL LIMITS ON STATE SPENDING

Direct political action will not fix the problem of excessive government spending. Occasionally citizens may elect some politicians supporting small government who will stem the tide, as in 2010. But pleas for greater political participation do not repeal the law of concentrated benefits and dispersed costs. That political action, which may occasionally reduce government spending or slow the *growth* of government, does not invalidate the proposition that representative government usually spends more than the average citizen prefers. The spending bias is like having the home field advantage in football, where when two equally matched teams play, the home team often wins. Home field advantage is not absolute, and home teams do lose, even sometimes to an inferior opponent. Similarly, the spending bias in politics leads government to normally, but not always, spend excessively. Thus, the federal government ran a budget surplus in the late 1990s, but has run deficits 38 of 42 years since 1969.

The playing field of representative government tilts in favor of excessive spending. To resolve this dilemma, one must look for insights from constitutional economics, which studies the choice of rules for limiting government. Constitutional economics focuses on limitations beyond normal democratic politics (e.g. elections) to regulate the pathologies of politics.[12] Sports leagues make rule changes during the off-season to maintain competitive balance. Similarly, when citizens realize that the rules of representative democracy favor concentrated benefits and excessive spending, the rules need to be changed.

A variety of constitutional constraints on fiscal policy have been adopted in different states. The evidence shows that constitutional constraints have limited state government, at least on the margin (Krol 2007). One such limit is the balanced budget requirement (BBR). It is often reported that 49 states have some form of balanced budget rule, with Vermont the lone exception. State BBRs are designed to prevent shortsighted government officials from burdening the state with excessive debt. State BBRs take a variety of forms, and quantifying them in any meaningful way has proven notoriously difficult and has led to disagreement in the literature as to their effectiveness (Krol and Svorny 2007). For example, while a National Association of State Budget Officers report in 2008 found that Tennessee has a constitutional requirement to have both the Governor submit a balanced budget and the Legislature pass a balanced budget, analysis by Hou and Smith (2006) found no such limitation. They note that the actual language of Tennessee's constitutional BBR stipulates that expenditures must not exceed revenues in that year, effectively making it a "de facto unbalanced budget"

---

[11] For a discussion of how these forces over time affect representatives and generate a "Culture of Spending," see Payne (1991).

[12] The best statement of the need for constitutional rules limiting government is Brennan and Buchanan (1985). Lee and McKenzie (1987) and Racheter and Wagner (1999) also provide good treatments.

requirement as borrowing must occur. More stringent rules, such as those which make explicit mentions of the governor signing only a truly balanced budget into law, are required to avoid exploiting the BBR.

Another popular example of such a constraint is tax and expenditure limits (TELs). As of 2008, thirty states had passed some type of TEL, most since the "tax revolt" of the 1970s, with Tennessee one of the earliest adopters of a TEL in 1978. Several types of limitations have been adopted. As the name implies, TELs can be designed to limit tax revenues collected or the level of expenditures. Several states, Tennessee among them, limit the rate of spending growth to the rate of growth in per capita personal income. Such limits are designed to prevent the government from growing faster than the private sector. Other states limit appropriations to some percentage of projected state revenue. Research on TELs has identified one of the most important differences across state provisions as whether the limit is part of the state constitution or merely a legislative statute.[13] Statutory limitations are not as effective as constitutional limits because state legislators have the ability to rescind a statutory limit should they want to increase spending to win reelection. Constitutional limits are much more difficult to change. Constitutional TELs are present in seventeen states, including Tennessee. Thirteen states have only a statutory TEL. While constitutional TELs are generally more effective than statutory limits, not all constitutional TELs are created equal. Tennessee's TEL, while codified in the state's constitution, contains two flaws which limit its effectiveness.

As noted above, constitutional TELs are more effective at slowing the growth of state government than statutory limits.[14] Figure 14.5 shows growth in real per capita state government direct expenditures between 1992 and 2010 for three groups of states, those with a constitutional TEL, those with only a statutory TEL, and states with no restriction. Per capita state government spending grew 42 percent in states with a constitutional TEL, 48 percent in states with a statutory TEL, and 51 percent in states with no TEL. Thus, a constitutional limit reduced spending growth by about 9 percent compared with a statutory TEL or no limitation.

Simply being codified in a state's constitution does not necessarily make a TEL effective, however. All TELs contain provisions for waiving the limitation, and the nature of these provisions is crucial to their effectiveness. These provisions range from the relatively weak simple legislative majority vote, to the exceedingly strict requirement of voter approval.[15] Figure 14.6 illustrates the effects of these different provisions, once again by showing the growth of per capita state direct expenditure growth between 1992-2010. TELs which may be waived by a simple majority vote of the legislature are the least effective, and state governments operating with such provisions actually grew *more* than states with no TEL whatsoever (48 percent compared to 51 percent). States featuring a TEL that can only be waived via a supermajority vote (typically two thirds) in the legislature exhibited less growth of government. For states where expenditures can only be increased by supermajority vote, per capita spending increased by 42 percent, and states where at least some tax rates can only be increased by such a vote saw spending grow by 45 percent. Those states where TELs may

---

[13] See, for example, Stansel (1994) and Amiel, Deller, and Stallmann (2009).

[14] See Holcombe (1999) and Vedder and Gallaway (1999) for additional analysis and an evaluation of the evidence.

[15] See Poulson (2005) for a thorough description of the differences in waiver provisions.

be broken only with voter approval saw the lowest growth of government from 1992-2010, at 37 percent.

Figure 14.5: The Effect of Tax and Expenditure Limits

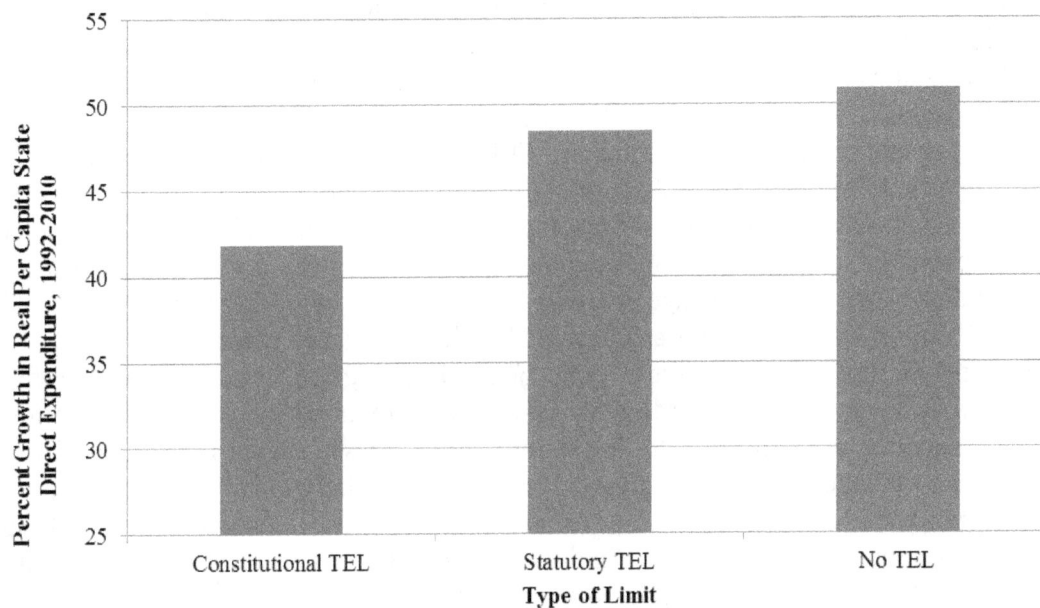

Sources: U.S. Census Bureau (2011a); Waisanen (2008); Bureau of Labor Statistics (2006).

Figure 14.6: The Effect of Provisions for Waiving TELs

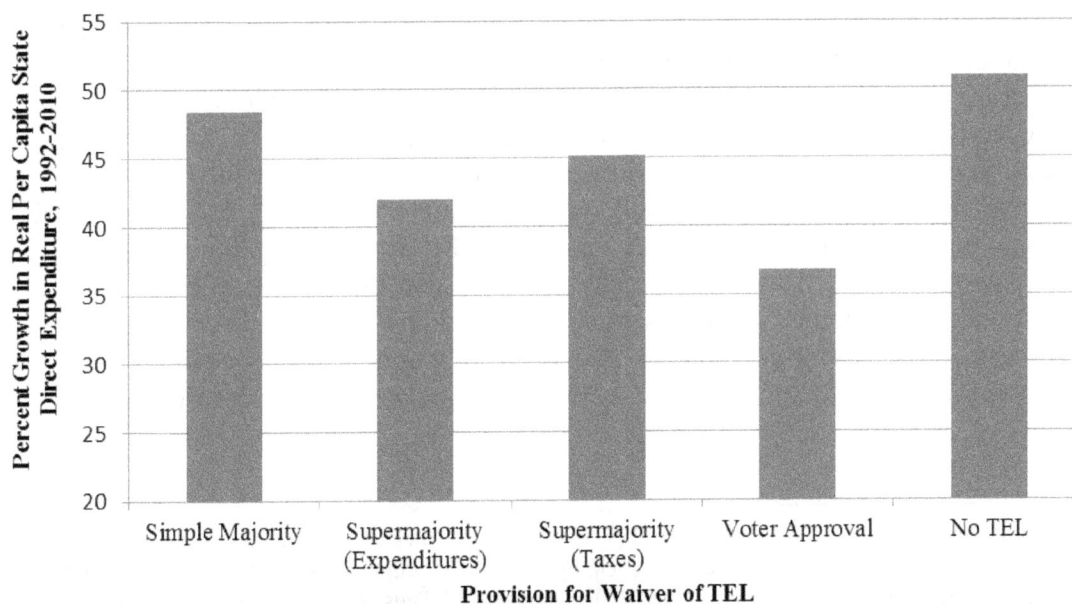

Sources: U.S. Census Bureau (2011b); Poulson (2005); Bureau of Labor Statistics (2006).

Tennessee is a state where a simple majority vote in the legislature is all that is required to break its constitutional TEL. Since the fundamental problem with statutory TELs is that the legislature may rescind them at its own discretion, this feature of Tennessee's TEL essentially strips it of the fundamental advantage of constitutional TELs. Constitutional TELs that can be waived with a simple majority vote (the same margin required to pass the budget) can be viewed as functionally equivalent to the less-effective statutory limits. Since its adoption in 1978, the Tennessee legislature has voted to waive its TEL 17 times as of the 2010-2011 fiscal year.[16] Waiving the TEL has essentially become a common standard practice of passing the state's budget (Zelinski 2011).

Another important factor in evaluating TEL effectiveness is what specific type of limit the TEL imparts. Limits may be tied to some measure of economic growth (such as personal income), expected revenues, or even arbitrary growth rates (such as Oklahoma's 12 percent). A form of expenditure limit receiving attention in recent years limits the annual growth of state expenditures to the percentage increase in population plus the inflation rate. These "popflation" limits on expenditure are designed to keep real per capital spending constant, only allowing increases in expenditure to accommodate changes in population or inflation. Typically, in order to increase spending above this level requires special approval, either by voters or a supermajority in the state legislature. Any excess revenues cannot be spent by lawmakers even if state tax revenues grow by more than popflation in a year, but must instead either be deposited in a rainy day fund or refunded to taxpayers. Colorado's TEL is designed following this model, and was widely considered the strictest in the country until it was suspended in 2005. Several other states have recently considered so-called Taxpayer's Bill of Rights (TABOR), which usually contain a popflation spending limit; Alaska has had such a limit since the early 1980s.[17]

A strict expenditure limit (such as those based on popflation) addresses the problem of state and local government spending booms during economic expansions. State tax systems are on net progressive, and thus tax revenues increase, often very rapidly, when the economy is strong even without an increase in tax rates. This makes TELs based on personal income growth or expected tax receipts problematic. If unconstrained, politicians will spend this money to increase reelection prospects. Here, once again, Tennessee's TEL falls short of being a truly strict constraint. In Tennessee, appropriations from state tax revenue sources cannot exceed the estimated growth of personal income in the state.[18] In other words, during economic expansions, spending is permitted to increase rapidly. In theory, the constraint should bind the other direction as well: when income growth is low or negative during recessions, the permitted appropriations under the TEL are similarly limited. As discussed above, however, the legislature may simply vote to waive the limit, and in fact has done so frequently during economic downturns, most recently doing so during fiscal years 2009-2010 and twice in 2010-2011 (see footnote 16). In other words, Tennessee's spending limit is overly-generous during economic booms and fails to bind at all during downturns.

---

[16] Tennessee Code Annotated Section 9-4-5203. The stipulation which allows the legislature to waive the TEL with a simple majority vote reads "the general assembly shall by law containing no other subject matter, set forth the dollar and the percentage by which the [TEL] is exceeded." Thus, the Tennessee Code actually contains explicit mentions of each time the limit was waived, and by how much.

[17] See National Conference of State Legislatures (2008).

[18] Tennessee Constitution, Section 24.

Figure 14.7: State Spending Growth in Tennessee

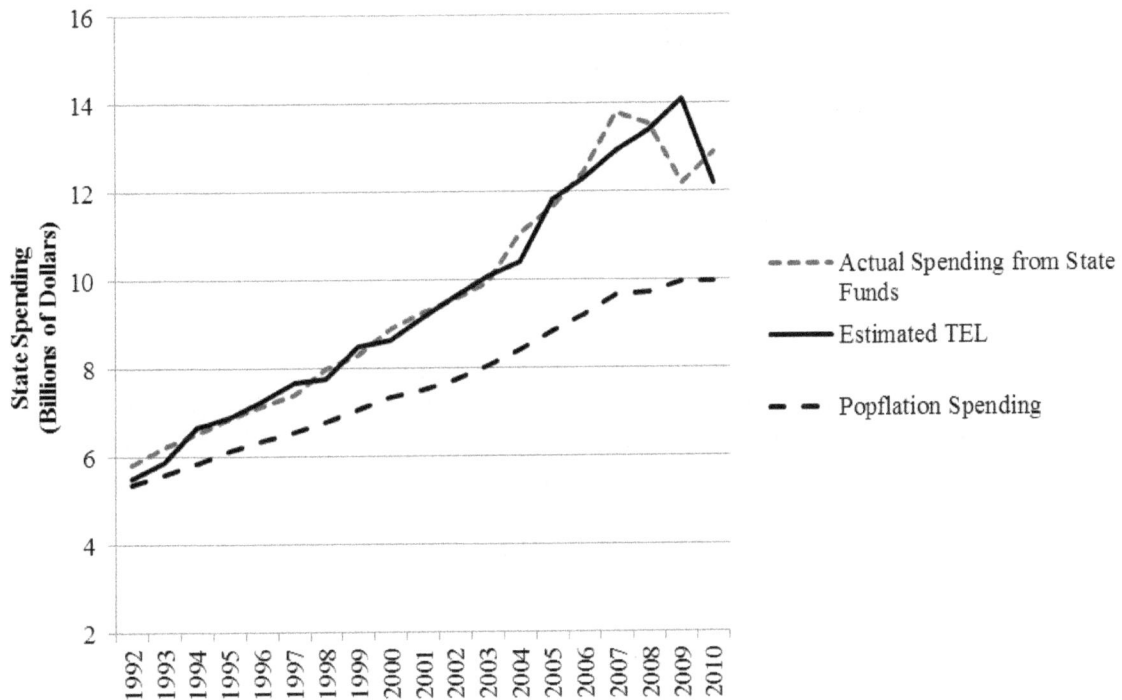

Sources: Tennessee Office of Legislative Budget Analysis (2012); Bureau of Economic Analysis (2012); Bureau of Labor Statistics (2006).

Figure 14.7 reflects this problem in Tennessee, showing the growth of expenditures from state revenue sources (the spending subject to the TEL) over 1992-2010. The figure graphs actual spending, the estimated growth rate allowed by the TEL, and the level of spending consistent with popflation in the state.[19] Over the period state spending grew about 40 percent more than the popflation value growing at roughly the same (much higher) rate allowed by the TEL, rarely dipping below the limit. As most of the time period showcased here could be characterized by economic expansion and rising personal income, state spending skyrocketed. Also readily apparent are the numerous cases where spending exceeded the personal income limit; in other words, periods where state spending growth exceeded growth in the private sector. Such spending sprees result in two problems. First, the new spending is often for pork barrel projects of questionable value. After all, state and local governments were already supplying important services like roads, police, courts, and prisons before the boom. Flush coffers allow politicians to fund wasteful projects which nonetheless win votes due to the law of concentrated benefits. Limiting the pork barrel spending spree will result in a better use of resources. Second, when the economy eventually goes into recession and tax revenues fall, states face a budget crisis, made worse by the spending boom. States often engage in unsustainable spending, hiring new employees, and beginning new programs requiring funding even when revenues fall. The fiscal crises that states confront

---

[19] The 'Estimated TEL' is based on actual growth of personal income and may not be fully reflective of the 'true' limit in place at the time, as it is based on an estimate of income growth.

with each recession are due primarily to excess spending booms, not inadequate revenue to fund core government services (Stansel and Mitchell 2008). Politicians often then manipulate a budget crisis to their advantage, exploiting agenda setting power to threaten to cut vital services instead of the new pork barrel spending if tax increases are not approved.[20] For instance, states which faced the worse fiscal crises during the 1990-91 recession were more likely to raise taxes, and then recovered from the recession more slowly (Poterba 1994). The tax hikes diminish economic freedom and set the stage for another cycle of excess spending when the economy recovers. A strict expenditure limit can help end this spending spree, budget crisis cycle once and for all.

Limiting the growth of government spending during a boom is likely to be easier politically than cutting existing programs. Before new spending is approved, no one knows exactly who will benefit from the new programs—who will be hired for new jobs and what companies will get contracts is not yet known. Consequently, we do not have individuals who face the loss of their jobs or reduction in income as when spending is reduced. Over time, the effect of avoiding excessive spending can be extensive. Spending in Tennessee was 40 percent greater in 2010 than it would have been if held to the popflation level since 1992. Cutting state government spending by 40 percent now would likely be a Herculean task, but the same effect could have been achieved merely by limiting spending since 1992.

Figure 14.8 illustrates the potential benefits of limiting excess spending during booms. For each of the contiguous states, the state and local spending in 1992 has been adjusted for state population growth and national inflation between 1992 and 2010, and then divided into the actual state spending in 2010 by the popflation limited level. The result creates a ratio of excess spending over the period. A ratio of 1, for example, means that state spending was at the level it would have been under a popflation rule, while a ratio of 2 means that actual spending was double the popflation limit level. Figure 14.8 then graphs the scatterplot of state income against our index of excess spending. States indulging in spending sprees above and beyond the popflation level were markedly poorer in 2010. The trend line shows that an excess spending ratio of 2 compared to 1 is associated with about 35 percent lower PCPI in 2010.

Tennessee currently has a constitutional TEL in place, was one of the first states to implement such a limitation, and yet has experienced reasonably fast growth in state spending. The state's excess spending ratio for 1992-2010 was 1.48. Tennessee's expenditure limitation suffers from several weaknesses (Poulson 2005). First, the limit may be waived by a simple majority vote in the legislature, the same vote required to pass the budget. In the roughly thirty years it has functioned under the limit, the legislature has voted to violate it seventeen times. Second, the state's TEL is tied to the growth of personal income which allows the state to rapidly expand spending during economic booms. This is especially problematic given the likely low-value nature of this excess spending. Finally, Tennessee's TEL makes no explicit mention of how excess revenues are to be treated. This lack of any explicit language likely means that any tax revenues collected in excess of what TEL permits will wind up in the general fund (Poulson 2005). A preferable limit would return excess revenues to taxpayers each year.

---

[20] Mitchell and Simmons (1994) label this the Washington Monument strategy after the Federal government's closing of national parks during the government shutdown in 1995. Similarly school boards will threaten to cut bus service or athletics or even close schools before the end of the year in advance of a school millage election instead of laying off administrators.

Figure 14.8: Spending Growth in Excess of Popflation and State Income

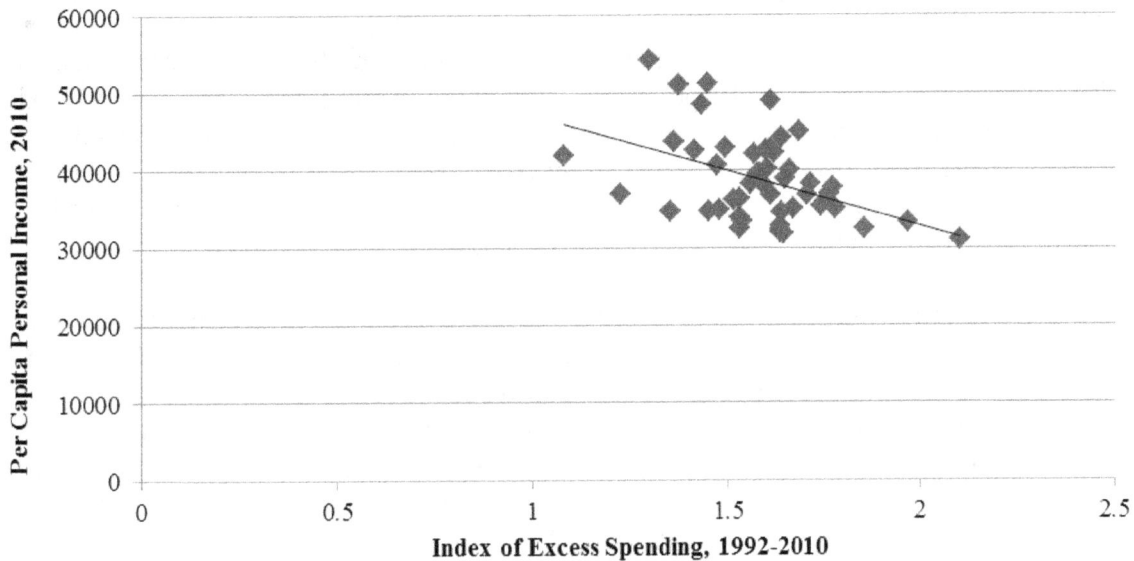

Sources: U.S. Census Bureau (2011b); Bureau of Economic Analysis (2012); Bureau of Labor Statistics (2006).

DECENTRALIZATION AND SEPARATION OF POWERS

Most of the time people debate whether government should provide a service, but *which* level of government should undertake a task is also an important question. The U.S. features multiple levels of government, with the federal government, the fifty state governments, county and city governments, and independent governmental units like school and water districts. Government in Tennessee is currently relatively decentralized, but the state could benefit from further decentralizing its government.

A guiding principle for assigning functions to different levels of government is to match the geographic scope of the benefits of government goods and services with political jurisdictions. A strong military defends an entire country, so defense is naturally a national government function, while parks and street repairs primarily benefit local residents and thus are appropriate municipal government functions. A well-designed system of fiscal federalism benefits society in several ways, perhaps most importantly by accommodating people's differing preferences for government goods and services. Where state government might adopt a one-size-fits-all approach, local communities can choose a combination of spending on parks, police, schools, and other services that reflects the preferences of their residents. When cities make these decisions, local residents can choose to spend more on the services they desire.

Of course the problems of politics might lead to a bias toward excessive spending by local governments, but when local government provides services, citizens now have an additional mechanism to limit spending: they can "vote with their feet" and leave a community which spends too much. Charles Tiebout (1956) proposed that mobility across communities lets citizens choose local government services in a manner analogous to the market place. If people move to communities with low crime rates and excellent parks, this lets politicians know that people value these government services, as opposed to say smaller class sizes in public schools.

Local government should be more responsive to citizen preferences. Albert Hirschman (1970) explains how political participation, or "voice," and voting with one's feet, or "exit," interact in controlling organizations, including government. Both exit and voice operate more effectively at the local level than at the state level. Political action by any one individual is more likely to be decisive in a small community, making voice more effective. In addition, exit is more effective because moving to the next town is less disruptive than moving to another state.

For all of these reasons, states with more decentralized government should outperform more centralized states. Figure 14.9 considers the relationship between real per capita personal income in 2010 and fiscal decentralization for the contiguous United States. We define decentralization in Figure 14.9 as the ratio of spending by all local governments in the state to the total amount of state plus local government spending for 2009 (but the ratio is relatively stable from year to year). Local government accounts for only 59 percent of total spending in Tennessee, which ranks 10th nationally, compared with an average across states of 50 percent, and local government accounts for about 65 percent of total state and local spending in the most decentralized states. The fitted line in Figure 14.9 shows that more decentralized states had about 10 percent higher PCPI in 2010 than the most centralized states. While Tennessee is one of the most decentralized states, these data suggest that further decentralization would be associated with higher income.

Figure 14.9: Benefits of Decentralization

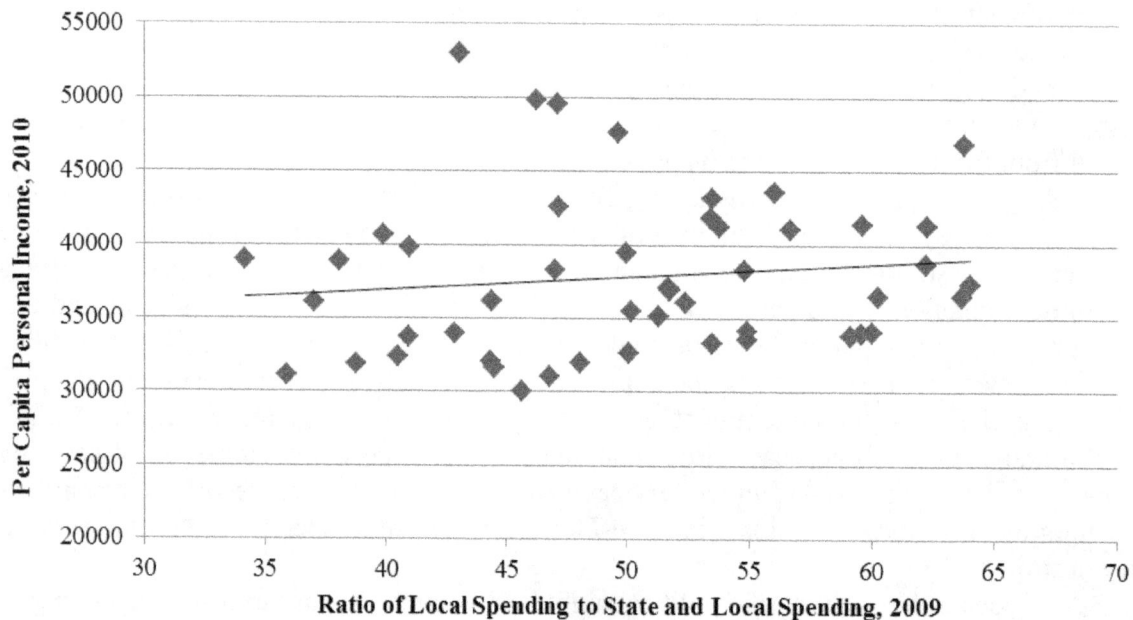

The separation of powers provides a means of making government more representative. A bicameral legislature, for example, elects representatives and senators from different districts. The differing districts divide up the constituency differently, and thus the views of representatives from a Tennessee county likely differ from the county's senator. Requiring approval of legislation by both houses increases the amount of support needed to pass a bill into law (Buchanan and Tullock 1962). The law of concentrated benefits warns that minorities can secure passage of spending measures. Tennessee could take further advantage of the separation of powers by strengthening its executive branch. The governor does have a line-item veto, which has proven to be a useful tool in restraining state spending (Krol 2007). However, the governor's veto can be overridden by a majority vote in both houses of the legislature, the same standard required to pass the legislation initially (Maddex 2006). This, like the simple majority vote required to waive the TEL, effectively nullifies the constraint on the legislature's power. Further strengthening the executive branch will serve to expand the support necessary for spending, and should help combat the spending bias of democracy.

A factor which strengthens legislative dominance is the direct election of a number of executive branch offices. Like the president at the federal level of government, the governor is the only statewide-elected member of the executive branch in Tennessee. Unlike the federal level, where the president may appoint the other executive officers, Tennessee's constitution stipulates that all other members of the executive branch be appointed by the legislature (Maddex 2006). This certainly weakens the executive branch relative to the legislature. In states with gubernatorial appointment of executive officers, a savvy governor will consider some of the political forces affecting the outcome of election contests in making appointments to these positions, so similar persons are often appointed to these positions. Legislative appointment, however, limits a governor's ability to form coherent policy initiatives. Executive officers appointed by members outside of the executive branch will sometimes have different coalitions of supporters, and could be from a different party. Governors are already held accountable for policy through elections, so greater use of gubernatorial appointment for executive branch positions does not make government less democratic; on the contrary, it would lessen the concentration of power in the legislature.

The judiciary represents the third branch of government in the separation of powers. And the judiciary plays a particularly important role in constitutional government as enforcer of the constitutional contract (Brennan and Buchanan 1985). A constitution serves to limit government, but government will naturally try to evade the constitutional limitations on its powers. Although judicial review was not explicitly included in the U.S. Constitution, judicial review of legislative and executive acts is implicit in the design of constitutional government (Wagner 1993). And judicial review by the Supreme Court served to limit the growth of government during the early 20th century under the doctrine of substantive due process (Siegan 1980). Tennessee's constitution provides for judges to be elected to the Supreme Court for terms of eight years (Article VI). Other courts subordinate to the Supreme Court are established by the legislature. Election of judges, particularly on a partisan basis, however, does not seem to be an improvement over appointed judges (Sobel and Hall 2007). Justices may be removed by a two-thirds majority of both houses of the legislature.

CONCLUSION: LIMITING GOVERNMENT TO UNLEASH CAPITALISM

Representative democracy is prone to spend too much, and a large, bloated government burdens the economy. The nature of representative democracy leads to excessive spending as a rule and not an accident. Despite steps taken by the state, Tennessee still suffers from a problem of large government. Only a change in the structure of government can effectively counter the pro-spending bias of politics. The following three changes are recommended for Tennessee to more effectively limit government spending:

- *Pass a revamped constitutional expenditure limit.* Tennessee's current limit has too high of a ceiling on expenditures, especially during economic expansions. Further, while Tennessee's TEL is codified in its constitution, it can be waived by a simple majority vote in the legislature, which makes it a "de facto" statutory limit which can be rescinded at the will of the legislature. We believe that a population plus inflation or popflation limit represents a more appropriate ceiling given the bias for excessive spending in democratic politics and the role of spending growth in fueling periodic fiscal crises. Further, spending above and beyond the TEL must require voter approval or, at the very least, a supermajority vote in the legislature. Finally, excess revenues should be refunded to citizens annually to prevent legislators from evading the constraint. In addition, rebating excess revenues to taxpayers each year would provide state residents a tangible reminder of the value of limiting government.

- *Greater fiscal decentralization.* While Tennessee ranks in the top ten of states in fiscal decentralization, further decentralization will allow competition between local governments to better serve citizens.

- *Strengthen the separation of powers.* Tennessee's executive branch is weak relative to its legislature. The executive branch can be strengthened by moving to gubernatorial appointment in place of legislative selection of executive branch positions. The line item veto could be given actual power by requiring a supermajority vote to override it; as it stands now, Tennessee's legislature can override a veto with the same simple majority required to pass the original bill. A stronger executive branch should better balance statewide interests against the more local interest of legislators.

Tennessee has a reasonably strong base of economic freedom, but the state is burdened by the legislature's continued circumvention of fiscal constraints. Cutting spending immediately would be desirable, but the power over time of limiting the growth of state spending should not be underestimated. State government in Tennessee was 40 percent larger in 2010 than it would have been had expenditure growth been held to population plus inflation over the previous eighteen years. Limiting spending growth to popflation for the next decade or two would bring spending in Tennessee under control, and allow the private sector room to grow. Public choice theory suggests that spending will be easier to prevent than to cut.

REFERENCES

Amiel, Lindsay, Steven Deller, and Judith Stallmann. 2009. "The Construction of a Tax and Expenditure Limitation Index for the U.S." Staff Paper No. 536. University of Wisconsin-Madison Department of Agricultural and Applied Economics. May. http://www .aae.wisc.edu/pubs/sps/pdf/stpap536.pdf.

Ashby, Nathan J., Avilia Bueno, and Fred McMahon. 2011. *Economic Freedom of North America: 2011 Annual Report*. Vancouver, BC: Fraser Institute.

Baumol, William. 1990. "Entrepreneurship: Productive, Unproductive and Destructive." *Journal of Political Economy* 98 (5): 893-921.

Brennan, Geoffrey, and James M. Buchanan. 1985. *The Reason of Rules*. Cambridge, MD: Cambridge University Press.

Brennan, Geoffrey, and Loren C. Lomasky. 1993. *Democracy and Decision: The Pure Theory of Electoral Preference*. Cambridge, MD: Cambridge University Press.

Buchanan, James M., and Gordon Tullock. 1962. *The Calculus of Consent*. Ann Arbor, MI: University of Michigan Press.

Buchanan, James M., and Richard E. Wagner. 1977. *Democracy in Deficit: The Political Legacy of Lord Keynes*. New York, NY: Academic Press.

Bureau of Economic Analysis, U.S. Department of Commerce. 2012. *Regional Economic Accounts—State Personal Income Summary SA1-3*. Washington, DC: U.S. Department of Commerce. http://bea.gov/iTable/iTableHtml.cfm?reqid =70&step =30&isuri=1&7028=-1&7040=-1&7083=Levels&7031=0&7022=21&7023=0&7024 =Non-Industry&7025=0&7026=XX&7027=1&7001=421&7029=21&7090=70&7033 =-1.

Bureau of Labor Statistics, U.S. Department of Labor. 2006. *Consumer Price Index—All Urban Consumers (CPI-U)*. Washington, DC: U.S. Department of Labor. ftp://ftp.bls .gov /pub/special.requests/cpi/ cpiai.txt.

Campbell, Noel D., and Tammy M. Rogers. 2007. "Economic Freedom and Net Business Formation." *Cato Journal* 27 (1): 23-36.

Caplan, Bryan. 2007. *The Myth of the Rational Voter: Why Democracies Choose Bad Policies*. Princeton, NJ: Princeton University Press.

Garrett, Thomas A., and Howard J. Wall. 2006. "Creating a Policy Environment for Entrepreneurs." *Cato Journal* 26 (3): 525-552.

Gwartney, James, Robert A. Lawson, and Joshua Hall. 2011. *Economic Freedom of the World: 2011 Annual Report*. Vancouver, BC: Fraser Institute.

Gwartney, James D., Randall G. Holcombe, and Robert A. Lawson. 2004. "Economic Freedom, Institutional Quality, and Cross-Country Differences in Income and Growth." *Cato Journal* 24 (3): 205-233.

Heston, Alan, Robert Summers, and Bettina Aten. 2011. *Penn World Table Version 7.0*. Philadelphia, PA: Center for International Comparisons of Production, Income, and Prices at the University of Pennsylvania. http://pwt.econ.upenn.edu/php_site /pwt_index.php.

Hirschman, Albert O. 1970. *Exit, Voice and Loyalty*. Cambridge, MA: Harvard University Press.

Holcombe, Randall G. 1999. "Tax Limits." In *Limiting Leviathan*, edited by Donald P. Racheter and Richard E.Wagner, 115-39. Northampton, MA: Edward Elgar.

Hou, Yilin, and Daniel L. Smith. 2006. "A Framework for Understanding State Balanced Budget Requirement Systems: Reexamining Distinctive Features and an Operational Definition." *Public Budgeting and Finance* 26 (3): 22-45.

Kreft, Steven F., and Russell S. Sobel. 2005. "Public Policy, Entrepreneurship, and Economic Freedom." *Cato Journal* 25 (3): 595-616.

Krol, Robert. 2007. "The Role of Fiscal and Political Institutions in Limiting the Size of State Government." *Cato Journal* 27 (3): 431-445.

Krol, Robert and Shirley Svorny. 2007. "Budget Rules and State Business Cycles." *Public Finance Review* 35 (4): 530-544.

Lawson, Robert A. 2007. "Economic Freedom and Property Rights: The Institutional Environment of Productive Entrepreneurship." In *Making Poor Nations Rich: Entrepreneurship and the Process of Economic Development*, edited by Benjamin Powell, 112-33. Palo Alto: Stanford University Press.

Lee, Dwight R., and Richard B. McKenzie. 1987. *Regulating Government: A Preface to Constitutional Economics*. Lexington MA: Lexington Books.

Maddex, Robert L. 2006. *State Constitutions of the United States*. 2nd ed. Washington, DC: CQ Press.

Mitchell, William C., and Randy T. Simmons. 1994. *Beyond Politics*. Boulder CO: Westview Press.

Mueller, Dennis C. 2003. *Public Choice III*. Cambridge, MA: Cambridge University Press.

National Association of State Budget Officers. 2008. *Budget Processes in the States*. http://www.nasbo.org/sites/default/files/BP_2008.pdf.

National Conference of State Legislatures. 2008. *State Tax and Expenditure Limits 2008*. Washington, DC: National Conference of State Legislatures. http://www.ncsl.org/issues-research/budget/state-tax-and-expenditure-limits-2008.aspx.

Niskanen, William A., Jr. 1971. *Bureaucracy and Representative Government*. Chicago, IL: Aldine-Atherton.

Norton, Seth W., and James D. Gwartney. 2008. "Economic Freedom and World Poverty." In *Economic Freedom of the World: 2008 Annual Report*, edited by James Gwartney and Robert A. Lawson. Vancouver, BC: Fraser Institute.

Olson, Mancur. 1982. *The Rise and Decline of Nations*. New Haven, CT: Yale University Press.

Payne, James L. 1991. *The Culture of Spending: Why Congress Lives Beyond Our Means*. San Francisco: ICS Press.

Poterba, James M. 1994. "State Responses to Fiscal Crises: The Effects of Budgetary Institutions and Politics." *Journal of Political Economy* 102 (4): 799-821.

Poulson, Barry W. 2005. *A Fiscal Discipline Report Card Grading the States' Tax and Expenditure Limits on State and Local Government*. Washington, DC: Americans for Prosperity Foundation.

Poulson, Barry W., and Jules Gordon Kaplan. 2008. "State Income Taxation and Economic Growth." *Cato Journal* 28 (1): 53-71.

Racheter, Donald P., and Richard E. Wagner, eds. 1999. *Limiting Leviathan*. Northampton, MA: Edward Elgar.

Siegan, Bernard H. 1980. *Economic Liberties and the Constitution*. Chicago, IL: University of Chicago Press.

Sobel, Russell S. 2008. "Testing Baumol: Institutional Quality and the Productivity of Entrepreneurship." *Journal of Business Venturing* 23: 641-655.

Sobel, Russell S., and Joshua C. Hall. 2007. "The Effect of Judicial Selection Processes on Judicial Quality: The Role of Partisan Politics." *Cato Journal* 27 (1): 69-82.

Stansel, Dean. 1994. "Taming Leviathan: Are Tax and Spending Limits the Answer?" Cato Institute Policy Analysis No. 213.

Stansel, Dean, and David T. Mitchell. 2008. "State Fiscal Crises: Are Rapid Spending Increases to Blame?" *Cato Journal* 28 (3): 435-448.

Tennessee Office of Legislative Budget Analysis. 2012. *Total State Budget Comparisons: Fiscal Years 1970-71 through Recommended 2012-13.* Nashville, TN: Office of Legislative Budget Analysis. http://www.capitol.tn.gov/joint/staff/budgetanalysis/docs /Total%20State%20Budget%20FY1970-01%20through%202012-13.pdf.

Tiebout, Charles M. 1956. "A Pure Theory of Local Expenditures." *Journal of Political Economy* 64: 416-424.

Tullock, Gordon. 1967. "The Welfare Costs of Tariffs, Monopoly and Theft." *Western Economic Journal* 5: 224-232.

U.S. Census Bureau. 1980. *Statistical Abstract of the United States: 1980.* Washington, DC: U.S. Census Bureau.

———. 2011a. *State and Local Government Finances: 2009.* Washington, DC: U.S. Census Bureau. http://www.census.gov/govs/estimate/.

———. 2011b. *State Government Finances: 1992-2010.* Washington, DC: U.S. Census Bureau. http://www.census.gov/govs/state/.

Vedder, Richard K., and Lowell E. Gallaway. 1997. "Constitutional Spending Limitations and the Optimal Size of Government." In *Limiting Leviathan*, edited by Donald P. Racheter and Richard E.Wagner, 96-114. Northampton, MA: Edward Elgar.

———. 1998. *Government Size and Economic Growth.* Washington DC: Joint Economic Committee.

———. 1999. *Tax Reduction and Economic Welfare.* Washington, DC: Joint Economic Committee.

Wagner, Richard E. 1993. *Parchment, Guns and Constitutional Order.* Brookfield VT: Edward Elgar.

Waisanen, Bert. 2008. "State Tax and Expenditure Limits—2008." *National Conference of State Legislatures.* http://www.ncsl.org/issues-research/budget/state-tax-and-expenditure-limits-2008.aspx.

Zelinski, Andrea. 2011. "State Again Pops Purported Spending 'Cap.'" *TNReport*, June 15. http://www.tnreport.com/blog/2011/06/15/state-again-pops-purported-spending-cap/.

SUMMARY

SUMMARY OF
CHAPTER CONCLUSIONS

Freedom and Prosperity
in Tennessee

SUMMARY OF CHAPTER CONCLUSIONS

PART I—GOVERNMENT AND ECONOMIC GROWTH IN TENNESSEE

CHAPTER 1   THE CASE FOR GROWTH
by Russell S. Sobel, J.R. Clark, and Susane J. Leguizamon

- Small differences in economic growth rates can produce substantial differences in the quality of life within a generation or two
- A better and richer Tennessee is possible to achieve within our lifetime
- This growth does not have to come at the expense of other things people value—to the contrary, these other areas, like a reduction in crime and increases in educational attainment, are also enhanced by economic growth

CHAPTER 2   THE SOURCES OF ECONOMIC GROWTH
by Russell S. Sobel, J.R. Clark, and Joshua C. Hall

- States relying more heavily on capitalism have higher income levels, faster average income growth, but also more even growth across the income distribution
- The key component in reforming policy is to ensure the security of private ownership rights
- Government must refrain from attempting to control the state's economy through the regulation and spending of citizens' incomes for them through high taxation and government expenditures
- The goal should be to increase the share of our state economy controlled through the private sector and diminish the share controlled through the public sector

CHAPTER 3   WHY CAPITALISM WORKS
by Russell S. Sobel, J.R. Clark, and Peter T. Leeson

- Specialization, division of labor, and capital investment are all characteristics of capitalism which increase labor productivity, prosperity, and individual wealth
- Capitalism embodies a process in which entrepreneurs continuously discover new and more valuable uses for our resources, generating higher incomes in the process
- Government central planning and economic control often create unintended consequences—the problem is not bad people in government, but bad incentives
- To encourage *freedom and prosperity*, policy reform must increase the reward to productive (market) entrepreneurship and decrease the reward to unproductive (political and legal) entrepreneurship

263

PART II—POLICY REFORMS IN TENNESSEE TO PRODUCE ECONOMIC GROWTH

CHAPTER 4   WHEN IT COMES TO TAXES IN TENNESSEE: FOCUS ON COMPETITIVE
ADVANTAGE
by Joshua C. Hall and Adam J. Hoffer

- Taxes are more costly than most people realize—$1.00 of taxes costs the Tennessee economy upwards of $1.50 when direct and indirect costs are summed
- Tennessee is able to avoid an income tax and keep its other tax rates in line because overall government is kept relatively small
- People change their behavior to avoid taxes, including deciding where to live, and that is where Tennessee's tax system positions itself at an advantage compared to other states
- Tennessee has seen a major surge of in-migration, primarily from states with a far less friendly tax system and a much larger tax burden
- Tennessee must find ways to keep its overall tax burden low while not allowing its sales tax rate or other taxes to deviate significantly from neighboring states

CHAPTER 5   SPECIFIC TAX AND SUBSIDY REFORMS TO PROMOTE ECONOMIC
PROGRESS IN TENNESSEE
by Art Carden and Joshua C. Hall

- A broad sales tax base is necessary to ensure that Tennessee has a simple and efficient tax system
- Sales tax exemptions (such as reduced food sales rate and sales tax holidays) slowly erode the sales tax base, necessitating higher sales tax rates
- Phasing out Tennessee's estate tax and eliminating its gift tax reduces a large amount of unproductive and distortionary economic activity
- Subsidization of sports facilities through preferential tax treatment or passage of new taxes should be eliminated to avoid both deterring and manipulating economic activity

CHAPTER 6   MAKING PROPERTY RIGHTS MORE SECURE IN TENNESSEE: LIMITING
DISCRETIONARY POWERS OF EMINENT DOMAIN
by Edward J. López

- The public interest is not served by using eminent domain in situations where private parties can achieve an agreement through continued negotiations
- Tennesseans can reform their laws to increase protection of property rights *without* a tradeoff of foregone economic development
- By eliminating the exemption for blighted properties and for private transfers that are merely incidental to an otherwise traditional public use and introducing these protections into the Tennessee Constitution, the state can become a more attractive environment for property owners, investors, and developers

Chapter 7   REDUCE LABOR RESTRICTIONS: FROM RIGHT-TO-WORK TO SCHOOL CHOICE
by Joshua C. Hall, Ashley S. Harrison, Nathan J. Ashby, and Susan S. Douglass

- Labor policies that encourage increased productivity and greater competition in labor markets increase the *freedom and prosperity* for all Tennesseans
- Whether the cause is minimum wage laws, occupational licensure, or prevailing wage laws, most regulations provide benefits only to special interest groups and impose significant costs on the rest of society
- Implementation of a school voucher program would greatly increase the competition among schools and provide significantly higher quality education for all Tennessee children
- Improvements are needed at the college level to transform the Tennessee Education Lottery Scholarship program to ensure that it increases the acquisition of human capital instead of merely subsidizing households who are able to afford college attendance

Chapter 8   REGULATORY REFORMS AND PROSPECTS FOR GROWTH
By Art Carden

- Economic freedom is an essential element of a pro-growth business environment
- The social cost of regulation includes the reduction in production and trade, as well as the loss in productive activities from resources re-allocated to special interest groups and lobbying activities
- Reducing occupational licensing requirements would create a more vibrant Tennessee economy without compromising the quality of the services people are able to enjoy
- Repealing Tennessee's law against price gouging would provide Tennessee entrepreneurs with the flexibility needed to respond to emergencies, expedite recovery, and create a larger quantity of needed goods and services available to consumers
- Potential policies such as higher minimum wages, employment protection laws, and protecting incumbent retailers from competition would harm all Tennessee consumers, but especially the poor and the young
- Firms seek regulation from the government in order to create barriers to entry that protect them from competition at the expense of consumers, who must pay higher prices or are unable to enjoy the newly-limited services, and potential competitors, who are shut out of the market by regulation

CHAPTER 9   EDUCATION REFORM IN TENNESSEE: SPENDING MONEY ON WHAT MATTERS
by Joshua C. Hall and Ashley S. Harrison

- More money does not always produce greater results in education
- Factors affecting school improvement are either outside the direct control of policymakers (family and peer effects) or related to how schools are structured, financed, and operated
- Providing families with a large number of school districts to choose among (without considering private schools or leaving the city) creates competition and is an important component of Tennessee's economic growth

CHAPTER 10   WELFARE REFORM AND INCENTIVES TO WORK IN TENNESSEE
by Art Carden

- Successful anti-poverty policies encourage growth when they include incentives that reward work effort and/or regaining employment
- Reforms that promote economic growth will help solve many social problems by increasing average incomes among Tennesseans
- Higher income states have better outcomes in health, crime, and family stability
- Eliminating disincentives to work will ultimately reduce demand for welfare services by addressing peoples' needs through voluntary channels

CHAPTER 11   GAMBLING ON LOTTERIES AND CASINOS IN TENNESSEE
by Douglas M. Walker

- Tax revenues are a primary catalyst for states to introduce lottery and casino gambling
- Gambling tax revenues offset the anxiety caused from the alternatives of spending cuts or raising taxes in the state
- A ban on gambling (except the lottery) is a highly inefficient policy because it prevents willing buyers and sellers of a popular entertainment industry from operating in Tennessee
- Since Tennessee currently has neither casinos nor online gambling, the introduction of these new forms of gambling would almost certainly increase the overall amount of tax revenues from legalized gambling

CHAPTER 12   COURT REFORM: "COMPETITION IN THE COURTROOM"
by Art Carden and Justin Owen

- A well-functioning legal system is an essential element of a pro-growth institutional environment
- A neutral and independent judiciary is necessary for a well-functioning legal system
- The process by which judges are selected should insure judicial independence from bias and undue outside influence
- Policies that substitute private solutions, such as Alternative Dispute Resolution for government planning, within the state's legal system should be considered

CHAPTER 13   LEGAL REFORM: SPECIFIC CHANGES TO FOSTER ECONOMIC GROWTH
by Justin Owen

- Economic growth is harmed by high tort and civil litigation cost
- Reforms to collateral source rule laws, which include remedies to deal with subrogation, lead to greater efficiency by decreasing the number of tort suits filed
- Reforms, if structured properly, can lead to a more balanced, fair, and efficient judicial system and ultimately more *freedom and prosperity*

CHAPTER 14   CONSTITUTIONALLY CONSTRAIN GOVERNMENT TO PROMOTE FREEDOM AND PROSPERITY
by George Crowley and Daniel Sutter

- The incentives within democratic politics create a strong tendency for government to spend and grow excessively—beyond the levels best for economic growth
- The size of government must be limited to increase economic prosperity
- Overall spending can be reduced and made more effective by further decentralizing spending to local governments
- Revamping constitutional requirements imposing either voter or supermajority standards, limiting spending growth to popflation, and refunding excess revenue to the citizens would bring spending in Tennessee under control and allow the private sector to grow
- The separation of powers could be enhanced by strengthening the executive branch

ABOUT THE AUTHORS

EDITOR:

J.R. Clark, Ph.D., holds the Probasco Chair at The University of Tennessee at Chattanooga and is a Vice President of the John Templeton Foundation. He has published extensively in the areas of economics, entrepreneurship, public finance, regulation, and education. He is Secretary/Treasurer of both the Southern Economic Association and The Association of Private Enterprise Education and a Vice President of The Mont Pelerin Society.

ASSOCIATE EDITORS:

Russell S. Sobel, Ph.D., is a Visiting Scholar in Entrepreneurship at The Citadel. He has published over 150 books and articles on economic policy, including a nationally-best-selling college Principles of Economics textbook.

Joshua C. Hall, Ph.D., is the Elbert H. Neese Professor of Economics at Beloit College and a Senior Fellow at the Center for College Affordability and Productivity. He was formerly an economist for the Joint Economic Committee of the U.S. Congress. In addition to being widely published in academic journals, Dr. Hall is an author of the annual *Economic Freedom of the World* report.

OTHER CONTRIBUTING AUTHORS:

Nathan J. Ashby, Ph.D., is a professor in Western Hemispheric Trade Research and Economics at The University of Texas at El Paso. His published research focuses on the impact of economic freedom on migration, inequality, and other economic outcomes.

Art Carden, Ph.D., is a professor in Economics at Samford University and a Senior Fellow at the Beacon Center of Tennessee. He has done extensive research on the "Wal-Mart effect" and published widely in the areas of economic history of the American South and economic development.

George Crowley, Ph.D., is a professor in Economics at Troy University. His research interests include public economics, constitutional economics, political economy, and state and local public finance.

Susan S. Douglass, MBA, is a research assistant in the Probasco Chair at The University of Tennessee at Chattanooga. Her published research concerns labor economics.

Ashley S. Harrison, MBA, is Assistant Director of the Center for Economic Education at The University of Tennessee at Chattanooga and teaches Finance in the College of Business. Her published research focuses on economic education. She is Assistant Secretary/Treasurer of both the Southern Economic Association and The Association of Private Enterprise Education.

Adam J. Hoffer, Ph.D., is a professor in Economics at the University of Wisconsin-La Crosse. His research focus is on the political economy and spatial aspects of cigarette excise tax.

Susane Leguizamon, Ph.D., is a professor in Economics at Tulane University. Her research fields include public economics, spatial econometrics, international economics, state and local finance, and urban economics.

Peter T. Leeson, Ph.D., is the BB&T Professor for the Study of Capitalism at George Mason University. Dr. Leeson was formerly a Visiting Fellow in Political Economy and Government at Harvard University and the F.A. Hayek Fellow at the London School of Economics. He has authored or co-authored over 100 publications and edits four economic journals.

Edward J. López, Ph.D., is the BB&T Distinguished Professor of Capitalism at Western Carolina University. He has published extensively in the areas of applied political economy, property rights, and eminent domain.

Justin Owen, J.D., is the President and Chief Executive Officer of the Beacon Center of Tennessee. Prior to joining the Beacon Center, Owen served as a law clerk to the U.S. Attorney in Memphis and at the Pentagon as a legal intern to the General Counsel of the United States Navy.

Daniel Sutter, Ph.D., is the Charles G. Koch Professor of Economics at Troy University and an Affiliated Senior Scholar at the Mercatus Center. His published research deals with public choice economics, the news media, and the economics of weather and natural hazards.

Douglas M. Walker, Ph.D., is professor of Economics at the College of Charleston. He has published extensive research on economic and social impacts of legalized gambling focusing on commercial casinos in the United States.